Cecilia 336 pocA2002

For my parents:
Mary R. Gilmore
and
the late John R. Gilmore (1909-69)

Dirty money

The evolution of international measures to counter money laundering and the financing of terrorism

Third edition
Revised and expanded

William C. Gilmore

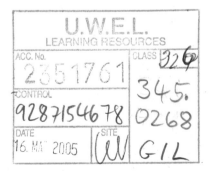
Council of Europe Publishing

French version:

L'argent sale – La communauté internationale face au blanchiment de capitaux et au financement du terrorisme

ISBN: 92-871-5465-1

Appendices I-VII are reproduced by kind permission of the FATF Secretariat.

Cover design: Graphic Design Workshop, Council of Europe
Layout: Pre-Press Unit, Council of Europe
© Council of Europe

Edited by Council of Europe Publishing
http://book.coe.int
F-67075 Strasbourg Cedex

ISBN 92-871-5467-8
© Council of Europe, November 2004
Printed in Germany by Koelblin-Fortuna-Druck

TABLE OF CONTENTS

ACKNOWLEDGEMENTS

Such is the pace of developments as the international community seeks to counter money laundering, and so numerous the fora which are contributing to that process, that I have found it necessary on many occasions to request assistance from those involved. Almost without exception such pleas have elicited positive and constructive responses. Particular thanks are due to Mr H Nilsson and Mr A Beverly in Brussels, Mr J Ringguth in Strasbourg and Mr P Csonka of Washington, DC. I would also like to take this opportunity to acknowledge the research assistance provided by Ms T Collier and Mr M Duff in relation to the human rights issues addressed in chapter VII and the financial support received from the School of Law of the University of Edinburgh in that regard. I am also in the debt of Ms C Croal for providing me with the opportunity to focus on the writing of this edition, at a critical period, at her house on the island of Iona. Finally, I would like to express my thanks to Ms F Raveney of Council of Europe Publishing for her kindness and support, and to Miss L Lawson whose friendship, secretarial skills and exceptional tolerance were relied upon throughout.

The views contained in the pages which follow are mine alone and are not intended to represent the perceptions of the Council of Europe or of any other institution or government with which I am associated. I am, of course, responsible for any deficiencies of style or substance which remain. The text seeks to represent the position as of 1 January 2004 although I have made use of materials of a more recent vintage where possible.

Old College   William C. Gilmore
Edinburgh

23 February 2004

FOREWORD

The Council of Europe has had a long engagement with the anti-money laundering issue. In 1980 it adopted the first international instrument against money laundering (Recommendation No. R (80) 10 on measures against the transfer and the safekeeping of funds of criminal origin). Since then it has developed its involvement with this issue on three fronts: as a standard setter, through the 1990 Council of Europe Convention on Laundering, Search, Seizure and Confiscation of the Proceeds from Crime; as a monitor of the effectiveness of anti-money laundering measures in place, through the MONEYVAL mechanism, under which twenty-seven European states are currently evaluated; and as a provider of technical assistance.

Money laundering is the process by which criminal proceeds are sanitised to disguise their illicit origins. It is a major international problem which confronts governments and policy makers worldwide. Criminals around the globe, whether drug barons in South America or fraudsters and racketeers in Europe, all have one thing in common. They need to distance themselves from their crimes by finding safe havens for their profits, where they can be made to look legitimate. Given the speed with which money can move around the globe the problem requires common international approaches.

At the domestic level, preventive action by states to counter the misuse of the financial system through money laundering, and repressive action in the courts are critical.

For many years, the Council of Europe has promoted action on these matters, particularly in the context of the fight against organised crime. Estimates suggest that of the billions laundered worldwide, most is laundered by, or on behalf of, organised crime groups. Money laundering is said to provide them with their cash flow and investment capital, which, as noted in this book, consolidates their economic power-base, allowing them to penetrate the legitimate economy. Moreover, a concentration of economic power by organised crime can all too easily, through the use of corruption and influence, infect the political process. Therefore there are risks for the rule of law and democracy in not attacking the power of organised crime by fighting money laundering.

Money laundering, of course, also matters economically, as it poses immediate threats to global financial institutions. Financial systems, both domestic and international, depend on confidence. Bankers (and governments) need to protect confidence in financial institutions and maintain their stability. If a bank or financial institution becomes known to be associated, however inadvertently, with criminal money, it is vulnerable: confidence can be undermined, leading to collapse and failure with multiple losses to investors.

Misuse of the financial system is not, however, limited to money launder-ing schemes designed to preserve and maximise proceeds from crimes which have been committed. The financial system is misused in similar ways to fund future terrorist atrocities. In the wake of the terrible attacks on the United States of America on 11 September 2001, the international com-munity rapidly recognised the important similarities between the processes involved in money laundering and in terrorist financing. This new edition of *Dirty money* explains how international action to counter money laun-dering has been developed in the last few years into a combined agenda to tackle both money laundering and terrorist financing. In particular it describes how the world's leading standard-setting body in the anti-money laundering area, the Financial Action Task Force (FATF), responded to the events of 11 September 2001, in an emergency plenary meeting in October of that year, which agreed a set of eight terrorist-specific recommendations (The Special Recommendations on Terrorist Financing), and incorporated action on terrorist financing into its mandate. The Committee of Ministers of the Council of Europe were also swift to extend the terms of reference of MONEYVAL, in 2002, to include the terrorist financing issue in its evaluations.

The Council of Europe is committed to fighting terrorism on many levels, not least, in partnership with the FATF (and more recently with the international financial institutions), through detailed and searching mutual evaluation to verify that states have implemented robust and effective measures to counter terrorist funding.

But it is not only in the area of terrorist funding that significant developments have occurred since the last edition of this work. As countries put in place pre-ventive safeguards in credit and financial institutions, so the launderers find new channels and techniques to hide their ill-gotten wealth. International standards have moved on to keep pace with these developments. In 2001 the European Union adopted Directive 2001/97/EEC, amending the 1991 EC Directive on Prevention of the Use of the Financial System for the Purpose of Money Laundering, and in June 2003 the FATF finalised its revised set of Forty Recommendations, which all states are urged to implement. Similarly new money laundering-specific provisions feature in the UN Convention against Transnational Organised Crime, which came into force in September 2003. At the time of writing, an expert committee within the Council of Europe is charged with elaborating a protocol to the 1990 Convention on Laundering, Search, Seizure and Confiscation of the Proceeds from Crime by the end of 2004. Thus, anti-money laundering (and now countering the financing of terrorism) are truly dynamic areas of activity.

Professor Gilmore's third edition of *Dirty money* is very timely. It brings together all recent developments and places them in their historical context. It will be required reading for all experts who are wrestling with these increas-ingly complex and multifaceted phenomena.

Chapter I – Transnational and Organised Crime: THE CONTOURS OF THE PROBLEM

The context

In the course of the past thirty years there has been ever-growing public anxiety and political concern with the threat posed by modern and sophisticated forms of transnational criminal activity. In stark contrast with the nineteenth century when issues of criminal justice policy were thought of in almost exclusively national terms, the need for enhanced international co-operation and co-ordination in this sphere now occupies an important position on the political agenda. This represents an inevitable recognition of the fact that reliance on unilateral domestic legislative and law enforcement measures is no longer sufficient. As Peter Wilkitzki has aptly remarked, "no domestic criminal legislator can afford to treat crime merely as a national phenomenon".[1]

Among the factors which have contributed to the growth of cross-border criminal activity pride of place must go to the technological revolution witnessed since the end of the second world war.[2] While this has brought about countless benefits of an economic and social nature, as with the growth in world trade and international travel, it has also provided the criminal entrepreneur with new opportunities and wider geographic horizons. As has been noted elsewhere:

> Modern technology has provided new impetus not only to legitimate trade and commerce, but also to criminal business enterprises. Thus, mass communications have facilitated contacts with associates in other countries and continents, modern banking has facilitated international criminal transactions, and the modern revolution in electronics has given criminal groups access to new tools enabling them to steal millions and to launder the huge illicit profits.[3]

Wider opportunities to engage in transborder illicit conduct are also emerging in several parts of the world as a consequence of the enhanced mobility of individuals and the decreasing significance of national frontiers brought about by economic integration movements and similar factors. This is perhaps most obviously the case for the member states of the European Union (EU) as they seek to come to terms with the criminal justice implications flowing from the creation of a single internal market and the free movement of goods, people, services and capital which it ensures.

Notwithstanding the absence of comprehensive data on the scale of transfrontier crime in the EU, and the widely acknowledged difficulty of quantifying
the contribution of border controls to law enforcement and crime deterrence,
the member states have accepted the need to take action to minimise the
possibilities of abuse by criminal elements of a Europe without internal borders.[4] Indeed, Title VI of the Treaty of European Union (the Maastricht Treaty)
underlined the importance of this dimension of the integration movement
by specifically acknowledging that justice and home affairs were to be treated
as matters of common concern.[5] Concrete expression has been given to this
commitment to improve co-operation and co-ordination in a number of ways
including the creation of a law enforcement body, known as Europol, charged
with co-ordinating the exchange and analysis of police intelligence. As will
be seen in greater detail in chapter VIII, while the initial mandate of Europol
was restricted to drug trafficking and related money laundering it has since
been broadened to include a large number of other areas of serious crime
possessing a transnational dimension. Further significant compensatory law
enforcement measures have been agreed[6] and the area of judicial co-operation is in the process of being transformed through the ever-increasing use
of the concept of mutual recognition. While the criminal justice dimension
to regional economic integration is at its most advanced within the EU it is
not, however, an exclusively European issue. Its wider significance can, for
example, be seen in the acceptance of the need for greater co-operation in
criminal matters to compensate for increased freedom of movement within
the Economic Community of West African States.[7]

This is not to say that the concept of international co-operation in criminal
matters is itself new. For example, the nineteenth century witnessed the
beginnings of the modern system of extradition which continues to provide
the basic international mechanism for the return of fugitives who have
sought refuge abroad to face justice in the territory where the crime was in
fact committed. At much the same time the international community started,
on a modest scale, to negotiate agreements designed to combat crimes of
particular concern. To early examples of treaty-based action to counter such
abuses as the slave trade, and forgery of currency have been added, particularly since 1945, a growing list of international instruments dealing with
such diverse subjects as terrorist offences, genocide and apartheid.[8] There
are, in addition, well-established structures for co-operation among law
enforcement authorities. These include, among others, the International
Criminal Police Organisation (ICPO/Interpol) with its headquarters in Lyons,
France[9] and the Brussels-based World Customs Organisation (formerly the
Customs Co-operation Council (CCC)).[10] However, the high political priority
currently accorded to the subject is of relatively recent origin. This change
can be attributed in large measure to the enhanced level of appreciation of
the magnitude and complexity of the problem which emerged in the early
1980s when international concern came to focus on the threat posed by
the international drugs trade.

That international drugs trafficking emerged as a central issue of concern for the world community was not merely a result of the escalating nature of the problem of drug abuse. It was also, and importantly, a reflection of an enhanced understanding of its negative social impact, its distortive effects on economies, and its implications for domestic political stability. The extent of the societal threat posed by trafficking syndicates was clearly demonstrated in Colombia in the late 1980s and early 1990s and seen most vividly in the murder, at the behest of the powerful cocaine cartels, of some of that country's leading politicians, judges and journalists. Less visible, but equally serious, were the efforts to penetrate and corrupt the central organs of state power. In its most extreme form, as evidenced by the US invasion of Panama, undertaken to remove General Noriega from power, the drugs trade can even pose an indirect threat to the maintenance of international peace and security.

In addition, drugs trafficking is by nature global in character, requiring the international movement of products from producer countries to the major drug consumer nations. For example, cocaine produced mainly in South America must be shipped through the transit countries of the Caribbean and Central America to reach its major market in the United States. Similarly, heroin, originating primarily in the Golden Triangle of Southeast Asia and the Golden Crescent of Southwest Asia must be moved, by land, air or sea, to meet demand in North America and western Europe. In the case of the latter, most of the product has traditionally been exported by road using increasingly diverse routes and posing major problems for the emerging democracies of central and eastern Europe.

It would, however, be unduly simplistic to think merely in terms of a movement from producer countries in the developing world to consumers located in the advanced industrialised economies. Producer and transit countries have their own, increasingly serious, problem of drug abuse. Furthermore, Europe is a major exporter of psychotropic substances to other regions of the world including Africa.[11] Another illustration of the geographical complexity of the situation is the dependence of developing-country drug producers on the chemicals, manufactured primarily in the industrialised world, which are essential to the process of converting the coca leaf into refined cocaine and raw opium into heroin. For example, a kind of "reverse Balkan route" exists to facilitate the transfer of precursor and essential chemicals, particularly acetic anhydride, from Europe, through the southern borders of Turkey to the Persian Gulf states and the nations of Southwest Asia.

For these reasons, among others, the drugs trade came to be universally recognised as a global problem requiring a global solution. Given this fact, major emphasis throughout the 1980s was placed on the need to improve the effectiveness and extend the scope of international co-operation in this area. One major achievement in this regard was the conclusion in Vienna in December 1988 of the United Nations Convention against Illicit Traffic in Narcotic Drugs and Psychotropic Substances (the 1988 UN convention). This important international agreement, which is examined in chapter III of this book, has attracted the participation of the overwhelming majority of states including many of the most important source, transit and consumer countries.

Subsequently, the members of the world community expanded their area of concern to encompass other forms of transnational criminal activity; initially organised crime, more recently corruption. In so far as the former is concerned, a major stimulus was provided by developments in central and eastern Europe. The end of the cold war, the dissolution of the Warsaw Pact, and the disintegration of the Soviet Union were events of major global significance. They also brought about unparalleled opportunities and challenges for the states concerned and their people as domestic political structures moved swiftly to embrace both liberal democracy and entrepreneurial capitalism.[12] Of the many problems confronted by these states in the period of transition one of the most serious, least wanted, and most heavily publicised, had to do with crime. In essence, the traumatic economic and political changes had the unintended but perhaps inevitable effect of increasing the potential for crime; opportunities which were enthusiastically seized upon by criminal elements.

In the overall context of this work one of the most alarming features was the emergence (in some cases the resurgence) of powerful organised crime groups which exploited the opportunities presented by the decline of existing structures of authority and legitimacy to further their own ends. Nowhere was the severity of this threat more obvious than in the Russian Federation. As a 1994 UN report was to explain:

> Perhaps the most striking recent example of the way in which transnational criminal organisations can thrive in an environment of political, social and economic upheaval can be seen in the States of the former Soviet Union. Russian criminal organisations are not new, but the demise of the Communist Party, the disintegration of the Soviet Union, and the collapse of the criminal justice system clearly produced conditions that were highly conducive to the consolidation of existing criminal organisations and the emergence of new ones.[13]

The growing importance attached by governments to this issue was well illustrated in November 1994 by the convening, under the auspices of the UN, of the World Ministerial Conference on Organised Transnational Crime in Naples, Italy. There, the threat posed by the activities of such crime groups was regarded as both serious and increasing. It was perceived to pose a threat to sovereignty, to national authority and state control, to democratic values and public institutions as well as to national economies, financial institutions and individuals. All states, including developing countries and nations in transition from communist rule to democratic governance, were seen to be vulnerable.[14]

In spite of such shared perceptions of the nature of the problem the conference was unable to resolve one fundamental issue; namely, the absence of a universally agreed definition of organised crime.[15] This difficulty – solved only six years later with the conclusion of the UN Convention against Transnational Organised Crime – stemmed not only from differences in national legal approaches and traditions but also from the considerable variations which exist among the groups themselves. There is no single model. As has been pointed out elsewhere:

> The groups vary in shape and size and in skills and specialisations. They operate in different geographical domains and different product markets and use a variety of tactics and mechanisms for circumventing restrictions and avoiding law enforcement. Transnational criminal organisations range from highly structured organisations to more fluid and dynamic networks.[16]

While some forms of organised crime groups are involved primarily in one form of criminal activity, others engage in diverse activities. These range from traditional fields such as gambling, extortion, prostitution, counterfeiting and arms trafficking, to emerging areas like environmental crime, computer-related crime, the theft of technology, industrial espionage, and copyright infringement. A particular concern for the world community is the involvement of a number of crime groups in criminal activities which have a major international dimension such as the smuggling of illegal migrants, the theft and smuggling of vehicles, and money laundering.[17]

In addition to a highly diversified "product base", the most mature of these criminal syndicates have developed extremely complex organisational structures, reminiscent of multinational corporations, which are designed to maximise profits and minimise risks. This analogy with international businesses can greatly assist an understanding of the forces which have helped the growth of this form of criminality. As two leading Australian scholars have stated:

> Just as the move to corporate identity allowed capitalism to flourish, the move to organised crime allows crime to flourish. Economies of scale and limited liability operate within criminal organisations just as they operate in corporate organisations such as General Motors. Both systems reward entrepreneurship, and profit maximization is the ultimate goal of both enterprises. Costs are internalised, and the possibility of monopolistic pricing is ever present.[18]

Notwithstanding such diversity, several organisations have attracted particular attention. Selected because of their involvement in operations which cross national boundaries, this priority group includes long-established networks such as the Chinese Triads, the Colombian cartels, the Japanese Yakuza, and the Sicilian Mafia. Also of concern are newer groups with home bases in the Caribbean, West Africa and central and eastern Europe.[19]

Although the threat posed by these organisations is greatest in their home countries, an increasing ability and willingness to operate across international frontiers in the pursuit of profit means that few states are completely unaffected by their activities. By way of illustration, "[g]roups like the Sicilian Mafia are spreading their activity into both Western and Eastern Europe, in addition to maintaining their traditional connections in the Americas".[20] Similar concerns are attached to the internationalisation of the activities of Russian and other central and eastern European organised crime groups and their impact.

One illustration of such east-west linkages in Europe is to be seen in the area of drug trafficking.[21] Other aspects of the east-west crime flow relate to involvement in a range of activities including the smuggling of illegal migrants and transborder prostitution. Some of the crime opportunities which have been exploited, however, go in the reverse direction. This is reflected, for example, in the west-east movement of luxury cars stolen in Germany and other western European countries.[22]

Available evidence also suggests an increasing degree of co-ordination and co-operation between such groups. As the 1994 Naples Conference was informed:

> Like transnational corporations, transnational criminal organisations are entering more and more frequently into strategic alliances. ... Strategic alliances permit them to cooperate with, rather than compete against, indigenous entrenched criminal organisations, enhance their capacity to circumvent law enforcement, facilitate risk sharing, make it possible to use existing distribution channels, and enable criminal organisations to exploit differential profit margins in different markets.[23]

This phenomenon was clearly illustrated by Operation Green Ice. This was an undercover police operation which "revealed evidence of collusion between the Colombian cocaine cartels and organised crime groups in Italy for the importation and distribution of cocaine into Europe".[24] It was brought to a conclusion in late September 1992 with co-ordinated police raids in Canada, the Cayman Islands, Colombia, Costa Rica, Italy, Spain, the United Kingdom and the United States. In the words of the US Department of State: "The raids resulted in seizures of $47.7 million, and the freezing of 140 bank accounts containing $7.3 million, and dozens of arrests ...".[25] That this is not an isolated example of co-operation is clear. For instance, a 1999 report of the Financial Action Task Force on Money Laundering (FATF) noted the formation of new alliances between Colombian drug traffickers and Russian organised crime groups.[26]

Also worthy of note in this context was the increasing recognition throughout the 1990s of the close relationship between organised crime and corruption. At the 21st Conference of European Ministers of Justice, held in Prague in June 1997, the Minister of Justice of the Czech Republic articulated the link between them as follows:

> In many cases … corruption is indeed one of the basic accompanying phenomena of organised crime. Organised crime tries, through corruption, to obtain the information it seeks, to minimise the risk of being subject to law enforcement measures and to acquire decisive influence in society. Organised crime has at its disposal considerable financial means, thus giving uncontrolled dimensions to corruption. If these phenomena are not effectively tackled and if, rather to the contrary, conditions are created – even if inadvertently – for their growth, the forms of corruption stemming from organised crime may endanger the very foundations of society, and official government structures may become mere puppets in the hands of the criminals.[27]

As will be seen in chapter III, the need to address these issues in combination has become the new orthodoxy; a fact well illustrated by the UN Convention against Transnational Organised Crime which entered into force in September 2003.[28]

The strategy

The drugs trade and organised crime are not only international in character, they are also exorbitantly profitable.[29] While it is notoriously difficult to estimate with any precision the sums generated by such activities, all indications are that they are enormous. As the Director-General of the UN Office in Vienna noted in opening the 1988 Conference for the Adoption of a Convention against Illicit Traffic in Narcotic Drugs and Psychotropic Substances: "The amount of money involved in illicit drug trafficking was staggering. A single drug, cocaine, was worth billions of dollars on the illicit market. … In some cases, the astronomical profits of the drug trade were used to create alternative economies and to undermine legislative and political systems."[30] Although a large number of individuals are involved at the many differing levels of this illicit trade, "most of the gains go to a rich, small elite that has come to wield impressive economic and political power. Some members are believed to have a personal worth that exceeds their country's national debt".[31]

The difficulties in seeking to make estimates in the context of organised crime more generally are even greater. As a June 1996 expert report explained:

> The Italian Mafia, the Japanese Yakuza, the Colombian cartels, Russian and eastern European criminal enterprises, American ethnic groups and other, similarly structured groups are involved in a wide range of criminal activities. In addition to drug trafficking, these enterprises generate funds from loan sharking, illegal gambling, fraud, embezzlement, extortion, prostitution, illegal trafficking in arms and human beings, and a host of other offences.[32]

Increasingly, domestic and international law enforcement strategies have come to emphasise the need to focus on the financial aspects of these forms of crime; that is, to target the huge profits which have been aptly described as "the lifeblood of organised and transnational crime".[33] Somewhat surprisingly, however, even in the early 1980s the necessary legal framework to permit effective action against organised crime through "financial devastation" was found to be lacking in most domestic legal systems and it was totally absent at the international level. Two central tools are now widely acknowledged to be required in order to give effect to this strategy. First, the criminal justice system must make provision for an efficient and effective method of tracing, freezing and eventually confiscating the proceeds derived from criminal activity. While some countries have had at least a limited ability to take such action for some time, legislation to permit the confiscation of criminal proceeds has become popular only in the course of the last fifteen years.[34]

The second basic requirement is that modern legislation must be enacted which both criminalises and counters the process known as money laundering. The term "money laundering" is one of fairly recent vintage. It appears to have first been coined by American law enforcement officials and to have entered popular usage during the Watergate inquiry in the United States in the mid-1970s.[35] The expression seems to have been used in a judicial or legal context for the first time, again in the United States, only in 1982 in the case of US v. $4,255,625.39.[36] Since then it has become widely accepted as a term of art at both the international and domestic level, being extensively used, for example, in the 1990 Council of Europe Convention on Laundering, Search, Seizure and Confiscation of the Proceeds from Crime – an important initiative examined in chapter VII – and in subsequent global and regional treaty instruments. As Tom Sherman, the then Chairperson of the Australian National Crime Authority, has explained: "Money laundering is the process of converting or 'cleansing' property, knowing that such property is derived from serious crime, for the purpose of disguising its origin. The concept of money laundering generally covers those who assist that process and ought reasonably to be aware that they are assisting such a process."[37] Here again the vast majority of the members of the international community lacked appropriate domestic legal remedies. For instance, in the United States the phenomenon of money laundering was addressed for the first time in the Bank Secrecy Act of 1970 and was criminalised as such only in October 1986 with the enactment of the Money Laundering Control Act. Similarly, in the United Kingdom a modern legal framework for drug-related money laundering had to await the passage of the Drug Trafficking Offences Act 1986 and the Criminal Justice (Scotland) Act 1987.

Over the last decade or more, and initially as a result of the 1988 UN drug trafficking convention, the need for a modern anti-money laundering strategy has become widely accepted in both law enforcement and policy making circles; so much so that it was characterised as "the white collar crime of the 1990s ...".[38] As Nadelmann has pointed out: "It was perceived as essential both to identifying and prosecuting the higher-level drug traffickers who rarely if ever came into contact with their illicit goods, and to tracing, seizing and forfeiting their assets."[39] Progress in this area is also seen to be a critical element in the fight against organised crime and, increasingly, as crucial in efforts to combat corruption. Consequently money laundering countermeasures have been afforded a central position in global and regional programmes, political declarations and treaties (most recently the 2003 UN Convention against Corruption).[40]

A further impetus for action has come from the increasing recognition of the negative impact which vast flows of "dirty money" can have on the financial sector. Here we are also confronted with serious difficulties in formulating estimates of any reliability and all such efforts must be regarded with caution.[41] However, the common perception in governmental circles is that the amounts in question are very substantial. For instance, in 1990 the FATF, the work of which is examined in chapters IV, V and VI, estimated that as much as US$85 billion could be available annually for laundering and investment from the proceeds of drug trafficking in the US and Europe.[42] A March 1998 report released by the US State Department's Bureau for International Narcotics and Law Enforcement Affairs placed the annual value of laundered funds derived from all crimes at between US$300 and US$500 billion. Similarly, in a February 1998 speech in Paris the Managing Director of the International Monetary Fund (IMF) underlined the magnitude of the issue of criminal profits in these words: "While we cannot guarantee the accuracy of our figures ... the estimates of the present scale of money laundering transactions are almost beyond imagination – 2 to 5% of global GDP would probably be a consensus range."[43]

It is widely acknowledged that these are but very rough estimates (a fact highlighted by the abandonment in 2000 of a FATF initiative to develop a methodologically sound basis for calculating the magnitude of money laundering).[44] However, for present purposes such uncertainty is not fatal. As Evans has remarked: "Fortunately there is no particularly compelling reason to spend much time on estimates. It is abundantly clear that the proceeds of crime have reached unacceptable levels and that action must be taken to contain criminal profits."[45]

The apparent magnitude of the sums involved has stimulated a growing concern about the adverse consequences which flow from the investment of the substantial profits derived from crime in the legitimate economy and the degree of power and control which results. As Lamberto Dini, the then Italian Minister of the Treasury, remarked in June 1994: "The social danger of money laundering consists in the consolidation of the economic power of criminal organisations, enabling them to penetrate the legitimate economy."[46]

It is, for instance, a commonly expressed view that the Mafia in Italy derives more income from its "legitimate" business interests than from its criminal activities. Although such businesses will, like any other, create wealth and employment, their control by criminal elements poses a number of difficulties and dangers. As one leading law enforcement official has remarked: "There are clear signs that when organised crime invests in legitimate business activity it will attempt to dominate that market and engage in predatory pricing, extortion and corruption. In other words, the organised criminal is not content simply with legitimate profit but to maximise profit, by fair means or foul."[47]

Also of interest in this context is the fact that increasing attention is now being paid to the possible impact of money laundering activities on the world financial system. As Vito Tanzi was to explain in an influential 1996 IMF working paper:

> The international laundering of money has the potential to impose significant costs on the world economy by (a) harming the effective operations of the national economies and by promoting poorer economic policies, especially in some countries; (b) slowly corrupting the financial market and reducing the public's confidence in the international financial system, thus increasing risks and the instability of that system; and (c) as a consequence ... reducing the rate of growth of the world economy.[48]

In recent years the finance ministers of the G7 have ensured that such issues were afforded a high priority by governments, international financial institutions, and other relevant actors.[49]

A final, and critical, element of the strategy to counter money laundering flows from the international nature of the crimes in question and the extent to which criminals resort to the use of the global financial system in an effort to launder their funds and protect them from possible confiscation by law enforcement. Thus, close international co-operation is recognised as essential. The ultimate overall goals of such international action "are to make the environment for transnational criminal organisations hostile and inhospitable, to infiltrate, disrupt, and destroy the network structures on which many of these organisations are based, and to make continued transnational criminal activities as difficult and as costly as possible".[50]

As will be seen in some detail in chapter V, this strategy of financial devastation has, particularly since the events of 11 September 2001, been employed in the fight against terrorism. The underlying philosophy has been explained thus:

> A successful terrorist group, like any criminal organisation, is ... necessarily one that is able to build and maintain an effective financial infrastructure. For this it must develop sources of funding, a means of laundering those funds and then finally a way to ensure that the funds can be used to obtain material and other logistical items needed to commit terrorist acts.[51]

In seeking to exploit this area of potential vulnerability, all of the dimensions of the strategy have been brought into play. That said, particular attention has been devoted to the campaign to freeze the funds and other assets of terrorists, terrorist organisations, and those who finance them. In addition to the immediate impact on the funds in question an effective freezing regime is also thought to combat terrorism by:

- deterring non-designated parties who might otherwise be willing to finance terrorist activity;

- exposing terrorist-financing "money trails" that may generate leads to previously unknown terrorist cells and financiers;

- dismantling terrorist-financing networks by encouraging designated persons to disassociate themselves from terrorist activity and renounce their affiliation with terrorist groups;

- terminating terrorist cash flows by shutting down the pipelines used to move terrorist-related funds or other assets;

- forcing terrorists to use more costly and higher risk means of financing their activities, which makes them more susceptible to detection and disruption; and

- fostering international co-operation and compliance with obligations under UN Security Council Resolution 1267 (1999) and UN Security Council Resolution 1373 (2001).[52]

Notes: I

1. Wilkitzki, P, "Development of an Effective International Crime and Justice Programme – a European View", in Eser, A and Lagodny, O (eds), *Principles and procedures for a new transnational criminal law*, Freiburg, Eigenverlag MPI, 1992, p. 267, at p. 270.

2. "Problems and Dangers Posed by Organised Transnational Crime in the Various Regions of the World", UN Doc. E/CONF. 88/2, 18 August 1994, p. 8.

3. "The Impact of Organised Criminal Activities Upon Society at Large: Report of the Secretary-General", UN Doc. E/CN.15/1993/3, 11 January 1993, p. 4.

4. See, for example, Bruggeman, W, "Transnational Crime: Recent Trends and Future Prospects", in Cullen, P and Gilmore, W (eds), *Crime sans frontières: international and european legal approaches*, Edinburgh, Edinburgh University Press, 1998, p. 85.

5. See generally, Anderson, M, et al., *Policing the European Union*, Oxford, Oxford University Press, 1995.

6. See, for example, Peers, S, *EU justice and home affairs law*, Harlow, Essex, Longman, 2000.

7. See, for example, Gilmore, W (ed), *Mutual assistance in criminal and business regulatory matters*, Cambridge, Cambridge University Press, 1994, at pp. ix-x.

8. See, for example, Clark, R, "Offences of International Concern: Multilateral State Treaty Practice in the Forty Years Since Nuremberg", *Nordic Journal of International Law*, 1988, at pp. 49-119.

9. See generally, Anderson M, *Policing the world: Interpol and the politics of international police cooperation*, Oxford, Oxford University Press, 1989.

10. See, Rigdon, A, "Aspects of International Police and Customs Cooperation", in *Action against transnational criminality: papers from the 1992 Oxford conference on international and white collar crime*, London, Commonwealth Secretariat, 1993, pp. 83-88.

11. See, for example, Council of Europe Doc. P-PG/Psychotropes (93) 3, 22 March 1993.

12. Joutsen, M, "Crime Trends in Central and Eastern Europe", Council of Europe Doc. PC-TP (94) 13, p. 1.

13. *Supra*, note 2, p. 10.

14. See, ibid., at pp. 24-29.

15. See, UN Doc. E/CONF./88/L.3/Add.1, 23 November 1994, at pp. 3-4. See also, European Parliament, "Report of the Committee on Civil Liberties and Internal Affairs on Criminal Activities in Europe", Doc. EN/RR/244/244371, 27 January 1994, at p. 9. There was, however, some harmonisation of approach within the law enforcement community. See, for example, memorandum submitted by Interpol and reproduced in House of Commons, Home Affairs Committee, "Organised Crime", HC Paper 18-II, 1994-95, at p. 150. See also,

Anderson, M, "Control of Organised Crime in the European Community", Working Paper IX, A System of European Police Co-operation after 1992, Department of Politics, University of Edinburgh, 1993, at p. 6; *supra*, note 3, at pp. 2-3; and, Nilsson, H, "Future Corruption Control in Europe", paper presented at the Fifth International Anti-Corruption Conference, Amsterdam, 7-12 March 1992 (typescript), at p. 3.

16. *Supra*, note 2, pp. 10-11.

17. See, ibid., at pp. 16-22.

18. Fisse, B and Fraser, D, "Some Antipodean Skepticisms About Forfeiture, Confiscation of Proceeds of Crimes, and Money Laundering Offenses", *Alabama Law Review*, 1993, p. 737, at p. 738.

19. See, Savona, E and De Feo, M, "Money Trails: International Money Laundering Trends and Prevention/Control Policies", paper presented to the International Conference on Preventing and Controlling Money Laundering and the Use of the Proceeds of Crime: A Global Approach, Courmayeur Mont Blanc, Italy, 18-20 June 1994 (hereafter the 1994 conference) (typescript), at pp. 10-16. Since reproduced in Savona, E U (ed), *Responding to money laundering: international perspectives*, Amsterdam, Harwood Academic Publishers, 1997. Subsequent references are to the original.

20. Ibid., p. 90.

21. See, Gregory, F, "Unprecedented Partnerships in Crime Control: Law Enforcement Issues and Linkages Between Eastern and Western Europe Since 1989", in Anderson, M and den Boer, M (eds), *Policing across national boundaries*, London, Pinter Publishers, 1994, p. 85, at p. 96.

22. See, for example, Adamoli, S et al., *Organised crime around the world*, Helsinki, Heuni, 1998, at pp. 51-52.

23. *Supra*, note 2, p. 23.

24. Sherman, T, "The Internationalisation of Crime and the World Community's Response", in *Action against transnational criminality: papers from the 1993 Oxford conference on international and white collar crime*, London, Commonwealth Secretariat, 1994, p. 1, at p. 5.

25. US Department of State, "International Narcotics Control Strategy Report: Executive Summary", Washington, DC, 1993, p. 111. See also, Wilson, G, "The Changing Game: The United States Evolving Supply-Side Approach to Narcotics Trafficking", *Vanderbilt Journal of Transnational Law*, 1994, p. 1163, at pp. 1204-1206.

26. See, "Financial Action Task Force on Money Laundering: 1998-1999 Report on Money Laundering Typologies", Paris, FATF, at p. 16.

27. Council of Europe Doc. MJU-21 (97) 1, p. 3.

28. See further, chapter III below.

29. See, Fisse and Fraser, op. cit., at p. 739.

30. UN Doc. E/CONF.82/SR.1, p. 3.

31. "International Narcotics Control", *US Department of State Dispatch* (10 September 1990), p. 83, at p. 85.

32. "Financial Action Task Force on Money Laundering: Annual Report 1995-1996", Paris, FATF, Annex 3, p. 2.

33. "Control of Proceeds of Crime: Report of the Secretary-General", UN Doc. E/CN.15/1993/4, 25 January 1993, p. 6.

34. See, ibid., at p. 18.

35. See, Vallance, P, "Money Laundering: The Situation in the United Kingdom", paper presented to the Council of Europe Money Laundering Conference, Strasbourg, France, 18-30 September 1992 (typescript), at p. 1.

36. (1982) 551 F Supp. 314.

37. Sherman, T, "International Efforts to Combat Money Laundering: The Role of the Financial Action Task Force", in MacQueen, H L (ed), *Money laundering*, Edinburgh, Edinburgh University Press, 1993, p. 12, at p. 13.

38. "Report on Financial Havens, Banking Secrecy and Money-Laundering", New York, UN Office for Drug Control and Crime Prevention, 1998, p. 34.

39. Nadelmann, E, *Cops across borders: the internationalization of US criminal law enforcement*, Pennsylvania, Pennsylvania University Press, 1994, p. 388.

40. See further, chapter III below.

41. See, for example, Gold, M and Levi, M, *Money laundering in the UK: an appraisal of suspicion-based reporting*, London, Police Foundation, 1994, at pp. 39-49.

42. See, Gilmore, W (ed), *International efforts to combat money laundering*, Cambridge, Cambridge University Press, 1992, p. 4, at p. 6.

43. "Financial Action Task Force on Money Laundering: Annual Report 1997-1998", Paris, FATF, Annex A, p. 37.

44. See, "Financial Action Task Force on Money Laundering: Annual Report 1999-2000", Paris, FATF, at pp. 26-27.

45. Evans, J, "The Proceeds of Crime: Problems of Investigations and Prosecution", paper presented to the 1994 conference (typescript), p. 1. Since reproduced in Savona, E U (ed), *supra*, note 19.

46. Dini, L, "Opening Remarks" to the 1994 conference, *supra*, note 19 (typescript), p. 2.

47. Sherman, *supra*, note 37, p. 13.

48. Tanzi, V, "Money Laundering and the International Financial System", IMF Working Paper, WP/96/55, May 1996, p. 2. See also, Quirk, P, "Macroeconomic Implications of Money Laundering", IMF Working Paper, WP/96/66, June 1996.

49. This area has been particularly prominent in the work of the G7 since 1998 with special emphasis being placed on the difficulties posed by so-called "offshore financial centres" and on encouraging international financial institutions to play a more proactive role in relevant spheres of activity.

50. "The Feasibility of Elaborating International Instruments, Including Conventions, against Organised Transnational Crime", UN Doc. E/CONF. 88/6, 29 September 1994, p. 2.

51. "Guidance for Financial Institutions in Detecting Terrorist Financing Activities", FATF-XIII, PLEN/39.REV 1, Paris, FATF, p. 2.

52. *Freezing of terrorist assets: international best practices*, Paris, FATF, 2003, p. 2.

Chapter II – Money laundering:
AN OVERVIEW OF THE PROCESS

Introduction

Governmental interest in seeking to combat money laundering is, as we have seen, of relatively recent origin. Similarly, the term itself has entered the accepted vocabulary of diplomacy and legislative drafting only in the course of the last fifteen years. Although the terminology may be relatively recent, the concept is one of very long standing in relation to financially motivated criminal conduct. As McClean has stated:

> From the point of view of the criminal, it is no use making a large profit out of criminal activity if that profit cannot be put to use. ... Putting the proceeds to use is not as simple as it may sound. Although a proportion of the proceeds of crime will be kept as capital for further criminal ventures, the sophisticated offender will wish to use the rest for other purposes. ... If this is to be done without running an unacceptable risk of detection, the money which represents the proceeds of the original crime must be "laundered", put into a state in which it appears to have an entirely respectable provenance.[1]

This is not to say that all criminals will have the need to resort to elaborate schemes in order to create the perception of legitimacy of the source and ownership of wealth and property. Small-time criminals will rarely do so. As Evans has pointed out: "They deal in cash and avoid financial institutions as much as possible. Their criminal associates and suppliers expect cash and they pay cash for most living expenses."[2] Even in more significant ventures the perception of the need to engage in laundering activity will differ widely from country to country. Here the judgment of those involved as to the effectiveness of the local criminal justice system and the associated level of risk of detection and prosecution will be central considerations. For example, in jurisdictions which have effectively embraced modern law enforcement strategies in which the confiscation of the proceeds of crime is used both as a deterrent and as a form of punishment, money laundering schemes are likely to be resorted to with greater frequency than elsewhere. As has been pointed out:

> As financial investigative and prosecutorial activity becomes more professional and effective, the more resources the criminal organisation tends to devote to lowering the risk of being traced and apprehended through the money trail and the risk of losing the criminal proceeds. ... Increased sophistication in prevention and control methods tends to be matched by increased sophistication in money laundering activities, until one side or the other reaches the point of diminishing returns.[3]

In much the same way considerable variations exist, both between countries and among sectors of criminality, as to the scope, complexity and sophistication of the money laundering schemes which are in fact resorted to. As the National Crime Authority of Australia was to note in a December 1991 report:

> Money laundering schemes uncovered so far are generally unsophisticated but some of the very large cases involve the use of complex corporate structures and trusts as part of the laundering process. Most money laundering activity is carried out by the primary offender, not by "professional" launderers, although the use of corrupt or complicit individuals is often crucial to the success of money laundering schemes.[4]

On the other hand, organised crime and drug trafficking groups have created diverse and sophisticated systems with a global reach in order to protect and legitimise the vast profits which are generated by their activities. One Colombian cocaine "kingpin", Rodriguez Gacha, is reputed to have laundered approximately US$130 million using eighty-two company and other accounts in sixteen countries located in Central and South America, the Caribbean, Asia and Europe. As a UN report has noted:

> The basic characteristics of the laundering of the proceeds of crime, which to a large extent also mark the operations of organised and transnational crime, are its global nature, the flexibility and adaptability of its operations, the use of the latest technological means and professional assistance, the ingenuity of the operators and the vast resources at their disposal. In addition, a characteristic that should not be overlooked is the constant pursuit of profits and the expansion into new areas of criminal activity.[5]

It should be stressed, however, that while the international movement of criminal proceeds is a hallmark of laundering activities carried out by or on behalf of such powerful organised groups, it is by no means restricted to them. Indeed, the transnational movement of funds is a common feature of sophisticated laundering activities. For example, an early report carried out by the Ministry of the Solicitor General of Canada, based on an examination of actual police files, revealed that an international dimension was present in over 80% of those cases.[6] While the evidence suggests that the Canadian figures may be higher, for a variety of reasons, than in some other jurisdictions, they do underline the fact "that crime, like much else, is increasingly international".[7]

There are sound reasons for resorting to such an international strategy. At one level, as the European Commission has noted, "[i]nternationalisation of economies and financial services are opportunities which are seized upon by money launderers to carry out their criminal activities, since the origin of funds can be better disguised in an international context".[8] In addition, such mechanisms take advantage of the delays and inefficiencies which confront regulators and the law enforcement community arising from such factors as differences in language and criminal justice systems. Finally, cross-border strategies reflect a natural displacement of activity from juris- dictions which have been active in addressing the issue, to countries and territories which possess no or insufficient anti-money laundering mea- sures. As Savona and De Feo have remarked, launderers are motivated by the desire:

> ... to find and to take advantage of the weakest link in the global regulatory and enforcement chain, by shifting transactions, communications or assets to the country which has the weakest or most corruptible regulatory or police and prosecution authorities, the most restrictive bank and professional secrecy, or extradition, or asset seizure law, the most ineffective bank supervision, etc.[9]

Terrorist organisations, of course, are not primarily motivated by financial gain. None the less, as was pointed out in the previous chapter, they are faced with the need to develop and sustain an adequate financial infra- structure through which to support their activities. While in some instances the required income stream is generated from the commission of profit- generating crimes such as drug trafficking, kidnapping and extortion, fund- ing may also include income derived from legitimate sources. As has been pointed out elsewhere: "A very effective means of raising funds that may eventually be used to finance terrorism is through community solicitation and fundraising appeals, often in the name of organisations with the status of a charitable or relief organisation."[10] Notwithstanding such differences, the preponderant view in law enforcement circles has been that there are significant areas of similarity and overlap. In the words of a February 2003 study:

> While terrorist groups may support themselves with funding from illicit and legit- imate sources, they "process" these funds – that is, move them from the source to where they will be used – in much the same way that non-terrorist criminal groups launder funds. ... [E]xperts continue to find that there is little difference in the methods used by terrorist groups or criminal organisations in attempting to hide or obscure the link between the source of the funds and their eventual destination or purpose.[11]

Accordingly, much of what follows is applicable both to money laundering, in its traditional proceeds-legitimation manifestation, and to terrorist funding activities. That said, there are aspects of the latter, including the relatively small size of the transactions typically involved, which make the effective- ness of countermeasures much more problematic. By way of illustration, "an examination of the financial connections between the September 11th hijackers and their overseas accounts showed that most of the individual transactions were small sums, that is, less that US$10 000, and in most cases the operations consisted of nothing more than wire transfers".[12]

The money laundering process

The stages of the process

It is important to bear in mind that money laundering is a process, often a highly complex one, rather than a single act. Furthermore launderers, as will be seen in greater detail below, make use of a wide variety of techniques in order to accomplish their ends.

In an effort to assist in the exposition and analysis of this phenomenon it has become common to use a three-part framework which seeks to encompass an ideal money laundering scheme. In the words of an Australian report: "Such a scheme would take raw proceeds of crime, held by the offender, manoeuvre them through a process that would conceal their source and confuse or break the money trail, and then return them to the offender legitimised and ready for further safe use."[13] This model can, in turn, be expressed by reference to the following three stages:

- *Placement stage:* where cash derived directly from criminal activity (for example, from sales of drugs) is first placed either in a financial institution or used to purchase an asset.
- *Layering stage:* the stage at which there is the first attempt at concealment or disguise of the source of the ownership of the funds.
- *Integration stage:* the stage at which the money is integrated into the legitimate economic and financial system and is assimilated with all other assets in the system.[14]

In many instances all three of these stages will be clearly discernible. In other cases, however, the basic steps "may occur simultaneously or, more commonly, they may overlap. How the basic steps are used depends on the available laundering mechanisms and the requirements of the criminal organisations".[15]

Money laundering techniques

The context

Money laundering techniques "are innumerable, diverse, complex, subtle and secret".[16] All, however, contain three common features in order to meet the normal requirements of those involved:

- launderers need to conceal the true ownership and origin of the proceeds;
- launderers need to maintain control of the proceeds;
- launderers need to change the form of the proceeds.

Taking these requirements, as well as the three-phased ideal of the process, into consideration, policy makers and agencies charged with the task of devising appropriate countermeasures have sought to identify those points where the launderer is most vulnerable to detection. Given the fact that drug trafficking was, as noted in the previous chapter, the original catalyst for concerted international action in this area it was inevitable that the initial focus would be on the placement stage. This flowed from the fact that drug trafficking, as with certain other forms of profit-generating criminal activity, is highly cash intensive. Indeed, "in the case of heroin and cocaine, the physical volume of notes received from street dealing is much larger than the volume of the drugs themselves".[17] The drug criminal is therefore faced with the problem of physically disposing of a significant volume of small denomination bank notes. It is of relevance to note that while there has been a marked move away from the initial preoccupation with the laundering of drug trafficking proceeds, cash placement continues to be a major focus of law enforcement activity.[18]

Deposit-taking institutions

As a senior Bank of England official has explained: "Because of the money launderer's need to get rid of cash, deposit-taking institutions are particularly vulnerable to being used. Hence, many of the efforts to combat money laundering have concentrated on the procedures adopted by deposit takers."[19] As will be seen in our examination of the recommendations of the Financial Action Task Force in chapter IV and of the European Union directives in chapter VIII, among other initiatives, it has become common practice to impose significant obligations on banks, building societies and other deposit-taking institutions in the fight against money laundering. Requirements for customer identification, the imposition of comprehensive record-keeping rules, and the need to report suspicious transactions are but some of the means used to ensure, through the creation of an audit or paper trail for use by law enforcement authorities and otherwise, that the risks for the criminal are maximised at the placement stage. This policy also recognises the wider attractiveness of deposit-taking institutions, as providers of an extensive range of services, to launderers at the layering and integration stages.

The imposition of obstacles to placement have generated a range of innovative responses from criminal money managers. For example, in the United States it has become common practice for criminals to engage the services of numerous individuals to convert cash of small denominations into larger bills – a process sometimes known as the "refining" of dirty money.[20] A similar modus operandi has been used in an effort to evade the US legal requirements for the mandatory reporting of all cash transactions over a specified threshold. Known as "smurfing", this involves the structuring of transactions in such a way as to avoid the automatic triggering of the system. As a law enforcement official has explained, this "involves the employment of 'smurfs', money couriers of innocuous appearance who make large numbers of small transactions, always under US$10 000, at various financial institutions. In this manner, large quantities of cash can enter the banking system without attracting undue attention".[21]

The task of the launderer is, of course, greatly eased if the integrity of bank employees can be compromised. In a small minority of cases banks themselves come to acquire a corrupt culture which lends itself to involvement as a willing partner in laundering operations. This was most strikingly the case with the Bank of Credit and Commerce International (BCCI).[22] The involvement of BCCI in facilitating the international movement of criminal proceeds first came to public attention in late 1988 with the culmination of a US customs undercover investigation known as Operation C-Chase. This identified some US$32 million of laundered funds and resulted in the arrest of a substantial number of individuals including nine high-ranking BCCI employees. In addition to the subsequent conviction of staff members in both the United States and the United Kingdom the bank itself was proceeded against. As the US Department of State noted: "BCCI Ltd. plead guilty to one count of conspiracy and twenty-eight counts of money laundering. BCCI SA plead guilty to one count of conspiracy and two counts of money laundering. BCCI's convictions resulted in the forfeiture of approximately US$15.3 million in criminal penalties to the US Government."[23]

Operation C-Chase was, as Ehrenfeld has noted, "the beginning of the end for BCCI"[24] and it was eventually closed down by co-ordinated international regulatory action in July 1991 leaving an estimated 530 000 creditors worldwide and a substantial "black hole" in its accounts.[25] In a 1993 report prepared on behalf of the UN Secretary-General it was alleged that this rogue bank was responsible for laundering some US$20 billion.[26]

In the vast majority of cases, however, launderers are confronted by non-corrupt credit institutions seeking to give effect to an increasingly sophisticated package of countermeasures. In these circumstances it was inevitable that there would be increased efforts by criminal money managers to shift the placement stage to less well regulated, or totally unregulated, jurisdictions. This can be accomplished in various ways including currency smuggling. As the International Criminal Police Organisation (ICPO/Interpol) has noted:

> The money courier fills suitcases with cash, hides cash in cargo, or sends cash in an international express package. The money is physically transported to a foreign country that has no currency controls and preferably has bank secrecy laws. ... In the tax haven country the cash will be deposited into a bank or other financial institution and from there it can be moved at will. The money is now indistinguishable from the legitimate funds that are routinely transferred throughout the world's financial systems.[27]

Resort to such a strategy of geographic displacement is not without risk. At a practical level the launderer must weigh both the possibility of loss or theft as well as the risk of detection and subsequent action by law enforcement. In so far as the latter is concerned, a growing number of countries have put in place legal structures which permit action to be taken to interdict certain categories of cross-border cash shipments. Three basic systems have been used. Some countries, including Australia and the United States, have imposed mandatory reporting of the import or export (or both) of international currency transfers above a stipulated threshold. Failure to comply with such requirements can result in the imposition of penalties and the forfeiture of the currency. In other jurisdictions, such as the United Kingdom, the legislature has given the relevant law enforcement authorities the right to seize large sums of cash which are being imported or exported in circumstances which give rise to reasonable grounds to believe that it represents the proceeds of criminal activity. Yet other jurisdictions are able to invoke provisions of their exchange control or other similar legislation.

In the event that cash placement, at home or abroad, is successful, the layering process can commence. Although a range of possibilities exist, in recent years particular concern has been expressed about the abuse of electronic fund or "wire" transfers. As Savona and De Feo have remarked: "wire transfers are probably the most important layering method available to money launderers. They offer criminals many advantages as they seek to cover their trail. Speed, distance, minimal audit trail, and increased anonymity amid the enormous daily volume of electronic fund transfers are all major benefits".[28]

Although there are numerous ways for launderers to abuse the system:

> … the objective for most money launderers is to aggregate funds from different accounts and move those funds through accounts at different banks until the origins of the funds cannot be traced. Most often this involves moving the funds out of the country, through a bank account in a country with strict bank secrecy laws, and possibly back.[29]

At this stage, detection becomes extremely difficult and full integration relatively straightforward.

While the major policy focus has been on the use of banks and other deposit-taking institutions for the purposes of laundering, it is clear that a wide range of other mechanisms, either alone or in combination, can be used for the same purpose. As Tom Sherman, a former President of the FATF, has stated: "Experience shows that money launderers will use almost any form of corporate and trust activity to launder their profits. The mainstream and underground financial systems in all their varieties are susceptible."[30] It is to this wider panorama that this study now turns.

Non-bank financial institutions

The introduction of measures to prevent banks being readily used for the purposes of money laundering has, without doubt, made life more difficult by increasing the costs and the risks for those involved. However, launderers have proved to be adept in identifying and exploiting weaknesses in such structures. This has been manifested not only in a resort to more complex techniques such as "smurfing" but also, and increasingly, in a diversion of activities from better to less well-regulated sectors of the economy. As the US Department of State has noted:

> In too many countries, the governments have concentrated on identifying cash deposits at the teller's window, and have failed to mount a total program against money laundering that takes into account all of the traditional and non-traditional resources used today to convert illicit proceeds. Traffickers are all too familiar with traditional customer identification procedures used by banks, so they have adopted new strategies.[31]

In recent years launderers have proved to be particularly innovative in the way in which they use "non-bank financial institutions and systems". This term will be used, for present purposes, to encompass "those businesses which provide bank-like services ... but which are historically less closely supervised than traditional financial institutions".[32] The activities most commonly mentioned within the FATF and other expert groups include, among others, bureaux de change; cheque cashers and money transmission services; securities and commodities brokers; life insurance companies; and underground and parallel banking systems.

Some of these activities, as with cheque cashers and bureaux de change, have a singular utility and significance in the cash placement stage of the process. Others, such as the life insurance industry, can be used for placement but are particularly associated with layering and integration. By way of example, cash could be used for the purchase of a single premium life insurance policy. With placement secured it could subsequently be sold or switched to other forms of investment. The final, or integration, stage would be represented by the redemption of the contract or by a switch to other forms of investment.[33] Resort to substantial cash transactions in this sector is, in many jurisdictions, sufficiently unusual as to generate suspicion. Accordingly, use at the placement stage is infrequent save with the complicity of an employee.

Somewhat similar considerations apply when the launderer seeks to engage in a strategy which involves investment in stocks and bonds. In an era characterised by the ever-increasing integration of financial markets and global trading, the securities sector holds an obvious attraction for the sophisticated money launderer. As a February 2003 report has explained:

> The securities sector on a global scale is characterised by its diversity, the ease with which trading can now take place (through electronic trading for example), and the ability to perform transactions in markets with little regard to national borders. These characteristics make securities markets attractive to the ordinary

investor looking for a good return on his or her money. These same characteristics, along with the sheer volume of transactions in many markets, also make the securities sector a potentially inviting mechanism for the laundering of funds from criminal sources.[34]

While there have been reported instances of the proceeds of such crimes as drug trafficking, insider dealing and market manipulation being laundered through securities investments, evidence suggests that its use is restricted to the more sophisticated and professional operations. A number of factors account for this. First, and most importantly, "in many jurisdictions, securities and futures brokers that are authorised to receive and hold customer funds do not, in most cases, accept such funds in the form of cash. For this reason, the securities and futures markets may not lend themselves to the 'placement' phase of money laundering".[35] In other words the use of cash as a means of settlement of securities transactions is likely, in most financial centre jurisdictions, to attract suspicion and thus greatly increase the risk of detection. Consequently, it is again only with the complicity of employees that launderers can readily avoid the need to convert cash into negotiable instruments, through a bank or otherwise, before seeking to access the securities markets.

The resulting emphasis on the layering and integration stages of the process acts as a further disincentive to the popularisation of its use. As has been pointed out elsewhere: "It is unlikely that this area will often be used as few people understand the workings of securities and futures markets. International experience seems to indicate that the securities and futures markets are only used in money laundering schemes by persons who are thoroughly familiar with the system."[36] For those able to access the markets for these purposes its attractive features can be brought fully into play in order to break or confuse the audit trail. In such circumstances, detection becomes difficult though not impossible. One method used to improve the prospects for detection has been to impose on market participants the obligation to report suspicious transactions to the authorities. In some jurisdictions, such as the United Kingdom, official guidance has been provided to assist brokers and others to more readily identify the kinds of dealing patterns and settlement methods which might be indicative of money laundering. In so far as the former is concerned, these include such things as entering into "a large number of securities transactions across a number of jurisdictions" and "buying and selling of a security with no discernible purpose or in circumstances which appear unusual, e.g. churning at the client's request".[37] A somewhat similar effort has been undertaken by others including the International Organisation of Securities Commissions (Iosco).[38]

In many countries money launderers also have the option of using alternative remittance systems; sometimes known as "money or value transfer services" (MTV). This refers to "a financial service that accepts cash, cheques, other monetary instruments or other stores of value in one location and pays a corresponding sum in cash or other form to a beneficiary in another location by means of a communication, message, transfer or through a clearing network to which the MTV service belongs. Transactions performed by such services can involve one or more intermediaries and a third party final payment".[39] There has been concern in specialist circles for many years that such underground or parallel banking systems were vulnerable to abuse by criminal elements.[40] Indeed, in the wake of the terrorist attacks of September 2001 and the indications of the use of such systems for terrorist purposes there has been significant additional focus on this issue.[41]

While there are numerous alternative remittance systems, three have attracted particular attention: Hawala/hundi; Chinese/East Asian systems; and the Black Market Peso Exchange. All share certain characteristics.[42] All pose major problems for law enforcement. For example:

> ... unregulated MTV services permit funds to be sent anonymously, allowing the money launderer or terrorist financier to freely send funds without having to identify himself or herself. In some cases, few or no records are kept. In other cases, records may be kept but are inaccessible to authorities. The lack of adequate records makes it extremely difficult, if not impossible, to trace the funds after the transaction has been completed.[43]

Non-financial institutions

As Ronald Noble, then a Vice-President of the FATF, put it in a paper prepared for a 1994 UN conference held in Courmayeur, Italy: "Money laundering is not simply a problem faced by the banking community and other mainstream financial institutions."[44] Non-financial businesses of various kinds have been identified as being of ever-increasing importance as vehicles for carrying out laundering operations.

Perhaps best known in this regard are the attractions offered by the use of companies in laundering schemes. As Beare and Schneider have noted: "The incorporation, financing and operation of companies satisfies the three prime objectives of a laundering vehicle. It allows criminals to convert illicit cash into other assets, create a perception of a legitimate source of funds, all the while effectively concealing the true beneficial owner – the criminal enterprise."[45]

Law enforcement experience has demonstrated that both active businesses and so-called "shell" companies are frequently used.

It is common for those involved in laundering operations to either establish or purchase a business of a highly cash-intensive type. These include, among others, retail shops, car washes, vending machine enterprises, restaurants and bars. It is then relatively simple to commingle illicit funds with those generated by the legitimate activities of the company. As has been pointed out elsewhere: "While the excess profits are subject to tax, the trafficker is now free to spend his profits since he has a legitimate source of income."[46] While such methods provide the launderer with both legitimacy and respectability they do present certain limitations. In the words of an Australian National Crime Authority report: "Smaller-cash businesses may be unattractive to some money launderers because they do not offer large-scale laundering opportunities."[47] Highly unrealistic revenue figures for the type of business concerned may attract suspicion and the consequent attention of investigators. This is well illustrated by a Canadian case in which a launderer established two retail outlets and then opened a corporate bank account locally. Thereafter, substantial funds moved through the account. Surveillance conducted on the stores revealed clearly insufficient business to generate the quantities of cash being deposited.[48] Such difficulties can be minimised. The criminal enterprise concerned can, for instance, extend the range and number of the businesses concerned. It can also resort to the use of other corporate techniques.

Of significance in this regard has been the establishment of shell corporations and similar entities such as "ghost" or "front" companies. As Beare and Schneider have noted: "They are legally incorporated and registered by the criminal organisation but have no real business apart from the manipulation of business and financial transactions for laundering purposes."[49] The evidence suggests that these are commonly established in offshore financial centres. For present purposes it will suffice to note that, from the perspective of the money launderer, several of the services often offered by such jurisdictions are highly attractive. Such features include "[e]ase of incorporation, especially where ownership can be held through nominees or bearer shares, or where off-the-shelf corporations can be acquired".[50] Such offshore shell corporations have a special utility at the placement and layering stages of the operation. In the latter context it is not uncommon for several such companies in different jurisdictions to be used in an effort to eliminate the audit trail. In many cases, however, the overall needs of the criminal will require that the funds are eventually "repatriated in such a way that it appears to have been legitimately acquired from abroad".[51]

There are a number of methods by which this goal can be achieved. One is by direct investment. Here, funds held offshore are invested in legitimate businesses in the criminal's own country with the foreign company shown as the purchaser. An interesting variant of this is the loan back method. As a 1997 UNDCP study has explained, in this situation a criminal:

> ... with illicit funds in a foreign account decides to make an investment, which he secures with a down payment of legitimate funds. To pay the balance, he takes out two loans, one legitimate, and the second from the foreign bank holding his illicit funds (probably offshore). He then repays the loans plus interest as if they were both legitimate. In some cases these repayments may be tax deductible. The income from the initial investment is sufficiently documented to appear entirely

legitimate, and the trafficker is free to use it in any way he chooses. As he repays the loan of his initial illicit funds, they are again available for him to "borrow" and the cycle can be repeated.[52]

A further technique is to resort to some form of invoice manipulation. This can involve entirely fictitious transactions as when an offshore shell company pays its domestic counterpart in full upon presentation of a false invoice. Alternatively, where the launderers own ostensibly legitimate businesses in both the country where the criminal proceeds are generated and in the jurisdiction where the money is to be placed, the transfer of funds can be disguised by the inflation of invoices relating to actual trading activities. Just such a method was used in the undercover operation known as Green Ice which was discussed in the previous chapter. In that instance American law enforcement officials, representing themselves as money launderers, established a chain of leather goods stores. As the then Chief of the Money Laundering Section of the US Department of Justice explained: "The leather stores were used by the money launderers as a means of shipping leather goods to the United States and padding the invoices to show more merchandise than actually was shipped. This enabled them to legitimise the export businesses and to justify the United States currency deposits in their bank accounts in Colombia."[53] It has been reported that in this case twenty tonnes of imported leather goods were listed for each tonne actually shipped.[54] Research in the United States has indicated that such practices are widespread.[55]

In all of the examples given so far, launderers exploit corporate techniques based on ownership and control to further their ends. However, there are also various ways in which legitimate non-financial institutions can be exploited by launderers without their knowledge or consent. Those that deal extensively in cash are particularly vulnerable. As Noble has remarked: "Such businesses range from casinos and other gambling operations to vendors of luxury goods of all kinds."[56]

In many jurisdictions gambling is legal. It is also often less well regulated than banking. Perhaps less fully appreciated among the general public is that many modern casinos offer a wide range of banking-type services to their customers. These include the sale and cashing of cheques, foreign currency exchange, the hiring of safety deposit boxes, and international wire transfers. Furthermore, the gambling industry is highly cash intensive thus affording an unusual degree of anonymity to an individual involved in the placement stage of a laundering scheme. At its most basic level the casino may be used for little more than the "refining" of small denomination banknotes. Another common practice is to seek to represent criminal proceeds as winnings thus both concealing the true origin of the funds and legitimising them. The simple process involved has been described by ICPO/Interpol thus:

> This method is accomplished by the money launderer when casino chips in large amounts are purchased for cash or when cash is deposited with the casino for

alleged further gaming activity. The money launderer then redeems his chips or closes his account and requests a cheque either in his name or a third party name. The cheque is then deposited in the money launderer's account. If there are any questions about the source of the deposit it is explained as gambling winnings.[57]

In one case reported by the Royal Hong Kong Police to the FATF some US$8 million, representing cash from street drug sales in that jurisdiction, was processed in this way through casinos in the United States. The cheques were then deposited in accounts in Hong Kong, being subsequently transferred to Australia for use in real estate purchases.[58] Such high-volume and high-value transactions are, however, the exception. Unwanted suspicion is likely to be aroused by large-scale operations unless the complicity of the casino management has been arranged in advance or the enterprise itself has come to be controlled by organised crime. The attractiveness of such methods will, of course, differ widely from country to country depending on a range of factors including the size and nature of the industry and the degree of regulation to which it is subject.

A number of other types of non-financial institutions have also been identified by the law enforcement community as being vulnerable to abuse. Many of these, such as art and antique dealers, auction houses, and sellers of luxury goods and precious metals deal in high-value items in an environment where the use of cash is by no means uncommon. These business sectors are traditionally also largely unregulated.

New possibilities for abuse continue to be revealed by practice. In the area of efforts to combat the financing of terrorism, for instance, significant concern has come to surround the possibilities of misuse of non-profit organisations in different parts of the world. By way of illustration:

> One non-profit organisation solicited donations from local charities in a donor region, in addition to fundraising efforts conducted at its headquarters in a beneficiary region. This non-profit organisation falsely asserted that the funds collected were destined for orphans and widows. In fact, the finance chief of this organisation served as the head of organised fundraising for Usama bin Laden. Rather than providing support for orphans and widows, funds collected by the non-profit organisation were turned over to al-Qaida operatives.[59]

As will be seen in chapter V, the first tentative steps have now been taken to minimise the potential to exploit charitable organisations, relief operations and other similar bodies for such purposes. Guidance has emphasised such issues as enhanced financial transparency, programmatic verification, and improved administrative procedures. However, it is recognised that the nature, scale and diversity of the sector, among other factors, militates in favour of risk-based and functional rather than mechanistic and legalistic solutions.

"Gatekeepers"

Throughout the second half of the 1990s there emerged a broad-based concern that international and domestic anti-money laundering measures had paid insufficient attention to the potential for the abuse of members of the legal professions and other "gatekeepers" to the international financial system (such as auditors and accountants). At the policy level this issue came to occupy a prominent position on the agenda of such bodies as the European Commission and the meetings of G7 finance ministers. All were significantly influenced in their thinking by the annual reports on money laundering methods and techniques produced under the auspices of the Financial Action Task Force (FATF). A constantly recurring concern within those expert reports was the role played (knowingly or unwittingly) by such professional service providers in money laundering schemes. For example, the relevant part of the 1996-97 FATF typologies report reads as follows:

> As anti-money laundering regulations have increased in many countries the criminals place increasing reliance on professional money laundering facilitators. The experts reported a significant number of cases involving lawyers, accountants, financial advisers, notaries, secretarial companies and other fiduciaries whose services are employed to assist in the disposal of criminal profits. Among the most common tactics observed have been the use of solicitors' or attorneys' client accounts for the placement and layering of funds. By this method the launderer hopes to obtain the advantage of anonymity, through the solicitor-client privilege. The making available of bank accounts and the provision of professional advice and services as to how and where to launder criminal money is likely to increase as counter measures become more effective.[60]

The level of concern over the vulnerability of the legal professions and other "gatekeepers" did not diminish over time. Indeed, the misuse of lawyers, notaries, accountants and other professionals was again a significant point of focus in the 2000-01 FATF typologies exercise.[61] Similarly, the report issued in February 2002 "stressed the urgent need to bring the non-financial professionals, when performing particular functions, under the same anti-money laundering rules as for other financial services".[62]

In the work of the FATF it is, however, acknowledged that not all of the professional services provided by such "gatekeepers" have the same attraction to or possibility of abuse by criminal elements. As a 2 February 2001 report was to note:

> Not all of these functions have the same utility to a potential laundering operation. The functions that are the most useful to the potential launderer include:
>
> • Creation of corporate vehicles or other complex legal arrangements (trusts, for example). Such constructions may serve to confuse the links between the proceeds of a crime and the perpetrator.

- Buying or selling of property. Property transfers serve as either the cover for transfers of illegal funds (layering stage) or else they represent the final investment of these proceeds after their having passed through the laundering process (integration stage).

- Performing financial transactions. Sometimes these professionals may carry out various financial operations on behalf of the client (for example, cash deposits or withdrawals on accounts, retail foreign exchange operations, issuing and cashing cheques, purchase and sale of stock, sending and receiving international funds transfers, etc.).

- Financial and tax advice. Criminals with a large amount of money to invest may pose as individuals hoping to minimise their tax liabilities or desiring to place assets out of reach in order to avoid future liabilities.

- Gaining introductions to financial institutions.

In some of these functions, the potential launderer is obviously not only relying on the expertise of these professionals but is also using them and their professional status to minimise suspicion surrounding their criminal activities. A solicitor representing a client in a financial transaction or providing an introduction to a financial institution lends a certain amount of credibility in the eyes of the transactor because of the ethical standards presumed to be associated with the work of such professions.[63]

It is of importance to note that the above range of possible abuses of the professional services provided by lawyers and other "gatekeepers" have a potential impact on all three stages normally used in the analysis of money laundering schemes.

A further source of insight on this subject was the material generated in the context of the FATF mutual evaluation process (described in chapter VI below). Although the individual country evaluations are confidential and thus not in the public domain, the FATF published, in February 2002, a "Review of FATF Anti-Money Laundering Systems and Mutual Evaluation Procedures 1992-1999". It reads, in part, thus: "Many reports also suggested that certain categories of professionals should be brought within the scope of anti-money laundering controls, due to the increasing involvement of such persons (knowingly or otherwise) in money laundering schemes."[64] In the light of such perceptions it is not surprising that both the FATF and the European Union have acted to bring such activities within the system of controls; initiatives which, as will be seen in subsequent chapters, have not been without controversy.

The emergence of new challenges

Given the range and complexity of money laundering methods it has come to be recognised that it is essential for law enforcement officials and regulators with a mandate in this area to have regular discussions with their counterparts abroad concerning trends, identified variations in methods and emerging threats. As was noted above, within the FATF, the nature and activities of which are examined in chapters IV to VI, this has assumed the form of an annual money laundering typologies exercise. The perceived value of this forum for the exchange of insights into enforcement issues has been such as to persuade other specialist anti-money laundering bodies, including the Caribbean Financial Action Task Force (CFATF) and the Asia/Pacific Group (APG) (as to which see chapter IX), to take similar steps.

At the FATF typologies meeting held in Rome in November 2002, a broad range of issues was discussed. Topics extended from money laundering through the securities sector to the vulnerability of the gold and diamond markets for money laundering purposes.[65] This forum is also used to monitor emerging challenges or threats. Some of these, as with the introduction of the euro, are of a short-term nature. Others, as with the emergence of new payment technologies, are ongoing and are consequently returned to from time to time.

The seriousness with which the latter is viewed was underlined in 1996 when the FATF elaborated a new recommendation which called upon its members to "pay special attention to money laundering threats inherent in new or developing technologies that might favour anonymity, and take measures, if needed, to prevent their use in money laundering schemes". In 2003 this recommendation was strengthened by the inclusion of a specific requirement that financial institutions have "policies and procedures in place to address any specific risks associated with non-face to face business relationships or transactions".[66]

Two aspects of developing "cyberpayments" technology have attracted particular attention in specialist circles to date; namely, smart cards and network-based systems. As has been noted elsewhere, smart cards are "credit card like devices containing a microchip on which value is encoded. The cards can be read by vending machines or terminals that deduct the amount of each transaction from the total stored value. When the card's value is used up, it may be re-loaded via ATM, telephone, "electronic wallet" or personal computer, or it may be discarded".[67] One aspect of this developing technology which has been a source of concern is the so-called "peer-to-peer" variant which would permit electronic cash to be transferred from card to card without recourse to a financial intermediary. Other features which present acute actual or potential challenges relate to the capacity of smart cards to operate in multiple currencies and without limits as to the value which can be stored. Taken together, for example, stored value card technology could significantly reduce the need for, or the vulnerability to detection associated with, the bulk smuggling of currency thus rendering efforts to detect cross-border flows difficult if not impossible. More recently, the implications of WAP technology have found a place in these discussions.[68]

The second aspect of this technological revolution of relevance in this context concerns those systems which use the Internet as a means of transfer of electronic or "e-money". Perhaps the most firmly entrenched manifestation of this dimension of the issue is represented by on-line banking. As has been pointed out elsewhere, this "has increasingly come to mean the method whereby certain types of financial transactions may be performed through the Internet website of those banks that offer this service. ... In its most basic form, the service provided includes verification of cheque account balances and transfers among accounts at the same institution. In those systems that allow payments or transfers to be made, the customer is often restricted in the amount of transaction or the identity of the beneficiary".[69] The provision of such services is growing very rapidly in many countries. Other network-based systems "contemplate the use of digital value or tokens, where the value is purchased from an issuer then stored on the computer rather than held in an account".[70]

A further element of complexity is presented by the potential to marry these sophisticated technologies in so-called "hybrid systems". As one report on the subject has noted:

> The interrelationship of the different features and the rapid move toward system interoperability (where stored value cards and/or network-based systems are compatible and accepted by each other) makes it difficult to identify distinct categories. Systems are now being developed that would allow stored value cards to be used interchangeably, regardless of issuer. Other developing systems would permit cards to be used in connection with network-based systems.[71]

Over recent years the FATF, among others, has sought both to develop a better understanding of the possible law enforcement and regulatory implications of these innovations and to enter into a dialogue with the leading private sector developers and providers of these technologies and products. Given its current stage of development, particular attention has been devoted to the implications of on-line banking for the efficacy of conventional money laundering countermeasures. These include, among others, the problems posed for traditional approaches to customer due diligence procedures in general and especially customer identification. As the Basel Committee on Banking Supervision noted in October 2001: "The impersonal and borderless nature of electronic banking combined with the speed of the transaction inevitably creates difficulty in customer identification and verification."[72] Regulatory and specialist bodies have devoted substantial attention to the formulation of measures designed to mitigate these and other risk factors.[73]

It is to be hoped that the ongoing consideration of these technological issues, and the associated but crucial dialogue with the private sector, will permit governments and industry to determine what steps they can "take together to ensure that these systems are developed in ways that minimize their potential abuse by criminals".[74]

Conclusions

From the limited and necessarily partial overview of money laundering techniques provided in this chapter some appreciation will have been gained of the range of options which are provided by a modern economic system to those who are intent on legitimising the proceeds derived from criminal activity or distancing themselves from the source of terrorist funds. There is an obvious truth in the contention of Beare and Schneider that the available methods "are limited only by the imagination of the criminal enterprise".[75]

While recourse to relatively simple schemes carried out by the perpetrator of the profit-generating offence still appears to be the norm in many jurisdictions, there is a clear trend towards greater complexity, sophistication and internationalisation of activities. This seems to be especially so for powerful organised crime groups which are able to call upon the expertise of accountants, lawyers and other professionals.

It is against this background that the problems confronted by the law enforcement and regulatory communities must be seen and the adequacy of the evolving programme of money laundering countermeasures must be assessed. It is to these issues that this study now turns.

Notes: II

1. McClean, J D, *International co-operation in civil and criminal matters*, Oxford, Oxford University Press, 2002, at p. 261.

2. Evans, J L, "The Proceeds of Crime: Problems of Investigation and Prosecution". Paper presented at the International Conference on Preventing and Controlling Money Laundering and the Use of the Proceeds of Crime: A Global Approach, Courmayeur Mont Blanc, Italy, 18-20 June 1994 (hereafter 1994 conference) (typescript) p. 2. Since reproduced in Savona, E U (ed), *Responding to money laundering: international perspectives*, Amsterdam, Harwood Academic Publishers, 1997. Subsequent references are to the original. For a somewhat broader view of the categories of offenders who, based on UK experience, do not launder the proceeds of their crimes in any systematic way see, the evidence of Professor M. Levi reproduced in, House of Commons, Home Affairs Committee, "Organised Crime", HC Paper 18-II, 1994-95 (hereafter Select Committee), at p. 187.

3. Savona, E U, and De Feo, M A, "Money Trails: International Money Laundering Trends and Prevention/Control Policies". Paper presented at the 1994 conference, *supra*, note 2 (typescript), p. 84, Since reproduced in Savona, E U (ed), *supra*, note 2. Subsequent references are to the original.

4. National Crime Authority, *Taken to the cleaners: money laundering in Australia*, Canberra, Australian Government Publishing Service, 1991, Vol. I, p. vii.

5. "Control of Proceeds of Crime: Report of the Secretary-General", UN Doc. E/CN.15/1993/4, 25 January 1993, p. 11.

6. See, Beare, M E and Schneider, S, *Tracing of illicit funds: money laundering in Canada*, Solicitor General of Canada, Ottawa, 1990, at p. 304.

7. Evans, op. cit., p. 14.

8. Reproduced in Gilmore, W (ed), *International efforts to combat money laundering*, Cambridge, Cambridge University Press, 1992, p. 243.

9. Savona and De Feo, op. cit., p. 93.

10. "Guidance for Financial Institutions in Detecting Terrorist Financing Activities", FATF XIII, PLEN/39. REV 1, Paris, FATF, p.2.

11. "Financial Action Task Force on Money Laundering: Report on Money Laundering Typologies 2002-2003", Paris, FATF, p. 3.

12. *Supra*, note 10, p. 4.

13. *Supra*, note 4, p. 31.

14. Drage, J, "Countering Money Laundering", *Bank of England Quarterly Bulletin*, November 1992, p. 418, at p. 420. For an interesting variant on this classic approach see, "Report on Financial Havens, Banking Secrecy and Money-Laundering", New York, UN Office for Drug Control and Crime Prevention, 1998, at pp. 4-5.

15. *Money laundering: guidance notes for mainstream banking, lending and deposit taking activities*, London, Joint Money Laundering Steering Group, 1993, paragraph 8.

16. "International Narcotics Control Strategy Report", Washington, DC, US Department of State, 1988, p. 46.

17. "Financial Action Task Force on Money Laundering: Report of 6 February, 1990", reproduced in Gilmore, W (ed), op. cit. p. 4, at p. 7.

18. See, "Financial Action Task Force on Money Laundering: Report on Money Laundering Typologies 2000-2001", Paris, FATF, at pp. 16-17.

19. Drage, J, "Countering Money Laundering: The Response of the Financial Sector", in MacQueen, H L (ed), *Money laundering*, Edinburgh, Edinburgh University Press, 1993, p. 60, at p. 61.

20. See, Chaikin, D A, "Money Laundering: An Investigatory Perspective", *Criminal Law Forum*, 1991, p. 467, at pp. 478-479.

21. Bowie, B W, "Money Laundering Techniques" (typescript), Drug Enforcement Directorate, Royal Canadian Mounted Police, February 1988, p. 3.

22. See generally, Adams, J R and Frantz, D, *A Full Service Bank*, New York, Pocket Books, 1992.

23. "International Narcotics Control Strategy Report", Washington, DC, US Department of State, 1991, p. 347.

24. Ehrenfeld, R, *Evil money: encounters along the money trail*, New York, Harper Business, 1992, p. 70.

25. See, for example, "Prison for Naqvi over BCCI Fraud", *The Times*, London, 20 October 1994.

26. See, "The Impact of Organised Criminal Activities Upon Society at Large: Report of the Secretary-General", UN Doc. E/CN.15/1993/3, 11 January 1993, at p. 12.

27. *FOPAC Bulletin*, No. 6, 1991, p. 3. The use of cash carriers by terrorist financiers is also a matter of growing concern.

28. Savona and De Feo, op. cit., p. 21.

29. Paper (untitled) presented by R A Small of the US Federal Reserve System to the Financial Action Task Force Money Laundering Symposium, Singapore, 21-23 April 1993 (typescript), p. 76.

30. Sherman, T, "International Efforts to Combat Money Laundering: The Role of the Financial Action Task Force", in MacQueen, H L (ed), *supra*, note 19, p. 12, at p. 14.

31. See, "International Narcotics Control Strategy Report", Washington, DC, US Department of State, 1994, at p. 472.

32. Savona and De Feo, op. cit., p. 19.

33. See, *Money laundering: guidance notes for insurance and retail investment products*, London, Joint Money Laundering Steering Group, 1993, at paragraph 8.

34. *Supra*, note 11, p. 11.

35. "International Organisation of Securities Commissions, Working Party Number 4, Report on Money Laundering" (typescript: 1992), p. 4.

36. *Supra*, note 4, p. 43.

37. *Money laundering guidance notes for the financial sector revised and consolidated June 1997*, London, Joint Money Laundering Steering Group, 1997, Appendix I.

38. See, *supra*, note 35, at p. 8.

39. *Combating the abuse of alternative remittance systems: international best practices*, Paris, FATF, 2003, p. 2.

40. See, for example, Cassidy, W L, "Fei-Ch'ien, Flying Money: A Study of Chinese Underground Banking". Paper presented at the 12th International Asian Organised Crime Conference, Fort Lauderdale, FL, USA, 26 June 1990 (typescript).

41. See, for example, chapter V below. See also, for example, the October 2001 report of the Asia/Pacific Group (APG) Typologies Working Group on alternative remittance and underground banking services. ICPO/Interpol has also been active in its study of this issue in recent years.

42. See, "Financial Action Task Force on Money Laundering: Report on Money Laundering Typologies 1999-2000", Paris, FATF, at pp. 4-8.

43. *Supra*, note 39, p. 2.

44. Noble, R, "The Financial Action Task Force Recommendations and their Implementation". Paper presented to the 1994 conference (typescript), *supra,* note 2, paragraph 28.

45. Beare and Schneider, op. cit., p. 183.

46. *Supra*, note 21, p. 4.

47. *Supra*, note 4, p. 47.

48. Beare and Schneider, op. cit., p. 188.

49. Ibid., p. 186.

50. *Supra*, note 31, p. 477.

51. Chaikin, op. cit., p. 488.

52. UNDCP, *World drug report*, Oxford, Oxford University Press, 1997, p. 39.

53. Greenberg, T S, "Anti-Money Laundering Activities in the United States", in *Action against transnational criminality: papers from the 1993 Oxford conference on international and white collar crime*, London, Commonwealth Secretariat, 1994, p. 53, at pp. 64-65.

54. See, Robinson, J, *The laundrymen*, London, Macmillan, 1994, at p. 227.

55. See, for example, "Cash at any price", *Economist*, 9 May 1992.

56. Noble, op. cit., paragraph 28.

57. *Supra*, note 27, p. 6.

58. See, "Typology of Money Laundering", in "Financial Action Task Force on Money Laundering: Annexes to the Report, 1990-1991", Paris, FATF, at pp. 26-27.

59. *Combating the abuse of non-profit organisations: international best practices*, Paris, FATF, 2002, p. 7.

60. "Financial Action Task Force on Money Laundering: Annual Report 1996-1997", Paris, FATF, Appendix A, p. 7.

61. See, *supra*, note 18, at pp. 12-15.

62. "Financial Action Task Force on Money Laundering: Report on Money Laundering Typologies 2001-2002", Paris, FATF, p. 25.

63. *Supra*, note 18, pp. 12-13.

64. Paris, FATF, 2001, paragraph 56.

65. See generally, *supra*, note 11.

66. FATF Recommendation 8 of 2003.

67. See, "Financial Action Task Force on Money Laundering: Annual Report 1995-1996", Paris, FATF, Annex 3, at p. 5.

68. See, *supra*, note 18, at pp. 18-19.

69. See "Financial Action Task Force on Money Laundering: Report on Money Laundering Typologies 1998-1999", Paris, FATF, at p. 8.

70. *Supra*, note 60, Appendix A, p. 18.

71. Ibid.

72. "Customer Due Diligence for Banks", Basel, Basel Committee Publication No. 85, 2001, p. 11.

73. See, for example, ibid., at p. 12.

74. *Supra*, note 60, p. 16.

75. Beare and Schneider, op. cit., p. xi.

Chapter III – Global responses to money laundering

The United Nations

Introduction: the focus on drugs

The initial impetus for co-ordinated international action to combat money laundering arose, as has been seen, out of a growing concern within the world community about the problems of drug abuse and illicit trafficking. These subjects have for long been recognised as being particularly suited for action at the global level. Indeed, the first international agreements which sought to regulate these matters, such as the International Opium Convention of 1912 and the 1931 Convention for Limiting the Manufacture and Regulating the Distribution of Narcotic Drugs, predate the creation of the United Nations.[1] In the years since 1945, the UN has built extensively upon these foundations. Its broad mandate in this area has provided the basis for the creation of a comprehensive and multifaceted strategy with initiatives linked to, among others, prevention, demand reduction, and the treatment and rehabilitation of offenders. It is, however, the actions taken on the supply side which are of the greatest interest in the present context.

Prior to 1988 there were two central pillars which supported that effort. The first was the 1961 UN Single Convention on Narcotic Drugs, as amended by a 1972 protocol, which has attracted substantial support from the international community. This "provides for international controls over the production and availability of opium and its derivatives, synthetic drugs having similar effects, cocaine and cannabis".[2] By 1 September 2003 some 179 states were parties to the convention and the protocol or to the convention alone. The second major plank of the supply-side system took the form of the 1971 UN Convention on Psychotropic Substances, with 174 state parties, which extends the concept of international control to a wide range of synthetic drugs.[3]

While these international treaties have made a highly positive contribution in controlling the production of drugs and seeking to prevent their diversion into the illicit market place it gradually became apparent that they were inadequate to the task of dealing with the range of complex issues raised by modern international drug trafficking. As Donnelly has remarked:

> An international drug control regime based primarily on controlling the production of and regulating legal trade in dangerous drugs has proved valuable in safeguarding medical and scientific uses. It has increased the costs and difficulties of illegal trafficking. It also provides a firm basis for further forms of international cooperation. Alone, however, it is completely inadequate to the problem – in large part because of its conceptual narrowness.[4]

A new initiative at the global level to supplement existing arrangements was clearly necessary. It was widely accepted that this would need to focus on transnational drug trafficking operations and make provision for greatly enhanced co-operation in law enforcement. The underlying philosophy was well articulated in the Comprehensive Multidisciplinary Outline of Future Activities in Drug Abuse Control, adopted by the 1987 UN Conference on Drug Abuse and Illicit Trafficking:

> ... it is necessary to ensure vigorous enforcement of the law in order to reduce the illicit availability of drugs, deter drug-related crime, and contribute to drug abuse prevention by creating an environment favourable to efforts for reducing illicit supply and demand. ... Coordination of activities and cooperation among national agencies within each country and between countries are vital for the achievement of the objective.[5]

Following an initiative taken by the Government of Venezuela, the UN General Assembly, on 14 December 1984, unanimously adopted a resolution in which it expressed the conviction that "the wide scope of the illicit traffic in narcotic drugs and its consequences make it necessary to prepare a convention which considers the various aspects of the problem as a whole and, in particular, those not envisaged in existing international instruments". The General Assembly requested the UN Economic and Social Council to instruct the Commission on Narcotic Drugs to prepare a draft convention "as a matter of priority".[6] Acting on that mandate the commission adopted, by consensus, on 14 February 1986 a resolution in which it identified fourteen elements for inclusion in a draft convention. This set in motion a detailed process of consultation, study and review which culminated in the holding in Vienna, from 25 November to 20 December 1988, of the UN Conference for the Adoption of a Convention against Illicit Traffic in Narcotic Drugs and Psychotropic Substances. This important gathering, attended by representatives from 106 countries, succeeded in adopting, again by consensus, a detailed treaty text (of the same name) consisting of thirty-four articles and one annex.

In spite of its scope and ambition this instrument, described by the then US President George Bush as "of fundamental importance to effective international cooperation to combat drugs",[7] entered into force on 11 November 1990 – a near record in terms of time for an instrument of this kind. By September 2003 it had attracted 168 states parties as well as the formal participation of the Commission of the European Communities. It is of interest to note in this regard that the United Kingdom, which embraced the convention regime in 1991, has since acted to extend its application to a number of jurisdictions for which it has responsibility in the foreign affairs sphere, several of which are significant offshore financial centres. Such extension took effect for Bermuda and the relevant Caribbean jurisdictions (including both the Cayman Islands and the British Virgin Islands) with effect from February 1995. In 1997 the convention was extended to the Bailiwick of Jersey and similar action was taken in relation to Guernsey in April 2003.

In addition to this impressive numerical total the quality of participation has also been very encouraging. Apart from the major consumer nations of North America and western Europe, it has attracted the support of key transit states in central and eastern Europe, the Caribbean and Central America. Of even greater significance is that a growing number of the world's major drug producers have accepted the convention's obligations. These include, among others, Afghanistan, Bolivia, Colombia, India, Iran, Lebanon, Mexico, Morocco, Myanmar, Nepal, and Pakistan. Such has been its reception that the 1988 UN convention is now widely regarded as constituting the essential foundation of the international legal regime in this important area of concern.[8] As Savona and De Feo have remarked: "Ratification of the Vienna Drug Convention is becoming virtually an indicator of responsible membership in the anti-drug and anti-money laundering world community."[9]

Major provisions of the 1988 UN convention

Money laundering and confiscation

At the very heart of an effective strategy to counter modern international drug trafficking is the need to provide the law enforcement community with the necessary tools to undermine the financial power of the cartels and other groups, and to do so in a way which is sensitive to the requirements of international co-operation. As was seen in chapter I, throughout the 1980s a broad consensus emerged that the criminalisation of money laundering and providing for the confiscation of criminal proceeds were the essential components of such a strategy. The 1988 UN convention addressed both of these issues – the first time that a convention of global reach had done so.

Critical to the approach adopted to the issue of money laundering was the imposition, in Article 3(1)(a), of a strict obligation for each participating country to criminalise a fairly comprehensive list of activities concerning drug trafficking which have a major international impact. These range from production and cultivation through to the organisation, management, and financing of trafficking operations. The latter was believed to be a particularly important component of the effort to reach those involved at the highest levels of the drugs trade. As Bassiouni has remarked: "The organisers of the international illicit traffic do not in most cases physically handle any drugs themselves, but instigate, finance and direct these operations which are carried out by underlings ...".[10] Subparagraph (b) then requires that drug-related "money laundering" be established as a criminal offence. The actual term was not (due to its novelty and for translation reasons) used in the text. Rather the concept was expressed in these words:

(i) the conversion or transfer of property, knowing that such property is derived from any offence or offences established in accordance with subparagraph (a) of this paragraph, or from an act of participation in such offence or offences, for the purpose of concealing or disguising the illicit origin of the property or of assisting any person who is involved in the commission of such an offence or offences to evade the legal consequences of his actions;

(ii) the concealment or disguise of the true nature, source, location, disposition, movement, rights with respect to, or ownership of property, knowing that such property is derived from an offence or offences established in accordance with subparagraph (a) of this paragraph or from an act of participation in such an offence or offences.

In addition, the same article of the 1988 UN convention requires each party, to the extent that it is not contrary to its constitutional principles and the basic concepts of its legal system, to criminalise "the acquisition, possession or use of property, knowing, at the time of receipt" that it was derived from drug trafficking (Article 3(1)(c)(i)) as well as conspiracy, aiding and abetting, and facilitating the commission of drug trafficking offences including money laundering (Article 3(1)(c)(iv)). The important issue of the appropriate burden of proof in relation to all such offences is addressed in Article 3(3) which provides that knowledge, intent or purpose "may be inferred from objective factual circumstances".

Many of the remaining provisions of this lengthy and complex article are designed to ensure that money laundering and other trafficking offences are treated with appropriate seriousness by the judiciary and the prosecutorial authorities of each participating state. By way of illustration, Article 3(5) requires that each party ensure that "their courts or other competent authorities" can take into account a non-exhaustive list of factors which make these offences particularly grave. Those specifically mentioned, and of obvious relevance to the world of money laundering, include the involvement of organised criminal groups, the use of violence, and "[t]he fact that the offender holds a public office and that the offence is connected with the office in question".

The significance of the approach adopted in Article 3 to drug-related money laundering for the future of international co-operation should not be underestimated. By requiring its criminalisation and treating it as a serious offence in paragraph 1, the drafters have sought to ensure that co-operation in respect of confiscation, mutual legal assistance and extradition will be forthcoming. For example, the United States delegation hailed the achievement of the convention in relation to extradition, a subject addressed in detail in Article 6, in these words:

> Because all parties are obligated to establish Article 3, paragraph 1, offences as criminal offences in their domestic law, any requirements of dual criminality, that is that the offence is criminal in both jurisdictions, in a Party's extradition law should be met. Although there has been almost universal recognition that illicit drug trafficking offences are extraditable offences, narcotics related money laundering is a new criminal offence for many states and has not been traditionally recognised as an extraditable offence. The universal recognition of narcotics related money laundering as an extraditable offence is one of the most important aspects of this article.[11]

A further indication of the sensitivity of the drafters of this convention to the transnational dimension of the problem is to be seen in Article 3(10) which seeks to restrict the possibility that narco-terrorists, money launderers and others involved in the drugs trade could take advantage of two traditional restrictions on international co-operation. It will be recalled that the concept that individuals who have been accused or convicted of offences of a political character should not be subject to extradition has a lengthy history and continues to find expression in domestic extradition laws and international treaty practice. Similarly, some arrangements for international co-operation do not extend to fiscal offences. The provision in question restricts, but does not entirely eliminate, the possibility of invoking such grounds in this context.

At a practical level, the mandatory wording of the 1988 UN convention in relation to money laundering and other serious offences means that many states wishing to become parties to this significant international instrument were faced with the need to enact complex implementing legislation in order to ensure that they could act in full compliance with its terms. Indeed, experience demonstrated that even states which possessed relatively modern legislative instruments governing money laundering might have to introduce amendments in order to bring the law into line with convention requirements. Thus, the United Kingdom Parliament had to include specific provisions in the Criminal Justice (International Co-operation) Act of 1990 in order to bridge the gap between section 24 of the Drug Trafficking Offences Act 1986 (the relevant statute at that time) and the money laundering requirements of Article 3.

A second major feature of the approach adopted in the drafting relates to the subject of the confiscation of the proceeds derived from, and the instrumentalities used in, drug trafficking. This is treated in detail in Article 5 which addresses both the measures to be taken at the national level and the necessary mechanisms to give effect to international co-operation in this vital area. It is of importance because confiscation measures aim to:

> ... incapacitate, by depriving a person of the physical or financial ability, power, or opportunity to continue to engage in proscribed conduct, to prevent offenders from

unjustly enriching themselves, by eliminating the advantages and benefits which the offender has gained through his or her illegality, to deter the offender and others from crime by undermining the ultimate profitability of the venture and to protect the community by curbing the circulation of prohibited items.[12]

The first three paragraphs of Article 5 treat the issue of confiscation at the level of domestic law and practice. They impose a series of broad obligations which are free from any limitations or safeguard clauses. Paragraph 1 reads:

> 1. Each Party shall adopt such measures as may be necessary to enable confiscation of:
>
>   (a) Proceeds derived from offences established in accordance with article 3, paragraph 1, or property the value of which corresponds to that of such proceeds;
>
>   (b) Narcotic drugs and psychotropic substances, materials and equipment or other instrumentalities used in or intended for use in any manner in offences established in accordance with article 3, paragraph 1.

It should be noted that, whilst framed in mandatory terms, this paragraph was deliberately worded so as to leave to each state a wide measure of discretion as to how best to achieve the desired result. This emphasis on flexibility also permitted due account to be taken of the differing approaches to confiscation which had evolved in domestic legislation. As the United States delegation pointed out, the wording "allows the option of forfeiting either the proceeds of the offence or, in their place, property which has a corresponding value".[13] In order to ensure the effectiveness of the confiscation procedure, paragraph 2 makes provision for necessary preliminary steps to be taken to "identify, trace, and freeze or seize proceeds, property, instrumentalities or any other thing referred to in paragraph 1 ...". The text, however, provides no guidance on how states are to handle a broad range of practical issues which arise in giving effect to these obligations. By way of illustration, experience has demonstrated:

> ... the pressing need to provide a coherent and adequately financed asset-management regime to deal with property subject to provisional measures and with confiscated property. It will be necessary for the appropriate authority to have the necessary power to take possession and control of, and to manage or otherwise deal with, the property in question. This might include the need, for example, to run restrained businesses, ranging from restaurants to ski resorts, to dispose of perishable or rapidly depreciating property, and to compensate innocent creditors.[14]

The Vienna conference also acted to ensure that the concept of bank secrecy did not needlessly hinder the search for and the eventual confiscation of the assets derived from this form of criminal activity. As was seen in chapter II, complex laundering schemes often seek to incorporate some aspect of the protection afforded by strict rules of customer confidentiality. Experience had shown that "existing bank secrecy laws are being used in many instances to obstruct cooperation and the provision of information needed for the investigation of allegations of drug-related offences".[15]

The solution which commended itself to the drafters of the convention, now reflected in Article 5(3), was to require that each state party empower its courts or other relevant authorities to order that bank, financial or commercial records be made available. Most importantly it is specifically provided that: "A Party shall not decline to act under the provisions of this paragraph on the ground of bank secrecy." The inclusion of this affirmative obligation has been widely characterised as a major breakthrough. In the words of Sproule and Saint-Denis: "The exclusion of bank secrecy as a justification to decline to act may prove to be one of the most important measures in combating drug money laundering operations."[16]

The centrality of this issue (which, as noted below, also arises in the context of mutual legal assistance under Article 7) was highlighted when, in March 1996, the instrument of accession deposited by the Government of the Lebanon included reservations to these bank secrecy provisions. In its 1996 report, the International Narcotics Control Board expressed concern over what it regarded as these "far-reaching reservations". It also expressed the view that "the validity of reservations going to the core of the 1988 convention, for example, by excluding important provisions on money laundering, is questionable from both the legal and policy perspectives".[17] It also drew attention to the relevant provisions of the Vienna Convention on the Law of Treaties which, in the absence of specific coverage of reservations in the 1988 text, are deemed to govern this issue.[18] In the course of the following year, eight states formally objected to the reservations made by the Lebanon. While Austria and Germany regarded them as "problematic", the remainder went further in that they considered them to be contrary to the object and purpose of the 1988 convention and thus inadmissible. As Sweden noted in March 1997:

> The convention establishes that bank secrecy shall not be a ground for a failure to act or for a failure to render mutual assistance. The Government of Sweden considers that these reservations therefore undermine the object and purpose of the convention as stated in article 2, paragraph 1, i.e. to promote cooperation among the parties in order to effectively address the international dimension of illicit traffic in drugs.

Notwithstanding the above, and other pressures placed on the Government of the Lebanon, this reservation has not been withdrawn.

While there is no doubt that the bank secrecy provision in Article 5(3) is of profound significance to the effectiveness of confiscation, as a criminal justice measure it has been argued that it does not go far enough. There has been a growing perception that the removal of such secrecy provides only an illusory benefit where additional layers of protection, such as anonymous trusts and shell companies, are available.[19] In this context particular concern has been expressed about the range of services provided in the ever-growing number of offshore financial centres. A detailed and hard-hitting 1998 study published by the UN expressed the following view:

> The common denominator in money laundering and a variety of financial crimes is the enabling machinery which has been created in the financial havens and offshore centres. The effectiveness of these centres in helping people and companies to hide assets is not the result of any single device. Changing bank secrecy rules alone will not help. Rather the centres have created a tool kit composed of new corporate instruments, foundations, trusts, trust companies, banks and bank accounts. The tools are mixed and matched with jurisdictions that have made a point of non-cooperation with the rest of the international community in criminal and tax investigations. What started as a business to service the needs of a privileged few has become an enormous hole in the international legal and fiscal system.[20]

As will be seen in chapter VI, one of the longstanding priorities of the Financial Action Task Force on Money Laundering (FATF) has been to secure further progress in this sphere; an interest which was eventually to stimulate its highly controversial name, shame and punish strategy commonly known as the NCCT (Non-Cooperative Countries and Territories) initiative.

It was also widely accepted by the drafters of the 1988 convention that action in the confiscation sphere when undertaken on a unilateral basis at the level of domestic law was unlikely to be fully effective in combating an activity, such as drug trafficking, which has conspicuous transnational features. As McClean has pointed out: "The facility with which assets, particularly in the form of financial credits of some sort, can be passed across national boundaries means that an order enforceable only in the country of origin may be of limited value."[21] The need for effective international co-operation in this context was therefore viewed as being critical. It too is treated in Article 5 of the 1988 text.

Here a mandatory framework is provided which, none the less, recognises the need for a substantial element of flexibility for national legislatures. Article 5(4)(a) is central to the approach adopted and reads, in full, as follows:

> 4. (a) Following a request made pursuant to this article by another Party having jurisdiction over an offence established in accordance with article 3, paragraph 1, the Party in whose territory proceeds, property, instrumentalities or any other thing referred to in paragraph 1 of this article are situated shall:
>
> (i) Submit the request to its competent authorities for the purpose of obtaining an order of confiscation and, if such order is granted, give effect to it; or
>
> (ii) Submit to its competent authorities, with a view to giving effect to it to the extent requested, an order of confiscation issued by the requesting Party in accordance with paragraph 1 of this article, in so far as it relates to proceeds, property, instrumentalities or any other things referred to in paragraph 1 situated in the territory of the requested Party.

Two different approaches to securing the co-operation of other states are thus contemplated. In the words of the chairman of the relevant conference committee:

Sub-paragraph (a)(i) dealt with the case of confiscation in a state where the proceeds were found. The order in that case would be issued by the local authorities of the requested state. It was immaterial whether an order by the requesting state had been issued or not. In sub-paragraph (a)(ii) an order by the requesting state was essential.[22]

In adopting this approach it was recognised that the former procedure was more in keeping with the traditional disinclination of members of the international community to directly enforce foreign criminal judgments. However, this was an area in which some countries, including the United Kingdom, had enacted legislation to permit them "under certain circumstances to recognise and enforce a foreign forfeiture judgment"[23] and it was thought appropriate that the 1988 convention reflect that fact. Provision is also made to ensure that a requested party shall take effective provisional measures, including tracing and freezing proceeds and property, "for the purpose of eventual confiscation to be ordered either by the requesting Party or, pursuant to a request under subparagraph (a) of this paragraph, by the requested Party". (Article 5(4)(b)).

Two further points deserve emphasis here. First, although these actions take place according to the domestic laws and procedures of the requested state its legal system must permit such assistance to be granted. Second, no further international action is required to perfect this obligation although states parties are encouraged to enter into detailed bilateral and multilateral agreements in order to make their confiscation arrangements as effective as possible. In the absence of such agreements the parties to the 1988 convention are obliged to regard it as sufficient.

The unparalleled ambition and intrusiveness of this new form of co-operation was bound to give rise to both difficulties and inefficiencies. To some extent the emphasis on flexibility has been an unintended source of problems at the practical level. Take, for example, the decision not to impose a single confiscation system, thus permitting the two principal approaches which had evolved in domestic legislation (property and value confiscation) to continue. As has been seen, states parties to the 1988 convention may select either (although there is nothing to prevent the adoption of both). Problems will arise when a request emerges from a country with one system and is directed at a state using the other, unless the domestic law of the requested state has been framed in such a way as to permit it to respond to either type of request. Subsequent international initiatives, such as the 1990 Council of Europe Convention on Laundering, Search, Seizure and Confiscation of the Proceeds of Crime, reviewed in chapter VII, have learned from and sought to improve upon this UN precedent in this and other areas in order to maximise the effectiveness of confiscation assistance.

Article 5 of the 1988 UN convention also requires states to provide the UN Secretary-General with the texts of relevant laws and regulations as well as any subsequent amendments. This enables the UN secretariat to act as an effective clearing house for information. Article 5 goes on to treat the important issue of the final disposition of the proceeds and property which are eventually confiscated. The basic rule is that such matters are to be determined in accordance with the domestic law of the state which gives effect to the confiscation. In many countries confiscated profits are simply used to supplement general government revenues. In others, such as the United States, the fruits of forfeiture are reinvested in federal, state, local and international law enforcement. In yet others, such as the United Kingdom, a distinction is made in terms of the eventual disposition of confiscated proceeds based on whether or not the case possessed an international element.[24]

In so far as confiscations resulting from international co-operation are concerned, paragraph 5(b) of Article 5 invites parties to give special consideration to contributing such funds to intergovernmental bodies specialising in efforts to counter trafficking or drug abuse or to concluding agreements for sharing the same with other states. "Since 1988, practice has tended to focus on the latter."[25]

Particularly in recent years, considerable emphasis has been placed on the practical benefits to be derived from asset sharing among states which have contributed to a successful confiscation. It is the view of the US Justice Department "that asset sharing among nations enhances international forfeiture cooperation by creating an incentive for countries to work together, regardless of where the assets are located or which jurisdiction will ultimately enforce the forfeiture order".[26] The sums in question can be substantial. This attitude towards asset sharing at the international level is but an extension of a well-established practice in relation to purely domestic cases.

While in some states it has been possible to use existing laws and administrative procedures as a basis for entering into the international asset sharing arena, in others new legislation has been required. In the case of Canada, for example:

> The Seized Property Management Act creates a statutory regime for international asset-sharing based on prior reciprocal agreements. The terms of the subsequent Forfeited Property Sharing Regulations of 1995 provide the necessary detail to make the scheme operational. This includes coverage of such matters as the determination of the amount available for sharing, the time at which any sharing will take place, and the rules by which, and the grounds upon which, the respective contributions of the jurisdictions in question will be assessed.[27]

The concept that confiscation of criminal proceeds is "a good way to make law enforcement pay for itself"[28] has an obvious attraction. Similarly, there is no doubt that such funding, whether resulting from national or international cases, can both reinforce the effectiveness of existing programmes and permit initiatives to take place which might not otherwise have been possible. In 1994, for instance, the FATF established a small Asian secretariat. Based in Sydney, Australia, it was paid for primarily out of the Australian confiscated assets fund. There are, however, obvious dangers which can flow from lax management of this new revenue source. As has been pointed out elsewhere:

> Poetic justice is not necessarily suitable justice. If the primary purpose of asset seizure becomes the maximisation of government profit or equipping enforcement agencies, there is the possibility that enforcement discretions will be exercised not on the basis of the seriousness of the offence or the dangerousness of the offender but on the wealth of the offender or what the agency sees as desirable to retain.[29]

Another provision particularly worthy of note in the context of money laundering is that contained in Article 5(6). This has as its focus the need to "ensure that proceeds derived from and instrumentalities used in illegal trafficking could not escape forfeiture simply because their form had been changed or they had been commingled with other property".[30] Here again the convention uses mandatory language – a decision of great practical importance given "the skill and speed with which large-scale traffickers are able to launder their profits".[31] Given this issue, and the nature of Article 5 as a whole, it was felt necessary to provide that its provisions "shall not be construed as prejudicing the rights of *bona fide* third parties" (Article 5(8)).

Finally, it should be noted that, pursuant to Article 5(7), each party may give consideration to reversing the burden of proof in regard to the lawful origin of the alleged proceeds of trafficking and several countries have done so.[32] It is, however, clear from both the wording of this provision and from its drafting history that there is absolutely no requirement to so act.

From the above overview of this highly complex and innovative article it is easy to see why it has attracted great praise from commentators. In the words of Sproule and Saint-Denis:

> The provisions now contained in this article are clear, specific, and in most cases, mandatory. They can be properly viewed as a major breakthrough in attacking the benefits derived from drug trafficking activities and are a forceful endorsement of the notion that attacking the profit motive is essential if the struggle against drug trafficking is to be effective.[33]

Other important provisions

The precedents established by the 1988 UN convention in the fields of money laundering and confiscation are supported by a range of other important mechanisms designed to promote international co-operation. Of these perhaps the most significant is its Article 7 dealing with the provision, on an interstate basis, of mutual legal assistance in investigations, prosecutions and judicial proceedings relating to money laundering and other serious convention offences.

In contrast with confiscation, the drafters of the 1988 text were able to build upon an established and developing international practice in this area in relation to which the Council of Europe had played a major role. The 1988 text envisages the provision of assistance in a number of highly practical areas. A non-exhaustive list includes: the taking of evidence or statements; effecting service of judicial documents; executing searches and seizures; examining objects and sites; providing information and evidentiary items; providing relevant documents and records including bank, financial, corporate or business records; and, identifying or tracing proceeds and instrumentalities for evidentiary purposes. As one leading commentator has stressed:

> Obtaining evidence from abroad ... is as essential to the success of prosecutions as collecting intelligence and obtaining the offender. It is also the most dependent upon legal formalities and affords the least latitude for the sorts of informal measures and understandings upon which the police normally rely in their international dealings.[34]

In the course of the conference at Vienna a number of delegations pressed for the specific inclusion of a statement to the effect that requests for assistance could not be refused on the ground of bank secrecy. Such concerns find reflection in the clear wording of Article 7(5) of the final text. The extent of the obligation so imposed was described by the United States Attorney-General as follows:

> First, it is an obligation to enact implementing legislation, if necessary, to modify domestic bank secrecy laws to permit execution of requests for bank records under the Convention. Second, with respect to an individual request for bank records under the Convention, it obliges a requested Party to grant the request, if the only basis for refusing would be bank secrecy laws.[35]

The authorised grounds for the refusal of a request are set out, in a broadly worded fashion, in such a way as to ensure the protection of the essential interests of the requested state. Similarly, and in common with pre-existing practice, Article 7 imposes restrictions on the use to which the assistance obtained may be put and places certain obligations on the requested state.

In spite of the detail contained in these and other substantive and procedural provisions in this article, it was clearly recognised that the complexity of this subject area is such that states might well wish to conclude further agreements of a bilateral or multilateral nature in order to more adequately address issues of importance. Account also had to be taken of the fact that a substantial number of such agreements already existed. The solution adopted has been summarised by the United Kingdom Home Office in the following way:

> By paragraph 20, the Parties are to consider the possibilities of bilateral or multi-lateral agreements to give effect to or enhance the provisions of the article, and if such an agreement is in force the procedures specified therein shall prevail over the normative procedures specified in Article 7.[36]

By embracing the concept of mutual legal assistance, the 1988 UN convention made a major contribution towards increasing its availability in areas of the world, and within legal traditions, where it was, at the time, underdeveloped or unknown. In addition, it provided a critical level of support for those charged with prosecuting money laundering offences containing a substantial international dimension. As Kriz has pointed out:

> ... mutual legal assistance can assist with attacking each of the basic steps in the money laundering process. Indeed, if the proceeds derived from a drug trafficking operation are physically carried out of country A in which it was obtained and deposited into a financial institution in country B (placement); transferred from that financial institution through various other financial institutions in various countries to another financial institution in country C (layering); and finally paid into a number of corporations in various countries in purported payments of share transfers (integration), then the investigators/prosecutors in country A would not have much hope in tracing, let alone confiscating, the proceeds of drug trafficking without using mutual legal assistance.[37]

Less innovative, though equally important, is the attention paid to the oldest and most firmly established method of co-operation; namely, extradition. This is the formal procedure governing the return of persons who have been accused or convicted of criminal offences in order that they may face prosecution or the execution of a sentence in a third country. It lies at the very heart of both the 1961 UN Single Convention, as amended, and the 1971 UN Convention on Psychotropic Substances and continues to occupy a position of significance in the 1988 arrangements.

The basic approach adopted in this regard is similar to that found in other multilateral instruments dealing with criminal activity of international concern. First, as is common, Article 6 requires that the domestic criminal offences which give effect to the obligations of the 1988 convention shall be deemed to be extraditable offences in any existing extradition treaty between the parties. This obligation is restricted to the more serious offences, including money laundering, provided for in Article 3(1). Similarly, the parties "undertake to include such offences as extraditable offences in every extradition treaty to be concluded between them" (Article 6(2)).

The second common element of practice reflected in the 1988 convention was summarised by Earl Ferrers, on behalf of the UK Government, in January 1990 in these words: "... where a party's extradition law depends on the existence of a treaty and there is no such treaty with another party, the convention may serve as a legal basis for extradition in respect of offences covered by it".[38]

In the course of the Vienna conference a number of delegations pressed for the inclusion of a mandatory provision in this regard. However, a majority favoured the use of permissive wording and it is this approach which finds reflection in the final treaty text. A number of states, including the UK, have used the option in a positive sense. By way of contrast the United States, which faces particular domestic law constraints in this regard, subjected its ratification of the convention to the specific understanding that: "the United States shall not consider this convention as a legal basis for extradition of citizens to any country with which the United States has no bilateral extradition treaty in force".

The third element common to international criminal conventions is to provide that "a party in whose territory an alleged offender is found shall itself either extradite or prosecute".[39] Though applicable in a number of different situations its greatest relevance is where extradition is refused because the individual concerned is a national of the requested state. Both prior to and during the Vienna conference a major effort was made to secure the inclusion of a provision which would have obliged states to extradite their own nationals. However, this particular innovation was resisted by a clear majority of delegations. As has been pointed out elsewhere "there was overwhelming opposition from countries which, for either political or legal reasons, would not accept any provision on the extradition of their nationals, even a hortatory provision".[40] For such countries, which include many from the civil law tradition, when extradition is refused on the ground of nationality the requirement is to submit the case to the competent authorities for the purpose of prosecution "unless otherwise agreed with the requesting Party" (Article 6(9)(a)).

While a full review of the 1988 convention's treatment of extradition lies beyond the scope of the present study it is fair to say that it does not, when taken as a whole, constitute a particularly radical departure from the traditional approach to this subject as reflected in international practice. None the less, in the words of Stewart, Article 6 makes it somewhat easier "for prosecuting states to obtain the extradition of narcotics traffickers and cartel chiefs from overseas".[41]

Finally, it should be stressed that the formal procedures for mutual assistance in the administration of justice contained in this important international instrument are intended to supplement, rather than to replace, existing channels of police-to-police co-operation. This subject is separately addressed in Article 9 which is entitled "Other forms of co-operation and training". As has been pointed out elsewhere:

> This Article is designed to preserve and enhance forms of cooperation which may exist on a less formal basis than the mutual legal assistance referred to in Article 7. It provides that parties shall cooperate more closely with each other in matters of intelligence in investigating offences. It also calls on them to facilitate coordination of the work of their competent agencies and promote exchanges of staff, to carry out suitable training programmes and to assist one another in their training and research programmes.[42]

Conclusions

From this brief overview of some of the central features of this multilateral treaty one can readily appreciate why it was so widely characterised by those involved in the efforts to combat money laundering as a major achievement. In particular it responded to many of the challenges faced by the law enforcement community in their efforts to address the traditional fragmentation of legal arrangements which are so frequently exploited by sophisticated money launderers. As the FATF stated in 1990:

> Many of the current difficulties in international cooperation in drug money laundering cases are directly or indirectly linked with a strict application of bank secrecy rules, with the fact that, in many countries, money laundering is not today an offence, and with insufficiencies in multilateral cooperation and mutual legal assistance.[43]

The 1988 convention has addressed each of these concerns and, in so doing, made an important contribution to future progress in this vital area of concern.

The UN conventions on transnational organised crime and corruption

In the light of what has been said above, it is perhaps surprising that over a decade was to pass before the international community concluded a major multilateral treaty of global reach which built on the foundations established by the 1988 precedent. The subject area selected was that of organised crime.

This UN initiative has its origins in the Political Declaration and Global Action Plan adopted at the World Ministerial Conference on Organised Transnational Crime held in Naples, Italy in 1994. The formal product of this high-level meeting, subsequently approved by the General Assembly in resolution 49/59 of 23 December 1994, was designed to strengthen and improve: "national capabilities and international cooperation against organised transnational crime and [to] laying the foundations for concerted and effective global action against organised transnational crime and the prevention of its further expansion".[44]

It should be noted here that action to combat organised crime has also formed a regular part of the G7/8 agenda since the Halifax Summit of June 1995.[45] Similarly, the topic has taken on a position of some importance within the European Union, especially in the work of the so-called "Third Pillar" which, as will be seen in chapter VIII, is devoted to justice and home affairs. This is evidenced by, among other things, the ambitious June 1997 Action Plan to Combat Organised Crime.

In late 1996, Poland, in effect, initiated discussion by submitting a draft treaty text to the UN General Assembly. The subsequent detailed negotiations were formally concluded when the Assembly adopted the UN Convention against Transnational Organised Crime and two protocols – against trafficking in persons and smuggling of migrants – on 15 November 2000.[46] A further protocol – on firearms – was finalised the following year. The convention in turn entered into force in September 2003, followed in December 2003 and January 2004 by the two original protocols.

The cornerstone of the 2000 convention is Article 3 which sets out its scope of application. In essence it clarifies that it applies to the prevention, investigation and prosecution of stipulated offences (including money laundering and corruption) and other serious crimes (defined in Article 2(b) by reference to a threshold of punishment). Two further criteria for application are also specified; namely that the offence involves "an organised criminal group" and is "transnational in nature".[47]

The discussions surrounding the former issue were complicated by the fact that there existed no universally agreed definition. This had, in turn, resulted in significant differences in approach in national legal systems. Similarly there were considerable variations in practice in the structure of such groups in different nations and regions. The preferred solution, embodied in Article 2(a), was to provide a broad definition of "organised criminal group"; one which ensures that the operation of the 2000 convention would not be confined or restricted to Mafia-type criminal organisations.[48] A similarly delicate judgment had to be brought to bear on how best to reflect the intention of participating states that the new instrument focus on the transnational manifestations of the problem, thus excluding purely domestic offences. This matter was addressed in Article 3(2) which is worded as follows:

2. For the purpose of paragraph 1 of this article, an offence is transnational in nature if:

(a) It is committed in more than one State;

(b) It is committed in one State but a substantial part of its preparation, planning, direction or control takes place in another State;

(c) It is committed in one State but involves an organised criminal group that engages in criminal activities in more than one State; or

(d) It is committed in one State but has substantial effects in another State.

Many of the detailed provisions which follow are designed to ensure that participating states have in place adequate domestic law powers and, from that base, are able to engage in meaningful international co-operation. The influence of the 1988 UN convention is clearly evident in both the internal structure of the 2000 text and in the drafting of specific provisions. This is, however, no mere clone of that earlier instrument. Among its innovative features one might mention the extension of coverage to new areas of concern such as the protection of witnesses and victims (Articles 24 and 25), and the manner in which it addresses the close interface between organised crime and corruption (Articles 8 and 9). Of perhaps even greater significance, the 2000 convention explicitly applies to prevention as well as to the investigation and prosecution of offences (Article 31).

Importantly for present purposes, the 2000 convention, as with its 1988 precursor, fully embraces the strategy of seeking to undermine and disrupt organised crime groups by focusing on their finances. As the 1997 EU action plan had noted: "the major driving force behind organised crime is the pursuit of financial gain. This both attracts it into an ever-increasing number of areas of activity where it sees possibilities for economic crime ... and also faces it with a need to launder the profits thereafter".[49]

The most interesting innovation in this context was, without doubt, the decision to include detailed provision on measures to prevent money laundering. The negotiations on this issue were highly charged and, as a consequence, the resulting text represents a (perhaps unsatisfactory) compromise. In particular, the generality and open-textured nature of the wording eventually adopted has attracted adverse comment. That said, in certain key areas, mandatory terminology is used. The approach adopted in this respect is well illustrated in Article 7(1)(a) which reads:

1. Each State Party:

(a) Shall institute a comprehensive domestic regulatory and supervisory regime for banks and non-bank financial institutions and, where appropriate, other bodies particularly susceptible to money-laundering, within its competence, in order to deter and detect all forms of money-laundering, which regime shall emphasise requirements for customer identification, record-keeping and the reporting of suspicious transactions.

Article 7(3) then calls upon participating countries "to use as a guideline" relevant international anti-money laundering initiatives in establishing their domestic regulatory and supervisory regimes. While the best known and most firmly established such guidance is contained in the Forty FATF Recommendations, there are no specific references to them in the text of the article. However, the interpretative notes for the official record make it clear that the terminology used was "understood in particular" to refer to FATF standards. While the alternative of identifying the core elements of the preventive approach and addressing them in greater detail in the text would no doubt have been more beneficial in securing an adequate level of harmonisation among participating countries, the fact remains that this dimension of the modern stance to countering money laundering had failed to find inclusion in the 1988 text. As noted above, it concentrated on the criminalisation of money laundering and providing for international co-operation in investigations and prosecutions.

The issue of the criminalisation of money laundering is treated in Article 6. As with other criminal justice and international criminal co-operation issues, the influence of the 1988 instrument, as well as of the 1990 Council of Europe Convention on Laundering, Search, Seizure and Confiscation of the Proceeds of Crime (examined in chapter VII), is clearly evident. While Article 6 owes much to those earlier treaties it does contain features of interest. One such is the manner in which it provides for the treatment of extraterritorial predicate offences. Article 6(2)(c) stipulates that:

> ... predicate offences shall include offences committed both within and outside the jurisdiction of the State Party in question. However, offences committed outside the jurisdiction of a State Party shall constitute predicate offences only when the relevant conduct is a criminal offence under the domestic law of the State where it is committed and would be a criminal offence under the domestic law of the State Party implementing or applying this article had it been committed there.

While a review of the many novel features contained in the 2000 convention lies beyond the scope of this work, two areas are perhaps deserving of attention for present purposes. The first relates to the issue of corporate liability – a matter afforded some prominence by the FATF in its anti-money laundering programme since 1990[50] but left untreated in the 1988 UN text.

Article 10 recognises the diversity of approaches which exist in this area within differing legal traditions. It does so by acknowledging that while liability of legal persons for participation in relevant offences (including money laundering) must be provided for in national legal systems, such liability "may be criminal, civil or administrative". However, the decision not to require common recourse to the concept of corporate criminal liability – understandable though that may be – does have direct and immediate implications for the provision of international co-operation. This is particularly so in instances in which the state requesting assistance has given effect to criminal liability and the requested jurisdiction has used a civil or administrative option.

The 2000 convention seeks to minimise this potential barrier to co-operation. For instance, Article 18(2) provides that "mutual legal assistance shall be afforded to the fullest extent possible ... with respect to investigations, prosecutions and judicial proceedings in relation to the offences for which a legal person may be held liable in accordance with article 10 of this Convention in the requesting State Party". While it thus emphasises the desirability of the provision of mutual assistance in such circumstances it does not require it; a point highlighted in Article 18(9) which permits mutual assistance to be declined "on the ground of absence of dual criminality".[51]

The second issue is that of the ultimate disposal of confiscated criminal proceeds. It will be recalled that the 1988 convention articulates the basic principle that the disposition of confiscated proceeds and property is to be determined by the law and practice of the jurisdiction in which such confiscation finally takes place. Asset sharing is encouraged but not required.

While this approach may well have been (and indeed remain) appropriate in the context of drug trafficking, the extension of money laundering and confiscation regimes to an ever-broader range of predicate offences has conspired to call into question the adequacy of this principle in international cases. Such concerns manifested themselves in the course of the elaboration of the 2000 convention. The outcome of those negotiations, reflected in Article 14, saw some progress recorded in the direction of the return of property. Although the traditional basic rule is repeated in the first paragraph of the article it is supplemented by the following provision:

> 2. When acting on the request made by another State Party in accordance with article 13 of this Convention, State Parties shall, to the extent permitted by domestic law and if so requested, give priority consideration to returning the confiscated proceeds of crime or property to the requesting State Party so that it can give compensation to the victims of the crime or return such proceeds of crime or property to their legitimate owners.

Asset sharing in such international cases remains, as with the 1988 precedent, optional in nature.

Significantly, the same issue was to become one of the central concerns when, shortly thereafter, the international community turned its attention to the negotiation of a global convention against corruption; a task completed when the resulting treaty (UN Convention against Corruption) was adopted and opened for signature in December 2003 .

The treatment of plundered state assets had been a source of concern for some time; a fact which owed much to highly publicised examples of the looting of national wealth by several rulers of developing countries. However, the perceived need to formulate new international standards in this area was not confined to victim states. For instance, in their July 2000 report to the Heads of State and Government meeting in Okinawa, Japan, G7 finance ministers identified "the clandestine diversion of public assets" as one of four money laundering-related issues requiring priority attention. This matter was similarly highlighted by the UN General Assembly in resolution 55/188 of 20 December 2000 on preventing and combating corrupt practices and illegal transfer of funds and repatriation of such funds to countries of origin.

From an early stage of the negotiations, it was apparent that securing progress on this matter would be both symbolically and substantially important for the process as a whole. Indeed, at the second session of discussions, the chairperson (the late Héctor Charry Samper of Colombia) mentioned that "the question of asset recovery, among other issues ... would serve as an indicator of the political will to join forces in order to protect the common good".[52] Its singular significance was underlined by the decision to set aside one day of that session for a technical workshop on the range of complex issues to which that subject gave rise.

In the event the whole of Chapter V of the 2003 convention was devoted to the asset recovery issue; one described in the text as constituting a "fundamental principle".[53] Article 57, entitled "Return and disposal of assets", is of special interest for present purposes. While this commences with a restatement of the orthodox rule,[54] participating states are required to take such steps as may be necessary to permit the return of confiscated property when requested so to do by another state party "taking into account the rights of *bona fide* third parties".[55] The exercise of the latter authority is governed by paragraph 3. Pursuant to this provision a requested state shall:

> (a) In the case of embezzlement of public funds or of laundering of embezzled public funds as referred to in articles 17 and 23 of this Convention, when confiscation was executed in accordance with article 55 and on the basis of a final judgment in the requesting State Party, a requirement that can be waived by the requested State Party, return the confiscated property to the requesting State Party;

> (b) In the case of proceeds of any other offence covered by this Convention, when the confiscation was executed in accordance with article 55 of this Convention and on the basis of a final judgment in the requesting State Party, a requirement that can be waived by the requested State Party, return the confiscated property to the requesting State Party, when the requesting State Party reasonably establishes its prior ownership of such confiscated property to the requested State Party or when the requested State Party recognizes damage to the requesting State Party as a basis for returning the confiscated property;

> (c) In all other cases, give priority consideration to returning confiscated property to the requesting State Party, returning such property to its prior legitimate owners or compensating the victims of the crime.[56]

One consequence flowing from the adoption of the above approach was the need to re-examine the treatment of the question of the costs associated with the execution of requests for confiscation assistance. As Stessens has remarked: "As a rule, the requested state both bears the costs of complying with a request and reaps the eventual benefits from it."[57] The simplicity and internal balance of this general rule is clearly lost with the introduction of the principle of asset recovery. Consequently, the 2003 convention provides that a requested state "may deduct reasonable expenses incurred in investigations, prosecutions or judicial proceedings leading to the return or disposition of confiscated property pursuant to this article".[58] The official *travaux préparatoires* will indicate that reasonable expenses "are to be interpreted as costs and expenses incurred and not as finders' fees or other unspecified charges".[59]

It was to be expected that a measure seeking to suppress corrupt practices would embrace those aspects of the modern international strategy, pioneered in the 1988 convention and further refined in the 2000 convention, which seek to focus on the profit motive. A full range of relevant provisions designed to strengthen domestic criminal justice systems and to promote international co-operation have found inclusion in the 2003 text. Some, such as Article 23 on the laundering of the proceeds of crime, draw heavily on those earlier precedents. Others, such as Article 24 on the concealment or retention of tainted property, have a more innovative quality.

However, what distinguishes the 2003 convention from earlier multilateral treaty initiatives at the global level is the extent to which it embraces, and articulates in detail, a strategy to prevent acts of corruption in both the public and private sectors. That said, Article 14 on measures to prevent money laundering owes much to the approach adopted in Article 7 of the 2000 Convention against Transnational Organised Crime examined above. However, the two are by no means identical. In this regard, it should be noted that the negotiators of the 2003 Convention against Corruption were in a position to take due account of both the eight special recommendations of the FATF on the financing of terrorism which were formulated in October 2001, and the amendments to the Forty FATF Recommendations which were finalised in June 2003.[60] Both are subject to detailed examination elsewhere in this book.[61] The influence of the former is particularly evident in the treatment of electronic fund transfers contained in Article 14(3).[62]

The 2003 FATF amendments have had an obvious impact on the formulation of Article 52 of the 2003 convention on the prevention and detection of transfers of proceeds of crime – a provision with no counterpart in the 2000 convention. This has as its primary purpose the imposition on financial institutions of obligations of enhanced scrutiny in relation to the affairs "of individuals who are, or have been, entrusted with prominent public functions and their family members and close associates".[63] The treatment of shell banks and correspondent banking relationships in Article 52(5) also echo distinct concerns embodied in the new version of the Forty FATF Recommendations.

The 1999 UN International Convention for the Suppression of the Financing of Terrorism

Given the lengthy engagement of the United Nations with terrorist-related issues and the range of relevant multilateral instruments which have been concluded under its auspices it is perhaps curious that until very recently the issue of terrorist finances had been largely ignored. However, as will be seen in chapter V, this posture of neglect was also evident in other international fora including the FATF. While many practical and political factors conspired to bring about this unfortunate state of affairs perhaps the most significant obstacle to co-ordinated international action was the absence of a universally accepted definition of terrorism.

In the late 1990s, however, the foreign ministers of the G8 identified action against the funding of terrorism as a priority issue. As has been pointed out elsewhere:"the President of France ... called for the negotiation without delay of a 'universal convention against the financing of terrorism' and, in December 1998, the UN General Assembly decided in resolution 53/108 that an ad hoc committee 'should elaborate a draft international convention for the suppression of terrorist financing to supplement related existing international instruments'".[64]

To the surprise of many, the ensuing negotiations progressed swiftly and the final text was adopted by the General Assembly on 9 December 1999 and opened for signature the following month. Its primary, but by no means exclusive, focus is on relevant activities which possess a transnational dimension.[65]

One of the keys to success was the unexpected ease with which agreement was reached on the critical issue of the definition of terrorism for the purposes of the convention.[66] In this regard the text of Article 2(1) is of particular importance. It is worded as follows:

> 1. Any person commits an offence within the meaning of this Convention if that person by any means, directly or indirectly, unlawfully and wilfully, provides or collects funds with the intention that they should be used or in the knowledge that they are to be used, in full or in part, in order to carry out:
>
> (a) An act which constitutes an offence within the scope of and as defined in one of the treaties listed in the annex; or
>
> (b) Any other act intended to cause death or serious bodily injury to a civilian, or to any other person not taking an active part in the hostilities in a situation of armed conflict, when the purpose of such act, by its nature or context, is to intimidate a population, or to compel a government or an international organisation to do or to abstain from doing any act.

The obligation for participating states to criminalise the provision or collection of funds[67] is thus triggered in two major ways. First, by reference to acts specifically prohibited in one of the pre-existing counter-terrorism conventions of global reach. These are listed in the annex to the 1999 convention and range from the unlawful seizure of aircraft to terrorist bombing. Secondly, and more innovatively, the prohibition is engaged by reference to what is, in effect, a freestanding mini-definition of terrorism. Contained in Article 2(1)(b), this is broad in scope. It is, however, subject to a specific "military carve-out" limitation. As the US Department of State was to explain in the formal Letter of Transmittal to President Clinton of 3 October 2000: "The intent, which was broadly shared by other delegations, was to define the terrorist activity meant to be addressed by the convention in a way that excluded the legitimate actions of the military forces of states by focusing on the intentional targeting of civilians as such."[68]

The prohibition contained in Article 2 extends, among other things, to attempts to commit such offences as well as to their organisation. Importantly, however, "for an act to constitute an offence set forth in paragraph 1, it shall not be necessary that the funds were actually used to carry out an offence referred to in paragraph 1, sub-paragraphs (a) or (b)".[69]

Several other provisions of the 1999 convention are designed to ensure that adequate powers exist in national legal systems to address the issue of the funding of international terrorism. Of particular significance for present purposes is the requirement, contained in Article 5, to introduce (if necessary) criminal, civil or administrative liability for legal persons and, in Article 8, to take appropriate measures for the tracing, freezing and confiscation: "of any funds used or allocated for the purpose of committing the offences set forth in article 2 as well as the proceeds derived from such offences ...". Curiously, however, there is no specific requirement to criminalise the laundering of such funds.

These and other obligations to enhance domestic legal powers are, as is common in UN treaty practice, then supplemented by a range of provisions designed to facilitate international co-operation in the investigation and prosecution of relevant offences. Significantly, domestic measures of prevention and associated international co-operation are also set out in some detail. Of particular relevance for present purposes is that Article 18(1)(b) requires states to take steps, including:

> Measures requiring financial institutions and other professions involved in financial transactions to use the most efficient measures available for the identification of their usual or occasional customers, as well as customers in whose interest accounts are opened, and to pay special attention to unusual or suspicious transactions and report transactions suspected of stemming from a criminal activity.

The 1999 text then sets out several illustrations of steps to be considered in this context, the content of which has been clearly influenced by the package of FATF countermeasures (although that source, as with the 2000 Convention against Transnational Organised Crime, Article 7, and the 2003 Convention against Corruption, Articles 23 and 52, is not specifically acknowledged).

In these and other ways, the 1999 UN International Convention for the Suppression of the Financing of Terrorism provides, for the first time, an agreed global framework within which the international community can collaborate more effectively in seeking to "tackle the difficult problem of financial 'godfathers', without whom most terrorist crimes would not be possible".[70] As will be seen in chapter V, this instrument was also to provide a base from which the international community could seek to build a more ambitious programme of measures in the terrorist financing sphere in the wake of the 11 September 2001 attacks against the United States.

Supportive UN activities

The conclusion of these global, crime-specific, suppression conventions and their entry into force are, without doubt, significant achievements. It is widely appreciated, however, that it is one thing to reach agreement on paper and quite another to secure effective operation in practice. Indeed, to date the results – as indicated by the raw and incomplete statistics which are available – tell a rather disappointing story even among the world's richest industrialised countries. For example, money laundering convictions have proved to be very difficult to secure in most jurisdictions.[71] As has been explained elsewhere: "Most legislation required evidence of three specific elements in order to bring a successful money laundering prosecution – the predicate crime ... the awareness of the launderer of the illegal source of the proceeds, and the action of removing or concealing the funds."[72]

A somewhat similar picture presents itself at the level of the confiscation of criminal proceeds. In a July 1998 report to the European Parliament, the Commission of the European Communities reflected upon the results achieved by its fifteen member states: "It does not appear that large amounts are being confiscated and there are indications, from certain member states, that much of the money seized or frozen ultimately has to be returned or released."[73]

In so far as international co-operation is concerned a review of the practice of FATF members published in 1997 acknowledged that "there has been relatively limited mutual assistance experience ... in the confiscation field, and asset sharing and co-ordinating seizure and confiscation proceedings are also in their infancy at present".[74]

While the reasons for this state of affairs are many, complex and varied, the experience of EU and FATF members helps, for present purposes, to underline the magnitude of the challenge facing developing countries and states in transition. Consequently, one of the priorities for the UN system has been to provide such states with both encouragement and technical and other forms of assistance in order to convert political momentum into practical reality.

While various agencies have a mandate in this area, the major focus of UN activities has been centred on its Vienna Office; the location of the UN Office on Drugs and Crime (UNODC). Among a broad range of other activities it provides – as have its predecessor bodies – vital assistance in the legal field including help to those jurisdictions faced with the challenge of enacting often highly complex legislation required to give domestic effect to the numerous obligations contained in the 1988 and subsequent conventions. This is a particular area of difficulty for small developing countries which suffer from a chronic shortage of appropriately trained professionals including legislative drafters.

In recognition of this fact the UN office at Vienna has, since the early 1990s, produced, revised and updated "model laws" on money laundering; one for use by civil law jurisdictions and another designed for common law countries. This latter was extended to include terrorist financing issues in 2003. At the time of writing the model for civil law countries was being similarly upgraded. It is of importance to note that from the outset these model laws have sought to reflect best international practice and have not been artificially constrained by the formal mandate as reflected in the texts of the UN treaties in question.

Indeed, especially in the second half of the 1990s, UN-based consideration of money laundering and related matters generally followed the same laudable pattern in going well beyond the confines of the 1988 convention. Increasingly, emphasis was placed upon the need to have resort to preventive strategies which fully engage the banking and financial sectors in the anti-money laundering effort as well as the desirability of extending the scope of money laundering predicate offences beyond drug trafficking. This is well illustrated in Resolution 5 (XXXIX) adopted by the UN Commission on Narcotic Drugs on 24 April 1996. This provided, among other matters, encouragement to states to require the establishment of customer identification, record keeping and other preventive strategies by banks and other financial institutions. It also urged countries to "broaden money-laundering countermeasures … to include the transit, conversion or other disposition of illegal proceeds from serious crime". The resolution, importantly, noted that the Forty Recommendations of the FATF "remain the standard by which the anti-money laundering measures adopted by concerned States should be judged".

This trend was consolidated by the UN General Assembly Special Session on the World Drug Problem which was held in New York from 8 to 10 June 1998. This high-level event was convened to mark the tenth anniversary of the 1988 convention and to provide an opportunity to develop a forward-looking strategy for the twenty-first century. One of the specific objectives set for the special session was to adopt further measures to prevent money laundering and to sanction the same. To this end the General Assembly embraced the need to tackle the laundering of profits derived both from drug trafficking and other serious crimes, stressed the centrality of the preventive strategy and emphasised the importance of the implementation of law enforcement measures including information-sharing mechanisms.

Of particular interest for present purposes is that part of UNODC now known as the Anti-Money Laundering Unit (Amlu) which is responsible for carrying out the Global Programme against Money Laundering (GPML) which was launched in 1997. This aims to increase the effectiveness of international action through, among other things, the provision to governments of technical assistance (for example, in the creation of financial intelligence units or FIUs), and the development of relevant research and analysis. In the latter context Amlu also maintains (in a joint effort with other international bodies) the innovative and well-regarded International Money Laundering Information Network (Imolin) website and the associated Anti-Money Laundering International Database (Amlid). The latter "is a world review of national anti-money laundering laws and regulations analysed according to 73 objective criteria".[75] The GPML has also facilitated the conduct of original research on central issues of concern. Of the resulting products perhaps the best known and most influential to date has been the May 1998 report entitled "Financial Havens, Banking Secrecy and Money Laundering",[76] prepared by four leading authorities in the field.

It should also be stressed that the remit of the Amlu has been extended, since the September 2001 terrorist attacks against the United States, to include matters related to the financing of terrorism. This flows, in part, from the entry into force of the 1999 convention on this subject which was examined at an earlier stage of this chapter. Furthermore, the Security Council in Resolution 1373 (2001), passed in the aftermath of that outrage, specifically noted the close interrelationship between international terrorism and other forms of criminality of international concern including money laundering.[77]

Finally, for present purposes, it should be recalled that in addition to providing a forum for the negotiation of crime-specific international instruments of global reach, the UN has sought to facilitate the provision of international co-operation in the criminal justice area more generally. Of particular significance has been the elaboration of UN model treaties, on such matters as mutual assistance in criminal matters and extradition (formally adopted by the United Nations Congresses on the Prevention of Crime and the Treatment of Offenders).[78] The model on mutual assistance in criminal matters, for example, was adopted by the 8th Congress held in Havana, Cuba, in 1990 and approved by the UN General Assembly later the same year. Designed to popularise this important form of co-operation and to facilitate the negotiation of bilateral agreements between interested states it is, unlike the

1988 convention, not restricted to drug trafficking offences. In its original formulation it contained an optional protocol on the subject of co-operation in the confiscation of the proceeds of crime.[79] However, in 1998 it was decided to amend the model so as to insert the proceeds of crime provisions into the main body of the text.[80] It does not, however, directly treat the issue of laundering. As has been pointed out elsewhere: "If all countries criminalise money laundering ... then in so far as the granting of assistance is governed by the principle of dual criminality, the Protocol would be available in respect of such conduct."[81]

Global law enforcement co-operation

The UN is not the only institution with a global constituency which has an interest in countering money laundering and promoting the tracing, seizing and confiscation of the proceeds of crime. These aims are shared by those charged with servicing the needs of the world's law enforcement community; namely, the International Criminal Police Organisation (ICPO/Interpol) and the World Customs Organisation (WCO) (formerly the Customs Cooperation Council (CCC)).

Interpol, the successor to the International Criminal Police Commission which was founded in 1923, is the principal facilitator of police-to-police co-operation on a global scale. With its headquarters in Lyons, France, to which it moved in 1989, it has a worldwide membership. Staffed by a mix of serving police officers and civilian employees it has four official working languages (English, French, Spanish and Arabic). Its major aims, as expressed in Article 2 of its constitution, are to promote the widest possible co-operation between police authorities in the spirit of the Universal Declaration of Human Rights, and to contribute to the "prevention and suppression of ordinary law crimes".[82]

It is of importance to stress that, contrary to popular belief, Interpol has no operational policing mandate. One of its two major functions is to facilitate communication between its members through the provision of a modern, safe and secure communications network. For this purpose each member has a National Central Bureau (NCB) which acts as the focal point for liaison with both the general secretariat in Lyons and the NCBs of other members. The second major function performed by Interpol is to act as a source of information on criminals and on developing trends and patterns of criminality. The emphasis on the sharing and analysis of information on an international basis continues:

> The most recent development is a unique system known as I-24/7. This is a high security, maximum efficiency system using the Internet as a tunnel for heavily encrypted data. It enables the Interpol community to access multiple databases

containing criminal information such as drug seizures, stolen vehicles, fraudulent travel documents, suspect individuals, weapons and explosives, fingerprints and DNA. Police can cross-reference data in seconds and pursue their investigations more quickly and effectively.[83]

The interest of Interpol in money laundering and related issues dates back to the early 1980s. Until relatively recently such matters fell primarily within the remit of the Fopac group; an acronym derived from the French *fonds provenant des activités criminelles*.

Established as a working group in 1983 and given permanent status in January 1990, Fopac had a variety of functions and responsibilities. A substantial part of the effort of its modestly sized staff was devoted to providing information on money laundering to national law enforcement agencies. One vehicle used was the Fopac *Bulletin*. This contained details on such matters as new, significant or unusual cases; developments, changes, trends and patterns; and, countermeasures initiated by member countries. It was also charged with maintaining contact with specialists in the anti-money laundering field and in this capacity it reached out to a range of international bodies, and parts of the private sector in addition to its core law enforcement constituency. Finally, it had an analysis and dissemination function.

Following extensive reorganisation within Interpol's general secretariat, in 2001 Fopac ceased to exist. The anti-money laundering issue is now dealt with by the Financial and High Tech Crime (FHT) Sub-Directorate which also has responsibility for a range of other offences. While many of the activities of Fopac continue, emphasis has been placed on enhancing the role of Interpol through "wider and more effective information sharing, an expanded database and better analysis of the available data".[84]

Unsurprisingly, Interpol has recently started to afford a high priority to the issue of terrorism including the funding of terrorist groups. In the latter context there has been a focus on:

> ... significant sources and methods of money transfer by terrorists, including alternative remittance systems and non-governmental organisations (NGOs) to discover links with suspicious entities, individuals or companies. Links between NGOs and front companies engaged primarily in import-export across different jurisdictions have been researched along with linkages with other significant sources of terrorist funding, including narcotics and weapons trafficking, precious metals and gems.[85]

As mentioned earlier, the Brussels-based WCO shares Interpol's concern with money laundering and has close links with Lyons on this and other matters of common concern. This includes the routine sharing of information and intelligence. Established in 1952 to meet the specialist international needs of customs administrations it has a somewhat smaller membership and staff than its policing counterpart. Its two central missions are "[t]o promote the simplification and harmonisation of customs procedures and to promote effective customs controls".[86]

In the discharge of its enforcement responsibilities, the WCO provides its members with somewhat similar services to those offered by Interpol. It too has no operational powers. In terms of subject areas there are, as with drugs, areas of overlap between them which can be the source of difficulties. In the specific instance of money laundering, the involvement of the WCO flows from the fact that in some jurisdictions the enforcement of the relevant legislation "is the responsibility of customs administrations or the finance ministries to whom they report".[87] Specific activities have included the provision of information and training and the promotion of appropriate legislation, and the formulation of best practice guidance. It has also been active in promoting international co-operation.

The Egmont Group

While Interpol and the WCO are long-established and formally structured international bodies in which the money laundering issue forms but a part of the overall mandate, the Egmont Group is an informal international grouping which has emerged in a specific anti-money laundering context. It is named after the Egmont-Arenberg Palace in Brussels where, in June 1995, the first meeting took place following a joint Belgian-US initiative. Since that time this grouping has met on a regular basis and has, in the words of the European Commission, "become a genuine international forum and, though having no official status, has become an essential element in the international fight against money laundering".[88]

Its origins are to be found in the challenges posed for national authorities in securing the effective implementation of agreed anti-money laundering measures. Of particular importance in this regard has been the creation of often extensive new and potentially valuable sources of financial information available to national authorities, arising out of the elaboration of those aspects of the evolving strategy which embrace the private sector. For example, both the 1996 recommendations of the FATF and the 1991 EC Directive on the Prevention of the Use of the Financial System for the Purpose of Money Laundering[89] call for the mandatory reporting of suspicious transactions to the relevant national authorities. However, in neither case is it specified what form such national authorities should take.

In consequence there has been little in the way of harmonisation of approach to this matter although the majority of countries have seen a need for some centralisation of this task.[90] These disclosure-receiving bodies, commonly known as financial intelligence units (FIUs), tend to be of any one of four types.[91] In the police model (as used, for instance, in the United Kingdom (NCIS)) such suspicious-transaction reports are made directly to law enforcement bodies for investigation. In the judicial model, as used in Portugal (UIF) among others, disclosures are addressed to the office of the public prosecutor. In a few instances reports are transmitted to a joint police-judicial unit (the mixed system). Finally, there is the intermediary or administrative model, variants of which have been created in a wide variety of jurisdictions, including the USA (FinCEN) and Australia (Austrac). These act as a buffer between the private sector and the police and prosecutorial authorities. As Verhelst, the Deputy Director of the Belgian unit (CTIF/CFI), which falls into this category, has remarked: "Reports are made to a specifically designated (and mostly newly created) administrative authority to be analysed and processed before being passed on for investigations and prosecution."[92]

This highly diverse institutional architecture has, in turn, been the source of some difficulties in achieving a further goal of the anti-money laundering system; namely, international co-operation. As Mitsilegas has remarked:

> It is extremely difficult for an independent or administrative unit to share information with a unit that constitutes part of the police of another state. Such an exchange, without sufficient guarantees, would undermine one of the fundamental missions of independent units, that is to avoid to the greatest possible degree the communication of sensitive everyday information to law enforcement authorities. On the other hand, independent units face problems in consulting foreign police data, as they "do not fit" in the international police communication system; at the same time, it is impossible sometimes even unconstitutional for many police units, as state units, to exchange information with independent, "non-state" bodies in other countries.[93]

In recognition of these difficulties, FATF Recommendation 32 of 1996 called upon its members to "make efforts to improve a spontaneous or 'upon request' international information exchange relating to suspicious transactions, persons and corporations involved in those transactions between competent authorities". The Egmont Group has emerged as the major international forum devoted to maximising co-operation between such national units.

At its meeting in Rome in November 1996, the Egmont Group adopted a definition of a financial intelligence unit. It reads as follows:

> A central, national agency responsible for receiving (and, as permitted, requesting), analysing and disseminating to the competent authorities, disclosures of financial information:
>
> i. concerning suspected proceeds of crime, or
>
> ii. required by national legislation or regulation in order to counter money laundering.[94]

By the time of its meeting in Sydney in July 2003, some eighty-four national bodies had been deemed to meet that definition.

In June 1997, at its meeting in Madrid, the Egmont Group reaffirmed this definition and formally adopted a statement of purpose.[95] Here, priority was afforded to the enhancement of international information exchange and other measures to improve co-operation between participating jurisdictions. One highly practical manifestation of its approach to the latter is the creation of the Egmont Group secure website. This permits members "to access information on FIUs, money laundering trends, financial analysis tools, and technological developments. The website is not accessible to the public; therefore, members are able to share this information in a protected environment".[96] Other priorities include the provision of training and fostering the development of similar units in further countries around the world.

That said, enhanced international co-operation remains the cornerstone of the mandate of the Egmont Group. The centrality of this concept is underlined by the fact that specific principles of information exchange between FIUs are annexed to and form part of the statement of purpose. The primary goal of such co-operation is embodied in paragraph 9 and reads thus:

FIUs should be able to exchange information freely with other FIUs on the basis of reciprocity or mutual agreement and consistent with procedures understood by the requested and requesting party. Such exchange, either upon request or spontaneously, should produce any available information that may be relevant to an analysis or investigation of financial transactions and other relevant information related to money laundering and the persons or companies involved.

This is, in turn, is supplemented by specific provisions which, among others things, clarify the restrictions on the use of the information so obtained, and emphasise the need for strict controls and safeguards to ensure consistency with national requirements on data protection and personal privacy. The Egmont Group has also elaborated a statement of "Best Practices for the Improvement of Exchange of Information Between Financial Intelligence Units".

Unsurprisingly, the Egmont Group has developed strong ties with the FATF; a situation which was formalised in February 2002 when it was granted observer status by the Paris-based anti-money laundering body.[97] Like the FATF, it moved speedily after the events of September 2001 to extend its mandate to include matters relating to the financing of terrorism.[98]

As will be seen in subsequent chapters of this book, the potential for enhanced international co-operation through the creation of national FIUs on the basis of the Egmont Group definition is now widely recognised. Initiatives are being taken in an increasing number of institutional contexts, including the UN[99] and the IMF/World Bank,[100] to encourage this process. Furthermore, the importance of FIUs to the effectiveness of the anti-money laundering effort is increasingly finding reflections in international treaty practice.[101] The Egmont Group has emerged as a key institutional player in that continuing effort.

Notes: III

1. See, Bassiouni, M C, "The International Narcotics Control Scheme", in Bassiouni, M C (ed), *International criminal law*, New York, Transnational Publishers, 1986, Vol. I, at pp. 507-524.

2. "Home Office Memorandum of December 1984", reproduced in House of Commons, Home Affairs Committee, "Misuse of Hard Drugs", HC Paper No. 66, Minutes of Evidence (27 March 1985) (1985-86).

3. See, Chatterjee, S K, A *guide to the international drugs conventions*, London, Commonwealth Secretariat, 1988, at pp. 17-19.

4. Donnelly, J, "The United Nations and the Global Drug Control Regime", in Smith, P H (ed), *Drug policy in the Americas*, Boulder, Colorado, Westview Press, 1991, p. 282, at p. 287.

5. *International Legal Materials*, 26, 1987, Washington, DC, American Society of International Law, p.1637, at p. 1686.

6. UN General Assembly Resolution 39/141.

7. "International Narcotics Control Strategy Report", Washington, DC, Bureau of International Narcotics Matters, US Department of State, 1988, p. 67.

8. US Department of Justice, *Manual for compliance with the United Nations Convention against Illicit Traffic in Narcotic Drugs and Psychotropic Substances*, Washington, DC, 1992, p.I. For a recent and comprehensive treatment of the criminal justice aspects of the global treaties in the drugs area including the 1988 convention, see, Boister, N, *Penal aspects of the UN drugs conventions*, Dordrecht, Kluwer, 2001.

9. Savona, E U and De Feo, M A, "Money Trails: International Money Laundering Trends and Prevention/Control Policies". Paper presented at the International Conference on Preventing and Controlling Money Laundering and the Use of the Proceeds of Crime: A Global Approach, Courmayeur, Mont Blanc, Italy, 18-20 June 1994 (hereafter 1994 conference) (typescript), p.96. Subsequently published in Savona, E U (ed), *Responding to money laundering: international perspectives*, Amsterdam, Harwood Academic Publishers, 1997. References in this work are to the original.

10. Bassiouni, op. cit., p. 521.

11. Reproduced in Gilmore, W (ed), *International efforts to combat money laundering*, Cambridge, Cambridge University Press, 1992, p.98, at p.120. There is evidence to suggest that the manner in which some countries have given effect to this obligation has resulted in a continuing element of difficulty with the dual criminality concept. See, Woltring, H F, "Money Laundering: Impediments to Effective International Co-operation". Paper presented at the 1994 conference (typescript), *supra*, note 9, at pp. 8-9.

12. Freiberg, A, "Criminal Confiscation, Profit and Liberty", *Australian and New Zealand Journal of Criminology*, 1992, p. 44, at pp. 45-46.

13. Gilmore, W (ed), op. cit., p. 112.

14. "Commentary on the United Nations Convention against Illicit Traffic in Narcotic Drugs and Psychotropic Substances 1988", New York, 1998 (hereafter "commentary"), UN Doc. E/CN.7/590, p. 141.

15. *Supra*, note 5, p. 1692.

16. Sproule, D W and Saint-Denis, P, "The UN Drug Trafficking Convention: An Ambitious Step", *Canadian yearbook of international law*, 1989, p. 263, at pp. 281-282.

17. "Report of the International Narcotics Control Board for 1997", New York, INCB, 1997, p. 5.

18. See, Gilmore, W C, *Combating international drugs trafficking: The 1988 United Nations Convention against Illicit Traffic in Narcotic Drugs and Psychotropic Substances*, London, Commonwealth Secretariat, 1991, at pp. 40-41.

19. "Money Laundering and Associated Issues: The Need for International Cooperation", UN Doc. E/CN.15/1992/4/Add.5, 23 March 1992, p. 22.

20. "Report on Financial Havens, Banking Secrecy and Money Laundering", New York, UN Office for Drug Control and Crime Prevention, 1998, p.v.

21. McClean, J D, "Seizing the Proceeds of Crime: The State of the Art", *International and Comparative Law Quarterly*, 1989, p. 334, at p. 339.

22. UN Doc. E/CONF.82/C.1/SR.7, at p. 2.

23. Gilmore, W (ed), op.cit., p. 114.

24. See, for example, "Financial Action Task Force on Money Laundering: Annual Report 1996-1997" (hereafter Report VIII), Paris, FATF, Annex B, at p. 10.

25. "Commentary", op. cit., p.150. The writer is aware of only one state, Luxembourg, which has opted in practice for the alternative approach.

26. Greenberg, T S, "Anti-Money Laundering Activities in the United States", in *Action against transnational criminality: papers from the 1993 Oxford Conference on International and White Collar Crime*, London, Commonwealth Secretariat, 1994, p. 53, at p. 58.

27. "Commentary", op. cit., p. 151.

28. Nadelmann, E, "Unlaundering Dirty Money Abroad: US Foreign Policy and Financial Secrecy Jurisdictions", *Inter-American Law Review*, 1986, p. 33, at p. 34.

29. Freiberg, *supra*, note 12, p. 68.

30. Gilmore, W (ed), op. cit., p. 118.

31. Sproule and Saint-Denis, op. cit., p. 284.

32. In the case of Cyprus, see, for example, section 7 of the Prevention and Suppression of Money Laundering Activities Law, 1996. See also, Ministry of Foreign Affairs, Republic of Cyprus, *Measures taken by the Republic of Cyprus on preventing and combating money laundering*, Nicosia, 1998. The significance of the easing or reversal of the burden of proof to the creation of an effective confiscation system is increasingly acknowledged in specialist circles. See, for example, Report VIII, *supra*, note 24, at p. 19.

33. Sproule and Saint-Denis, op. cit., p. 281.

34. Nadelmann, E A, *Cops across borders: the internationalization of US criminal law enforcement*, Pennsylvania, Pennsylvania University Press, 1993, p. 313.

35. "United Nations Convention against Illicit Traffic in Narcotic Drugs and Psychotropic Substances", 101st Congress, 1st Session, Senate, Executive Report 101-15, p. 185.

36. "Criminal Justice (International Cooperation) Bill: Explanatory Memorandum on the Proposals to Implement the Vienna Convention against Illicit Traffic in Narcotic Drugs and Psychotropic Substances", London, HMSO, 1989, p. 29.

37. Kriz, G, "International Co-operation to Combat Money Laundering: The Nature and Role of Mutual Legal Assistance Treaties", *Commonwealth Law Bulletin*, 1992, p. 723, at p. 726.

38. Parliamentary debate in, *Hansard*, HL, Vol. 514, No. 24, 22 January 1990, col. 896.

39. Ibid.

40. Gilmore, W (ed), op. cit., pp. 119-120.

41. Stewart, D, "Internationalising the War on Drugs: The UN Convention against Illicit Traffic in Narcotic Drugs and Psychotropic Substances", *Denver Journal of International Law and Policy*, 1990, p. 387, at p. 397.

42. *Supra*, note 36, p. 29.

43. Reproduced in Gilmore, W (ed), op. cit., p. 4, at p. 14.

44. UN *Crime Prevention and Criminal Justice Newsletter*, Nos. 26/27, 1995, p. 17.

45. See, Wrench, P, "The G8 and Transnational Organised Crime", in Gilmore, W and Cullen, P (eds), *Crime sans frontières: international and European legal approaches*, Edinburgh, Edinburgh University Press, 1998, at pp. 39-43.

46. See, *International Legal Materials*, 40, 2001, Washington, DC, American Society of International Law, at p. 335 et seq.

47. Article 3(1).

48. See also, Article 2(c) for the associated definition of "structured group".

49. *Official Journal of the European Communities*, No. C 251/1, 15 August 1997, p. 2.

50. See, FATF Recommendation 7 (1990) and Recommendation 6 of the 1996 revised text.

51. An alternative solution is to be found in the 1990 Council of Europe convention on money laundering which specifically provides (in Article 18(8)(a)) that "the fact that the person under investigation or subject to a confiscation order by the authorities of the requesting Party is a legal person shall not be invoked by the requested Party as an obstacle to affording any co-operation under this chapter". The approach (contained in Article 3) of the EU Convention on Mutual Assistance in Criminal Matters of 2000 is also worthy of attention.

52. "Report of the Ad Hoc Committee for the Negotiation of a Convention against Corruption on the Work of its First to Seventh Sessions", UN Doc. A/58/422, 7 October 2003, p. 6.

53. Article 51.

54. See, Article 57(1).

55. Article 57(2).

56. Article 57(3)(b) should be read in conjunction with Article 53(c).

57. Stessens, G, *Money laundering: a new international law enforcement model*, Cambridge, Cambridge University Press, 2000, p. 417.

58. Article 57(4).

59. "Interpretative Notes for the Official Record (*Travaux Préparatoires*) of the Negotiation of the United Nations Convention against Corruption", UN Doc. A/58/422/Add.1, 7 October 2003, p. 11.

60. See, ibid., at p. 4.

61. Chapters V and IV respectively.

62. See also, the references to informal money transmission services in Article 14(1).

63. Article 52(1).

64. Johnson, C M, "Introductory Note to the International Convention for the Suppression of the Financing of Terrorism", *International Legal Materials*, 39, 2000, Washington, DC, American Society of International Law, p.268.

65. See, for example, Article 4.

66. See, Aust, A, "Counter-Terrorism – A New Approach", *Max Planck UN yearbook*, 2001, p. 1, at pp. 4-17.

67. A term broadly defined in Article 1(1).

68. "International Convention for Suppression of Financing of Terrorism: Message from the President of the United States", 106th Congress, 2nd Session, Senate, Treaty Doc. 106-49 (2000), VII.

69. Article 2(3).

70. *Supra*, note 66, p. 4.

71. For details concerning the then fifteen member states of the European Union see "Second Commission Report to the European Parliament and the Council on the Implementation of the Money Laundering Directive", Brussels, 1 July 1998, COM (1998) 401, final, at Annex 9, pp.43-44.

72. UNDCP, *World drug report*, Oxford, Oxford University Press, 1997, p. 137.

73. *Supra*, note 71, p. 21.

74. Report VIII, *supra*, note 24, p. 20.

75. Anti-Money Laundering Unit, *2003 activity report*, Vienna, 2003, p. 19.

76. See, *supra*, note 20.

77. See further, chapter V below.

78. See, Clark, R S, "Crime: The UN Agenda on International Cooperation in the Criminal Process", *Nova Law Review*, 1991, at pp. 475-500.

79. See, ibid., at pp. 490-493.

80. See, "Commission on Crime Prevention and Criminal Justice: Report on the Seventh Session (21-30 April 1998)" UN Doc. E/CN.15/1998/11, at p. 11.

81. *Supra*, note 19, p. 20.

82. See generally, Anderson, M, *Policing the world: Interpol and the politics of international police co-operation*, Oxford, Oxford University Press, 1989.

83. Information kindly supplied to the writer by the Assistant Director, Financial and High Tech Crime, Interpol General Secretariat, January 2004.

84. Ibid.

85. Ibid.

86. Rigdon, A M, "Aspects of International Police and Customs Cooperation", in *Action against transnational criminality: papers from the 1992 Oxford Conference on International and White Collar Crime*, London, Commonwealth Secretariat, 1993, p. 83, at p. 83.

87. Ibid., p. 84.

88. *Supra*, note 71, p. 14.

89. Discussed in chapter IV and chapter VIII respectively.

90. See generally, Thony, J-F, "Processing Financial Information in Money Laundering Matters: The Financial Intelligence Units", *European Journal of Crime, Criminal Law and Criminal Justice*, 1996, p. 257. See also, Schott, P A, *Reference guide to anti-money laundering and combating the financing of terrorism*, Washington, DC, World Bank, 2003, chapter VII.

91. See, Verhelst, B, "The Organisation of a Financial Intelligence Unit". Paper presented to a training seminar for Council of Europe evaluators, Brussels, 25 March 1998 (typescript).

92. Ibid.

93. Mitsilegas, V, *Money laundering counter-measures in the European Union: a paradigm of security governance versus fundamental legal principles*, New York, Aspern Publishers, 2003, p. 170.

94. For the "Interpretative Note Concerning the Egmont Definition of a Financial Intelligence Unit" visit www.egmontgroup.org This site also contains all of the key formal texts mentioned in the following paragraphs of the section.

95. This text was amended both in 2001 and 2003.

96. US General Accounting Office, "Money Laundering: FinCEN's Law Enforcement Support, Regulatory, and International Roles", GAO/T-GGD-98-83, Appendix III, p. 19.

97. See, "Financial Action Task Force on Money Laundering: Annual Report 2001-2002", Paris, FATF, at p. 12.

98. *Suppressing the financing of terrorism: a handbook for legislative drafting*, Washington, DC, Legal Department, International Monetary Fund, 2003, p. 62.

99. See, for example, *supra*, note 93, at pp. 173-174.

100. For a discussion of the role of the IMF and World Bank in this area and in the anti-money laundering effort more generally see, chapter VI below. For a valuable research contribution see, *Financial Intelligence Units: An Overview*, Washington, DC, International Monetary Fund, 2004.

101. See, Article 7(1)(b) of the 2000 UN Convention against Transnational Organised Crime, and Articles 14(1)(b) and 58 of the 2003 Convention against Corruption.

Chapter IV – The Financial Action Task Force

The background

In any assessment of efforts at the international level to ensure the utility and effectiveness of money laundering countermeasures, pride of place must be given to the work of the Financial Action Task Force (FATF).[1] Best known for its Forty Recommendations, it has become the single most important international body in terms of the formulation of anti-money laundering policy and in the mobilisation of global awareness of the complex issues involved in countering this sophisticated form of criminality.[2] Furthermore, and as detailed in chapter V, since September 2001 it has emerged as an influential actor in the associated sphere of action to suppress the financing of terrorism.

The origins of the FATF are firmly rooted in the growing concern, evident particularly in the 1980s, with the increasing extent of the problem of drug abuse and heightened sensitivity with the associated issue of the financial power of drug trafficking syndicates and other organised crime groups. When these matters arose for discussion at the July 1989 Paris Summit Meeting of the Heads of State or Government of the seven major industrial nations (G7), joined by the President of the Commission of the European Communities, it was concluded that there was an "urgent need for decisive action, both on a national and international basis" to counter drug production, consumption and trafficking as well as "the laundering of its proceeds".[3] In this context the decision was taken to create the Task Force. Its initial mandate was:

> ... to assess the results of co-operation already undertaken in order to prevent the utilisation of the banking system and financial institutions for the purpose of money laundering, and to consider additional preventive efforts in this field, including the adaptation of the legal and regulatory systems so as to enhance multilateral judicial assistance.[4]

In addition to the summit participants (Canada, France, Germany, Italy, Japan, United Kingdom, United States and the Commission of the European Communities) eight other states (Australia, Austria, Belgium, Luxembourg, Netherlands, Spain, Sweden and Switzerland) were invited to take part in this initiative which was convened under French chairmanship. This expansion of the Task Force was undertaken "in order to enlarge its expertise and also to reflect the views of other countries particularly concerned by, or having particular experience in the fight against money laundering, at the national or international level".[5]

In the months which followed "[m]ore than one hundred and thirty experts from various ministries, law enforcement authorities, and bank supervisory and regulatory agencies met and worked together".[6] The fruits of these labours are to be found in an impressive report of 6 February 1990. This contains an analysis of the extent and nature of the money laundering process, an overview of international instruments and national programmes then in place to counter the problem and, most importantly, forty separate recommendations for action. These recommendations are reproduced in full at Appendix I.

Building on the firm foundations established by the 1988 UN Convention against Illicit Traffic in Narcotic Drugs and Psychotropic Substances, and the statement of principles for the guidance of bank supervisors issued on 12 December 1988 by the Basel Committee on Banking Supervision, which is outlined below, the 1990 FATF recommendations were to focus on three central areas: (i) improvements to national legal systems; (ii) the enhancement of the role of the financial system; and (iii) the strengthening of international co-operation.[7]

This report was endorsed at the ministerial level by all participating countries in May 1990 and submitted to the G7 summit in Houston in July. There it was agreed that the FATF would be reconvened for a further year "to assess and facilitate the implementation of the Forty Recommendations and to complement them where appropriate. It was agreed that all OECD and financial centre countries that would subscribe to the recommendations of the Task Force should be invited to participate in this exercise".[8]

Strengthened by the addition of eight further OECD countries (Denmark, Finland, Greece, Ireland, New Zealand, Norway, Portugal and Turkey) as well as Hong Kong and the Gulf Cooperation Council to its list of members,[9] several meetings were held in Paris, again under French presidency, and a second report was issued on 13 May 1991. Importantly, this recorded an agreement "to continue FATF for a period of five years, with a decision to review progress after three years ...".[10] The decision taken to extend the lifespan of the FATF was but one of a number of measures designed to ensure the coherence, flexibility and efficiency of this initiative. Of these one of the most significant was that "membership should not be further widened".[11] An exception was, however, agreed in respect of those who had been invited to participate in FATF II but who had yet to accept the recommendations. It was on this basis that Iceland and Singapore joined in the course of the FATF III session.[12]

The promised mid-term review in turn took place during the 1993-94 round (FATF V) at which time it was unanimously agreed that the group should remain in being until 1998-99.[13] At that time the possibility of accommodating "a very limited expansion" was signalled but did not, in fact, take place.[14]

The issue of the future of the FATF was revisited in the course of the 1997-98 session (FATF IX) and again the conclusion was reached that there remained "an obvious need for continued mobilisation at the international level to deepen and widen anti-money laundering action".[15] Consequently, a ministerial meeting of members held in Paris in April 1998 extended its life, though with a somewhat revised mandate, until 2004. This decision swiftly gained the support of OECD ministers, G7 finance ministers, and the heads of state and government of the G8. On 17 May 1998 the latter "welcomed the FATF decision to continue and enlarge its work to combat money laundering in partnership with regional groupings".[16] Significantly, that revised mandate envisaged the long-awaited increase in numbers. Such expansion was, however, to be both modest and targeted:

17. The minimum and *sine qua non* criteria for admission are as follows:

- to be fully committed at the political level: (i) to implement the 1996 Recommendations within a reasonable timeframe (three years), and (ii) to undergo annual self-assessment exercises and two rounds of mutual evaluations;

- to be a full and active member of the relevant FATF-style regional body (where one exists), or be prepared to work with the FATF or even to take the lead, to establish such a body (where none exists);

- to be a strategically important country;

- to have already made the laundering of the proceeds of drug trafficking and other serious crimes a criminal offence; and

- to have already made it mandatory for financial institutions to identify their customers and to report unusual or suspicious transactions.[17]

The first phase of this process sought to address the lack of members in Latin America and resulted in the admission, in 2000, of Argentina, Brazil and Mexico. This was followed in 2003 by the election of the Russian Federation and South Africa, bringing the total membership, at the time of writing, to thirty-one jurisdictions and two international institutions.[18] Some further expansion in the years ahead is not unlikely.[19] In this regard it should also be noted that in May 2004 the decision was taken to extend the life of the Task Force for a further eight years; that is, to December 2012.

The structure and purpose of the FATF

Steps were agreed in the course of FATF II to strengthen the institutional structure of the grouping and to regularise its methods of operation. Of particular importance in this context was the decision to institute a rotating presidency involving a one year term of office. "The President would be chosen by the FATF, taking into account as much as possible geographical locations and membership of various international groupings."[20]

The nature of the internal working structure of the FATF has not been characterised by excessive rigidity and has been permitted to evolve and mature. For example, initially working groups played a significant part in its work. This was made possible by the multidisciplinary character of many national delegations which remains a major strength of this body. As a senior delegate explained, the FATF "brings together policy makers and experts from a wide range of disciplines, finance and justice ministries, banking and other financial regulators, as well as law enforcement and legal agencies. This multidisciplinary approach is essential to the FATF's work and indeed to the effectiveness of action to combat money laundering".[21]

The strength of the working group structure was, however, bound to have an impact on the nature of the role and contribution of the plenary meetings. The issue of working practices was consequently examined in the course of FATF V and it was decided "that following the completion of their current work programmes, the committee structure should be discontinued and the functions of the plenary strengthened. ... However, ad hoc groups might be created to carry out specific tasks in line with specific terms of reference approved by the plenary".[22]

The Task Force meets several times each year. Normally one meeting is held in the country of the presidency with the remainder being convened at OECD headquarters in Paris. The latter houses a modest (but growing) FATF secretariat. This was established following FATF II and services the regular meetings and facilitates other aspects of the ongoing work programme including the processes for the evaluation of the progress of the membership in implementing the Forty Recommendations, and arranging an ambitious range of external relations activities (detailed in chapter VI below).

Though located within the OECD it is important to note that FATF is not formally a part of that or any other international organisation. Similarly, as the Head of the Financial Affairs Division of the OECD remarked: "It is not a permanent international organisation nor a body managing a legally-binding convention."[23] It is, rather, an ad hoc grouping of governments and others with a complex but highly focused agenda. As has been pointed out elsewhere: "Their common purpose is, and will remain, their determination to pursue convergent and comprehensive money laundering strategies based on international co-operation while preserving both the efficiency of the financial system and the freedom to engage in legitimate financial transactions."[24] Central to the achievement of that ambition is the package of recommended countermeasures which was first elaborated in the February 1990 report.

The 1990 FATF recommendations

The context

The major goal of the FATF when first established in 1989 was "the establishment of standards in the form of recommendations that could be endorsed by national authorities and applied internationally in a consistent manner".[25] As was noted above, this effort to formulate a comprehensive anti-money laundering programme was to be based on a prior study of the nature and extent of the problem and a critical examination of existing domestic and international countermeasures.[26]

Out of the above, a multitrack approach to the problem gradually emerged. First, it calls for the strengthening of the criminal law with a particular emphasis on the development of legislative and enforcement techniques, such as the confiscation of the proceeds of crime, designed to undermine the financial power of trafficking networks and organised crime groups. Thus, as with the 1988 UN convention, there is a clear recognition that in the fight against money laundering major reliance must be placed on criminal justice mechanisms. However, in contrast to that UN precedent, the FATF recognised that sole reliance on such measures would be insufficient. As one commentator has stated: "The criminal law cannot by itself carry the burden of reducing, or even containing, money laundering. A broad range of measures is required."[27]

This perception resulted in the inclusion of a second and more highly innovative element in the FATF programme. It is reflected in the decision to involve, in an unprecedented fashion, participants in financial sector activity in the strategy to combat money laundering. This decision flowed from the analysis of money laundering techniques and the identification of the stages in the process where the launderer was most vulnerable to detection. As the February 1990 report noted: "Key stages for the detection of money laundering operations are those where cash enters into the domestic financial system, either formally or informally, where it is sent abroad to be integrated into the financial systems of regulatory havens, and where it is repatriated in the form of transfers of legitimate appearance."[28]

However, the decision of the FATF to place banks and other financial institutions "in the front line against laundering"[29] was not based exclusively on an assessment of the key role that they could play in the detection process. A further important factor was the enhanced appreciation of the negative impact which "dirty money" can have on the credit and financial institutions through which it passes or in which it is deposited or invested in the course of laundering operations.[30] As Tom Sherman, the then President of the FATF, was to state in September 1992: "Combating money laundering is not just a matter of fighting crime but of preserving the integrity of financial institutions and ultimately the financial system as a whole."[31]

While "[c]riminal and regulatory, or control and preventive, policies are necessarily connected"[32] they are not, when conceived of in traditional national terms, sufficient to deal with this complex problem. Modern money laundering techniques, as was demonstrated in chapter II, commonly, and increasingly, include a transnational dimension. The FATF recognised from the outset that the possibilities of success for any strategy which sought to combat laundering depended in a critical way on the range, scope and quality of the mechanisms of international co-operation.[33] This was, accordingly, made the third central feature of its programme of action.

The nature of the 1990 recommendations

The package of countermeasures formulated by FATF I, which is reproduced at Appendix I, consisted of forty separate recommendations for action. Although viewed as constituting "a minimal standard in the fight against money laundering"[34] it should be noted that some failed at the time to attract unanimous support. As the 1990 report admits, "the minimal standard we recommend can be viewed as rather ambitious".[35] It should also be stressed that these recommendations possess no binding force as a matter of international law; customary or conventional.[36] A number are, however, also embodied or reflected in the provisions of existing multilateral conventions and are, to that extent, binding on the parties *inter se*. Beyond that, their force and authority derive from their endorsement by member governments and their practical implementation.[37]

A minority of the original forty "action steps" in essence called only for further study or for consideration to be given to particular matters, or articulated alternative approaches. Even those of a more mandatory character were commonly, and deliberately, formulated in a fairly open-textured manner.[38] As has been pointed out elsewhere, it was recognised:

> ... that there can be significant differences between the legal systems, financial systems and, indeed, the money laundering situations of different countries. So the Recommendations allow considerable flexibility in how they are applied and concentrate on laying down the general principles for combating money laundering rather than prescribing in great detail what should be done.[39]

It is also of relevance to note that individual member countries of the FATF were permitted to adopt stricter measures should they so wish;[40] an opportunity which has been resorted to in practice.[41]

The general framework of the 1990 recommendations

The 1990 FATF report identifies three measures which were unanimously regarded as constituting the overall general framework for its many specific proposals. All were intended to cure major difficulties and inefficiencies in international co-operation. The specific recommendations were as follows:

1. Each country should, without further delay, take steps to fully implement the Vienna Convention [1988 UN convention] and proceed to ratify it;

2. Financial institutions secrecy laws should be conceived so as not to inhibit implementation of the recommendations; and,

3. An effective money laundering enforcement programme should include increased multilateral cooperation and mutual legal assistance in money laundering investigations and prosecutions and extradition in money laundering cases where possible.[42]

In formulating the specific elements for inclusion in the general framework delegates were conscious of the fact that at that stage no FATF member country had become a party to the 1988 UN convention (which is referred to throughout the FATF document as the Vienna Convention) and that it had yet to enter into force. Indeed, it was feared that, given the ambition and complexity of that international instrument, "some countries could have difficulties in ratifying and implementing it for reasons that are not related to the issue of money laundering".[43]

Given the need to make rapid money laundering-specific progress, the decision was taken to include in the recommendations "important steps which are implied by this convention".[44] For example, at least in so far as drug-related money laundering is concerned, Recommendation 2 on financial secrecy finds reflection, as was seen in the previous chapter, in Articles 5(3) and 7(5) of the 1988 UN convention. In addition, the concerns of Recommendation 3 relating to improved international legal co-operation are addressed by a number of central provisions of that instrument including Articles 5 to 11.

The drafters of the FATF programme did not, however, feel constrained by the 1988 UN convention which, as has been seen, came to be regarded throughout much of the 1990s as representing a minimum standard of responsible international behaviour in this area. In this regard they were prepared to recommend a "reinforcement of its provisions applicable to money laundering issues"[45] and to venture into areas, as with the enhancement of the role of the financial sector, which fell entirely outside the scope of the 1988 exercise.

Improvement of national legal systems

The first of three distinct sets of specific recommendations (4 to 8) were directed towards securing improvements in national legal systems. A number of these, for reasons given above, represented primarily a reaffirmation of the principles contained in the 1988 UN convention. This was explicitly the case, for example, in the call to criminalise drug-related money laundering (Recommendations 4 and 6) and to make appropriate provision for the confiscation of proceeds and related provisional measures (Recommendation 8).

Two of the recommendations, however, sought to broaden the approach adopted in Vienna. Thus, Recommendation 5 encouraged member countries to "consider extending the offense of drug money laundering to any other crimes for which there is a link to narcotics; an alternative approach is to criminalize money laundering based on all serious offenses, and/or on all offenses that generate a significant amount of proceeds, or on certain serious offenses".[46] Similarly, Recommendation 7 concerning the possible extension of corporate criminal liability to this area of concern has no parallel in the 1988 UN text.

Enhancement of the role of the financial system

The second set of area-specific measures (Recommendations 9 to 29) articulated a strategy to engage the financial system in the effort to combat laundering while, at the same time, seeking to ensure the retention of the conditions necessary for its efficient operation. As Pecchioli has stated: "The common thread underlying these recommendations is the view that financial institutions are the key element in the detection of illicit transactions given their unique function in a country's payments system and in the collection and transfer of financial assets."[47]

In approaching this matter the Task Force decided to build upon the precedent established by the December 1988 "Statement on Prevention of Criminal Use of the Banking System for the Purpose of Money Laundering" issued by the Basel Committee on Banking Supervision. Its basic purpose is to encourage the banking sector, through "a general statement of ethical principles", to adopt a common position in order to ensure that banks are not used to hide or launder funds acquired through criminal activities and, in particular, through drug trafficking. To that end, it enunciated several key principles including proper customer identification, compliance with the law and ethical standards, and co-operation with law enforcement agencies.[48] In an effort to increase the impact of this statement the committee took the step of commending it to supervisory authorities in other countries.

It is important to note that the Basel statement, unlike the 1988 UN convention, is not a treaty in terms of public international law. Similarly it has no direct legal effect in the domestic law of any country. An exclusive concentration on the formal status of the text would, however, be extremely misleading. As was pointed out in the 1990 FATF report:

> Although it is not itself a legally binding document, various formulas have been used to make its principles an obligation, notably a formal agreement among banks that commits them explicitly (Austria, Italy, Switzerland), a formal indication by bank regulators that failure to comply with these principles could lead to administrative sanctions (France, United Kingdom), or legally binding texts with a reference to these principles (Luxembourg).[49]

The influence of that 1988 initiative can be clearly discerned in the more detailed FATF treatment of these and related matters. However, while the FATF approach owed much to the Basel statement it was, without doubt, a far more ambitious undertaking. This was so both in terms of the areas common to both texts, and in the willingness of the 1990 report to break new ground. By way of illustration of the former, while both address the critical question of customer identification, the FATF reached out to the close-ly associated issues of obtaining information on the beneficial ownership of funds (Recommendation 13) and the retention of records, for a period of at least five years, "sufficient to permit reconstruction of individual trans-actions ... so as to provide, if necessary, evidence for prosecution of criminal behaviour" (Recommendation 14).

Among the measures with no obvious counterparts in the Basel statement, one might mention the FATF effort to cope with the problem of countries with no or insufficient anti-money laundering measures (Recommendations 21 and 22), its treatment of the monitoring of cross-border flows of cash (Recommendation 23), and suggestions made as to the role of regulatory and other administrative authorities in order to ensure effective implemen-tation (Recommendations 26 to 29). Most importantly, while the financial recommendations "appear to have been developed primarily with deposit-taking institutions in mind"[50] they were specifically extended to non-bank financial institutions (Recommendations 9 to 11). They also have an impact on "certain other professions dealing with cash, which are unregulated or virtually unregulated in many countries".[51] While this expansion of the reach of the countermeasures in question has been the source of considerable dif-ficulty it was, as underlined by the analysis of money laundering methods in chapter II, an innovation of great practical importance. As a past president of the FATF has explained: "Much of the preoccupation of anti-money laundering activity has been with the banking system. But experience shows that money launderers will use almost any form of corporate and trust activity to launder their profits."[52]

As was to be expected, however, it was not possible to achieve a consen-sus on all central issues in this sensitive sphere. This is well illustrated by the divergence of views as to the effectiveness of a system of mandatory and routine reporting of domestic and international currency transactions above a fixed threshold. The two member countries which had opted to establish such a system, the United States and Australia, viewed it as a vital part of any comprehensive package of countermeasures. The majority, however, were not convinced.[53] Accordingly, Recommendation 24 merely called upon FATF participants to "consider the feasibility and utility" of this approach.

Strengthening of international co-operation

As emphasised in chapter II, modern money laundering techniques contain conspicuous transnational features. While national countermeasures, such as criminalisation, confiscation, and the institution of comprehensive preventive strategies, are a precondition for making substantial progress it has been accepted from the outset that "[w]ithout appropriate international cooperation, all these efforts could yield few results while incurring large costs".[54] The facilitation of international interaction between law enforcement and prosecutorial authorities and financial regulators and supervisors was the central thrust of Recommendations 30 to 40 inclusive. The majority of the proposals to enhance co-operation between legal authorities (Recommendations 33 to 40) reaffirmed the processes and sought to consolidate the progress achieved in the 1988 UN convention. This was particularly so in respect of such areas as co-operation in the seizure and confiscation of the proceeds of crime, mutual assistance in criminal matters, and extradition.

As with the 1988 UN convention, the Task Force gave explicit recognition to the fact that "international cooperation should be supported by a network of bilateral and multilateral agreements and arrangements based on generally shared legal concepts with the aim of providing practical measures to affect the widest possible range of mutual assistance".[55] The work then being done within the Council of Europe, which was to result in the conclusion later the same year of the 1990 Convention on Laundering, Search, Seizure and Confiscation of the Proceeds from Crime, received positive support. This highly significant European initiative is examined in chapter VII.

The 1990 FATF report also sought to pave the way for the improved exchange of information relating to suspicious transactions (Recommendation 32), and to enhance "the knowledge of international flows of drug money, noticeably cash flows, and the knowledge of money laundering methods, to enable a better focus of international and national efforts to combat this phenomenon".[56]

The 1996 revised FATF recommendations

The context

In the years since its creation, the FATF has consistently demonstrated an awareness of the need to take action to ensure the continuing relevance and utility of its programme of action. In particular, it was anticipated from the outset that the process would be a dynamic one and that changes in strategy would be brought about by, among other factors, an enhanced understanding of the techniques used by criminals and the impact thereon of the increasingly effective countermeasures of FATF members. Consequently, it was recognised in the 1990 FATF report that "our recommendations will probably need periodic re-evaluation".[57] In this regard, however, the conscious decision was taken "not to amend the Recommendations before the completion of the first round of mutual evaluations of FATF members so that they could all be assessed against the same standard".[58] This highly innovative process of peer review, designed to facilitate the international monitoring of the implementation of the recommendations by members, is discussed in chapter VI.

Until the end of the first mutual evaluation period was reached, the grouping had to content itself with adopting what are known as "interpretative notes" to the original recommendations. Griffiths explained the formal position thus: "These do not change the scope or substance of the recommendations but clarify or provide supplementary guidance on their application."[59] A significant number of such clarifications were issued.[60] Of these, the great majority related specifically to one or more of the original recommendations. For example, Recommendation 23 was a rather weakly worded measure directed at the detection and monitoring of cross-border flows of cash. Following further consideration of this important point of vulnerability in actual money laundering operations, a specific interpretative note was formulated in the course of FATF III. This recorded agreement that, in spite of its wording, "this recommendation is not limited to currency, but also covers cash equivalent monetary instruments and other highly liquid valuables (for example, precious metals and gems)".[61] A minority, however, as with those adopted during FATF III on shell corporations, and on the issue of deferred arrests and seizures,[62] were not tied to particular recommendations in this way.

The nature of the process is well illustrated by the active consideration in various early rounds of problems associated with the use of shell companies. Such entities, particularly those registered in offshore jurisdictions, as has been seen earlier in this work, have been widely used in complex international money laundering schemes. Initial consideration of this matter resulted in the formulation, during FATF III, of an interpretative note. This urged members to take heed of the potential for abuse which they represented and to "consider measures to prohibit unlawful use of such entities".[63] The issue was returned to in the following year. It was concluded that "[a] key factor which makes shell corporations attractive to money launderers is the ability in many jurisdictions to conceal or obfuscate the true beneficial ownership of the entity".[64] However, as the study progressed into FATF V, "the importance of applying the principle of transparency of ownership to corporate bodies in general was emphasised since not only shell corporations but virtually any legal entity could be used in money laundering schemes".[65] These insights in turn provided the basis for a further interpretative note to Recommendations 12, 13 and 16 to 19 concerning the use in money laundering schemes of accounts in the names of customers who are not natural persons.[66]

There was, of course, a certain artificiality associated with the notion that such notes "do not add to or change the scope or the substance" of the original recommendations.[67] With the end of the first phase of the mutual assessment process in sight it was announced that "a stocktaking exercise will be conducted in 1995, taking in [sic] account experience gained over the last four years, including the Interpretative Notes which have been developed".[68]

The 1996 revisions

The first steps in this major stocktaking review of the 1990 recommendations were undertaken during the Dutch presidency. A questionnaire was circulated to members seeking views on what alterations might be made to the recommendations and the interpretative notes. The results of this survey were prepared in summary form in May 1995.[69] Most members indicated the need for caution in conducting this exercise in order, for example, not to undermine the extensive efforts to encourage the broadest possible geographic extension of the Task Force programme of action. However, initially there was less agreement on where these changes should fall. Indeed, the responses to the consultation questionnaire included suggestions for either substantive or stylistic modifications to be made to all forty of the original recommendations.

In order to facilitate progress the then FATF President, Leo Verwoerd, proposed that "the review should focus on a relatively limited number of major issues of substance which have been identified by the consultation exercise".[70] He identified eight such issues:

- the extension of the predicate offences for money laundering beyond drugs trafficking;
- the expansion of the financial recommendations to cover non-financial businesses;
- the expansion of treatment of customer identification;
- the imposition of a requirement for the mandatory reporting of suspicious transactions;
- cross-border currency monitoring;
- asset seizure and confiscation;
- shell corporations;
- controlled delivery.

Once agreement had been achieved on issues of substance, a policy-neutral review could be undertaken of stylistic changes and consequential amendments.

This course of action was agreed to and the detailed work commenced early in the 1995-96 round of meetings under the presidency of the United States. However, further consultations resulted in the inclusion of two further issues of importance; namely, the treatment of bureaux de change and the challenges posed by new technologies. The former had been the subject of an interpretative note and was, in addition, perceived to be a practical problem of considerable significance. Indeed, FATF experts "observed that criminal abuse of this industry is reaching epidemic proportions".[71] The latter issue, placed on the agenda by the United States, sought, in essence, to anticipate a future threat to the integrity of the anti-money laundering system.

While the changes of substance under discussion in the stocktaking review were thus not insignificant in numerical terms, the changes actually in contemplation were not particularly radical. As FATF President Ronald Noble was to remark to the membership in early 1996:

> Virtually all of the proposals advanced involve refinements to existing Recommendations as opposed to introducing entirely new concepts. Most entail nothing more than elevating material set out in the Interpretative Notes to the text of the Recommendations. (In this vein, members should keep in mind that the Interpretative Notes were designed to further clarify the Recommendations and were also adopted by consensus.) A few involve strengthening the character of extremely permissive Recommendations. Consequently, even if all of the proposals were adopted, members would not be confronting onerous new burdens.[72]

In the final event it proved possible to reach agreement in all of the key areas which had been identified with the exception of the proposed incorporation of the note on asset seizure and confiscation which would have urged consideration of the establishment of domestic asset forfeiture funds and the introduction of procedures to promote international asset sharing.

The agreed amendments, along with stylistic and consequential alterations to the 1990 recommendations and the interpretative notes, were published along with the annual report on 28 June 1996. The revised text of the former is reproduced in full at Appendix II of this book for ease of reference. It is of some interest to note that the total number of recommendations remained the same as in 1990. This outcome was not mere happenstance. Indeed, in the course of the discussions this emerged as a separate and distinct goal. As the FATF President noted:

> Whatever changes to the substance of the recommendations the membership accept, the total number of recommendations will remain at forty. The Forty Recommendations have become synonymous with the FATF and its mission. They have gained a measure of notoriety that has been helpful to the external relations effort. Any reduction or increase in the total might adversely affect that recognition.[73]

As we have seen, the major purposes of this stocktaking exercise were to bring the 1990 recommendations "fully up to date with current trends and developments and to anticipate future threats".[74] In relation to the former the most important change was, without doubt, the decision to extend money laundering predicate offences beyond narcotics trafficking. While the new position, embodied in Recommendation 4, represented a significant departure from the hesitant approach taken in 1990 it is perhaps best viewed as an effort to bring the countermeasures into line with actual domestic and international practice. Since 1990, a firm trend had emerged in favour of decoupling money laundering from drug trafficking. This had, in turn, been increasingly reflected in domestic legislation. For example, while in 1992 the FATF stated that few of its then twenty-six members had criminalised laundering beyond the narcotics predicate, its June 1996 report was able to note that "nineteen members have enacted an offence which covers the laundering of the proceeds of a wide range of crimes in addition to drug trafficking".[75] Such developments in national legislation had found increasing reflection in, and been reinforced by, a number of international instruments and political declarations. As will be noted in subsequent chapters, an early position of leadership in this sphere had been taken by the Council of Europe and thereafter by the member states of the European Union. It was thus essential for the continued credibility of the FATF programme of action that its formal stance be brought into line with this new reality.

At the other end of the spectrum was the entirely new Recommendation 13, which called upon FATF members to "pay special attention to money laundering threats inherent in new or developing technologies that might favour anonymity, and take measures, if needed, to prevent their use in money laundering schemes". The inclusion of this hortatory provision was explicitly proactive rather than reactive. It was admitted that there was no concrete evidence of the abuse of "cyberpayments" technologies for money laundering. However, as was seen in chapter II, it was also clear that these developing technologies have the potential to undermine the efficacy of anti-money laundering systems. Consequently, it was felt to be appropriate to require "countries to note the potential threat posed by new technologies and to adopt the appropriate measures to minimise this threat".[76]

A further inducement to take account of possible future vulnerabilities in the course of the review flowed from the uncertainty which then surrounded the future of the Task Force after its then mandate came to an end in 1999. As has been seen, this matter was resolved in the course of the 1997-98 round where it was agreed to keep the FATF in being for a further five years. It was acknowledged at the same time that it might prove to be necessary to undertake a further updating exercise of this kind in 2003-04.[77]

The 2003 revised FATF recommendations

The context

The years immediately following the conclusion of the 1996 amendments were, at least formally, characterised by the relative stability of the FATF package of anti-money laundering measures. This is well illustrated by the fact that prior to June 2003 only one new interpretative note was adopted.

It was this device which was chosen in 1999 to treat a concern raised by G7 finance ministers in advance of the Birmingham Summit the previous year. Perhaps the central focus of ministers at that meeting was the subject of harmful tax competition, one aspect of which relates to the interface with international efforts to combat money laundering.[78] The intention of finance ministers in this area was set out in paragraph 16 of the resulting communiqué. It was worded thus:

16. In addition we encourage international action to enhance the capacity of anti-money laundering systems to deal effectively with tax related crimes. Action here would both strengthen anti-money laundering systems and would also be an essential component of a coherent programme to increase the effectiveness of tax information exchange arrangements. Action could be based on furthering the following objectives:

(a) Effective anti-money laundering systems must ensure that obligations to report transactions relating to suspected criminal offences continue to apply even where such transactions are thought to involve tax offences.

(b) Money laundering authorities should be permitted to the greatest extent possible to pass information to their tax authorities to support the investigation of tax related crimes, and such information should be communicated to other jurisdictions in ways which would allow its use by their tax authorities. Such information should be used in a way which does not undermine the effectiveness of anti-money laundering systems.

It was subsequently agreed that the FATF would concentrate on the issue of suspicious transaction reports leaving the Committee on Fiscal Affairs of the OECD to assume primary responsibility on how money laundering information might best be provided to tax authorities to support the investigation of tax crime.[79] In the discharge of this responsibility the Task Force issued, in July 1999, the following interpretative note:

In implementing Recommendation 15, suspicious transactions should be reported by financial institutions regardless of whether they are also thought to involve tax matters. Countries should take into account that, in order to deter financial institutions from reporting a suspicious transaction, money launderers may seek to state *inter alia* that their transactions relate to tax matters.

While this was the sole formal and public modification to the programme of measures it was not long before private consideration started to be given to the possibility of initiating a further formal review of the recommendations. Substantive discussions within the FATF on this issue resulted in a decision in October 2000 to undertake such an exercise.[80] Several factors contributed to the decision to update and reinforce the FATF standards.

Among them one might mention the deficiencies identified in the course of the non-co-operative countries and territories (NCCT) exercise, the lessons learned from the mutual evaluation process, and the changes in money laundering techniques studied in the annual typologies exercises.[81] Also of considerable significance was the pressure for reform emanating from the G7. It will be recalled that in their July 2000 report to heads of state and government, meeting in Okinawa, G7 finance ministers called upon the FATF to consider the scope for revising its recommendations in four areas:

- "Gatekeepers" to the international financial system (ie, professionals such as lawyers and accountants);
- The international payments system (especially the inclusion of originator identification in international wire transfers);
- Corporate "vehicles" (with particular reference to the obtaining and sharing of information on the beneficial ownership and control of such "vehicles");
- Stolen state assets (in particular enhancing cooperation to address this issue).

It was clear from an early date that this process would be far deeper and more comprehensive in nature than the stocktaking exercise of the mid-1990s.[82] This was underlined by the decision to create three working groups to facilitate progress. These would deal with the following major issues: (i) customer identification and suspicious transaction reporting; (ii) corporate vehicles; and (iii) "gatekeepers".[83] It was also announced that the review would extend to other areas "including topics such as the scope of Recommendation 4 dealing with the offence of money laundering, how to enhance the recommendations dealing with international co-operation, and the need for adequate resources and specialised units to combat money laundering".[84]

In addition to the inherent complexity of some of the issues selected for consideration, the initial stages of the review had to contend with the fact that several important initiatives being undertaken in other fora had yet to be finalised. These included the second EC money laundering directive (examined in chapter VIII), the report by the Basel Committee on Customer Due Diligence for Banks, and a report by the OECD Steering Group on Corporate Governance on the misuse of corporate vehicles for illicit purposes. Fortunately, however, all were at a sufficiently advanced stage of evolution for their basic thrust to be known from the outset. In marked contrast, those charged with the review process also had to take stock of the aftermath of the terrorist attacks of September 2001 against the United States.

As is noted in some detail in chapter V of this study, those tragic events brought about a near immediate extension of the FATF mandate to embrace the problem of the financing of terrorism, and the formulation of eight special recommendations on that subject in October 2001. The latter were, however, not designed to be freestanding but rather to be combined with and supplement the existing Forty Recommendations (none of which was terrorist-specific). The consequential need to integrate terrorist financing into the overall anti-money laundering package thus added a further element of complexity to the review process.

It should be stressed that, in contrast to the stocktaking exercise of the mid-1990s, it took place with commendable openness. This approach was, in turn, fully consistent with the desire expressed by G7 finance ministers in Rome in July 2001. They called "on the FATF, as an international standard-setting organisation, to ensure that the revision process is open, transparent and consultative. In particular this should include dialogue with FATF-style bodies, IFIs [international financial institutions] and other relevant international organisations, non-FATF members and private sector experts". A major element in this new approach was the release by the Task Force, on 30 May 2002, of a detailed consultation paper.[85] This concentrated on a number of key areas of concern and the options under consideration for addressing them: namely, measures currently applicable to the financial sector, corporate vehicles, and non-financial businesses and professions. In addition to soliciting views in this manner, the FATF held, in October 2002, a private sector forum on the review.[86] "As the process developed … further informal consultation with industry took place in April 2003, which provided the sectors most directly affected with the chance to put forward final proposals on the recommendations."[87]

To the surprise of many, the new version of the Forty Recommendations, along with revised and updated interpretative notes, was agreed at a special plenary session shortly thereafter and formally adopted in June 2003 in Berlin.[88] That the process was brought to such a timely conclusion owes much to the drive and determination of the German presidency.

The 2003 revisions

The 2003 version of the Forty Recommendations, reproduced in full at Appendix III, contains numerous amendments. These range from stylistic modifications to additions and deletions. Even the overall structure of the package has been altered. It will be noted in particular that the introductory or framework section – which had remained unchanged since 1990 – has been removed, its substance being subsumed elsewhere. While this step no doubt provided a much needed element of flexibility in the effort to accommodate new subject areas, it also has a broader symbolic significance. It will be recalled that all of the original framework (Recommendations 1-3) was directly derived from obligations contained in the 1988 UN drug trafficking convention. Indeed Recommendation 1 called upon all members to ratify and implement it. Such a close reliance on that, or any other, international instrument is no longer considered appropriate. In a note prepared by the FATF secretariat in early 2001, the following explanation appears:

> 10. It is now widely accepted that the FATF Forty Recommendations are the leading international anti-money laundering standard. They are intended to apply to all countries, and cover all aspects of a national anti-money laundering system. They provide an international standard against which countries in all parts of the world are now assessing themselves, through mutual evaluation and self-assessment procedures. They do not need to rely on, but could refer to, other international instruments that deal with money laundering, as appropriate. Taking all these matters into account, the content of the Recommendations is the most important issue, but it is also important for the framework and order of the Recommendations to reflect and accurately convey the message that the Forty Recommendations are the international standard.[89]

The revised structure consists of four sections.

1. Legal Systems (Recommendations 1 to 3).

2. Measures to be Taken by Financial Institutions and Non-Financial Businesses and Professions to Prevent Money Laundering and Terrorist Financing (Recommendations 4 to 25).

3. Institutional and Other Measures Necessary in Systems for Combating Money Laundering and Terrorist Financing (Recommendations 26 to 34).

4. International Co-operation (Recommendations 35 to 40).

This is supplemented by an important glossary of definitions which forms an integral part of the text.

While it is clear from the above headings that the new FATF Forty Recommendations extend to terrorist financing, the decision was taken not to integrate the eight special recommendations on this subject which were adopted in October 2001 into the text.[90] As the introductory note to the former puts it:

> The revised Forty Recommendations now apply not only to money laundering but also to terrorist financing, and when combined with the Eight Special Recommendations on Terrorist Financing provide an enhanced, comprehensive and consistent framework of measures for combating money laundering and terrorist financing.

As a consequence, for example, the treatment of originator information in wire transfers – a subject of particular interest to G7 finance ministers in 2000 – is to be found primarily (though not exclusively[91]) in Special Recommendation VII and its interpretative note.

Amendments of interest and importance have been made in all four sections of the text. For instance, Recommendation 1 revisits the critical issue of the criminalisation of money laundering. It will be recalled that in the 1996 revised recommendations the original link with drug trafficking in this context was broken and replaced with a reliance on serious offences. However, at that time each jurisdiction was left to determine for itself what offences should be so regarded. The new text seeks to bring some element of harmonisation of approach to this matter. Recommendation 1 embodies the view that jurisdictions "should apply the crime of money laundering to all serious offences, with a view to including the widest range of predicate offences". It acknowledges, however, that this goal can be achieved in a number of different ways: on an all-crimes basis, through recourse to a "threshold" system, by using a "list" approach, or indeed through a combination of such devices. However, it is further stipulated that: "Whichever approach is adopted, each country should at a minimum include a range of offences within each of the designated categories of offences." These designated categories, some twenty in number, are listed in the glossary and range from the curious (piracy) to the orthodox (drugs). Importantly, given what has been said above, the list includes both "terrorism, including terrorist financing" and "corruption and bribery".

Similarly, the recommendations relating to international co-operation have been improved and extended; a process clearly influenced by the criteria used in the NCCT exercise. By way of illustration, the specific removal of "fiscal matters" as a basis for refusal of co-operation[92] owes much to the treatment afforded to this matter in NCCT criteria 18 and 22. However, in the view of the Task Force:

> The most significant addition is Recommendation 40, which deals with international co-operation other than mutual legal assistance and extradition, e.g., co-operation between administrative and law enforcement authorities concerned with combating money laundering and terrorist financing, including FIUs. This prescribes the need for the widest possible co-operation, and for clear and effective gateways.[93]

No doubt for reasons of timing, Recommendation 35, which urges countries to ratify and implement a range of global and regional conventions relevant to money laundering and terrorist financing, makes no mention of the 2003 UN Convention against Corruption. More significantly, the recommendations and interpretative notes fail to reflect the important precedent established in that treaty concerning the return of plundered state assets. It is to be hoped that this will not act to inhibit Task Force members or other jurisdictions from embracing that advance in their domestic law and practice.

Important though these and other changes are for the strengthening of national legal systems and the enhancing of co-operation in the effort to combat laundering, the most significant evolutionary dimensions to the 2003

FATF text are to be found elsewhere. Nowhere is this more evident than in section B which addresses measures to be taken by financial institutions and non-financial businesses and professions.

Among other things this section embraces modern regulatory thinking as reflected in the highly influential October 2001 report by the Basel Committee on Banking Supervision entitled "Customer Due Diligence for Banks". As has been pointed out elsewhere, the new FATF requirements "set firmer and more detailed standards, but also provide the necessary degree of flexibility, and are in line with current industry practice".[94] For instance, Recommendation 5 calls for customer due diligence (CDD) measures to be undertaken when financial institutions are establishing business relations or carrying out specified transactions, when there is a suspicion of money laundering or terrorist financing, or where "the financial institution has doubts about the veracity or adequacy of previously obtained customer identification data". The steps to be taken are the identification of the customer and beneficial owner, the obtaining of information on the purpose and intended nature of the relationship, and "[c]onducting ongoing due diligence on the business relationship and scrutiny of transactions undertaken throughout the course of that relationship to ensure that the transactions being conducted are consistent with the institution's knowledge of the customer, their business and risk profile, including, where necessary, the source of funds".

It will be widely appreciated in the private sector that the Task Force has been willing in this and other specified spheres to make provision for the application of risk-based approaches to implementation. For instance, Recommendation 5, having first set out the expected customer due diligence steps, then provides as follows:

> Financial institutions should apply each of the CDD measures ... but may determine the extent of such measures on a risk sensitive basis depending on the type of customer, business relationship or transaction. The measures that are taken should be consistent with any guidelines issued by competent authorities. For higher risk categories, financial institutions should perform enhanced due diligence. In certain circumstances, where there are low risks, countries may decide that financial institutions can apply reduced or simplified measures.

Certain high risk areas are, in turn, identified and afforded specific treatment. One such relates to politically exposed persons. Pursuant to Recommendation 6 financial institutions are, in addition to their normal measures, required to:

- Have appropriate risk management systems to determine whether the customer is a politically exposed person.
- Obtain senior management approval for establishing business relationships with such customers.
- Take reasonable measures to establish the source of wealth and source of funds.
- Conduct enhanced ongoing monitoring of the business relationship.

Given the significance of this issue to the associated international effort to combat corruption it is perhaps unfortunate that the glossary defined "politically exposed persons" in terms of those who are or have been entrusted with prominent public functions "in a foreign country". The relevant interpretative note merely encourages the extension of the concept to similar individuals in a domestic setting.

Another area in which this section of the text transforms the pre-existing FATF standards is in the extension of a broad range of countermeasures to vulnerable activities and professions. It will be recalled that the G7 had called for this step to be taken in respect to "gatekeepers" to the international financial system such as lawyers and accountants in advance of the Okinawa Summit in July 2000.

It was perhaps fortunate that the fifteen FATF countries which are members of the EU had decided to tackle this highly complex and controversial issue in advance of the Task Force. The results of their efforts, embodied in the second EU money laundering directive, are examined in some detail in chapter VIII. Given the obvious influence which this precedent exerted in the course of the review processes of the FATF it will suffice for present purposes to note that Recommendations 12 and 16, along with their respective interpretative notes, are of central importance. In addition to legal professionals and accountants, trust and company service providers, casinos, dealers in precious stones and metals, and real estate agents are also brought within the system explicitly for the first time.

Other developments worthy of note for present purposes and addressed in section B of the 2003 FATF text include the strengthening of the mandatory system for suspicious transaction reporting (Recommendation 13), the prohibition of shell banks (Recommendation 18), and the treatment of the vulnerabilities which arise in correspondent banking relationships (Recommendations 7 and 18).[95]

Significant developments are also to be found in section C on institutional and other measures necessary in systems for combating money laundering and terrorist financing. One such relates to the establishment of financial intelligence units (FIUs). As was noted in the previous chapter, a peculiarity of the 1996 FATF recommendations was its failure to directly treat this key issue. However, the centrality, de facto, of the FIU concept to the creation of a modern and comprehensive anti-money laundering programme had manifested itself in the work of the Task Force over a number of years notwithstanding the deficiencies in the treatment of this subject in those recommendations. This was evident, for example, in the mutual evaluations carried out to assess the progress of its members.[96] This aspect of FATF thinking was also clearly revealed in the NCCT initiative. It will be recalled that criterion 25 identified "lack of a centralised unit (i.e., a financial intelligence

unit) or of an equivalent mechanism for the collection, analysis and dissemination of suspicious transactions information to competent authorities" as a
detrimental factor in the assessment of national anti-laundering programmes.[97]

The new Recommendation 26, which requires the establishment of FIUs
and details their core tasks, is intended to fill this gap. The associated interpretative note calls upon countries to consider applying for Egmont Group
membership and highlights the utility of certain of its key texts, such as its
principles for information exchange, in providing guidance on the proper roles
and functions of such bodies. From this foundation, the recommendations
and interpretative notes covering other spheres of activity, such as suspicious
transaction reporting (Recommendation 13), domestic co-ordination of relevant policies and activities (Recommendation 31), and international co-operation outside the judicial sphere (interpretative note to Recommendation 40),
provided further specificity as to the critical involvement of FIUs in efforts
to combat laundering and terrorist financing.

Section C also contains the major elements of the response of the Task
Force to the July 2000 call by G7 finance ministers for the review process
to consider the misuse of "corporate vehicles" for money laundering and
other illicit purposes. In its report to heads of state and government, entitled
"Actions Against Abuse of the Global Financial System", they expressed
their concerns thus:

> Corporations are sometimes established simply in order to gain access to the
> financial system. If there is obscurity about their ownership, banks and other
> financial institutions may not be able to discover the identity of the beneficiary of
> the account and will be unable to meet their "know your customer" obligation.
> The combination of market access and obscurity of ownership can facilitate money
> laundering and market abuse.

This G7 statement was, however, but a reflection of a wider concern within
the international community. The issue of transparency had, for example,
played a central role in the controversial efforts of the OECD to counter
harmful tax competition from tax havens.[98] Furthermore, in the course of
2001, the OECD Steering Group on Corporate Governance released a
detailed report on the "Misuse of Corporate Vehicles for Illicit Purposes".[99] The
Task Force was able to draw on such experiences and insights in its consideration of this complex matter. The subject was by no means new to the
FATF. It will be recalled, for instance, that in 1996 it had amended its recommendations so as to encourage countries to "take notice of the potential
for abuse of shell corporations by money launderers" and "to consider
whether additional measures are required to prevent unlawful use of such
entities".[100] It subsequently returned to this area in the context of its NCCT
exercise.[101] It was against this background that the FATF came to include
Recommendations 33 and 34 on the issue of transparency of legal persons

and arrangements in the 2003 text. As has been noted elsewhere, they "set out the key objective of ensuring that adequate, accurate and timely information on the beneficial ownership and control of legal persons and arrangements is obtainable or accessible. In particular, countries must be able to show that companies issuing bearer shares cannot be misused for money laundering".[102]

From the above overview it is clear that the review exercise has been an ambitious one. In announcing their formal adoption of the amended recommendations in Berlin on 20 June 2003 it was noted that the FATF "set a new standard, which FATF members will immediately start working to implement. The FATF encourages other countries and jurisdictions to do likewise".[103] The mechanisms available to it in the promotion of this goal and in the monitoring of progress towards its achievement are examined in chapter VI. It can be anticipated, however, that even within its own membership the pace of implementation will be uneven and (perhaps especially in relation to "gatekeepers") not without substantial difficulty.

1. Also known as GAFI derived from its French title, Groupe d'Action Financière sur le Blanchiment de Capitaux.

2. In an address delivered to the FATF plenary meeting in February 1998 the Managing Director of the IMF described it as "the main body for dealing with money laundering". See, "Financial Action Task Force on Money Laundering: Annual Report 1997-1998" (hereafter Report IX), Paris, FATF, Annex A, p. 37.

3. Reproduced in Gilmore, W (ed), *International efforts to combat money laundering*, Cambridge, Cambridge University Press, 1992, at p.3. See also, Zagaris, B and Kingma, E, "Asset Forfeiture International and Foreign Law: An Emerging Regime", *Emory International Law Review*, 1991, p.445, at pp. 460-461.

4. Gilmore, W (ed), op. cit.

5. "Financial Action Task Force on Money Laundering: Report of 6 February, 1990" (hereafter Report I), Paris, FATF, reproduced in Gilmore, W (ed), op. cit., p. 4, at p. 4.

6. Ibid.

7. See, for example, Drage, J, "Countering Money Laundering: The Response of the Financial Sector", in MacQueen, H L (ed), *Money laundering*, Edinburgh, Edinburgh University Press, 1993, p. 60, at p. 65.

8. "Financial Action Task Force on Money Laundering: Report 1990-1991" (hereafter Report II), Paris, FATF, reproduced in Gilmore, W, (ed), op.cit., p. 31, at p. 33.

9. See ibid., at p. 44. See also, "Financial Action Task Force on Money Laundering: Annual Report 1991-1992" (hereafter Report III), Paris, FATF, at p. 5, note 1.

10. Report II, *supra*, note 8, p. 31.

11. Ibid., p. 53.

12. See, Report III, *supra*, note 9, at p. 5.

13. See, "Financial Action Task Force on Money Laundering: Annual Report 1993-1994" (hereafter Report V), Paris, FATF, at p. 6. The length of time that FATF has remained operational is one of the main points of contrast with the 1990 G7 initiative to create a Chemical Action Task Force (CATF). See, "Chemical Action Task Force: Final Report", Washington, DC, June 1991. In the following year it was determined that this task force should not be maintained and that the necessary follow up should be "assumed by the competent UN and treaty-based bodies, as provided for under the UN Convention". "Chemical Action Task Force: Status Report for the 1992 Economic Summit", Washington, DC, June 1992, p. 14.

14. See, Report V, op. cit., at p. 7.

15. Report IX, *supra*, note 2, p. 7.

16. Ibid., p. 7.

17. "Financial Action Task Force on Money Laundering: Annual Report 1999-2000" (hereafter Report XI), Paris, FATF, p. 7.

18. Argentina; Australia; Austria; Belgium; Brazil; Canada; Denmark; European Commission; Finland; France; Germany; Greece; Gulf Co-operation Council; Hong Kong, China; Iceland; Ireland; Italy; Japan; Luxembourg; Mexico; Netherlands; New Zealand; Norway; Portugal; Russian Federation; Singapore; South Africa; Spain; Sweden; Switzerland; Turkey; United Kingdom; United States.

19. It is widely acknowledged that the FATF wishes to see China join Hong Kong as a full participant and a range of efforts have been made to develop closer ties. See, for example, "Financial Action Task Force on Money Laundering: Annual Report 2002-2003" (hereafter Report XIV), Paris, FATF, at p. 25. A major difficulty, however, relates to the fact that Taiwan is a member of the relevant regional group (the APG); something which, in effect, precludes participation by China in that body but which would be a normal requirement for a new member. India has also been actively discussed.

20. Report II, *supra*, note 8, p. 53.

21. Noble, R, "The Financial Action Task Force Recommendations and their Implementation". Paper presented to the International Conference on Preventing and Controlling Money Laundering and the Use of the Proceeds of Crime: A Global Approach, Courmayeur, Mont Blanc, Italy, 18-20 June 1994 (hereafter 1994 conference), (typescript), p. 2.

22. Report V, *supra*, note 13, p.8. In recent years working groups have again emerged as a significant feature of the Task Force.

23. Pecchioli, R M, "The Financial Action Task Force". Paper presented at the Council of Europe Money Laundering Conference, Strasbourg, France, 28-30 September 1992 (hereafter Strasbourg conference) (typescript), p. 1.

24. Report III, *supra*, note 9, p. 22.

25. Pecchioli, op. cit., p. 2.

26. See, Report I, *supra*, note 5, at pp. 5-13.

27. Evans, J L, "The Proceeds of Crime: Problems of Investigation and Prosecution". Paper presented at the 1994 conference, *supra*, note 21 (typescript), p. 28. A revised version of this appears in Savona, E U (ed), *Responding to money laundering: international perspectives*, Amsterdam, Harwood Academic Publishers, 1997, p. 189.

28. Report I, *supra*, note 5, p. 9.

29. Noble, op. cit., p. 3.

30. See, for example, Hogarth, J, "Beyond the Vienna Convention: International Efforts to Suppress Money Laundering". Paper presented at the 1994 conference, *supra*, note 21 (typescript), at pp. 6-13.

31. Sherman, T, "Opening Session Speech", Strasbourg conference, *supra*, note 23 (typescript), p. 6.

32. Savona, E U, and De Feo, M A, "Money Trials: International Money Laundering Trends and Prevention/Control Policies". Paper presented at the 1994 conference (typescript), *supra*, note 21, p. 28. Subsequently published in Savona, E U (ed), *supra*, note 27, p. 9. All references are to the original.

33. See, e.g., Report I, *supra*, note 5, at p. 14.

34. Report I, *supra*, note 5, p. 15.

35. Ibid.

36. See, e.g., Sherman, T, "International Efforts to Combat Money Laundering: The Role of the Financial Action Task Force", in MacQueen, H L (ed), *supra*, note 7, p. 12, at p. 18. Some have characterised the recommendations as "soft law". See, for example, Zagaris, B and Castilla, S M, "Constructing an International Financial Enforcement Subregime: The Implementation of Anti-Money Laundering Policy", *Brooklyn Journal of International Law*, 1993, p. 871, at p. 879.

37. See, Pecchioli, op. cit., at p. 3; and Noble, op. cit., at p. 2.

38. See, for example, Fisse, B, "Money Laundering, Regulatory Strategy and International Corporate Controls". Paper presented to the 1994 conference, *supra*, note 21 (typescript), at p. 9. Subsequently published in Savona, E U (ed), *supra*, note 27, p. 283.

39. Noble, op. cit., p. 2.

40. See, Report I, *supra*, note 5, at p. 15.

41. See, for example, Report V, *supra*, note 13, at p. 13.

42. See, Report I, *supra*, note 5, at p. 14.

43. Ibid., p. 14.

44. Ibid.

45. Ibid.

46. Ibid., p. 15.

47. Pecchioli, op. cit., p. 3.

48. See, for example, Drage, op. cit., at p. 65. The committee, in September 1997, formulated twenty-five core principles for effective banking supervision. Principle 15 requires banking supervisors to ensure that the banks which they supervise have adequate anti-money laundering procedures in place. See, Schott, P A, *Reference guide to anti-money laundering and combating the financing of terrorism*, Washington, DC, World Bank, 2003, at pp.III-12 to III-15.

49. Report I, *supra*, note 5, p. 11.

50. "International Organisation of Securities Commissions, Report on Money Laundering" (hereafter Iosco report), Montreal, 1992, p. 5.

51. Report I, *supra*, note 5, p. 17.

52. Sherman, op. cit., p. 14.

53. See, Report I, *supra*, note 5, at pp. 20-21.

54. "Money Laundering and Associated Issues: The Need for International Cooperation", UN Doc. E/CN.15/1992/4/Add.5, 23 March 1992, p. 4.

55. Report I, *supra*, note 5, p. 23.

56. Ibid., p. 22.

57. Ibid., p. 15.

58. Noble, op. cit., p.6. See also, Report III, *supra*, note 9, at p. 16; "Financial Action Task Force on Money Laundering: Annual Report 1992-1993" (hereafter Report IV), Paris, FATF, at pp. 17-18; and Report V, *supra*, note 13, at p. 22.

59. Griffiths, D, "International Efforts to Combat Money Laundering: Developments and Prospects", in *Action against transnational criminality: papers from the 1993 Oxford Conference on International and White Collar Crime*, London, Commonwealth Secretariat, 1994, p. 11, at p. 12. See also, Report III, *supra*, note 9, at p. 16.

60. See, Report III, *supra*, note 9, at pp. 16-18; Report IV, *supra*, note 58, at pp. 18-19; and Report V, *supra*, note 13, at pp. 31-34.

61. Report III, *supra*, note 9, p. 17.

62. See, ibid., at p. 18.

63. Report III, *supra*, note 9, p. 18.

64. Report IV, *supra*, note 58, p. 19.

65. Report V, *supra*, note 13, p. 23.

66. See, ibid., at pp. 31-32.

67. Report III, *supra*, note 9, p. 16.

68. Report V, *supra*, note 13, p. 7.

69. "Stocktaking Review of the Forty FATF Recommendations: Summary of Responses to the Consultation Questionnaire", FATF VI, PLEN/40, Paris, FATF.

70. "Stocktaking Review of the Forty FATF Recommendations: Paper by the President", FATF VI, PLEN/48, Paris, FATF.

71. "Stocktaking Review of the Forty FATF Recommendations: Proposals by the President", FATF VII, PLEN/23, Paris, FATF.

72. Ibid.

73. Ibid.

74. "Financial Action Task Force on Money Laundering: Annual Report 1995-1996" (hereafter Report VII), Paris, FATF, p. 6.

75. Ibid., p. 11.

76. Ibid., p. 8.

77. See, Report IX, *supra*, note 2, at p. 8.

78. See, for example, *Tax competition: broadening the debate*, London, European Financial Forum 2000.

79. See, Gilmore, B, "Money Laundering and International Tax Cooperation: Exploring the Interface" in ibid., p. 26, at p. 29.

80. See, "Financial Action Task Force on Money Laundering: Annual Report 2000-2001" (hereafter Report XII), Paris, FATF, at p. 18.

81. See, ibid., at p. 17. See further, chapter VI below.

82. See, for example, "The Review of the Forty Recommendations and Interpretative Notes – Issues for Consideration", FATF XII, PLEN/30, Paris, FATF.

83. See, Report XII, *supra*, note 80, at pp.17-18. The internal structure of the review process matured and altered somewhat thereafter. See, e.g., Report XIV, *supra*, note 19, at p. 4.

84. Report XII, *supra*, note 80, p. 18.

85. See, "Review of the FATF Forty Recommendations: Consultation Paper", Paris, FATF, 2002.

86. See, Report XIV, *supra*, note 19, at p. 4.

87. Ibid.

88. Ibid.

89. *Supra*, note 82, p. 3.

90. See further, chapter V below.

91. See Recommendation 5.

92. See Recommendations 36 and 40.

93. Report XIV, *supra*, note 19, p. 7.

94. Ibid., p. 5.

95. See, for example, "Report on Correspondent Banking: A Gateway to Money Laundering", Washington, DC, Minority Staff of the US Senate Permanent Sub Committee on Investigations, 2001.

96. "Review of FATF Anti-Money Laundering Systems and Mutual Evaluation Procedures 1992-1999", Paris, FATF, 2001, pp. 29-33.

97. "Review to Identify Non-Cooperative Countries or Territories: Increasing the World-Wide Effectiveness of Anti-Money Laundering Measures", Paris, FATF, 2002, p. 29.

98. See, for example, Gilmore, W, "The OECD, Harmful Tax Competition and Tax Havens: Towards an Understanding of the International Legal Context", in Biswas, R (ed), *International tax competition: globalisation and fiscal sovereignty*, London, Commonwealth Secretariat, 2003, p. 289, at pp. 301-303; and Gilmore, W, "The OECD, Harmful Tax Competition and Tax Havens: An Update",

Commonwealth Law Bulletin, 2001, at pp. 1227-1230. For an interesting comparison of this OECD initiative with the NCCT process see, Hartman, B R, "Coercing Cooperation from Offshore Financial Centers: Identity and Coincidence of International Obligations against Money Laundering and Harmful Tax Competition", *Boston College International and Comparative Law Review*, 2001, pp. 253-290.

99. OECD, Paris, 2001.

100. See 1996 FATF Recommendation 25.

101. See, for example, criteria 13 and 14.

102. Report XIV, *supra*, note 19, p. 7.

103. "New Anti-Money Laundering Standards Released", Paris, FATF Press Release, 20 June 2003, p. 1.

CHAPTER V – THE FINANCIAL ACTION TASK FORCE
AND THE FINANCING OF TERRORISM

Background and context

Notwithstanding the ever-increasing emphasis throughout the 1990s on the need to target the financial base of drug trafficking syndicates, organised crime groups and those engaged in "grand" corruption, international counter-terrorism initiatives were slow to embrace this strategy. Prior to the conclusion of the UN International Convention for the Suppression of the Financing of Terrorism in December 1999, specific treatment of the tracing, freezing and confiscation of terrorist funds was typically omitted from global and regional treaties dealing with this serious form of criminal activity.[1] Similarly, the issue had failed to secure a central place on the agenda of specialist bodies with a mandate in relation to financial crimes; a point well illustrated by the absence of terrorist-specific measures in either the 1990 or 1996 recommendations of the Financial Action Task Force on Money Laundering (FATF).

Several issues, practical, technical, and political, played a part in bringing about this state of affairs. For instance, it is often pointed out that there are obvious differences in objectives between those involved in terrorism and those engaged in forms of profit maximisation criminal activity. Furthermore, whilst some terrorist groups rely on the proceeds of crime (kidnapping, extortion, drug trafficking, bank robbery) to fund their activities others derive their income, in whole or in part, from lawful sources, for example, "through community solicitation and fundraising appeals, often in the name of organisations with the status of charitable or relief organisations".[2] It is this latter aspect, in particular, which conspired to ensure that the issue of terrorist financing could not be addressed adequately by simply extending the range of money laundering predicate offences. As has been stated elsewhere:

> It is not their criminal origin that makes them "tainted", but their use, or intended use, to finance terrorist acts, or to provide support to terrorists or terrorist organisations. Thus, to rely exclusively on the offense of money laundering to criminalize terrorist financing would leave a significant gap in the legislation, as terrorist funding offenses would be established in cases where the funds intended to finance a terrorist act were of illicit origin, but the funding of terrorist acts out of legally obtained funds could not be prosecuted.[3]

That said, there are also important common features. For instance: "A successful terrorist group is therefore, as with a criminal organisation, one that is able to build and maintain an effective financial infrastructure." For this it must develop sources of funding, a means of laundering those funds and then finally a way to ensure that the funds can be used to obtain material and other logistical items needed to commit terrorist acts.[4] Similarly, even in the case of funds derived from legitimate sources, there is a perceived need to obscure or disguise the links to such sources and expert opinion suggests that terrorists generally resort to the same methods as traditional criminal groups in order to achieve this goal.[5]

It is also of interest to note that even when specific initiatives were elaborated, as with the 1999 UN International Convention on the Suppression of the Financing of Terrorism (examined in chapter III), there was initially little sense of urgency evident within the international community to take advantage of the promise for co-ordinated action which they afforded. For instance, by 11 September 2001 only four of the twenty-two ratifications needed to bring the convention into force had been deposited with the UN Secretary-General (Botswana, Sri Lanka, United Kingdom and Uzbekistan). This somewhat relaxed attitude was to be transformed by the terrorist outrage perpetrated on the United States that day.

The aftermath of 11 September 2001

Given the nature and scale of the attacks against the United States on 11 September 2001, it was to be expected that action to combat international terrorism would be propelled to the top of the political agenda. Nor is it surprising, given what has been said above, that initiatives to combat the financing of terrorism would emerge as a major element of focus. While initiatives of relevance in this sphere have been taken in various settings[6] the most significant so far have emerged under the auspices of the UN Security Council and within the FATF.

The UN Security Council

The UN Security Council was the natural candidate to take the lead in responding to these events. It will be recalled that under Chapter VII of the UN Charter it is provided with extensive powers to maintain or restore international peace and security. These include, in Articles 41 and 42 of the charter, both the taking of measures which involve the use of armed force and those which do not. Furthermore, as was emphasised in the October 1995 judgment of the appeals chamber of the International Tribunal for the Former Yugoslavia in the case of *Prosecutor* v. *Dusko Tadic:* "These powers are *coercive* vis-à-vis the culprit State or entity. But they are also *mandatory* vis-à-vis the other member states, who are under an obligation to co-operate with the Organisation ... and with one another ... in the implementation of the action or measures decided by the Security Council."[7]

Though initially drafted with traditional interstate tension and conflict in view, the remit of the Security Council is not explicitly confined to instances of those kinds. Indeed it is now widely acknowledged that the Security Council possess a broad discretion both in the determination of what constitutes a threat to international peace and security and as to the most appropriate measures to adopt in relation thereto. On several previous occasions, acts of international terrorism have provided the catalyst for the use of such Chapter VII powers. Of these perhaps the best known relate to the involvement of the Security Council in the Lockerbie affair.[8]

In the wake of the attacks in New York, Washington, DC, and Pennsylvania, the Security Council, in Resolution 1373 (2001), unanimously affirmed that such acts of international terrorism constitute a threat to international peace and security. Then, specifically acting under Chapter VII, it adopted a wide range of measures in which mandatory action for the suppression of the financing of terrorism was afforded a prominent position. As Ward has remarked:

> Paragraph 1, regarded as setting out the core principles of the resolution, requires that States prevent and suppress the financing of terrorist acts; criminalise all forms of financial support for terrorist acts; freeze without delay funds and other financial assets associated with acts of terrorism; and prohibit their nationals or any persons and entities within their territories from providing any form of financial support to terrorists. Its principal aim is to cut off the financial life-support to terrorism.[9]

While the legal obligations so imposed overlap with those contained in the 1999 convention (as, for instance with Articles 2 and 8) in some respects they go beyond the ambit of those obligations. This is so, for example, in the case of operative paragraph 1(d) which "sets out an autonomous obligation, not contained in the Convention ...".[10] The resolution also established a committee of the Security Council (the Counter-Terrorism Committee, CTC) to monitor the implementation of its obligations by members of the international community.

While a comprehensive examination of this crucial initiative is beyond the scope of this study,[11] certain of its features should be mentioned for present purposes. First, Resolution 1373 creates legally binding international obligations to prevent and suppress the financing of terrorist acts where, given the then status of the 1999 convention, none previously existed. Second, it has imposed these obligations on a universal basis in a manner which anticipates permanent alterations being made to national criminal justice systems. Finally, the action taken is not directed against Afghanistan or Mr bin Laden and his associates but rather against international terrorism more generally. Consequently, the legal impact of the action taken by the Security Council will not be curtailed by the destruction or disruption of the network which brought about the US attacks or by the removal of the Taliban regime which provided its membership with a safe haven. As its then Chairperson, Sir Jeremy Greenstock, was to remark at a press conference on 19 October 2001:

> The Counter-Terrorism Committee is concerned with the medium to long-term end of the fight against terrorism and is there to implement the intention of Resolution 1373 to establish the broadest possible legislative and executive defence against terrorism in every territory of members of the United Nations.

It should also be noted at this juncture that, notwithstanding the view of the Security Council that there is a close connection between international terrorism and, among other things, drugs, money laundering and organised crime, the opportunity for it to use its extensive Chapter VII powers in other criminal justice contexts in the absence of such a demonstrable terrorism nexus is severely restricted by political, legal, and practical considerations.[12] The ongoing and important work the CTC must, in turn, be distinguished from the obligation, imposed by the Security Council, to freeze without delay funds and other financial assets or economic resources of listed individuals and entities. Here, legal authority flows from various resolutions passed under Chapter VII of the UN Charter; the two most significant of which pre-date 11 September 2001. Resolution 1267 of 15 October 1999 is directed at the funds and other relevant assets owned or controlled by the Taliban, the targets for such action being designated by a committee of the Security Council established by the same text. In Resolution 1333 of 19 December 2000, it was decided to extend such measures. Operative paragraph 8 requires all states:

> (c) To freeze without delay funds and other financial assets of Usama bin Laden and individuals and entities associated with him as designated by the Committee, including those in the Al-Qaida organisation, and including funds derived or generated from property owned or controlled directly or indirectly by Usama bin Laden and individuals and entities associated with him, and to ensure that neither they nor any other funds or financial resources are made available, by their nationals or by any persons within their territory, directly or indirectly for the benefit of Usama bin Laden, his associates or any entities owned or controlled, directly or indirectly, by Usama bin Laden or individuals and entities associated with him including the Al-Qaida organisation and requests the Committee to maintain an updated list, based on information provided by States and regional organisations, of the individuals and entities designated as being associated with Usama bin Laden, including those in the Al-Qaida organisation.[13]

The above mandates were confirmed and extended on 16 January 2002 by Security Council Resolution 1390. At the same time it requested the committee established under Resolution 1267 to, among other things, regularly update the (now consolidated) list on the basis of relevant information provided by member states and regional organisations; to "promulgate expeditiously such guidelines and criteria as may be necessary to facilitate the implementation of the measures ..."; and, to make the list publicly available. Importantly the guidelines now contain detailed provisions on the process for securing both additions to and deletions from that list.[14]

The approach adopted by the Security Council in this important strand of its activities contains two novel (and controversial) features. As the IMF Legal Department has noted:

> First, they require that each member state freeze the assets of persons and entities independently of any suspicion or belief on the part of the member state that such persons and entities are engaging in terrorist activities. Second, the resolutions require the freezing of assets of listed persons, without providing any time frame for such freezing. The resolutions thus transform what is usually a temporary measure, intended to prevent assets from being removed from a country during an investigation or a trial, into a potentially permanent measure.[15]

For these reasons, the subsequent decision of the Security Council, in Resolution 1452 of 20 December 2002, to introduce an element of flexibility in respect of the meeting of basic expenses (including such matters as payment for food, shelter, medical treatment and legal representation) from such frozen funds and assets was most welcome.[16] Somewhat similar blacklisting exercises have also been conducted by, among others, the EU[17] and individual states (most actively by the United States).[18] Such exercises have also given rise to a range of both process and human rights and civil liberties concerns, the examination of which lie beyond the scope of this work.[19] The range and proliferation of such lists also raise a series of practical and legal issues for the banks and other financial institutions which are called upon to play a key role in the identification of the funds of the individuals and legal persons concerned.[20]

The Financial Action Task Force

Prior to the events of 11 September 2001, the issue of terrorist financing had not, as noted earlier, assumed a position of any prominence in the activities of the FATF. However, in the immediate aftermath of those events, the fifteen EU members called for the mandate of the FATF to be broadened to specifically embrace this subject. Similarly, on 6 October 2001, G7 finance ministers called upon the FATF to issue special recommendations on this matter and to include specific treatment of terrorist funding in the revision of the Forty Recommendations. They also called upon it to issue focused guidance to financial institutions, to develop a process to identify countries that facilitate terrorist financing, and to propose a course of action to achieve co-operation from such jurisdictions.

To these ends, an emergency plenary meeting of the FATF was held in Washington, DC, on 29 and 30 October 2001. There, agreement was reached on a set of terrorist-specific recommendations. In the words of the FATF press release of 31 October, these commit members to:

- Take immediate steps to ratify and implement the relevant United Nations instruments.

- Criminalise the financing of terrorism, terrorist acts and terrorist organisation.

- Freeze and confiscate terrorist assets.

- Report suspicious transactions linked to terrorism.

- Provide the widest possible range of assistance to other countries' law enforcement and regulatory authorities for terrorist financing investigations.

- Impose anti-money laundering requirements on alternative remittance systems.

- Strengthen customer identification measures in international and domestic wire transfers.

- Ensure that entities, in particular non-profit organisations, cannot be misused to finance terrorism.

The underlying philosophy was that these measures, when combined with the existing Forty Recommendations, would provide an appropriate framework for the prevention, detection and suppression of the financing of terrorism and terrorist acts.

Several of these special recommendations, which are reproduced in full at Appendix IV, interrelate closely with initiatives taken at the global level. For example, Special Recommendation I on ratification and implementation of UN instruments applies both to the 1999 UN convention and all of the key UN Security Council resolutions outlined above. However, even within this category some go further than the global instruments. By way of illustration, Special Recommendation II not only requires (as does the 1999 UN convention) the criminalisation of the financing of terrorism, it extends this requirement to ensure that such offences are designated as money laundering predicate offences in national law. Formal guidance from the FATF clarifies the fact that this must be done in such a way as to cover the laundering of proceeds from relevant offences committed in third countries.[21]

While the first five of the special recommendations contain substantial similarities with the 1999 convention and Security Council Resolution 1373, the remainder cover new ground; namely, alternative remittance systems, wire transfers, and non-profit organisations. That said, the potential for the abuse of all but the last of these in the laundering of the proceeds of crime had been a source of concern in law enforcement circles for some time.

Take, by way of illustration, the issue of the use of wire transfers in laundering schemes. Early study within the FATF had highlighted the need to take additional steps to lessen the possibility that the audit trail could be broken by having resort to such systems. A particular problem was that "payment orders ... frequently omit the name of the true originator and beneficiary of the payment".[22] In the search for a practical solution the Task Force mandated, in 1992, the creation of an ad hoc group to study this matter. It, in turn, initiated discussions with the Society for Worldwide Interbank Financial Telecommunications (Swift) which is the primary carrier of wire payment messages. In addition, Swift has a presence in many jurisdictions and enjoys a broad participant-base ranging from banks, to securities brokers/dealers and trust or fiduciary services companies.

As a consequence of this initiative the chairman of Swift asked, in July 1992, "all users of its system to ensure that when sending Swift MT 100 messages (customer transfers), the fields for the ordering and beneficiary customers should be completed with their respective names and addresses".[23] Following further discussions between the FATF and Swift, the latter officially brought the 1992 broadcast to the attention of both the Basel Committee and the Offshore Group of Banking Supervisors.[24] Although these and related developments brought about improvements, difficulties continued to be encountered as a result of which further discussions took place during the 1996-97 round of Task Force activities.[25]

In the wake of the events of 11 September 2001 – and the associated reliance of the hijackers on wire transfers of relatively small sums to fund their activities[26] – the issue was revisited as a matter of urgency. The outcome was Special Recommendation VII. It reads thus:

> Countries should take measures to require financial institutions, including money remitters, to include accurate and meaningful originator information (name, address and account number) on funds transfers and related messages that are sent, and the information should remain with the transfer or related message through the payment chain.

> Countries should take measures to ensure that financial institutions, including money remitters, conduct enhanced scrutiny of and monitor for suspicious activity funds transfers which do not contain complete originator information (name, address and account number).

It was acknowledged within the Task Force that further guidance on the implementation of this new recommendation would be necessary in order to avoid unnecessarily negative consequences for the operation of these payments systems. To this end, and following consultations with the private sector, an interpretative note was issued in February 2003. It is reproduced in full at Appendix V.[27] As has been pointed out elsewhere: "Jurisdictions will have until February 2005 to fully implement SR VII in recognition of the fact that they will need time to make relevant legislative or regulatory changes and to allow financial institutions to make necessary adaptations of their systems and procedures."[28]

Somewhat similar issues were to arise concerning the implementation of Special Recommendation VI on money or value transfer services (MTV services). Importantly, this category includes underground or parallel banking systems (such as hawala, hundi and fei-chien) which were discussed in chapter II of this work. As has been noted elsewhere: "Unregulated MVT services permit funds to be sent anonymously, allowing the money launderer or terrorist financier to freely send funds without having to identify himself or herself. In some cases, few or no records are kept. In other cases, records may be kept, but are inaccessible to authorities."[29]

Special Recommendation VI seeks to address the threat posed by such systems in three principal ways: (i) by requiring the licensing or registration of the natural and legal persons providing them; (ii) by ensuring that relevant FATF recommendations are applied to their activities; and (iii) through the imposition of sanctions for non-compliance.[30]

An interpretative note (reproduced at Appendix VI) has been adopted to provide further particulars as to the nature and scope of this provision. Furthermore, an international best practice paper was issued on the abuse of alternative remittance systems which provides, among other things, guidance on the detection of such systems in practice.[31]

Even more acute difficulties have been encountered in developing a consensus within the Task Force as to the implementation of Special Recommendation VIII which is worded as follows:

> Countries should review the adequacy of laws and regulations that relate to entities that can be abused for the financing of terrorism. Non-profit organisations are particularly vulnerable, and countries should ensure that they cannot be misused:
>
> (i) by terrorist organisations posing as legitimate entities;
>
> (ii) to exploit legitimate entities as conduits for terrorist financing, including for the purpose of escaping asset freezing measures; and
>
> (iii) to conceal or obscure the clandestine diversion of funds intended for legitimate purposes to terrorist organisations.

In addition to the imperfect nature of the understanding of law enforcement bodies as to the nature of the vulnerabilities presented by the charitable sector and the extent to which they are exploited in practice, the Task Force has also had to take cognisance of the great diversity of approaches found in the law and practice of its membership. Consequently, it has proceeded with marked caution in this area since October 2001. As the FATF annual report issued on 20 June 2003 notes:

> It adopted a best practices paper for SR VIII in October 2002, which among other things suggests certain strategies for non-profit organisations, including verification of programme activities and ensuring financial transparency. Given the complexity of issues relating to SR VIII, the FATF continues to examine ways of implementing this SR and will likely provide additional guidance on this subject in the future.[32]

At the October 2001 emergency plenary, the mandate for the remainder of the Hong Kong presidency of the FATF was revised in order to promote the early implementation of these new recommendations. A key element was the decision to conduct a self-assessment exercise[33] to gauge the level of compliance.

The initial focus of activity was on implementation by FATF members. A detailed questionnaire was developed (SAQTF) containing a range of questions on each of the new recommendations and responses were submitted in January 2002. The process was not, however, without its difficulties. In particular, it should be noted that while the SAQTF elicited information on each of the special recommendations, the decision was subsequently taken to exclude the data on Special Recommendation VIII from the analysis. This course of action was adopted in the light of the then lack of agreement within the FATF as to the exact scope and consequences of the wording as agreed to at the October 2001 meeting.

As the FATF annual report, issued on 21 June 2002, was to note: "The results are encouraging. ... The overall picture that emerges from these results appears to show that FATF members have made a great deal of progress in a very short time (eight months) in putting counter-terrorist financing measures into place."[34]

Annex C of that report contains a table showing the overall results for each FATF member. The report also recorded the intention to update this on a periodic basis. This was done in the June 2003 report.[35] While recording continued progress with the seven recommendations under assessment, only two member states (France and Italy) judged themselves to be fully compliant. By way of contrast, Mexico was fully in line with only two and Greece with but one.[36]

A second dimension of the assessment process was to seek, from the outset, to promote the exercise on a global basis. In the words of the October plan of action: "All countries around the world will be invited to participate on the same terms as FATF members." In order to encourage participation in this exercise, and to mobilise international support for the standards articulated in the special recommendations, the FATF held, on 1 February 2002, a special forum on terrorist financing at the conclusion of its plenary meeting in Hong Kong. As the June annual report notes: "Sixty-five jurisdictions from the FATF and from the FATF-style regional bodies in Asia, Eastern and Southern Africa, South America, Caribbean and Europe, and the Offshore Group of Banking Supervisors participated in the Forum. In addition, nine international organisations also attended."[37] At the same time, the FATF called upon non-member states and territories to undertake self-assessment on or before 1 May 2002. This time-frame was subsequently extended to 1 September 2002.

To facilitate this process a slightly modified version of the SAQTF was developed and posted on the FATF website. Furthermore, "it was decided that additional guidance would be drafted and published to assist non-FATF members to understand some of the concepts contained in the special recommendations on terrorist financing and to clarify certain parts of the SAQTF. Therefore, in March 2002, the FATF published 'Guidance Notes for the Special Recommendations on Terrorist Financing and the Self-Assessment Questionnaire'".[38]

It was the expectation of the Task Force secretariat that non-members would use its questionnaire and associated guidance and submit their responses directly to it in Paris for analysis, and approximately 100 jurisdictions did so.[39] A somewhat different approach was taken by the member states of MONEYVAL; the FATF-style regional body for non-FATF European countries.[40] It took the view that while its members were free to submit their responses to the FATF should they so wish, they must provide the same to MONEYVAL for separate analysis. This exercise was, in turn, completed in May 2003 and the results will, as with the Task Force, be updated from time to time.[41] As was noted above, G7 finance ministers also requested that a process be put in place to identify jurisdictions which have failed to take appropriate steps to counter terrorist financing. The eventual imposition of countermeasures against delinquent states and territories was specifically contemplated. Such a development would, of course, give rise to a range of issues of difficulty and concern. These include the nature of the relationship between such an exercise, on the one hand, and the discharge by the Security Council of its formal responsibilities in respect of the monitoring and enforcement of compliance with the legal obligations imposed under its resolutions, on the other. For this and other reasons (no doubt including the difficulties in promoting full compliance by its own members), more recent statements within the FATF (and by G7 finance ministers) have emphasised the provision of technical assistance to such states.[42] Indeed, in September 2003 the FATF announced a new initiative, taken in conjunction with the UN and other donors, to identify and meet technical assistance needs in this area.[43]

At a somewhat different level, the Task Force has also met the call, made by G7 finance ministers in October 2001, to issue focused guidance to financial institutions in detecting terrorist financing activities. This represents practical advice from operational experts "as to factors associated with financial transactions that should trigger further questions on the part of the financial institution".[44]

Conclusions

The pace at which the developments outlined in this chapter have taken place in the period since the attack on the Twin Towers is, from an international criminal justice perspective, unprecedented. Similarly, there can be little doubt that (at least in the short and medium term) the effort to disrupt international terrorist activity by undermining its financial base will continue to be a key concern at the intergovernmental level. Both the UN Security Council and the FATF can be expected to continue to refine and reinforce their strategies and activities in this sphere in order to enhance their effectiveness.[45]

It is important, however, not to harbour exaggerated expectations as to the likely contribution of this element of the counter-terrorism effort. The results of the attempt over the last decade or more to trace, seize and confiscate the huge profits derived from the drugs trade and organised crime demonstrate the difficulties encountered in practice in trying to implement a strategy which seeks to disrupt criminal activity through a focus on money. The challenge is all the greater in the sphere of terrorism where, as the financial profile of the 11 September 2001 hijackers demonstrates, much can be accomplished at relatively modest cost.[46] Focusing on the financial aspect of terrorism is, in short, a useful weapon but is no panacea.

Notes: V

1. See, e.g., McClean, D, *International co-operation in civil and criminal matters*, Oxford, Oxford University Press, 2002, Chapter 7.

2. "Guidance for Financial Institutions in Detecting Terrorist Financing Activities", FATF XIII, PLEN/39. REV1, Paris, FATF, p. 3.

3. *Suppressing the financing of terrorism: a handbook for legislative drafting*, Washington, DC, IMF, 2003, p. 49.

4. "Financial Action Task Force on Money Laundering: Report on Money Laundering Typologies 2001-2002" Paris, FATF, p. 2.

5. See, *supra*, note 2, at p. 3.

6. See, for example, Gilmore, W, "The Twin Towers and the Third Pillar: Some Security Agenda Developments" (EUI working paper Law 2003/7), Florence, European University Institute, 2003.

7. *International Legal Materials*, 35, 1996, p. 32, at paragraph 31. Washington, DC, American Society of International Law. Emphasis in the original.

8. See, for example, Beveridge, F, "The Lockerbie Affair", *International and Comparative Law Quarterly*, Vol. 41, 1992, at p. 907; and Aust, A, "Lockerbie: The Other Case", *International and Comparative Law Quarterly*, Vol. 49, 2000, at p. 278.

9. Ward, C A, "Legal Imperatives for Implementation of Resolution 1373 (2001)". Paper presented to the Caribbean Regional Conference of the International Law Association, Barbados, 26-29 March 2003 (typescript), p. 4.

10. *Supra*, note 3, p. 20.

11. But see, for example, "Report of Expert Working Group on Legislative and Administrative Measures to Combat Terrorism", London, Commonwealth Secretariat, 2002; and, Rosand, E, "Security Council Resolution 1373, the Counter-Terrorism Committee, and the Fight against Terrorism", *American Journal of International Law*, Vol. 97, 2003, at pp. 333-341.

12. Also of interest in this regard is the declaration of ministers of foreign affairs annexed to Security Council Resolution 1456 (2003).

13. There exists a close but unarticulated relationship between these blacklisting measures and operative paragraph 1(c) of Security Council Resolution 1373 (2001).

14. See, *supra*, note 3, at p. 23. Security Council Resolution 1455 (2003) also contains measures designed to improve the implementation of the blacklisting strategy. As of 9 September 2003, some 266 individuals and 99 entities appeared on the list; 4 individuals and 11 entities had been de-listed by that date.

15. *Supra*, note 3, p. 57.

16. Operative paragraph 1(b) also establishes a system, ultimately controlled by the Security Council committee, whereby such funds can also be used to meet other ("extraordinary") expenses.

17. See, for example, Hinterseer, K, *Criminal finance: the political economy of money laundering in a comparative legal context*, New York, Aspen, 2002, at pp. 454-458.

18. See, for example, Alexander, K, "United States of America", in Graham, T (ed), *Butterworths international guide to money laundering law and practice*, 2nd edn, London, Butterworth, 2003, p.628, at pp.660-663.

19. See, for example, Cameron, I, "Targeted Sanctions and Legal Safeguards", Faculty of Law, Uppsala University, 2002.

20. Of interest in this regard is the formal statement on the suppression of the financing of terrorism issued by the Wolfsberg Group of leading international banks. See, e.g., Srivastava, A P, "Terrorist Funding", in Clark, A and Burrell, P (eds), *A practitioner's guide to international money laundering law and regulation*, Old Woking, Surrey, City & Financial Publishing, 2003, p. 297, at pp. 313-315.

21. See, "Guidance Notes for the Special Recommendations on Terrorist Financing and the Self-Assessment Questionnaire", Paris, FATF, 27 March 2002, at p. 2. A formal interpretative note on this Special Recommendation was adopted in July 2004.

22. "Financial Action Task Force on Money Laundering: Annual Report 1991-1992", Paris, FATF, p. 15.

23. *Money laundering guidance notes for mainstream banking, lending and deposit taking activities*, London, Joint Money Laundering Steering Group, 1993, paragraph 104.

24. See, "Financial Action Task Force on Money Laundering: Annual Report 1993-1994", Paris, FATF, at p. 25.

25. See, "Financial Action Task Force on Money Laundering: Annual Report 1996-1997", Paris, FATF, at pp. 7-8.

26. See, *supra*, note 4, at p. 6.

27. The text of Recommendation 5 of the 2003 version of the FATF Forty Recommendations makes specific reference to this interpretative note.

28. "Financial Action Task Force on Money Laundering: Annual Report 2002-2003", Paris, FATF, p. 8. Some difficult technical issues, especially the treatment of batch transfers, remain to be resolved and are under active consideration within the FATF.

29. "Financial Action Task Force on Money Laundering: Combating the Abuse of Alternative Remittance Systems – International Best Practices", Paris, FATF, 20 June 2003, p. 2.

30. See, *supra*, note 21, at p. 5.

31. See, *supra*, note 29.

32. *Supra*, note 28, p. 7.

33. The nature of FATF self-assessment exercises is discussed in chapter VI below.

34. "Financial Action Task Force on Money Laundering: Annual Report 2001-2002", Paris, FATF, p.5.

35. See, *supra*, note 28, at Annex C.

36. New member states the Russian Federation and South Africa were not included in this exercise.

37. *Supra*, note 21, p. 6.

38. Ibid., p. 6.

39. See, *supra*, note 28, at p. 9.

40. The activities of which are discussed in chapter VII below.

41. See, "Self-Assessment of 'MONEYVAL' member states against the Special Recommendations on Terrorist Financing: the Position as of 30 September 2002", Council of Europe Doc. MONEYVAL (03) 12. An updated version was finalised at its July 2004 plenary meeting in Strasbourg.

42. See, for example, *supra*, note 28, at p. 9. See also, G7 finance ministers' statement, Deauville, 17 May 2003 and the G8 paper "Building International Will and Capacity to Combat Terrorism: A G8 Action Plan" issued at the Evian Summit, 2003.

43. See, for example, the FATF press releases of 10 September 2003 (Paris), and 3 October 2003 (Stockholm).

44. *Supra*, note 1, p. 1.

45. For example, in October 2003 the FATF issued an interpretative note to Special Recommendation III on freezing and confiscating terrorist assets. The text is reproduced in full at Appendix VII. See also, "Financial Action Task Force on Money Laundering: Freezing of Terrorist Assets – International Best Practices", Paris, FATF, 3 October 2003. A major review of the use of cash couriers in a terrorist context was under way in the FATF at the time of writing.

46. See, for example, "Financial Action Task Force on Money Laundering: Report on Money Laundering Typologies 2002-2003", Paris, FATF, at pp. 25-26. See also, *supra*, note 4, at p. 6.

CHAPTER VI – THE CONTINUING WORK OF THE FINANCIAL ACTION TASK FORCE

Mandate and priorities

The elaboration of the Forty Recommendations in the 1990s, while a major accomplishment, was not an end in itself. The Financial Action Task Force has been kept in being since then in order to ensure both the continuing utility of its comprehensive programme and to maximise its practical impact. To these ends it has traditionally concentrated on three priorities: (i) monitoring the implementation of the recommendations by its members; (ii) keeping track of developments in money laundering methods and examining the adequacy of its countermeasures in the light thereof; and (iii) carrying out an ambitious "outreach" or external relations programme to promote the greatest possible mobilisation of effort in the wider international community to counter this problem.

In the course of the review undertaken during FATF IX, it was resolved that these would continue to be central concerns over the next five years although there would be significant new elements in its approach to the issue of geographic expansion. As seen in the previous chapter, to these was added, in the aftermath of the September 2001 terrorist attacks on the United States, the countering of the financing of terrorism.

Monitoring implementation by FATF members

In the conclusion to the 1990 FATF report, it was recognised that "a regular assessment of progress realised in enforcing money laundering measures would stimulate countries to give to these issues a high priority ...".[1] Two principal procedures have since been developed to this end. The first of these, established in the course of the 1990-91 round, takes the form of a process of annual self-assessment, originally based on two detailed questionnaires circulated to each member country or territory. As was pointed out in the June 1997 report: "These responses are then compiled and analysed, and provide the basis for assessing to what extent the forty recommendations have been implemented by both individual countries and the group as a whole."[2]

The self-assessment system has been refined on several occasions. In the early years, particular attention was paid to measures designed to enhance the objective nature of the exercise. After the 1996 amendments to the remit, issues such as the extension of anti-laundering to all crimes were added to the questionnaires. Other modifications, such as the introduction of a question and answer session at a plenary meeting, were introduced in order to improve the practical utility of the process.

In the June 1998 FATF annual report it was announced that an "enhanced self-assessment" procedure would be afforded a position of prominence in the years up to 2004. The enhancements in question were agreed to at the September 1999 FATF plenary. Two alterations are of particular significance. As an interpretative note by the secretariat puts it:

> First, those Recommendations which are not mandatory, which are vague, or which do not require specific action against which compliance can be assessed ... will not be subject to compliance analysis through the self-assessment process. Second, greater attention will be paid to areas of non-compliance or partial compliance, rather than the areas where full compliance has already been achieved.[3]

In addition an effort was made to simplify and streamline the process. This included combining the previous questionnaires into one document and considerably reducing its size.[4] While there continued to be problems with the self-assessment procedure, such as divergences in the interpretation of certain of the recommendations, the end product appeared to be more useful than ever before.[5]

In a move at that time without precedent in international practice in the criminal law sphere, FATF II decided to supplement self-assessment with a system of mutual evaluation. As the 1991 report stated: "Individual members would be chosen for examination by the FATF with the examination carried out by selected other members of the FATF, according to an agreed protocol for examination and agreed selection criteria. The objective would be to examine every FATF member by the end of 1996."[6] The initial round of mutual evaluation, the major purpose of which was to assess the degree of formal compliance with the recommendations, was completed in 1995. A second round, with a focus on the effectiveness in practice of the measures taken by members, was initiated in the following year and was completed in mid-1999. The remit here also included an assessment of "any follow-up action taken in response to the suggestions for improvement made in the first round".[7] It is of importance to note that the benchmark for the second round continued to be the original Forty Recommendations of 1990 rather than the amended version. This is because the round began in February 1996 with the evaluation visit to France, while the amendments were agreed to only in June of that year. To avoid members being evaluated against different formal standards, this necessitated the continued use of the original text. As a subsequent review noted, however, this drawback "was compensated for by focusing on the effectiveness of the anti-money laundering systems, which required consideration of issues that had been adopted in the 1996 recommendations, as well as other factors which affected the effectiveness of the system".[8]

Initially this issue was due to be addressed in preparations for a third round of evaluations which was also expected to take on a somewhat more simplified character. As the June 1998 FATF report noted, it would focus "exclusively on compliance with the revised parts of the recommendations, the areas of significant deficiencies identified in the second round and generally the effectiveness of the countermeasures".[9] However, in the light of developments including the initiation of the process of revising the Forty Recommendations, the formulation of the eight Special Recommendations on Terrorist Financing, and the evolving relationships with the IMF and World Bank,[10] the third round was delayed. This exercise, based on the existing FATF standards, and comprehensive in nature, is expected to commence in late 2004. In the intervening period, only a restricted programme of mutual evaluations focusing on members of the Gulf Cooperation Council[11] and new FATF members[12] was carried out.

Mutual evaluation is, in essence, an international system of periodic peer review under which each member is subject to a form of on-site examination. As Patrick Moulette, the current FATF Executive Secretary, has pointed out:

> Each evaluation team usually comprises three examiners (four for the larger countries) of different nationalities whose expertise must cover all aspects of the fight against money laundering. Each team therefore comprises a legal expert (a judge or justice ministry representative), a financial expert (from a finance ministry, central bank or regulatory authority for the financial sector), and an operational services (law enforcement) expert (from the police, the customs or an agency receiving and analysing suspicious transaction reports, such as FinCEN in the United States).[13]

Formally, the team of examiners is selected by the FATF President (in reality, by the secretariat), and thereafter, the country to be examined is advised as to both the composition of the team and the dates of the on-site visit.[14] While it is "an underlying principle of the mutual evaluation process … that all members should participate in the process", this goal was not fully satisfied in the first round. In the second, all members provided at least one evaluator although efforts to secure a better balance in terms of overall involvement were not completely realised.[15]

The examination team visits the country in question, normally for three days, during which time it meets those ministries and institutions (public and private) with a mandate or substantial practical involvement in the anti-money laundering sphere. The team then prepares a detailed report, including the identification of deficiencies and suggestions for improvement, which is discussed in and adopted by a plenary meeting of the Task Force. Although each such report is and remains confidential, agreement was reached to make executive summaries public. These are contained in the annual reports of the work of the FATF, which can now be accessed by the general public on the Internet.[16]

Detailed procedures, rules and expectations have been developed to govern all of the stages of this innovative and intrusive process, the comprehensive exposition of which lies beyond the scope of this chapter.[17] However, while the system has evolved over time, a significant effort has been made from the outset to ensure equality and consistency of treatment of evaluated jurisdictions and an internal review in 2001 concluded that, by and large, these goals had been met.[18]

Although the self-assessment and mutual evaluation procedures were developed with existing member states and territories in mind they have, in practice, been used in two situations which were not fully envisaged at the outset; in relation to institutional members and in the context of the recent limited programme of geographic expansion of membership. In so far as the former is concerned, it will be recalled that the European Commission and the Gulf Cooperation Council (GCC) are full participants within the FATF. While fifteen European Union states also enjoy that status,[19] none of the six members of the GCC (Bahrain, Kuwait, Oman, Qatar, Saudi Arabia and the United Arab Emirates) are Task Force participants in their own right.

Over time, the absence of regular monitoring procedures for these countries emerged as a source of concern. In May 1997 agreement was reached on how to carry out an evaluation of the measures taken by them. The first step was to distribute self-assessment questionnaires. Unfortunately, the partial and incomplete nature of the subsequent returns made it impossible to form a view as to the state of compliance. Consequently, it was agreed that a high-level FATF mission would be despatched to the GCC secretariat to seek further information and "to discuss how to improve the implementation of effective anti-money laundering systems in the Gulf region".[20] This mission eventually took place in January 1999 and resulted in a commitment to provide all outstanding information required for the self-assessment exercise. In addition, the discussions set in train a process which was to result in all GCC members agreeing to undergo mutual evaluation. However, "given the unique position of the GCC ... it was decided that mutual evaluations of its member states should be a joint FATF/GCC process".[21] The series of on-site visits commenced in June 2000 and all evaluations have now been concluded.[22] Similarly, the GCC states have completed the self-assessment exercise and responsibility for future such surveys has been assumed by the GCC secretariat.[23]

The second innovative context in which the process of mutual evaluation has been resorted to is in the vetting of new applicants for membership. In June 1998, the FATF decided to permit the first limited expansion of its membership since the early 1990s. As was noted in chapter IV, the focus was to be on broadening the geographic base to include:

> ... strategically important countries which already have certain key anti-money laundering measures in place (criminalisation of money laundering; mandatory customer identification and suspicious transactions reporting by financial institutions), and which are politically determined to make a full commitment towards the implementation of the Forty Recommendations, and which could play a major role in their regions in the process of combating money laundering.[24]

The subsequently elaborated criteria for admission included a political commitment "to undergo annual self-assessment exercises and two rounds of mutual evaluations".[25]

Pursuant to this policy of strategic influence, Argentina, Brazil and Mexico, which had been admitted to observer status in September 1999, had their anti-money laundering systems positively evaluated the following year and were admitted to full membership in June. While the public summaries indicate that the evaluations were broad in scope, their "principal objective" was to determine compliance with the restricted but "fundamental" anti-laundering measures mentioned above.[26] This process was again followed in 2003 in relation to the Russian Federation and South Africa[27] and will continue to be used as the FATF seeks to progressively strengthen its representation from other regions.[28]

There is no doubt that, in practice, the prospect of a mutual-evaluation visit frequently acts as a catalyst for governmental action. As Dilwyn Griffiths, the then FATF Executive Secretary, noted in his address to the 1993 Oxford Conference on International and White Collar Crime: "I do not think that progress in implementing the recommendations would have been as swift and substantial without it. Countries are concerned to have a good story to tell examiners and there is thus an impetus to get things done which would otherwise be lacking."[29] Similarly, the detailed reports indicate often quite extensive areas in which improvements in laws, regulations and practices could and should be made. As was noted above, one of the functions of the second round was to check on the measures adopted in response to the deficiencies identified in the earlier report.[30]

While these periodic reviews have been sufficient to secure substantial improvements in many FATF members, they have not eliminated the problem of inadequate compliance by some with the Forty Recommendations. For this reason, the Task Force has formulated a policy which reflects a graduated approach. At its most basic, and frequently invoked, level this takes the form of a requirement for the country concerned to make periodic reports. As one insider has noted:

> … when a country fails to comply with a large number of FATF recommendations, we initiate a follow-up procedure, a major feature of which is the obligation to submit regular progress reports on the implementation of the recommendations. There would be no point in completing an evaluation and then ignoring the result.[31]

When this tactic for increasing peer pressure fails, the policy on non-complying members envisages the taking of additional steps. This is well illustrated by action taken in connection with Turkey in 1995-96. Its failure, among other things, even to enact basic anti-money laundering legislation had placed it in a position of serious non-compliance with the recommendations. Accordingly, the FATF President first wrote to relevant ministers in that member country expressing concern. Subsequently, a high-level mission was sent to Ankara to encourage the government to take urgent action or face the possibility of having more serious steps taken against it. Finally, on 19 September 1996, the FATF issued a public statement in which it invoked its Recommendation 21 procedure against a member for the first time.[32]

This prospect of financial and reputational damage seems to have had the effect of stimulating the attention of policy makers and others in Ankara, and in November 1996, Turkey enacted and brought into force the Law on the Prevention of Money Laundering. The Recommendation 21 measures were then lifted.

Concerns over partial non-compliance by other FATF members have been frequently expressed. Of these the most serious to date related to Austria, which had declined to abolish anonymous passbooks for Austrian residents in spite of the fact that this was regarded as a clear breach of the requirements of Recommendation 10. As a result, the FATF policy was triggered. The FATF President first wrote to the Austrian Government about this matter but when this did not lead to change, a high-level mission was dispatched to Vienna, without success. The Task Force then invoked Recommendation 21 and called on financial institutions to give special attention "to transactions with bank cheques issued by Austrian banks and denominated in Austrian schillings, as these funds might be the result of the closing of anonymous passbook savings accounts". In a news release of 11 February 1999 which announced this measure, the FATF indicated that it would continue to monitor the situation.

When even this robust stance failed to bring about the desired change in policy, the Task Force, at its February 2000 meeting, took the unprecedented step of agreeing to suspend Austria from membership unless, by 20 May:

> 1. The Austrian government issues a clear political statement that it will take all necessary steps to eliminate the system of anonymous passbooks in accordance with the 40 FATF Recommendations by the end of June 2002.

2. The Austrian government introduces and supports a Bill into Parliament to prohibit the opening of new anonymous passbooks and to eliminate existing anonymous passbooks in accordance with the above paragraph.[33]

Whether to mitigate public shaming or from fear of economic consequences, the Austrian Government soon took the required steps, leading to the lifting of the threat of suspension.[34]

In governmental circles in the major economies, the FATF experience with mutual evaluation has been widely perceived as a success. In a public lecture, delivered in Edinburgh in 1993, Mr Tom Sherman, the then FATF President, characterised it as "a very effective mechanism indeed".[35] In subsequent years this positive characterisation has, if anything, strengthened. By way of illustration, the June 1999 annual report described it as "an irreplaceable monitoring mechanism".[36] A recent internal review concluded that the process had "proven to be, by and large, an effective and efficient one, which uses relatively few resources to obtain significant results".[37] A broadly similar view has been taken in the literature. Sansonetti perhaps captured the preponderant tone when stating that the process "is one of the cornerstones of the FATF and has proven to be the most successful element of its activities".[38]

Perhaps the clearest illustration of the depth of this perception is to be found in the increasing resort being made to the FATF process, or variants of it, in other fora. As will be seen in subsequent chapters, mutual evaluation has been introduced as a key part of anti-money laundering efforts elsewhere (for instance, in the work of the Council of Europe and the Caribbean Financial Action Task Force). It has also started to be introduced in other contexts. It is, for example, an important feature of European Union efforts to combat both organised crime and terrorism and plays a central role in the ambitious agenda of the Council of Europe to counter corruption. It is not without interest that the concept now also finds expression in Article 12 of the 1997 OECD Convention on Combating Bribery of Foreign Public Officials in International Business Transactions.

For the sake of completeness, it should be noted that the FATF has a third mechanism through which it can seek to monitor implementation by its membership; namely, cross-country reviews. This is a little-used device intended to provide an analysis of the implementation of specific recommendations by the membership as a whole. For example, in 1996-97 such evaluations were carried out in relation to asset confiscation and provisional measures, and on measures taken to deal with customer identification.[39] While such studies have generated some interesting insights the process itself has failed to win a significant place in the thinking of the membership. It is anticipated that it will be resorted to fairly infrequently in the years ahead.

In each of its annual reports, the Task Force has been in a position to report progress by its members on the implementation of the Forty Recommendations. It is fair to say, however, that the pace of progress towards full formal compliance – let alone effective implementation – has been uneven; both geographically and in terms of specific issues. By way of illustration, the June 1998 report noted that "a large majority of members have reached an acceptable level of compliance with the 1996 Forty Recommendations". It went on to warn, however, that there was a need for some countries to take further steps and that it was of importance "that these changes be brought in as soon as possible".[40] As of June 2003, fifteen members were in a position to report formal satisfaction of all twenty-eight of the 1996 recommendations requiring specific action.[41] Many of the others were also nearing this goal. A minority (most notably Mexico, which was in full compliance with only twelve of these standards) was still some way away.

Reviewing developments in money laundering methods and countermeasures

One of the major tasks of the FATF has been, and will continue to be, to monitor developments in money laundering methods and to assess their implications. Central to this aspect of its work is an annual review known as a "typologies exercise". As has been stated elsewhere:

> The purpose of the annual FATF typologies exercise is to bring together experts from the law enforcement and regulatory authorities of the FATF member countries to exchange information on significant money laundering cases and operations. It thus provides a critical opportunity for operational experts to identify and describe current money laundering trends and to comment on the effectiveness of countermeasures.[42]

In this manner, the Task Force has sought to chart the increasing sophistication, complexity and professionalism of the money laundering process. In recent years, attention has been paid to such matters as the role of lawyers and other "gatekeepers" to the international financial system, the development of "cyberpayments" technologies, the exploitation of correspondent banking relationships, and the abuse of the securities sector. As pointed out in the previous chapter, practices associated with the funding of terrorism are now a primary source of concern and focus in this context.

A major function of these typologies exercises and related dialogue has been to provide a basis upon which to judge the continuing relevance and coherence of the FATF package of countermeasures. They have in this way contributed to the processes which culminated in both the 1996 and 2003 amendments to the recommendations. In the latter context, for example, the articulation of new standards for the treatment of members of the legal professions has its origins firmly (and clearly) in concerns expressed over time in these annual discussions.

The typologies meetings are mainly attended by operational experts drawn from member jurisdictions. On occasion, however, as during the 1995-96 round, representatives from the financial sector have also been invited to attend. This is but one illustration of a wider aspiration; namely, to establish strong links between the Task Force and the financial services industry with a view to working "in partnership with the private sector in combating money laundering".[43] To this end, the FATF has organised major meetings with private sector representatives. The first such forum was held in January 1996 with a second taking place in Brussels during FATF IX. As the June 1998 report noted: "The purpose of this event was to discuss with the private sector areas of common interest and ways to best develop measures to prevent and detect money laundering through the financial community."[44]

It will be recalled from chapter IV that this process was taken a stage further in the course of the discussions leading up to the revision of the recommendations in 2003. In contrast to the stocktaking exercise of the mid-1990s, this review took place with commendable openness[45] and included the release of a detailed public consultation paper.[46] In addition to soliciting views in this manner, the FATF convened, in October 2002, "a forum with representatives from the financial and other sectors from all parts of the globe. This included delegates from the banking, securities and insurance industries, as well as representatives from the legal and accounting professions".[47] More than 160 participants were involved in this dialogue; one supplemented at a later stage by informal consultations with the sectors most directly affected by the proposed changes to the recommendations.[48]

It is also of relevance to note in this context the increasing frequency with which the Task Force is formulating common guidance on matters of concern to the private sector rather than merely urging members to do so on an individual and consequently non-harmonised basis (as with Recommendation 28 in both the 1990 and 1996 versions).[49] One such initiative was the publication in June 1998 of a set of best practice guidelines entitled "Providing feedback to reporting financial institutions and other persons".[50]

More recently, the FATF has (as seen in chapter V) issued guidance to financial institutions to assist in the detection of terrorist finances. It has also indicated its intention to produce similar guidance on the detection of suspicious transactions related to money laundering.[51] These efforts to build a more meaningful relationship with the private sector are to be warmly welcomed.

The FATF external relations activities

The strategy in overview

It has been emphasised on a number of occasions that modern money laundering is highly sophisticated in nature and money managers have proved to be adept in identifying loopholes and exploiting weaknesses in the structures, both national and international, which have been constructed to combat their operations. Internationally, this has involved displacement from jurisdictions which have been active in securing improvements to countries and territories which possess no or insufficient anti-money laundering measures. Given its restricted membership base, the need to tackle the problem of geographic displacement has been a priority of the FATF from the outset and is addressed in a number of its recommendations. For instance, Recommendation 21 stipulates that, among other things, financial institutions "should give special attention to business relations and transactions with persons, including companies and financial institutions, which do not or insufficiently apply the recommendations".[52] Recommendation 20 of the 1996 text calls upon FATF member country financial institutions to apply certain principles to their branches and majority-owned subsidiaries located abroad to the extent that the laws of the host state permit. This applies "especially in countries which do not or insufficiently apply these recommendations ...".[53] In spite of the difficulties which flowed from the disinclination of the FATF throughout the 1990s to establish a common definitive list of such jurisdictions, an issue to which this study will return, progress was recorded. For instance, as of 1998, banks in twenty-two of the then twenty-six members reported paying special attention, pursuant to Recommendation 21, to transactions involving countries which did not or insufficiently applied the FATF package of countermeasures. In a further three countries, partial compliance by banks with this recommendation was reported. The position was only slightly less satisfactory in relation to non-bank financial institutions. Similarly, the vast majority of members have reported positively on compliance with the obligations set out in Recommendation 20.[54]

Although the absence of a common blacklist of delinquent jurisdictions made the application of the above measures difficult, practice demonstrated that, at least in extreme cases, they could be activated. For example, the first use of Recommendation 21 by the FATF in relation to a non-member took place in early 1996 regarding developments in the small Indian Ocean island state of the Seychelles. In November 1995 its National Assembly enacted the Economic Development Act, the stated purpose of which was "to ensure a very high level of sustainable economic development for Seychelles and its people".[55] In order to do so, however, it was deemed necessary to offer certain highly controversial "comforts and guarantees" to investors.

Among the concessions granted under section 5 of the 1995 act were the following:

> (7)   For the purposes of this section a concession or incentive includes -
>
> (a) immunity from prosecution for all criminal proceedings whatsoever except criminal proceedings in respect of offences involving acts of violence and drug trafficking in Seychelles;
>
> (b) immunity from compulsory acquisition or sequestration of the assets belonging to an investor other than a confiscation or forfeiture made by the court in relation to a criminal proceeding which is excepted under paragraph (a).

Furthermore, to set the minds of potential investors at rest, the legislation sought to ensure that these concessions, among others, could not readily be retracted or withdrawn. To this end, the decision was taken to afford the 1995 act a level of constitutional entrenchment.[56]

These developments were considered by the FATF in February 1996. Its then president characterised the enactment as being clearly designed "to attract capital by permitting international criminal enterprises to shelter both themselves and their illicitly-gained wealth from pursuit by legal authorities".[57] Given the threat which it was deemed to pose to the effectiveness of international money-laundering countermeasures, the FATF resolved to place all available pressure on the Seychelles Government to repeal the legislation. It also invoked Recommendation 21 and "urged financial institutions world-wide to scrutinise closely business relations and transactions with persons, companies and financial institutions domiciled in the Seychelles".

Faced with the above, and other manifestations of deep diplomatic unease, the Seychelles Government acted. In particular, on 2 April 1996 it introduced into the National Assembly the Anti-Money Laundering Bill which was enacted shortly thereafter. Furthermore, the government refrained from bringing the provisions of the 1995 act into operation.

These measures were not regarded as sufficient. Within the Task Force the repeal of the offending legislation was identified as the necessary precondition for the lifting of the Recommendation 21 measures; a matter made more complex by the manner in which it had been entrenched. Internally, the constitutionality of the act was subject to an unsuccessful challenge. As Venchard, Justice of Appeal of the Seychelles Court of Appeal remarked, in joining his fellow judges in dismissing the petition, in April 1997:

> ... it is for the Executive and the Legislature to devise ways and means to attract investments for the development of this country. It is open to the Legislature, in its wisdom, to determine the nature and extent of the concessions and incentives to be provided to potential investors. It is not open to the Court, in compliance with the doctrine of separation of powers, to substitute itself for the Legislature and to strike down any of these concessions.[58]

It was not until July 2000 that the Seychelles National Assembly passed the Economic Development (Repeal) Act which was assented to by President René the following month.[59] In the light of this development, the FATF lifted its Recommendation 21 warning at its next plenary meeting.[60]

The Seychelles fiasco outlined above serves as a vivid illustration of what is possible within the Task Force, at least in the most extreme cases, where there is a perception that a member of the international community has departed in a radical way from the standards of conduct reflected in the recommendations. At an even more practical level, the Economic Development Act saga was instructive. The evidence suggests that with the emergence of high-profile attention those interested in taking advantage of this law quickly made themselves scarce. As the *Economist* noted at the time: "Nasty noises from abroad have had their effect. ... The initial batch of interested 'investors' – some South Africans, Italians and Britons among them – have fled, many leaving high piles of large and unpaid hotel bills behind them to show the height of their calibre".[61]

In order to further minimise the "diversion" problem a major effort has been made throughout to secure the active co-operation of others. At the G7 summit in Houston all non-members "were invited to participate in the fight against money laundering and to implement the recommendations of the FATF".[62] In the course of the 1990-91 round it was determined that the first step should involve explaining the nature of the FATF action plan in different parts of the world "with a view towards obtaining formal endorsements and, as far as possible, universal effective implementation of these recommendations".[63] This emphasis on obtaining the endorsement of and political commitment to its programme of action remained as a central priority throughout the 1990s.

A further major element of the external relations strategy has been to reach out to non-member countries through a process of regional mobilisation.[64] Although all areas of the globe have received some attention, the FATF concentrated its efforts initially on the Caribbean, central and eastern Europe, and Asia.[65] The means adopted included, among others, the convening of regional conferences, undertaking country-specific missions, and co-operating closely with other organisations with a mandate in the money laundering area including the formulation of joint ventures with them. The organisational contacts which have been developed over the years are extensive.[66] They range from global bodies such as ICPO/Interpol, the World Customs Organisation, UNODC and international financial institutions such as the International Monetary Fund to specialised bodies with a more restricted membership such as the Egmont Group, the International Organisation of Securities Commissions (Iosco), the Offshore Group of Banking Supervisors (OGBS) and regional development banks. Joint ventures have not been uncommon. For example in April 1993, November 1994 and December 1995 the FATF combined with the Commercial Crime Unit (as it then was) of the Commonwealth Secretariat to organise major conferences in Singapore, Malaysia and Japan intended to raise the awareness of Asian and Pacific governments about the nature and extent of the money laundering threat and the evolving international response to it. In 1996 the same partnership sponsored the first Southern and Eastern African Money Laundering Conference which was convened in Cape Town in October.

Such co-operation with others is of considerable importance for a number of reasons. For example, given the small size of its Paris secretariat, co-operation is essential in order to ensure the appropriate provision of technical assistance and other follow-up activities in non-FATF member countries. It also helps to reduce, though by no means to eliminate, the problems which inevitably flow from the involvement of a number of different bodies in the same general sphere of concern. As the FATF report of June 1993 remarked: "It is clearly important that the international community avoids overlap and duplication and draws strength from collective action. In conjunction with the other major organisations, FATF is therefore taking steps to promote a more co-ordinated approach in this area."[67] This has most frequently taken the form of co-ordination meetings held on the margins of FATF plenary meetings. More recently, however, the co-ordination function has been further strengthened with regular meetings among the international organisations with an anti-money laundering mandate.

Early efforts of the outreach programme concentrated on securing progress in a region which had for many years been a major source of concern to law enforcement officials and others involved in anti-laundering investigations; namely, the Caribbean.[68] It is no doubt for this reason that the FATF has been active in promoting its programme among the countries of that region since as early as June 1990 when an important conference on the subject was held in Aruba. As will be seen in chapter IX, these efforts resulted, among other things, in the creation of the Caribbean Financial Action Task Force (CFATF). This precedent of regional action to combat money laundering was followed, in September 1997, by the establishment of a similar body for European jurisdictions which were not FATF members. MONEYVAL (formerly, and better known as the Select Committee of Experts on the Evaluation of Anti-Money Laundering Measures (PC-R-EV)) is based at the headquarters of the Council of Europe in Strasbourg. It is subject to analysis in chapter VII. It had for long been hoped that the same path might eventually be followed by Asian countries. It is of interest to note that in 1994 a first step in that direction was taken with the establishment, by the FATF, of a small unit, based in Sydney, Australia, which was tasked with providing support for initiatives in that region. This unit was "funded by advances from Australia's Confiscated Assets Trust Fund".[69] In 1997, following a fourth and final awareness-raising seminar held in Bangkok, Thailand, agreement was reached on the establishment of an autonomous regional body known as the Asia/Pacific Group on Money Laundering (APG). The APG held its first annual meeting in Tokyo in March 1998; a development which was warmly welcomed by the Task Force.[70]

In the light of these developments it is no surprise that encouraging the creation of new FATF-style regional bodies (FSRBs) was to become the cornerstone of Task Force effort to spread the anti-money laundering message. In this regard it was agreed that:

> ... the ideal model for a FATF-style regional body would be: a local group exerting peer pressure among its members and whose mutual evaluation procedures had

been endorsed by the FATF; one or several FATF members present in it and a secretariat which would liaise regularly with the FATF. Moreover, the presidents/secretariats of each FATF-style regional body should become full members of the FATF. The FATF-style regional bodies should also be committed to the Forty Recommendations and to any other anti-money laundering principles they wish to endorse to reflect local problems. The main tasks of these bodies should include conducting mutual evaluations of their members and carrying out self-assessment surveys and regional typologies exercises.[71]

New such groupings have since been created in both South America and eastern and southern Africa and yet others are in prospect.[72] Closely associated with this emphasis on regionalism has been the gradual, targeted and limited expansion in Task Force membership outlined at an earlier stage of this work. One of the criteria for admission is that the country "be a full and active member of the relevant FATF-style regional body (where one exists), or be prepared to work with the FATF or even to take the lead, to establish such a body (where none exists)".[73]

The NCCT initiative

As was seen in the previous section, throughout the 1990s the many efforts of the Task Force to spread the anti-money laundering message to all regions of the world resulted in substantial progress being recorded. However, as the decade drew to a close a more proactive stance on compliance with anti-money laundering standards emerged, the G7 nations playing an important role in moulding the new agenda. It will be recalled that in May 1998, G7 finance ministers drew attention to their concerns "at the number of countries and territories, including some financial offshore centres, which continue to offer excessive banking secrecy and allow screen companies to be used for illegal purposes". Ministers called upon the FATF to review the position and to make recommendations as to a course of action to rectify such abuses.

In response, the Task Force established a working group on non-co-operative countries and territories. It afforded priority to the identification of the criteria to be used in defining non-co-operation and in agreeing on the process through which to identify specific jurisdictions considered to meet such criteria in practice. The fruits of these deliberations are embodied in a report issued on 14 February 2000.[74]

Central to the initiative detailed in that document was the formulation of some twenty-five criteria – said to be consistent with the Forty Recommendations – which identify "detrimental rules and practices" in the international effort to combat money laundering. The criteria cover a broad range of matters from loopholes in financial regulations to the allocation of inadequate anti-money laundering resources. They are formulated in such a manner as to embrace both jurisdictions suffering from formal non-compliance as well as those where the anti-laundering regime is ineffective in fact. The report also established a review procedure through which jurisdictions would be subject to examination, and classified the concrete steps which could be taken against delinquent countries or territories to encourage compliance. These include a range of countermeasures which can be deployed against those which might be disinclined to fall into line. Ultimately, it was noted, these might include conditioning, restricting, targeting or even prohibiting financial transactions with non-co-operative jurisdictions. As the report put it:

> 54. FATF members should also consider determining whether it is desirable and feasible to condition, restrict, target or even prohibit financial transactions with such jurisdictions. Such measures could serve as an ultimate recourse should a country or territory have decided to preserve laws or practices that are particularly damaging for the fight against money laundering. In the event that there was no legal basis for taking these measures, FATF members should consider adopting the relevant legislation. FATF members should also examine ways to prevent financial institutions located in identified non-cooperating countries or territories from using facilities (for example, information technology facilities) located in the FATF members' territory.

By June 2000 this process had resulted in the creation of a blacklist of some fifteen jurisdictions where serious problems had been identified. While the majority were offshore centres in the Caribbean, the Pacific and elsewhere, it also included states as diverse as Israel, the Russian Federation, and the Philippines. None were FATF members. All were urged to address the specified deficiencies as a matter of priority. As an initial encouragement to do so, the FATF invoked its Recommendation 21 procedure for all on that list and warned that failure to respond in a positive manner would result in consideration being given to the adoption of further countermeasures. Immediate resort to Recommendation 21 was unexpected as the February text had envisaged its use only in relation "to countries or territories which are unwilling to take constructive action".[75]

In July of that year these developments were warmly welcomed by the G7. Heads of state and government, meeting in Okinawa, Japan, while expressing the wish for dialogue and offering to provide advice and assistance to support reform, reiterated their willingness to compel change. Their statement of 21 July reads, in relevant part, as follows:

> We are prepared to act together when required and appropriate, to implement co-ordinated countermeasures against those NCCTs that do not take steps to reform their systems appropriately, including the possibility to condition or restrict financial transactions with those jurisdictions and to condition or restrict support from IFIs [international financial institutions] to them.

In the period since, the initiative was further refined. In particular, a detailed policy was agreed and made public concerning the steps which need to be taken in order for a jurisdiction to be removed from the NCCT list (thus curing one of the more blatant omissions in the original report).[76] As the 2001-02 annual report noted:

> 73. To decide whether a jurisdiction should be removed from the list, the FATF must first be satisfied that the jurisdiction has addressed the deficiencies previously identified by enacting significant legislation and regulations. In assessing progress by NCCTs, the FATF gives particular importance to the relevant aspects of criminal law, financial supervision, customer identification, suspicious transactions reporting and international co-operation. Any new legislation or regulations must not only have been enacted but also have come into effect. Furthermore, the FATF also takes steps to ensure that the jurisdictions concerned are indeed implementing effectively the necessary changes. The FATF has also designed a rigorous monitoring mechanism to ensure sustained efforts in implementation.[77]

The FATF has monitored developments with some care, and the NCCT process and its application is addressed at each plenary meeting. As a consequence, several countries have been removed from the list whilst others have been added to it. As of July 2004, six jurisdictions remained on the blacklist.[78] The great majority of those which have been listed have been deemed to have made sufficient progress to avoid the immediate threat of additional countermeasures.[79] While there have been several public threats to go down this route such action had, as of early 2004, been initiated only in three instances. Of these, the action taken in December 2002 against Ukraine was short lived.[80] The impoverished Pacific island micro-state of Nauru has been less fortunate. As the 2002-03 NCCT annual review explained:

> Due to Nauru's failure to enact appropriate legislative measures and the existence of numerous shell banks, countermeasures have been in effect with respect to Nauru since December 2001. The FATF welcomes Nauru's recent legislative measures to eliminate shell banks. The FATF would like Nauru to take additional steps to ensure that previously licensed offshore banks are no longer conducting banking activity and are no longer in existence. When it is shown that Nauru has fully co-operated with the international community and has taken every step to ensure that shell banks no longer operate, the FATF can consider the removal of countermeasures.[81]

Myanmar joined this select group in November 2003.

Given what has been said above, it will come as no surprise that virtually every central aspect of this name, shame and punish policy has been subject to criticism. Of the objections which have been voiced, perhaps the most compelling relate to the use of what is widely seen as a double standard. In essence, this revolves around the nature and application of the twenty-five criteria. First, it may be pointed out that while the criteria are no doubt consistent with the 1996 version of the Forty Recommendations, in a number of obvious respects they go beyond those standards. This is well illustrated by criteria 13 and 14 relating to lack of identification of the beneficial owners of legal and business entities. While there was a growing appreciation of the practical importance of this matter, and a widespread acknowledgement of the need to develop and enforce appropriate international standards, the NCCT criteria in question projected well beyond the scope of Recommendations 9, 11 and 25 and the relevant interpretative notes as then worded.[82]

Second, while non-members have been assessed against the NCCT criteria, the FATF agreed in September 2001 merely to carry out a self-assessment exercise among its own members in order to determine their level of compliance. The results of that exercise were expected to be formulated during the 2002-03 round of FATF activities but have (at best) been further delayed. This fact, taken with other indications of the low priority afforded to this exercise, has served to reinforce the perception of inequality of treatment.

Finally, it should be noted that the criteria used to judge states and territories caught up within the NCCT process were far more exacting than those used in the admission to full membership of the Task Force of Argentina, Brazil, and Mexico in June 2000 and of South Africa and the Russian Federation in June 2003. It will be recalled that in 1998 the FATF decided to permit the first limited expansion of membership since the early 1990s. The substantive hurdle for admission was, however, set at a relatively low level being tied to the satisfaction of a limited range of "fundamental" principles. As noted at an earlier stage of this chapter, these included, in addition to the requisite political commitment to implement the recommendations within a reasonable time-frame, that the jurisdiction had already criminalised money laundering (beyond drug trafficking) and had made it mandatory for financial institutions to identify their customers and to report suspicious transactions. The membership assessments appear to have been conducted with sensitivity and flexibility both of which qualities were seemingly needed in arriving at a positive outcome.[83] These attributes are not, however, normally associated with the early stages of the NCCT process.

While for these and other reasons this FATF initiative has been controversial, it has also resulted in significant progress being recorded in the strengthening of the anti-money laundering regimes and practices of a number of target countries and territories (best illustrated by the transformation of the Russian Federation from blacklisted 'delinquent' to Task Force member).[84] Such successes have, however, not been achieved without cost. As the June 2001 annual report of the FATF noted: "this effort has also had the unintentional effect of straining the relationships between the FATF and the FATF-style regional bodies. The FATF has therefore discussed possible solutions to improve its relationships with the FATF-style regional bodies in the NCCT area".[85]

The evolving relationship with the IMF and the World Bank

Fortunately, there are relatively strong indications that the process of securing enhanced compliance with international anti-money laundering standards may now be moving into a less confrontational and coercive phase. This flows, in the main, from the greatly enhanced involvement of the International Monetary Fund and the World Bank in this sphere in the period since the terrorist attacks against the United States of 11 September 2001; an event which, as seen in chapter V, resulted in the formal extension of the mandate of the FATF to embrace the financing of terrorism and the formulation of eight special recommendations in relation to the same.

Throughout the 1990s, these international financial institutions (IFIs) had, at best, been semi-detached participants in the anti-money laundering effort. While some work of relevance was undertaken (and some pioneering research produced)[86] the anti-money laundering agenda was widely perceived to be marginal to their core responsibilities. Indeed, notwithstanding increasing pressure from the influential G7 finance ministers (concerned at the onset of the new millennium not only with countering money laundering but also with other perceived abuses of the global financial system)[87] the IMF and the World Bank showed little inclination to fully engage with this issue.[88] Unsurprisingly, however, much of this residual institutional reluctance abated in the wake of the terrorist attacks of September 2001.

Of particular relevance for present purposes were the decisions by the respective boards to recognise the FATF recommendations on money laundering (AML) and terrorist financing (CFT) as the relevant international standards, and to add these subjects to the list of areas in which they would carry out compliance inspections.[89] It was further agreed to conduct a twelve-month pilot programme of such "AML/CFT assessments and accompanying reports on the Observance of Standards and Codes (ROSCs) that would involve participation of the IMF and the World Bank, the Financial Action Task Force, and FATF-Style Regional Bodies (FSRBs)".[90]

These decisions were not taken lightly. For example at its 26 July 2002 meeting, the IMF Executive Board subjected its decision to the satisfaction of four conditions including that "the FATF does not undertake a further round of the non-cooperative countries and territories (NCCT) initiative, at least during the 12-month pilot project".[91] At the same time, the board articulated four key principles which would guide the nature of its involvement. One such was that "all assessment procedures should be transparent and consistent with the mandate and core experience of the different institutions involved, and compatible with the uniform, voluntary, and co-operative nature of the ROSC exercise".[92]

At the October 2002 FATF plenary, the necessary commitments were forthcoming and the pilot project commenced later the same month. Assessments within the scope of this exercise were carried out using a common and highly detailed methodology document[93] which had been elaborated by the IFIs and the FATF in consultation with other standard-setting bodies.[94] Interestingly, while based primarily on the FATF recommendations (inclusive of those on terrorist financing), it "also includes relevant elements from United Nations Security Council resolutions and international conventions and from supervisory/regulatory standards for the banking, insurance and securities sectors".[95]

In the pilot period, there were two types of assessment using the common methodology. First, there were those conducted by the FATF itself; a move agreed to at the October 2002 plenary. However, given that the third round of mutual evaluations would not commence until after the period in question, its use was limited primarily to the evaluation of new members.[96]

It should also be noted that it was also used, to varying extents, in the activities of FATF-style regional bodies. By way of illustration, MONEYVAL, the activities of which are examined in chapter VII, endorsed its use in the relevant period only in respect to the evaluation of its new members (Armenia, Azerbaijan, Serbia and Montenegro, and Bosnia and Herzegovina). However – as with the FATF itself – it will use the common methodology in its next full round of evaluations. The detailed work to revise and update the text to reflect the 2003 amendments to the FATF recommendations was completed in the first half of 2004, and it is this revised version which will be used in the future.[97]

The second type of pilot project assessment was that carried out by the staff of the World Bank and the IMF in the context of the Financial Sector Assessment Programme (FSAP) and the IMF's offshore financial centre (OFC) assessments. Evaluations of more than thirty jurisdictions were completed by the expiry of the twelve-month period. IFI-led assessments differed in one major respect from those conducted by the Task Force. As has been pointed out elsewhere:

> ... staff (and experts under staff supervision) assess compliance with all criteria except those relating to the implementation of (i) criminal justice measures, and (ii) preventive measures for financial activities that are not of macroeconomic relevance (e.g., foreign exchange dealers). For these two areas, one or more independent AML/CFT experts (IAEs) are provided by the members of the FATF, FSRBs, or the Egmont Group. The substantive work of the IAE is not supervised by Bank/Fund staff and their participation is not financed by the Fund/Bank.[98]

This self-imposed limitation, viewed – entirely properly – by many as having an Alice in Wonderland quality, had its origins in the rather strained process through which the IMF and the World Bank came to engage with the money laundering agenda. It carried with it such obvious difficulties and drawbacks, however, that it was revisited and, in effect, reversed in March 2004. At the same time it was decided to make such assessments a regular part of their work.

The reputation of both institutions for objectivity and professionalism, their capacity to deliver technical assistance and to produce research and analysis of quality, among other factors, make them obvious and welcome participants in the mobilisation of the international community in this important area of common concern. Such continuing involvement will, in all probability, also act so as to preclude a return by the FATF to coercive policies such as those which were manifested in the NCCT exercise. On 24 March 2004, it should be noted, IMF Directors "agreed on the importance of continuing collaboration with the FATF in light of its indication that it has no plans at present to conduct a further round of the Non-Co-operative Countries and Territories (NCCT) exercise".[99]

Future challenges

Looked at in the overall there can be no doubt that the Task Force experiment, initiated by the G7 in 1989, has been highly successful to date. In spite of the apparent drawbacks of its limited, western-dominated membership and its informal legal status, it has become the single most important body in terms of the formulation of international anti-money laundering policy and in the mobilisation of global awareness of the complex issues involved in countering this sophisticated form of criminality. Central to this achievement has been the comprehensive set of forty recommendations which have come to be generally accepted as setting the benchmark for members of the international community. As the Task Force put it in June 2003: "The 1996 Forty Recommendations have been endorsed by more than 130 countries and are the international anti-money laundering standard."[100] As has been detailed in earlier stages of this book, in the course of the last few years the FATF has expanded its mandate to meet the challenges posed by the funding of terrorist activities. It has also substantially revised the 1996 recommendations so as to address perceived insufficiencies.

In unveiling the modified package of countermeasures in June 2003 the Task Force called upon "all countries to take the necessary steps to bring their national systems for combating money laundering and terrorist financing into compliance with the new FATF recommendations, and to effectively implement these measures".[101] It is clear, however, that there is a major onus on the membership of the FATF to take the lead in this area. There can be little doubt that the credibility and influence of the Task Force will be undermined unless its own members are seen to move forward with expedition to full and effective compliance with these new standards. In meeting this major challenge the FATF has at its disposal the innovative and intrusive monitoring mechanism of mutual evaluations as well as other supportive procedures such as self-assessment. The early and rigorous deployment of these procedures, coupled with the willingness to resort to compliance-enhancing measures against those of its members that fail to take timely action, would have a highly positive demonstration effect for the FATF-style regional bodies and other relevant international actors.

This is, however, but one of a series of matters of importance which will, or should, arise for consideration within the Task Force. Others include consideration of at least some of the implications which flow from the enhanced level of involvement of the IMF and the World Bank in the AML/CFT arena. To this end, among others, it was decided at the February 2003 plenary to establish a working group to focus on IFI matters.[102] It is to be expected that short-term and technical issues, such as co-ordination of assessment activities and associated procedural matters will be the dominant concerns of this group.

It is to be hoped, however, that an opportunity will also be created to revisit some policies of long standing in the light of the emergence of the IFIs in the money laundering and terrorist financing sphere. For instance, the question arises as to whether it still makes sense to afford the customary priority to fostering the creation of new FATF-style regional bodies in all parts of the world. The participation of the IMF and the World Bank in the process of compliance assessment, their ability to provide technical assistance, and the global reach of their activities raises the issue of whether the establishment of such regional structures in geographic areas characterised by significant levels of economic underdevelopment and lack of impact on the functioning of the global financial system can still be justified on either policy or practical grounds. In the longer term, if the commitment of these bodies to the anti-money laundering agenda becomes firmly established, important issues concerning the nature and scope of the activities of the existing FSRBs and of the Task Force itself will inevitably also arise for active consideration.

Notes: VI

1. Reproduced in Gilmore, W (ed), *International efforts to combat money laundering*, Cambridge, Cambridge University Press, 1992, p. 24.

2. "Financial Action Task Force on Money Laundering: Annual Report 1996-1997" (hereafter Report VIII), Paris, FATF, p. 9.

3. "Analysis of the 1999-2000 Self-Assessment Exercise: Note by the Secretariat", FATF, PLEN/46. REV 1, Paris, FATF.

4. See, "Financial Action Task Force on Money Laundering: Annual Report 1999-2000" (hereafter Report XI), Paris, FATF, at p. 20

5. See, "Financial Action Task Force on Money Laundering: Annual Report 2000-2001" (hereafter Report XII), Paris, FATF, at pp. 13-14. As was noted in the previous chapter, regular self-assessments have now also been undertaken in respect of the eight Special Recommendations on Terrorist Financing. In July 2004, however, it was decided to de-emphasise the traditional self-assessment procedure in favour of a process of follow-up reports to mutual evaluations.

6. *Supra*, note 1, p. 51.

7. Report VIII, *supra*, note 2, p. 10.

8. "Financial Action Task Force on Money Laundering: Review of FATF Anti-Money Laundering Systems and Mutual Evaluation Procedures" (16 February 2001), Paris, FATF, p. 36.

9. "Financial Action Task Force on Money Laundering: Annual Report 1997-1998" (hereafter Report IX), Paris, FATF, p. 8.

10. Outlined later in this chapter.

11. See, "Financial Action Task Force on Money Laundering: Annual Report 2002-2003" (hereafter Report XIV), Paris, FATF, at p. 29.

12. See, ibid., at p. 29. See also, "Financial Action Task Force on Money Laundering: Annual Report 2003-2004" (hereafter Report XV), Paris, FATF, p. 8.

13. Moulette, P, "The Mutual Evaluation Process of the Financial Action Task Force on Money Laundering", Council of Europe Doc. PC-R-EV(98) 1, 29 January 1998, p. 23, at p. 25.

14. See, *supra*, note 8, at p. 37.

15. See, ibid., at pp. 37-38.

16. Visit www.fatf-gafi.org

17. See, for example, *supra*, note 8, at pp.35-42; and Sansonetti, R, "The Mutual Evaluation Process: A Methodology of Increasing Importance at International Level", *Journal of Financial Crime*, Vol. 7, 2000, at pp. 218-220.

18. See, Report XII, *supra*, note 5, at p. 13.

19. While none of the ten states which joined the EU in 2004 are members of the FATF all are members of MONEYVAL, the FATF-style regional body for Europe. See, discussion in chapter VII below.

20. Report VIII, *supra*, note 2, p. 11.

21. Report, XI, *supra*, note 4, p. 24.

22. See, "Financial Action Task Force on Money Laundering: Annual Report 2001-2002" (hereafter Report XIII), Paris, FATF, at p.20 and at Annex G. For Saudi Arabia, see Report XV, *supra*, note 12, p. 8, and at Annex C.

23. See, Report XII, *supra*, note 5, at pp. 14-15.

24. Report IX, *supra*, note 9, p. 8.

25. Report XI, *supra*, note 4, p. 7. See also, Report XIV, *supra*, note 11,p. 10.

26. See, Report XI, *supra*, note 4, at pp. 8-13. These members have since been subject to a second round evaluation. See, Report XV, *supra*, note 12, p. 8, and at Annex G.

27. See, Report XIV, *supra*, note 11, at pp. 10-18.

28. One country frequently discussed in this context is the People's Republic of China with which a dialogue is underway. See, for example, Report XIV, *supra*, note 11, at p. 25.

29. Griffiths, D, "International Efforts to Combat Money Laundering: Developments and Prospects", in *Action against transnational criminality: papers from the 1993 Oxford Conference on International and White Collar Crime*, London, Commonwealth Secretariat, 1993, p. 11, at p. 13.

30. As was noted in the FATF 2001 review, *supra*, note 8, p. 34: "When averaged out across all the members ... approximately the same number of suggestions were implemented as those that were not."

31. *Supra*, note 13, p. 27.

32. Recommendation 21 was then worded as follows: "Financial institutions should give special attention to business relations and transactions with persons, including companies and financial institutions, from countries which do not or insufficiently apply these Recommendations. Whenever these transactions have no apparent economic or visible lawful purpose, their background and purpose should, as far as possible, be examined, the findings established in writing, and be available to help supervisors, auditors and law enforcement agencies."

33. OECD, news release, Paris, 3 February 2000.

34. See, Report XI, *supra*, note 9, at pp. 20-22. Actual satisfaction in practice of these FATF expectations was, however, achieved only over a period of years. See, Report XIV, *supra*, note 11, Annex D, at p. 4.

35. Sherman, T, "International Efforts to Combat Money Laundering: The Role of the Financial Action Task Force", in MacQueen, H L (ed), *Money laundering*, Edinburgh, Edinburgh University Press, 1993, p. 12, at p. 19.

36. "Financial Action Task Force on Money Laundering: Annual Report 1998-1999" (hereafter Report X), Paris, FATF, p. 4.

37. *Supra*, note 8, p. 49.

38. Sansonetti, *supra*, note 17, p. 218.

39. See, Report VIII, *supra*, note 2, at pp. 19-20.

40. Report IX, *supra*, note 9, p. 11.

41. See, Report XIV, *supra*, note 11, Annex D, at p. 3.

42. Report XII, *supra*, note 5, p. 15.

43. "Financial Action Task Force on Money Laundering: Annual Report 1995-1996" (hereafter Report VII), Paris, FATF, p. 9.

44. Report IX, *supra*, note 9, p. 28.

45. This was, in turn, consistent with the call made by G7 finance ministers meeting in Rome in July 2001 for the process to be "open, transparent and consultative".

46. See, "The Review of the FATF Forty Recommendations: Consultation Paper" (30 May 2002), Paris, FATF.

47. Report XIV, *supra*, note 11, p. 4.

48. See, ibid.

49. This was renumbered and somewhat reworded in 2003. See, Recommendation 25.

50. The interpretative note to Recommendation 25 of 2003 calls upon countries to "have regard" to the 1998 guidance.

51. See, "Financial Action Task Force on Money Laundering: Report on Money Laundering Typologies 2002-2003", Paris, FATF, p. 1.

52. Recommendation 21 as it emerged from the amendment process in 2003 contains some minor changes in wording and one substantive addition. It now contains the following injunction: "Where such a country continues not to apply or insufficiently applies the FATF Recommendations, countries should be able to apply appropriate countermeasures."

53. Recommendation 22 in the 2003 text.

54. See, Report IX, *supra*, note 9, Annex D, at p. 70.

55. Economic Development Bill 1995 (Bill No. 21 of 1995), objects and reasons.

56. See, ibid.

57. FATF press release, Paris, 1 February 1996.

58. *Mancienne v. Attorney General*, Seychelles Court of Appeal, Civil Appeal No. 15 of 1996, judgment of 3 April 1997 (unreported). I am in the debt of the Registrar of the Supreme Court for providing the text.

59. Act 9 of 2000.

60. FATF press release, Paris, 11 October 2000.

61. *Economist*, London, 17 February 1996, p. 59.

62. *Supra*, note 1, p. 33.

63. Ibid., p. 44.

64. "Financial Action Task Force on Money Laundering: Annual Report 1991-1992" (hereafter Report III), Paris, FATF, pp. 46-47.

65. See, for example, "Financial Action Task Force on Money Laundering: Annual Report 1992-1993" (hereafter Report IV), at pp. 21-23. See also, *supra*, note 29, at p. 14.

66. See, for example, Report XIV, *supra*, note 11, at p. 3 for the extensive list of bodies which attended FATF meetings during the 2002-03 round.

67. Report IV, *supra*, note 65, p. 23.

68. See, for example, Gilmore, W., "International Action against Drug Trafficking: Trends in United Kingdom Law and Practice", *International Lawyer*, 1990, p. 365, at pp. 379-391.

69. "Financial Action Task Force on Money Laundering: Annual Report 1993-1994" (hereafter Report V), Paris, FATF, p. 27.

70. See, Report IX, *supra*, note 9, at p. 31.

71. "Review of the Future of FATF: Strategic Issues", FATF IX, PLEN/12. BIS. REV 1, Paris, FATF.

72. See, for example, Report XIV, *supra*, note 11, at p. 19; and Report XV, *supra*, note 12, p. 12.

73. Report XIV, ibid., p. 10.

74. See, "Financial Action Task Force on Money Laundering: Report on Non-Co-operative Countries and Territories" (14 February 2000), Paris, FATF.

75. Ibid., p. 8.

76. See, for example, "Review to Identify Non-Cooperative Countries or Territories: Increasing the World-Wide Effectiveness of Anti-Money Laundering Measures", Paris, FATF, 21 June 2002, at pp. 30-31.

77. Report XIII, *supra*, note 22, p. 15.

78. They were: Cook Islands; Indonesia; Myanmar; Nauru; Nigeria; and Philippines.

79. See, "Financial Action Task Force on Money Laundering: Annual Review of Non-Cooperative Countries or Territories" (20 June 2003), Paris, FATF, at p. 5 for the range of possible measures.

80. The measures were lifted in February 2003. See, ibid., p. 1.

81. Ibid., pp. 1-2.

82. As a consequence of the 2003 revisions to the Forty Recommendations there now exists a greater convergence between them and the NCCT criteria. See, chapter IV above.

83. See, Report XI, *supra*, note 4, at pp. 7-13; and Report XIV, supra, note 11, at pp. 10-18. For instance, South Africa was admitted to membership notwithstanding the conclusion that it was "materially non-compliant with Recommendation 11". Report XIV, p. 14.

84. It should be noted that the NCCT blacklists have also been afforded relevance in a number of subsequent international initiatives. This was so, for example, in the October 2001 report of the Basel Committee on Banking Supervision entitled "Customer Due Diligence for Banks". See, for example, p. 12 and p. 15.

85. Report XII, *supra*, note 5, p. 11.

86. See, for example, Tanzi, V, "Money Laundering and the International Financial System", IMF Working Paper, WP/96/55, May 1996; and Quirk, P, "Macroeconomic Implications of Money Laundering", IMF Working Paper, WP/96/66, June 1996.

87. See, for example, "Actions against Abuse of the Global Financial System: Report from G7 Finance Ministers to the Heads of State and Government", Okinawa, 21 July 2000; and "Fighting the Abuses of the Global Financial System: Report of G7 Finance Ministers and Central Bank Governors", Rome, 7 July 2001.

88. See, for example, the paper prepared by the staffs of the IMF and World Bank entitled "Enhancing Contributions to Combating Money Laundering: Policy Paper", Washington, DC, 26 April 2001.

89. See, for example, Schott, P A, *Reference guide to anti-money laundering and combating the financing of terrorism*, Washington, DC, World Bank, 2003, at pp. x-2 and 3.

90. "IMF Advances Efforts to Combat Money Laundering and Terrorist Finance", IMF Public Information Notice No 02/87, 8 August 2002.

91. "Report on the Outcome of the FATF Plenary Meeting and Proposal for the Endorsement of the Methodology for Assessing Compliance with Anti-Money Laundering and Combating the Financing of Terrorism (AML/CFT) Standards", IMF, 8 November 2002, p. 2.

92. Ibid.

93. Entitled "Methodology for Assessing Compliance with Anti-Money Laundering and Combating the Financing of Terrorism Standards".

94. *Suppressing the financing of terrorism: a handbook for legislative drafting*, Washington, DC, IMF, 2003, p. 24.

95. *Supra*, note 93, p. 3.

96. See, Report XIV, *supra*, note 11, at p. 22 and p. 29.

97. See, ibid., at p. 22. See also, Report XV, *supra*, note 12, pp. 8-9.

98. "Status Report of the Work of the IMF and the World Bank on the Twelve-Month Pilot Program of AML/CFT Assessments and Delivery of AML/CFT Technical Assistance", September 2003, p. 5.

99. "IMF Executive Board Reviews and Enhances Efforts for Anti-Money Laundering and Combating the Financing of Terrorism", IMF Public Information Notice No. 04/33, 2 April 2004.

100. "Financial Action Task Force on Money Laundering: The Forty Recommendations", Paris, FATF, 20 June 2003, at Introduction. Reproduced at Appendix III.

101. Ibid.

102. Report XIV, *supra*, note 11, p. 22.

CHAPTER VII – PAN-EUROPEAN RESPONSES TO MONEY LAUNDERING

The context

Although, as will be seen in chapter VIII, the member states of the European Union have sought to promote enhanced co-operation in criminal law matters for some time, the leading role within the European region in this area has traditionally been played by the Strasbourg-based Council of Europe. Established in 1949, its "principal aims are to promote European unity, foster social and economic progress and protect human rights".[1] Its membership was, until the early 1990s, limited to the countries of western Europe (including for this purpose, both Iceland and Turkey). However, with the demise of communist rule and the end of the cold war it played a key role in reaching out to embrace the countries of central and eastern Europe. The overwhelming majority of these new democracies have now obtained full membership. Importantly, the Russian Federation was admitted to this grouping in 1996. As the Secretary General of the Council of Europe remarked: "The recent member states have varied backgrounds: some lived under dictatorship for more than forty years, others for over seventy years; some had previously experienced democracy, while others never had; and some had never existed before as an independent state."[2] This process has now extended to cover such states as Armenia, Azerbaijan and Georgia as well as the post-conflict Balkan nations (most recently Bosnia and Herzegovina, and Serbia and Montenegro). It is now a truly pan-European organisation.

The Council of Europe has, for many years, afforded a high priority to activities in the legal sphere.[3] Its efforts to promote the modernisation of the law and closer co-operation between its members have resulted in the conclusion of an extensive network of treaties and conventions. Some of these relate to specific crimes of concern while others promote a broad range of forms of international co-operation. Recent areas of focus have included "cybercrime", and corruption. The latter instruments are closely tied to an ambitious agreement, concluded in 1998, which established the Group of States Against Corruption (Greco) which has a critical role in monitoring compliance with commitments made by member states in what is an increasingly important area of interest.[4]

Among the most significant achievements of the Council of Europe in facilitating international co-operation in criminal matters has been the elaboration of two multilateral conventions which have come to be regarded as the central pillars of European co-operative efforts to combat crime; namely the 1957 European Convention on Extradition, and the 1959 European Convention on Mutual Assistance in Criminal Matters.[5] The former, which emerged from intensive diplomatic negotiations in the early 1950s, sets out in detail provisions governing all aspects of extradition law and practice which were then thought to be of importance. By early 2004 it had been ratified by forty-three member states including all but one of the new members from central and eastern Europe. The 1959 instrument, which represented the first major breakthrough in fostering this highly practical form of co-operation at the multilateral level and has proved to be highly influential elsewhere, has been nearly as popular since its entry into force in 1962. Yet again, there is now significant participation by the new member states.

In the years since these texts were agreed, the Council of Europe has both monitored their implementation and sought to improve upon their effectiveness in practice. This has been done, in part, through a series of recommendations issued by the Committee of Ministers. Such recommendations "although lacking any direct binding effect under international law, are of great value in applying and interpreting the conventions ...".[6] In addition, this process of monitoring and review has resulted in the conclusion of two modernising protocols to the 1957 European Convention on Extradition and two which relate to the operation of the 1959 text. The process continues.

It was thus within a well-established tradition of awareness of the importance of the transnational dimension to effective crime control that the Council of Europe became, in 1977, the first international organisation to focus, in a systematic manner, on the problem of money laundering.

Money laundering initiatives

The context

Concerned over the growing number of acts of criminal violence such as kidnapping, the Council of Europe's European Committee on Crime Problems (CDCP) decided, in 1977, to establish a select committee of experts to examine various aspects of this issue. As the first phase of the exercise, the select committee was directed to focus on "the serious problems raised in many countries by the illicit transfer of funds of criminal origin frequently used for the perpetration of further crime".[7] This set in train a process of study and deliberation which was to conclude with the adoption by the Committee of Ministers, on 27 June 1980, of a formal recommendation on measures against the transfer and safekeeping of funds of criminal origin.

It is of interest to note that this recommendation fully embraces the philosophy of prevention so central to the programme of countermeasures subsequently adopted by the FATF. This stance flowed from the conviction that "the banking system can play a highly effective preventive role, while the co-operation of the banks also assists in the repression of such criminal acts by the judicial authorities and the police".[8] Within the package of measures which was recommended for consideration, particular emphasis was placed on the "know your customer" rule. It was felt that all private and public banks should "as a minimum" undertake identity checks on customers whenever "an account or securities deposit is opened; safe deposits are rented; cash transactions involving sums of a certain magnitude are effected, bearing in mind the possibility of transactions in several parts; interbank transfers involving sums of a certain magnitude are made, bearing in mind the possibility of transactions in several parts".[9] In spite of the fact that these and certain other recommended measures, such as staff training, are now generally regarded as central aspects of any comprehensive anti-money laundering programme, the 1980 initiative failed to find a receptive audience and was not widely implemented. As Nilsson has observed, "[t]he Council of Europe was probably ahead of its time ...".[10]

In the years which followed, work on the confiscation of the proceeds of drug trafficking was carried out under the auspices of the so-called "Pompidou Group". Formed in 1971 at the suggestion of the then President of the French Republic, the Co-operation Group to Combat Drug Abuse and Illicit Trafficking in Drugs, to use its formal title, has, from 1980, operated under the umbrella of the Council of Europe.[11]

A further impetus for progress was provided by European ministers of justice in 1986 when it was decided to request that the European Committee on Crime Problems undertake the formulation "in the light *inter alia* of the work of the United Nations, of international norms and standards to guarantee effective international co-operation between judicial (and where necessary police) authorities as regards the detection, freezing and forfeiture of the proceeds of illicit drug trafficking".[12] It, in turn, established in 1987 a select committee of experts which enjoyed fairly wide terms of reference. In particular, it was not obliged to restrict its focus to the proceeds derived from drug trafficking alone.

The 1990 Council of Europe convention

The select committee, which initially consisted of experts drawn from sixteen member states, was chaired by Mr G Polimeni of Italy. Interestingly, the committee also had the benefit of the direct participation of, among others, Australia, Canada, the United States, and the Commission of the European Communities. Its work was to culminate, in September 1990, in the adoption by ministers of a new Convention on Laundering, Search, Seizure and Confiscation of the Proceeds from Crime. It was opened for signature in

Strasbourg that November and entered into force in September 1993. While the initial pace of ratification was somewhat disappointing, recent years have witnessed a significant upsurge of activity. Consequently by early 2004, forty-four states had become parties. It is hoped in Strasbourg that it will eventually count among the participants a broad cross-section of non-member and, indeed, non-European states. As Hans Nilsson, the secretary to the committee of experts, explained: "In order to encourage worldwide cooperation in combating money laundering, the convention does not use the word European in its title. This reflects the drafters' opinion that the instrument should from the outset be open to like-minded states outside the framework of the Council of Europe."[13] Australia and Monaco are the only non-members to have taken this step to date.

In the preparation of the convention, the committee was anxious to ensure that its activities and product were sensitive to and complemented already existing Council of Europe conventions in the penal field. Following an examination of the relevant law and practice, the decision was taken that the new instrument would seek:

> ... to provide a complete set of rules, covering all the stages of the procedure from the first investigations to the imposition and enforcement of confiscation sentences and to allow for flexible but effective mechanisms of international co-operation to the widest extent possible in order to deprive criminals of the instruments and fruits of their illegal activity.[14]

It was primarily for this reason that the resulting text is one of considerable length and complexity. It is, however, limited in its ambition in the sense that it is, in contrast to the 1980 recommendation (see above), essentially an international criminal law agreement. It does not, therefore, include comprehensive measures intended to enhance the role of the private sector in preventing money laundering activities.

A second major concern of the drafters was to protect the advances which had so recently been secured by the 1988 UN (drug trafficking) convention. As the official explanatory report noted:

> The relevant provisions of the United Nations Convention were constantly taken into consideration: on the one hand, the experts tried as far as possible to use the terminology and the systematic approach of that convention unless changes were felt necessary for improving different solutions; on the other hand, the experts also explored the possibilities of introducing in the Council of Europe instrument stricter obligations than those of the United Nations Convention on the understanding that the new Convention – in spite of the fact that it is open to other States than the member states of the Council of Europe – will operate in the context of a smaller community of like-minded states.[15]

By way of illustration, the basic definition of the crime of money laundering, contained in Article 6(1) of the 1990 Council of Europe text, is based on that used in Article 3 of the1988 UN convention.

However, Article 6 also provides a clear example of the willingness of the Council of Europe to go beyond the 1988 precedent. Its greater ambition is revealed in a number of different ways. First, and most importantly, the obligation to criminalise money laundering is not restricted to drug trafficking offences. Instead it extends to any predicate offence. This approach under-lies the 1990 convention as a whole. As has been pointed out elsewhere:

> One of the purposes of the Convention is to facilitate international co-operation as regards investigative assistance, search, seizure and confiscation of the proceeds from all types of criminality, especially serious crimes, and in particular drug offences, arms dealing, terrorist offences, trafficking in children and young women ... and other offences which generate large profits.[16]

It was not felt, however, that the point had yet been reached where it would be appropriate to impose an absolute obligation to have in place domestic legislation on an all-crimes basis. For this reason, it was decided to permit the formulation of reservations as to scope. This element of flexibility is provided by Article 6(4) which reads:

> Each Party may, at the time of signature or when depositing its instrument of rat-ification, acceptance, approval or accession, by declaration addressed to the Secretary General of the Council of Europe declare that paragraph 1 of this article applies only to predicate offences or categories of such offences specified in such declaration.

Taken as a whole, the approach adopted may best be regarded as an implicit invitation for domestic money laundering legislation to be as broad in scope as possible. This interpretation is supported by the drafting history of this provision and also that of Article 2 which deals with confiscation of proceeds and which gives expression to the same philosophy. For example, the committee of experts agreed that states which took advantage of the reservations facility in the latter context "should review their legislation periodically and expand the applicability of confiscation measures, in order to be able to restrict the reservations subsequently as much as possible. They also agreed that such measures should at least be made applicable to serious criminality and to offences which generate huge profits".[17]

While the expansion of the definition of money laundering beyond its 1988 association with drug trafficking had no precedent in a binding international agreement, it was a development which was not, even in 1990, unexpected. For example, it was a proposal which, as was seen in chapter IV, had attracted the cautiously worded support of the FATF in the fifth of the Forty Recommendations contained in its February 1990 report. Furthermore, it had support in the legislative practice of a small minority of countries including Switzerland. Article 305 (*bis*) of its Penal Code, which came into effect on 1 August 1990 (the month before the convention was adopted by the Council of Europe Committee of Ministers), rendered money laundering in respect of all forms of crime a criminal offence.

After 1990 a firm trend emerged in favour of decoupling money laundering from drug trafficking and this was, as noted earlier in the study, increasingly reflected in domestic legislation elsewhere. Indeed, many of the parties have declined to avail themselves of this limiting facility. These ranged from Belgium to Croatia; and Slovenia to Australia. One of the early participants which took advantage of Article 6(4) was the United Kingdom. It elected (as an interim measure) to restrict money laundering "to offences the commission of which constitutes drug trafficking as defined in its domestic legislation". The explanation for the British position was primarily historical in that its original (and pioneering) legislation, passed in 1986 and 1987, was confined to drug trafficking. Since that time, however, its scope has been progressively expanded. Initially this was done to include proceeds relating to terrorist activities. This was followed by a further extension to cover the proceeds of all serious crimes.[18] As a consequence, the UK was able to withdraw this reservation on 1 September 1995. It is also of relevance to note that some recent conventions on particular crimes of international concern elaborated under the auspices of the Council of Europe have contained specific provisions on the criminalisation of money laundering within the meaning of Article 6 of the 1990 text. This stance was, for instance, adopted in its 1999 Criminal Law Convention on Corruption.[19]

This strong trend away from drug-related definitions of money laundering mirrors a near consensus among commentators and practitioners concerning the practical and policy disadvantages of the narrow approach. As the UN secretariat has stated:

> The international community, through the adoption of the 1988 Convention, has expressed its universal abhorrence of drug-related money laundering. However ... there would seem to be little policy justification for the proscription of money laundering arising from some profit-generating criminal activities and not others. Double standards, particularly in criminal law, are not conducive to the maintenance of the rule of law or to international cooperation, and there may be difficulties in proving that particular proceeds are attributable to particular predicate offences. In any event, drug trafficking may not remain – or for that matter still be – the most profitable form of transborder criminal activity.[20]

The extension of money laundering beyond the narcotics predicate is not, however, the sole difference in approach contained in the Council of Europe instrument as compared to the 1988 UN drug trafficking convention. One clear improvement is the manner in which it treats the question of jurisdiction in circumstances in which the predicate offence was committed extraterritorially. Given the transnational nature of many sophisticated money laundering operations it is of great significance for the effective functioning of international co-operation that a state be in a position to prosecute an individual for involvement in such activities in its jurisdiction even when the underlying criminal activity (the "predicate offence") which generated the proceeds in question took place elsewhere. For this reason it was unfortunate that the 1988 UN convention did not specifically require its parties to adopt legislative provisions in this area with such an extraterritorial reach. By way of contrast, Article 6(2)(a) in the 1990 Council of Europe convention stipulates that for the purposes of implementing and applying the substantive provisions "it shall not matter whether the predicate offence was subject to the criminal jurisdiction of the Party". Specific provision to this effect has been included in the legislation of numerous participating countries, including the UK.

Also worthy of note is the fact that Article 6(3) of the 1990 convention permits, but does not require, the criminalisation of certain acts, including negligent laundering, in addition to those contained in the 1988 UN text. Such an approach to negligent behaviour in this context is compatible with Recommendation 2 of the FATF Forty Recommendations and finds expression in the domestic legislation of a number of European countries.

In addition to Article 6 on money laundering, Chapter II of the 1990 Council of Europe convention, which addresses the measures to be taken by participating states at the national level, contains a number of interesting and innovative provisions. Thus, Article 2 imposes "a positive obligation for states to enact legislation which would enable them to confiscate instrumentalities and proceeds".[21] As with money laundering, this is done on an all crimes basis while holding out the possibility of formulating a reservation as to the categories of offences covered. For instance, the Netherlands has acted to remove the proceeds of taxation and customs and excise offences from the scope of the confiscation obligation, while Ireland took steps to ensure that Article 2(1) applied only "to drug trafficking offences as defined in its domestic legislation and other offences triable on indictment". In so far as the United Kingdom is concerned, a reservation was inserted in the 1992 instrument of ratification to restrict the obligation as it applied to Scotland to drug trafficking. This reflected the fact that in Scotland, which enjoys a separate legal system and legal tradition from that of England and Wales, there was at that time no legislation in place similar to that of the Criminal Justice Act 1988 which extended confiscation in respect of other serious offences to England and Wales. However, in September 1994 the Scottish Law Commission produced a report on confiscation and forfeiture containing proposals intended to update the law.[22] The process culminated with the enactment of legislation in 1995 which introduced a confiscation regime for the proceeds of crime more generally. Notwithstanding this fact, significant delays in putting in place the necessary technical and detailed arrangements in relation to the enforcement of external confiscation orders prevented the UK from withdrawing this reservation in a timely fashion. Indeed, it was not until September 1999 that it was able to take this step.

As with money laundering, subsequent treaty practice within the Council of Europe has sought to extend the scope of the confiscation obligation. In the course of 1998, for example, new multilateral instruments dealing with corruption[23] and the protection of the environment through criminal law[24] adopted this stance.

States parties must also be able to identify and trace property liable to confiscation and to take appropriate provisional measures to ensure that the property in question cannot be dissipated before a final confiscation order is made and implemented. In an approach similar to that used in the 1988 UN convention, Article 4(1) requires appropriate steps to be taken to facilitate access to banking, financial and commercial records. It stipulates that: "A Party shall not decline to act under the provisions of this article on grounds of bank secrecy." Finally, for present purposes, it is of interest to note that parties are to consider the domestic adoption of a number of special investigative techniques "which are common practice in some states but which are not yet implemented in other states".[25] Specifically mentioned in Article 4(2) are monitoring orders, observation, interception of telecommunications, access to computer systems, and orders to produce specific documents. However, it is clear that this list was not intended to be exhaustive. The permissive wording used is sufficiently flexible to encompass other investigative tools which commend themselves to the law enforcement community because of their utility in this new and complex sphere of policing.

This would include, for example, the investigative technique, frequently used in drug trafficking cases, known as "controlled delivery". In that context the "procedure involves allowing a delivery of illicit drugs, once detected, to proceed, under constant and secret surveillance, to the ultimate destination envisaged by the traffickers".[26] The purpose is to allow the investigation to proceed in order to maximise the possibility of identifying the principals in the criminal scheme rather than merely those with a lower level involvement such as drug couriers. The 1988 UN convention and the 1990 Schengen Convention, among others, contain provisions to pave the way for the use of this technique at the international level. The potential of controlled delivery to contribute positively to the outcome of money laundering investigations has been studied by the FATF. In the course of the 1992-93 round, the conclusion was reached that controlled delivery operations should be encouraged and that appropriate steps should be taken to remove legal impediments to its use both domestically and internationally. The Task Force experts felt that the technique had an even greater use in money laundering cases than those involving trafficking in drugs. As the original interpretive note explained:

> In the latter, it is easy to establish if the substances are illegal. However, it may not be readily apparent whether or not particular funds are the proceeds of crime. Further investigations are generally necessary to determine this and controlled delivery is a very effective method in this context. Even where it is clear that funds are of criminal origin, a controlled delivery operation … can be of great value in helping to identify and gather evidence against as many as possible of the criminals involved. In particular, it offers a route to the higher level criminals and the beneficial owners of the funds.[27]

It was no surprise therefore that in the course of the stocktaking exercise of the mid-1990s within the FATF, which was discussed in chapter IV, it was agreed to amend Recommendation 36 "so as to give greater recognition to the benefits of such a technique, and to encourage countries to support its use, where possible".[28] Interestingly, the many abstract advantages of controlled delivery have only infrequently been manifested in practice in a money laundering context and, perhaps for this reason, the 2003 revised recommendations and interpretative notes pay significantly less attention to it.[29]

The drafters of the 1990 Council of Europe convention anticipated that any new law enforcement techniques made available in domestic law could also be used to further the process of international co-operation. It is to the removal of obstacles to such co-operation that the numerous provisions of chapter III of the convention are directed. In the words of Article 7:

> 1. The Parties shall co-operate with each other to the widest extent possible for the purposes of investigations and proceedings aiming at the confiscation of instrumentalities and proceeds.
>
> 2. Each Party shall adopt such legislative or other measures as may be necessary to enable it to comply, under the conditions provided for in this chapter, with requests:
>
> > a. for confiscation of specific items of property representing proceeds or instrumentalities, as well as for confiscation of proceeds consisting in a requirement to pay a sum of money corresponding to the value of proceeds;
> >
> > b. for investigative assistance and provisional measures with a view to either form of confiscation referred to under a. above.

In order to give effect to these general principles and measures of international co-operation, subsequent provisions establish, in some detail, the necessary rules and procedures. Separate sections are devoted to investigative assistance, provisional measures, confiscation, refusal and postponement of co-operation, notification and protection of third parties' rights, and procedural and other general rules. In certain respects this scheme seeks merely to reflect established and accepted forms of best practice. In other areas, however, the text seeks to improve upon and extend the co-operative mechanisms embodied in pre-existing international agreements.

By way of illustration, a number of innovations were included to assist the law enforcement authorities in their investigative tasks. Thus, Article 8 of the 1990 Council of Europe convention, which requires that parties afford each other "the widest measure of assistance" at the investigative stage, goes further than the 1959 Council of Europe Convention on Mutual Assistance in Criminal Matters. As the secretary to the committee of experts noted: "The paragraph is to be interpreted broadly. It allows for police cooperation that does not involve coercive action."[30] Police-to-police contact is also facilitated by other provisions. For instance, Article 24 permits direct contact between such competent authorities internationally when no use of coercive authority is contemplated. Perhaps more importantly, Article 10 permits the spontaneous provision of information relating to instrumentalities and proceeds in circumstances where it is felt that this might be of practical assistance to the authorities of another participating state. This was one of the first occasions in which a multilateral convention on criminal matters had specifically contemplated the provision of assistance without a prior request to do so.[31]

A further area, and one of crucial importance, where progress was achieved by the drafters is that of international co-operation in the confiscation of the proceeds of crime. As was seen in chapter III, one source of difficulty under the 1988 UN convention arises out of the failure of the international community to impose a single mandatory approach to confiscation. Instead, it gives recognition to both the property and value confiscation systems which had been used in pre-existing domestic legislation. The Council of Europe text does likewise but goes further in requiring, in Article 7(2)(a), that each participating state be in a position to respond to both types of request. As has been pointed out elsewhere, "if a state applies only the system of property confiscation of proceeds, it will need to take such legislative measures as would enable it to grant a request from a state that uses value confiscation".[32] In this and other provisions,[33] the drafters were able to place both systems on an equal footing.[34]

As with the 1988 precedent, the Council of Europe convention recognises two basic options in giving effect to international confiscation assistance: namely, either to seek a domestic order or to give direct effect to an order made by the competent authorities of the requesting state.[35] In such cases, it is necessary to focus on the status to be accorded to a final judicial order issued in the requesting state. Although it remains untreated in the 1988 UN convention, the committee of experts considered it to be of crucial importance to resolve the issue specifically and in a manner which placed confidence in the standards of justice prevailing in the foreign country.[36] Article 14(2) accordingly provides: "The requested Party shall be bound by the findings as to the facts in so far as they are stated in a conviction or judicial decision of the requesting Party or in so far as such conviction or judicial decision is implicitly based on them."

Here, the courts of the requested state cannot make an independent assessment of the evidence. This does not, however, apply to the legal consequences which flow from such facts, or to the hearing of new evidence if such was not available for some valid reason in the original hearings.[37]

A further issue of concern to the drafters was how most appropriately to accommodate the differences which had evolved in national legal systems. Particular problems arise when states resort to forms of confiscation which are not based on a prior conviction for a relevant criminal offence. For example, in the United States at the time of the negotiations (and thereafter) much of the emphasis in practice has been on civil, *in rem*, procedures.[38] It is of relevance to note that in recent years both the Republic of Ireland[39] and the United Kingdom[40] have also firmly embraced the concept of civil asset recovery. The majority of international instruments concluded to date, however, either explicitly or implicitly require a criminal conviction to trigger confiscation. A similar requirement is also evident in the domestic legislation of a significant number of states. In the view of the committee of experts there was an obvious need for an added element of flexibility in addressing this issue. Thus, in discussing the obligation to confiscate at the request of another party, contained in Article 13, the official explanatory report states: "Any type of proceedings, independently of their relationship with criminal proceedings and of applicable procedural rules, might qualify in so far as they may result in a confiscation order, provided that they are carried out by judicial authorities and that they are criminal in nature, that is, that they concern instrumentalities or proceeds."[41] Action on the basis of purely administrative procedures is, however, not covered by the terms of the 1990 text.

These were but some of the innovative features contained in an agreement which, in many respects, reflected the state of the art in what was, in 1990, a new area of international concern. In the ensuing years it has come to occupy a prominent place in anti-money laundering policy discussions and political declarations both in Europe and beyond. In the latter context the significance attached to it is well illustrated by the fact that Recommendation 35 of the FATF package of countermeasures makes specific reference to it in formulating general encouragement to states to ratify and implement relevant international conventions on money laundering. The reasons for such treatment are not hard to identify. As we have seen, its general approach is entirely consistent with the philosophy of the Task Force. Indeed, many of its specific provisions act to reinforce, in treaty form, the measures designed to enhance the role of national legal systems and to strengthen international co-operation.

In Europe, however, it has come to be regarded as a critical element in the fashioning of an effective stance against profit-generating crimes of international concern. Thus securing the broadest possible geographic participation emerged in the 1990s as an important goal. This can be illustrated by two developments in 1997. In June, European ministers of justice, meeting in Prague, examined the links between organised crime and corruption. The first substantive provision of the resolution which emerged from their deliberations was to call for the speedy ratification of Council of Europe instruments on international co-operation in criminal matters and, in particular, of the 1990 convention. The priority thus afforded to the 1990 text was further underlined by the heads of state and government of the member states of the Council of Europe at their second summit which was held in Strasbourg in October 1997. In that part of the resulting action plan devoted to fighting corruption and organised crime, they also called upon all states to ratify the 1990 convention.

A similar importance has been afforded to the 1990 convention by the European Union. For instance, in the 1997 action plan to combat organised crime it was included as one of a limited number of multilateral conventions regarded as "essential to the fight against organised crime ...".[42] Similarly, in the 1998 Pre-Accession Pact on Organised Crime between the member states of the EU and the applicant countries of central Europe and Cyprus, agreement was obtained from the latter, as recorded in Principle 2, to adopt and implement the 1990 Council of Europe convention, among others, as soon as possible.

The protocol process

Notwithstanding what has been said above, it should not be thought that the 1990 convention is a totally comprehensive let alone perfect instrument. For example, it does not impose an obligation to ensure that corporations and other legal persons can be held liable for money laundering. In this regard, it contents itself, in Article 18(8), with provisions which seek to minimise the possibility of international co-operation being refused on the basis that the request arises out of investigations or proceedings in relation to such legal persons. It will be recalled that the concept of corporate criminal liability poses particular difficulties for states from the civil law tradition. However, some movement towards the wider acceptance of it (most recently in Poland) can be identified in state practice. Furthermore, it has become common for modern treaties in the criminal justice sphere to directly address the subject of corporate liability; a practice well illustrated by Article 12 of the 2001 Council of Europe Convention on Cybercrime which permits such liability to be criminal, civil or administrative.

Similarly, the gradual extension, outlined above, of money laundering and confiscation legislation from the initial focus on drug trafficking to a much broader range of predicate offences has conspired to call into question the adequacy of the approach adopted by the drafters to the important question of the final disposition of confiscated proceeds in international cases. At present Article 15, following the precedent set in the 1988 UN convention in the context of "victimless" drug crimes, simply provides that this matter is to be dealt with in accordance with the domestic law of the country where the confiscation is, in fact, effected. Disquiet over this stance became evident at a major Council of Europe gathering in Strasbourg in late 1994 which examined the problem of money laundering in the states of central and eastern Europe. There, delegates from the participating states approved the recommendation in the report of the General Rapporteur, Mr L-O Broch of Norway, that the Council of Europe assess the possibility of drafting a protocol which would have the effect of facilitating the return of confiscated proceeds, in certain cases such as the theft of property in the course of the privatisation process, to the jurisdiction where the predicate offence was committed.[43]

The case for the establishment of a mechanism to review the adequacy of the treatment of such issues, among others, was strengthened by the fact that updating measures have been taken by the FATF in relation to its package of countermeasures and, as will be seen in the following chapter, a similar process has also been concluded in respect of the 1991 EC money laundering directive. Perhaps even more compelling is the fact that, as will be seen in some detail at a later stage of this book, on 3 December 1998 the member states of the European Union adopted a Joint Action with the primary intention of enhancing the operation of the 1990 Council of Europe convention in their mutual relations.

Support for such a modernising initiative emerged in the second half of the 1990s within the context of the Council of Europe itself. At a general level, the 21st Conference of European Ministers of Justice, meeting in Prague in June 1997, requested the European Committee on Crime Problems (CDPC) "to submit proposals on the possible review and update of the existing conventions in the field of international cooperation in criminal matters, in order to take due account of the new demands to combat organised crime and corruption". In November of 1998 a high-level multilateral meeting held in Strasbourg on pan-European co-operation in the fight against organised crime and corruption concluded that the 1990 convention "should be reinforced with new provisions to facilitate the conducting of enquiries and confiscation of unlawful proceeds at international level, with the help of measures such as the elimination of tax havens and offshore zones, the lifting of bank secrecy or the sharing of confiscated assets".[44]

However, the question of whether an updating protocol to the 1990 text should be formulated remained somewhat contentious. Some expressed the view that practical experience of its operation has not yet been sufficient to permit conclusions to be drawn as to its adequacy and that, consequently, it would be premature to undertake a modernising initiative of this type. Many others, however, felt that only if the convention provisions were updated and its scope supplemented would it be able, in fact, to fully satisfy its potential in the efforts to combat profit-generating crime. Given these differences in view, "a questionnaire-based enquiry was conducted on the subject in 2000. It emerged from this enquiry that a clear majority of states were in support of an early opening of negotiations on a protocol to the convention".[45]

In the light of this outcome, the CDPC established a reflection group (PC-S-ML) in June 2001 under the chairmanship of Mr J-F Thony of France. It was entrusted with:

- taking stock of the experience of the parties to the Convention in implementing it, in particular with respect to the criminalisation of money laundering in domestic law and its prosecution in practice; the use of provisional measures and confiscation in practice; the channels and types of assistance used or needed in international co-operation related to money laundering or to confiscation cases; the structures, competence and training of national authorities dealing with confiscation;

- identifying specifically the problems that need to be addressed in the above-mentioned areas and explore issues arising out of recent developments;

- making concrete suggestions to the CDPC on possible solutions.[46]

In its deliberations, the Thony Committee considered a wide range of options but in the end advised that a comprehensive protocol be negotiated.[47] Among its core recommendations was that the new instrument should contain enhanced provisions on the disposition of confiscated proceeds (including asset sharing and restitution) and the management of seized assets and instrumentalities. It should also address the issue of corporate liability, incorporate treatment of FIUs, and (controversially) treat both the financing of terrorism and preventive measures.

After a further period of discussion, the CDPC agreed to establish the necessary mechanism. This takes the form of a committee of experts (PC-RM) consisting of delegations from each state party, supplemented by a range of other representatives and observers. It met for the first time in December 2003 and is expected to complete its work in late 2004 or early in the following year. Its terms of reference call upon it to draw up an additional protocol to the 1990 text, "in order to update it and complement it as necessary". However, the PC-RM was instructed to give priority consideration to the advisability of including preventive measures and the feasibility of treating the funding of terrorism. It subsequently reported to the CDPC on these matters, in March 2004, when the final decision was taken to permit contextual coverage of these matters to be further considered for protocol inclusion. This decision was, at the time of writing, subject to confirmation by the Committee of Ministers.

Mutual evaluation

From what has been said above, it is clear why in the years following its conclusion the 1990 Council of Europe convention was so positively viewed by both governments and commentators.[48] However, it was appreciated within the Council of Europe from the outset that it would achieve its full potential only if it were both widely adopted and effectively implemented by the countries of Europe.

In this regard it should be noted that the 1990 convention does not contain specific provision for the creation of any mechanism through which the manner and quality of the implementation of its obligations by participating countries could be subject to periodic review. Something of a functional equivalent did, however, exist for the European members of the FATF. This, as described in some detail in the previous chapter, takes the form of the self-assessment and mutual evaluation procedures designed to test compliance with the Forty Recommendations. Given the limited membership of the FATF, this did not extend to numerous member countries of the Council of Europe, including the new democracies of central and eastern Europe. A further cause for concern arose out of the fact that the 1990 convention does not reach out to embrace the important preventive aspects of the anti-laundering strategy articulated by the FATF. As will be seen in chapter VIII, the great majority of the relevant recommendations in this sphere have obtained concrete expression for the states of the European Union in the form of the 1991 money laundering directive (as amended). Notwithstanding the efforts of the European Commission and the Council of the EU to extend the geographic impact of that measure, there have remained important gaps in its coverage.

From as early as 1991, the external relations activities of the FATF came to focus on the extent to which the states of central and eastern Europe, in particular, were willing to introduce comprehensive money laundering countermeasures. This attention was not, in the first instance, dictated by their importance in the global money laundering process. Rather, it flowed from the identification of both the problems and opportunities presented by the transition from state control to market economies in the aftermath of the collapse of communist rule. As the FATF report of 25 June 1992 was to note:

> … as the economies of these countries become more integrated into the world financial system and their currencies move to convertibility, they will become attractive to money launderers. At the same time, the reform and restructuring of the Eastern European financial sector presents an ideal opportunity for these states to take measures which would help them to protect themselves against money laundering.[49]

In its first direct contact with the region, the FATF steering group held discussions with representatives from Hungary, Poland and Czechoslovakia (as it then was) in Paris during the third round.[50] An opportunity to build upon and extend this dialogue was provided by a major conference on money laundering which was convened by the Council of Europe in Strasbourg in late September 1992. The FATF President and other representatives of the group addressed a number of the formal sessions of this gathering. They also took the opportunity to hold "meetings with delegates from most central and eastern European countries to find out more about the money laundering situations within these countries and discuss how the FATF might assist them".[51] These contacts, in turn, paved the way for the Task Force to arrange two specialist seminars in the region (at Budapest and Warsaw) early the following year. A further such meeting was convened in Moscow in November 1993.[52] This engagement was subsequently continued and, indeed, extended.[53]

Such developments were critical in paving the way for an unprecedented initiative within the Council of Europe to introduce a highly intrusive system of peer review based on the FATF model. As has been pointed out elsewhere:

> In September 1997, the Committee of Ministers of the Council of Europe established a Select Committee (PC-R-EV) to conduct self and mutual assessment exercises of the anti-money laundering measures in place in … Council of Europe countries, which are not members of the Financial Action Task Force (FATF). The PC-R-EV takes into account the practices and procedures of the FATF in its work. The PC-R-EV is a sub-committee of the European Committee on Crime Problems of the Council of Europe (CDPC).[54]

This grouping was subsequently renamed as MONEYVAL.

The relationship between this Council of Europe procedure and the Paris-based FATF is intended to be particularly intense. This is well illustrated by the fact that full membership of MONEYVAL has been extended to the past and current presidencies of the FATF. In addition, observer status has been accorded to other members of the FATF as well as to its secretariat. Furthermmore, the terms of reference for MONEYVAL call upon it to structure its key activities "taking into account the procedures and practices used by the FATF". Finally, for present purposes, the secretariat of MONEYVAL is increasingly involved in participation in the activities of the Task Force.

It should not be thought, however, that this Council of Europe committee is but a mirror of a "parent" body. FATF precedents have not been slavishly followed. Indeed, in some respects the Council of Europe exercise is more ambitious and exacting. Of special significance in this context is the fact that the process of self-assessment and mutual evaluation is undertaken against a more extensive set of anti-laundering standards. Thus, in addition to the Forty Recommendations and the eight Special Recommendations on the Financing of Terrorism, participating countries are assessed in relation to their compliance with the 1988 UN and 1990 Council of Europe conventions, and both of the EU directives.

Another significant difference in approach relates to the self-assessment exercise. Though the importance of this dimension of the monitoring system is acknowledged, the decision has been taken not to have resort to it with the same frequency. However, a broadly similar purpose is served by the MONEYVAL system under which all members report back to a plenary meeting one year after being subject to mutual evaluation on the progress made towards implementation of the recommendations contained therein.[55] Also worthy of mention is the fact that while the Strasbourg Committee has a graduated strategy available for use in respect of non-compliance, it is not identical to that used by the Task Force in Paris. Thus members cannot be suspended, though the Recommendation 21 procedure for "special attention" to relationships and transactions may be applied.[56]

MONEYVAL held its first plenary meeting in December 1997 at which it paved the way for the first round of mutual evaluations to take place. This commenced in the following year with the on-site visit to Slovenia (the jurisdiction of the first chairperson of the group) and was brought to a conclusion with the mission to Albania in December 2000. Each team consisted of three experts drawn from the MONEYVAL membership who were joined by two colleagues drawn from the FATF. On each occasion, the resulting country reports were unanimously agreed by the examiners. While the reports remain confidential, an extensive summary is made public and posted on both the Council of Europe and FATF websites.[57]

At its January 2001 plenary, MONEYVAL decided that the teams used in the second round should include at least one FATF evaluator. This was put into effect when on-site visits, which focused on the effectiveness of national systems to combat money laundering, commenced later that year. The last of the second round reports was debated and adopted during 2004. At the time of writing, plans for a further evaluation round were at an advanced stage of preparation. It will include an emphasis on efforts to prevent the financing of terrorism – a subject area added to the MONEYVAL mandate in the wake of the events of 11 September 2001.[58] It has also been agreed that the teams will use the new "common methodology" which has been prepared by the IMF/World Bank and the FATF (with the participation of MONEYVAL and its secretariat).[59]

While the relationship between the Council of Europe select committee and the FATF has been an extremely close and constructive one, it has not been without its difficulties. This was particularly evident during the controversial NCCT process which was outlined in chapter VI. At its most obvious level, these strains flowed from the fact that two MONEYVAL members (the Russian Federation and Liechtenstein) were on the original blacklist; a fate subsequently shared by both Hungary and Ukraine. The depth of negative feeling was, however, exacerbated by a widespread disquiet over both the procedures used by the Task Force in the assessment of jurisdictions in this context and the standards to which non-members of that body were being held. In the latter context, there was particular concern that the NCCT criteria, while consistent with the Forty Recommendations as then formulated, went beyond those standards and thus imposed a higher benchmark of antici-pated achievement. Negative sentiment was reinforced by the failure of the FATF to afford any real priority in practice to its September 2001 decision to conduct a self-assessment exercise to gauge the extent to which its own membership complied with those standards.

It is not surprising therefore that the NCCT issue and the associated subject of relations with the Task Force came to be debated at length and with some frequency at plenary meetings in Strasbourg. Expressions of significant dis-content in this and other similar contexts have been acknowledged by the FATF. In the words of the June 2001 annual report:

> ... the FATF recognises that this effort has ... had the unintentional effect of straining the relationship between the FATF and the FATF-style regional bodies. The FATF has therefore discussed possible solutions to improve its relationships with the FATF-style regional bodies in the NCCT area. Possibilities include giving greater weight to the mutual evaluations conducted by FATF-style regional bodies when assessing potential NCCTs, provided the regional body takes into account the 25 NCCT criteria as part of its mutual evaluation process.[60]

This MONEYVAL decided to do; in essence, "deeming" the NCCT criteria to fall within its terms of reference. Consequently, the second round of evalu-ations incorporated this dimension.

More recently, the above strains and tensions have abated significantly as the Task Force, influenced by the IMF and the World Bank, has de-empha-sised coercive strategies. It is to be hoped that the relationship between these two important anti-money laundering bodies will, as a consequence, now be able to deepen and mature.

It will be apparent from what has been seen above that MONEYVAL has accomplished much in a relatively brief period of time. That it has been able to do so owes much to the leadership shown by the chair (which has been held by Slovenia and Malta) and its bureau. It has also been fortunate in having excellent support from its (very) small secretariat. It is well positioned to build upon these achievements as it enters its third round of evaluations if provided with the necessary human and financial resources to do so.

The human rights dimension

From what has been said earlier in the chapter it is clear that the 1990 con-vention, like other instruments designed to combat laundering and deprive criminals of their illicitly acquired profits, is highly intrusive in nature. This is especially so in relation to the imposition of obligations which impact directly on the domestic criminal justice system of each participating state. Thus, in addition to requiring a high level of international co-operation, in which considerable trust is placed in the standards of justice prevailing in other countries, the convention requires or permits radical changes in domestic criminal law.

In an area of concern such as this, where progress is very much driven by a law enforcement and criminal policy agenda, it is imperative to ensure that human rights and civil liberties issues are not lost sight of. As Dolle has remarked: "In the efforts to stamp out the canker presented by organised crime we have to be careful not to overreact and bend the rules so far that we contribute to the destruction of the very democratic values we are trying to protect."[61]

Such concerns are of particular centrality to instruments elaborated under the auspices of the Council of Europe which, in Article 3 of its Statute, makes respect for human rights a condition of membership. Furthermore, "[t]he importance of human rights is emphasised in several other provisions of the Statute, ... and Article 8 even provides that serious violations of human rights and fundamental freedoms are grounds for suspending or expelling a member state from the Council".[62]

It is clear from the record that Mr Polimeni and his colleagues on the committee of experts which drafted the 1990 convention were sensitive to the importance of striking an appropriate balance between the needs of crime suppression and international co-operation, on the one hand, and the rights of affected individuals, on the other. Such concerns are most clearly reflected in those provisions which seek to afford protection to the rights of *bona fide* third parties. That this is a highly practical rather than a merely theoretical issue is beyond doubt. As the official explanatory report has noted: "Practice has shown that criminals often use ostensible 'buyers' to acquire property. Relatives, wives, children or friends might be used as decoys. Nevertheless, the third parties might be persons who have a legitimate claim on property which has been subject to a confiscation order or a seizure."[63] In order to ensure that the latter group are adequately protected, Article 5 requires each party to the convention to have in its domestic law an effective set of legal remedies through which they can preserve their rights. The scope of this obligation has been officially described thus:

> The legal provisions required by this article should guarantee "effective" legal remedies for interested third parties. This implies that there should be a system where such parties, if known, are duly informed by the authorities of the possibilities to challenge decisions or measures taken, that such challenges may be made even if a confiscation order has already become enforceable, if the party

had no earlier opportunity to do so, that such remedies should allow for a hearing in court, that the interested party has the right to be assisted or represented by a lawyer and to present witnesses and other evidence, and that the party has a right to have the court decision reviewed.[64]

Having required such measures to be taken at the national level, the convention goes on to mandate complementary protection in cases involving international co-operation. In this regard, Article 21 addresses the issues of the serving of judicial documents on third parties affected by provisional measures and confiscation orders which have been taken or handed down abroad. The following article then sets out the general rule that a state which receives a request from another party will recognise any judicial decision which has been made regarding rights claimed by third parties. This does not apply, however, where the matter has not been considered in the requesting state. In such cases, the individual concerned has the right to invoke the protection of the law of the requested state. The general rule is subject to a number of exceptions which are specified in Article 22(2). For example, recognition of the foreign judicial decision may be refused in instances where "third parties did not have adequate opportunity to assert their rights".

The concern of the drafters of the convention extended beyond the protection of the interests of innocent third parties. This wider effort to promote a balance between the need for effective law enforcement and the protection of the rights of the individual is reflected in Article 18, which sets out a detailed and broad range of discretionary grounds for the refusal of requests for international co-operation. For example, co-operation may be declined where "the action sought would be contrary to the fundamental principles of the legal system of the requested Party". In the course of their deliberations, a number of examples were given by members of the expert committee of cases which might properly trigger this provision. These included, among others, "where the proceedings on which the request are based do not meet basic procedural requirements for the protection of human rights such as the ones contained in Articles 5 and 6 of the Convention for the Protection of Human Rights and Fundamental Freedoms".[65]

The committee of experts also took the opportunity afforded by the official explanatory report to signal its conviction that certain possible interpretations of convention articles which might raise human rights and civil liberties concerns were invalid. One such example, which had provoked lively debate and controversial litigation in the United States, related to the payment of legal fees by money launderers and others subsequently convicted of relevant offences for which confiscation is either permitted or required.[66] In the words of the explanatory report:

> The question has been raised, in relation to the United Nations Convention, whether it would be illegal for a lawyer's fees to be paid out of funds related to

a laundering offence. Some lawyers have even suggested that the United Nations Convention would, by its wording, make it criminal to hire a lawyer or accept a fee. In the view of the experts, the wording of the present Convention cannot be misinterpreted to that effect.[67]

Finally, it should be noted that the same commentary indicates that the provisions of the 1990 money laundering treaty, in so far as they impact on individuals, remain subject to the requirements of the European Convention on Human Rights (ECHR), which was opened for signature on 4 November 1950 and entered into force in September 1953.[68]

The Convention for the Protection of Human Rights and Fundamental Freedoms (short title, the European Convention on Human Rights, ECHR) has come to be viewed as the crowning achievement of the Council of Europe and was drafted with the intention of providing a system of collective guarantees for the protection of human rights in post-second world war Europe. The ECHR, together with a number of amending protocols concluded in later years, is primarily concerned with safeguarding a broad range of civil and political rights.[69] Relevant examples include the right to a fair and public hearing within a reasonable time by an independent and impartial tribunal established by law (Article 6), and the prohibition of retroactive criminal legislation (Article 7). Parties to the ECHR must, pursuant to Article 1, secure these rights for everyone within their jurisdiction and not merely, as with the traditional approach of international law, for foreign nationals.

In order to ensure that these important obligations are upheld in practice, the ECHR created machinery for the determination of violations which constituted, at that time, a near revolutionary precedent. Among other matters, it created the European Commission of Human Rights to determine the admissibility of complaints alleging violations, to undertake the tasks of fact finding and conciliation, and where no friendly settlement could be reached, to express a view as to whether the facts disclosed a violation of the Convention. In addition to contemplating orthodox interstate complaints, it also provided for the right of individual petition to the Commission, "provided that the state complained against has declared that it recognises the competence of the Commission to receive such petitions".[70] It is important to appreciate that, as with the orthodox approach in the international law of diplomatic protection, no such application can be entertained unless all domestic remedies have first been exhausted. An inability to satisfy this and other requirements relating to admissibility resulted, in practice, in a majority of applications failing to progress beyond this initial stage.

A further innovation of great significance was that the ECHR provided for the creation of a judicial body to supplement the process of political settlement available in the form of the Committee of Ministers. Known as the European Court of Human Rights, it was granted the power to hand down binding decisions concerning the interpretation and application of the Convention. This too constituted a departure from the cautious diplomatic traditions of the time and it was accordingly decided that the Court would have jurisdiction only as regards those states which had voluntarily accepted it by making a declaration to that effect under Article 46.

The intervening years have witnessed a major transformation in the way in which the states of Europe perceive both the ECHR and its control mechanisms. For example, it eventually became a *de facto* requirement of membership of the Council of Europe that a state be prepared both to become a party to the ECHR and accept the jurisdiction of the Court.[71] In addition, as Finnie noted in 1994, "there has again crystallised a convention that the acceptance of individual petitions is a condition of entry to the Council of Europe".[72] In practice, resort by aggrieved individuals to the Commission in Strasbourg became commonplace and the case load of the European Court of Human Rights soared. As the Office of the Registrar of the Court noted:

> ... the number of applications registered annually with the Commission increased from 404 in 1981 to 2,037 in 1993. By 1997 that figure had more than doubled (4,750). By 1997 the number of unregistered or provisional files opened each year in the Commission had risen to over 12,000. The Court's statistics reflected a similar story, with the number of cases referred annually rising from seven in 1981 to 52 in 1993 and 119 in 1997.[73]

Given these factors and the additional strains expected to arise out of the continuing expansion of membership, the decision was taken to streamline and modernise these ECHR procedures. Agreement on this important matter was reached and embodied in the terms of Protocol No. 11, which entered into force on 1 November 1998. While a detailed examination of the new structure brought about by the protocol lies beyond the scope of this work, it is important to note that it significantly alters the internal structure of the European Court of Human Rights, eliminates the Commission, and abolishes the adjudication role of the Committee of Ministers. In addition, it gives formal legal effect to certain of the practices and conventions which had evolved over the years. Particularly worthy of note in this context is the fact that "Protocol No. 11 made automatic the acceptance of both the right of individual petition and the compulsory jurisdiction of the court ...".[74]

The ease and immediacy with which an individual can invoke the protection of the rights set out in the ECHR differs from jurisdiction to jurisdiction. It depends, in large measure, on the approach which has been adopted nationally to the issue of the relevance of international legal obligations in domestic law. In many European countries, such as Germany, the process of approval of international treaties involves the legislature, with the result that their terms gain the force of law unless and until amended by a subsequent inconsistent statute. Individuals can therefore invoke the ECHR before their national courts in the same manner as purely domestic legal rights. A variant of this approach is found in the Netherlands. As Schermers has stated: "The Netherlands' government is not allowed to ratify any international treaty without parliamentary approval. Once it has been ratified the treaty becomes part of domestic law and has superior rank over all domestic legislation."[75]

By way of contrast, in the United Kingdom the executive branch of government exercises the treaty making power. International obligations contained in such instruments become part of domestic law only if subsequently incorporated by act of parliament. In the case of the ECHR no such statute was enacted until 1998. Consequently, the provisions of the ECHR could not be directly invoked by an aggrieved individual.[76]

A profound change in this regard was brought about when the 1998 Human Rights Act entered into force in the United Kingdom in October 2000. This measure, but part of an ambitious programme of constitutional reform initiated by the Labour government following its election in 1997, incorporates specific provisions of the ECHR and its protocols into UK law for the first time. Although this is accomplished in a manner which reflects the somewhat idiosyncratic nature of the constitution, including procedures and norms which attempt to reconcile this measure with the principle of the sovereignty of the Westminster parliament, it holds out the prospect of minimising the number of instances in which the UK is subject to adverse rulings from the Strasbourg Court.[77]

When faced with the need to formulate legislation in new fields such as money laundering and confiscation of proceeds, it has become common practice for governments and their advisers to seek guidance on what is acceptable by examining the text of the ECHR and its relevant protocols. Such an examination reveals that the Convention is not hostile to the needs of law enforcement. As Duffy has remarked: "Throughout the text of the Convention, provision is made for the legitimate policing and security needs of states. Powers of arrest, necessary interferences with privacy for investigative purposes, use of force – all were expressly recognised in the Convention's drafting."[78]

The outer limits of such provisions have been tested on a number of occasions with the result that there is also a fairly extensive jurisprudence to assist the legislative drafter. For example, of relevance in the present context are past decisions relating to Convention requirements in respect of such issues as the conduct of the criminal investigation, the use of preliminary or preventive measures, and the conduct of the eventual trial.[79] One area which has generated case-law of undoubted practical significance is the increasing resort to special investigative measures such as telephone interception and the use of undercover police agents. Cases emerging from the use of such techniques have required an examination of their consistency with various ECHR provisions including respect for privacy (Article 8) and the right to a fair trial (Article 6). In the 1992 case of *Ludi v. Switzerland,* the Court held that the use of telephone tapping in conjunction with the involvement of an undercover law enforcement agent was, in the *de facto* circumstances before it, consistent with the right to privacy.[80] However, in its June 1998 judgment in *Teixeira de Castro v. Portugal,* the Court set further limits on covert techniques. In holding that the deployment of police officers as *agents provocateurs* had resulted in a violation of the right to a fair trial it remarked:

> The use of undercover agents must be restricted and safeguards put in place even in cases concerning the fight against drug trafficking. While the rise in organised crime undoubtedly requires that appropriate measures be taken the right to a fair administration of justice nevertheless holds such a prominent place ... that it cannot be sacrificed for the sake of expediency. ... The public interest cannot justify the use of evidence obtained as a result of police incitement.[81]

Increasingly, the body of precedents is being enriched by individual petitions arising directly out of money laundering investigations or confiscation actions. One early example is provided by the September 1991 decision of the Commission on the admissibility of an application against the United Kingdom made by one Mr Nazir Chinoy.[82]

Mr Chinoy was wanted in the United States on a variety of criminal charges including drugs-related money laundering and a warrant was subsequently issued in England for his arrest with a view to his extradition. A vital element of the evidence adduced by the United States Government in the subsequent extradition proceedings took the form of tape recordings of telephone conversations made by US agents while Mr Chinoy was in France. It was alleged that these recordings had been made in violation of French law. Before the English courts it was argued, without success, that the evidence in question should be excluded.[83] Mr Chinoy then complained to the Commission alleging a violation of Article 8 of the ECHR (respect for his private life, home, family and correspondence). He also contended that "although his extradition was not unlawful under English law the lawfulness of his detention under Article 5 paragraph 1(f) of the Convention pending extradition was fundamentally tainted by virtue of the unlawfulness of the tape recordings under French law".[84]

The Commission, by a majority, disagreed and found the application to be manifestly ill-founded and hence inadmissible. In the course of its decision it remarked:

> The purpose of the extradition proceedings in which the United Kingdom authorities were involved was to further the international campaign against the drugs trade and the laundering of the proceeds of drug trafficking, and those proceedings were pursuant to the United Kingdom's international treaty obligations

(in this case to the United States of America). Moreover, while the unlawfulness alleged in respect of the recordings in the present case is, at least, in some doubt, the domestic courts clearly considered the evidence of the tapes and transcripts to be relevant. In these circumstances, the Commission finds that the use made by the United Kingdom authorities in the present case of the recordings of the applicant's conversations does not disclose any lack of respect for his private and family life, his home or his correspondence.[85]

Given its relative novelty, the jurisprudence under the ECHR relating to the confiscation of the proceeds of crime has developed only relatively recently and is not yet comprehensive in its coverage. Importantly, decisions of both the Commission[86] and the Court[87] in the early 1990s relating to Italian confiscation measures upheld their consistency with the right to property enshrined in Article 1 of Protocol No. 1. For example, in 1991 the Human Rights Commission held "that the confiscation of nearly all the property of a suspected member of the Camorra (including the property of his wife and children) pending his trial on mafia charges was compatible with the right to property ...".[88] In its 1994 judgment in the case of *Raimondo v. Italy*, the Court addressed a range of issues in the area of both seizure and confiscation. In the latter context, it made the following revealing statement:

> The Court is fully aware of the difficulties encountered by the Italian State in the fight against the mafia. As a result of its unlawful activities, in particular drug-trafficking, and its international connections, this "organisation" has an enormous turnover that is subsequently invested, *inter alia*, in the real property sector. Confiscation, which is designed to block these movements of suspect capital, is an effective and necessary weapon in the combat of this cancer. It therefore appears proportionate to the aim pursued ... .[89]

Several other ECHR issues are also raised by some of the draconian confiscation legislation enacted by European states. For example, the case of *Welch v. United Kingdom* related to a submission that a confiscation order imposed under the Drug Trafficking Offences Act of 1986 was retroactive in nature and thus violated Article 7 of the ECHR. This provides, among other things, that no "heavier penalty be imposed than the one that was applicable at the time the criminal offence was committed". In its report of 15 October 1993, the Commission, which was evenly split, decided, on the casting vote of the acting president, that the United Kingdom had not exceeded its competence in this regard.[90] However, in its 1995 judgment, the Court unanimously disagreed.[91] It concluded that such a confiscation order was properly classifiable as a penalty for the purposes of Article 7 and that its retroactive application must, therefore, be regarded as a breach of that fundamental obligation.[92]

It should be stressed that the judgment in *Welch* did not directly call into question the compatibility of the rebuttable post-conviction presumption, contained in the same enactment, that property currently held or acquired in the previous six years was the proceeds of drug trafficking. This issue was, however, central to the subsequent application of one Bryan Leslie Elton against the United Kingdom.

The applicant had been convicted of drug offences in 1993 and a confiscation order had been made pursuant to the provisions of the Drug Trafficking Offences Act 1986. Having exhausted his domestic remedies in the UK, he invoked the Strasbourg machinery of protection. In particular, he complained that the making of the confiscation order had violated his rights under Article 6(2) which provides thus: "Everyone charged with a criminal offence shall be presumed innocent until proved guilty according to law." In September 1997 the Commission held, unanimously, that the complaint was manifestly ill-founded and that the application was thus inadmissible.

In arriving at this determination the Commission, citing the 1988 judgment of the Court in *Salabiaku v. France*,[93] stressed that the ECHR did not prohibit recourse to presumptions in the sphere of criminal law so long as they were confined within reasonable limits which took into account the importance of what was at stake and maintained the rights of the defence. It also recalled that in *Welch*, the Court had stated, in paragraph 36, that its judgment "does not call into question in any respect the powers of confiscation conferred on the courts as a weapon in the fight against the scourge of drug trafficking".[94] The detailed judgment of the Strasbourg Court, delivered on 5 July 2001, in the case of *Phillips v. United Kingdom*[95] on the acceptability of the use of such presumptions in a modern, post conviction-based, confiscation system will also greatly assist in drawing to a close the controversy which has surrounded this policy for over a decade.[96] It is of interest for present purposes that the Court has also adopted a positive posture in cases relevant to the use of confiscation and forfeiture in a preventive rather than post-conviction context. The decisions on admissibility in *Arcuri and three others v. Italy*[97] in 2001 and in *Butler v. United Kingdom*[98] the following year will be welcomed by those European states contemplating adding civil asset recovery to their arsenal of initiatives to take the profit out of criminal activity. As was noted in the former case:

> The enormous profits made by these [criminal] organisations from their unlawful activities give them a level of power which places in jeopardy the rule of law within the state. The means adopted to combat this economic power, particularly the confiscation measure complained of, may appear essential for the successful prosecution of the battle against the organisation in question ....

Although the great majority of issues arising before the control mechanisms in Strasbourg relate to the consistency of domestic law and practice with the requirements of the ECHR, it is of relevance to recall that both the

Commission and the Court have also revealed a willingness to subject arrangements for international co-operation in criminal matters to critical scrutiny. For example:

> In the *Soering* case the European Court has held that both Article 3 (prohibition of torture or inhuman or degrading treatment or punishment) and 6 (right to a fair trial) of the European Convention can be applicable to extradition. This decision is of crucial importance: it indicates that, in the future, extradition relations, at least for the member states of the Council of Europe, may in part be governed by general human rights instruments.[99]

This case, which arose out of extradition proceedings involving the United Kingdom and the United States, also underlines the fact that the ECHR remains relevant, in certain circumstances, even when the violation would take place in a state which has not become formally subject to its obligations.[100]

The potential of the ECHR to have an impact on the co-operative relationships between states which are and those which are not parties to it is of obvious relevance in the context of the 1990 Council of Europe Convention on Laundering, Search, Seizure and Confiscation of the Proceeds from Crime which, as we have seen, is open to non-Council of Europe countries. The jurisprudence on the extraterritorial application of the ECHR is by no means fully developed and it continues to emerge from time to time.[101] For example, the 1992 case of *Drozd and Janousek v. France and Spain*[102] dealt, in part, with prisoner transfer arrangements between Andorra and France. The former, in which the proceedings subject to challenge had taken place, was not then a member of the Council of Europe or a party to the ECHR. These facts did not, however, make the ECHR irrelevant. In the view of the Court:

> As the Convention does not require the Contracting Parties to impose its standards on third States or territories, France was not obliged to verify whether the proceedings which resulted in the conviction were compatible with all the requirements of Article 6 of the Convention. To require such a review of the manner in which a court not bound by the Convention has applied the principles enshrined in Article 6 would also thwart the current trend towards strengthening international cooperation in the administration of justice. ... The Contracting States are, however, obliged to refuse their cooperation if it emerges that the conviction is the result of a flagrant denial of justice ....[103]

This brief discussion of the ECHR will, it is hoped, have provided a timely reminder that those charged with elaborating measures to counter money laundering and other forms of serious crime do not, and should not, have a completely free hand. They must balance the law enforcement goals which they wish to pursue against the need for all members of society to be protected against the use of arbitrary state power. At least for the member states of the Council of Europe there exists a relatively effective mechanism to ensure that the proper balance is in fact struck.

Notes: VII

1. Benyon, et al., *Police co-operation in Europe: an investigation*, Leicester, University of Leicester, 1993, p. 177.

2. Tarschys, D, "The Council of Europe: strengthening European security by civilian means", *NATO Review*, 1997, p. 4, at p. 8.

3. See, for example, Muller-Rappard, E, "The European System", in Bassiouni, M C (ed), *International criminal law*, New York, Transnational Publishers, 1989, Vol. II, at pp. 95-119.

4. Also of significance in this context is Resolution (97) 24 on the twenty guiding principles for the fight against corruption, which was adopted by the Committee of Ministers on 6 November 1997.

5. See, Anderson, M et al., *Policing the European Union*, Oxford, Oxford University Press, 1995, chapter 7.

6. Wilkitzki, P, "Development of an Effective International Crime and Justice Programme – A European View", in Eser, A and Lagodny, O (eds), *Principles and procedures for a new transnational criminal law*, Freiburg, Eigenverlag MPI, 1992, p. 267, at p. 291.

7. "Measures against the Transfer and Safekeeping of Funds of Criminal Origin: Recommendation No. R. (80) 10 adopted by the Committee of Ministers of the Council of Europe on 27 June 1980 and Explanatory Memorandum", reproduced in Gilmore, W (ed), *International efforts to combat money laundering*, Cambridge, Cambridge University Press, 1992, p.169, at p.171.

8. Ibid., p. 169.

9. Ibid., p. 170.

10. Nilsson, H, "The Council of Europe Laundering Convention: A Recent Example of a Developing International Criminal Law", *Criminal Law Forum*, 1992, p. 419, at p. 423.

11. See, e.g., Carlson, S and Zagaris, B, "International Cooperation in Criminal Matters: Western Europe's International Approach to International Crime", *Nova Law Review*, 1991, p. 551, at pp. 565-567. See also, *Origin, functioning and achievements of the Pompidou Group*, Strasbourg, Council of Europe Publishing, 1997.

12. "Explanatory Report on the Convention on Laundering, Search, Seizure and Confiscation of the Proceeds from Crime" (hereafter ER), reproduced in Gilmore, W (ed), *supra*, note 7, p. 192, at p. 192.

13. Nilsson, op.cit., p. 423. The text of the convention is reproduced in Appendix VIII.

14. ER, *supra*, note 12, p. 195.

15. Ibid., p. 197.

16. Ibid., p. 193.

17. Ibid., p. 204.

18. See generally, *Confiscation and money laundering: law and practice – a guide for enforcement authorities*, London, Organised and International Crime Directorate, Home Office, 1997. For the present position see, in particular, part 7 of the Proceeds of Crime Act 2002, UK.

19. See Article 13.

20. "Money Laundering and Associated Issues: The Need for International Cooperation" UN Doc. E/CN.15/1992/4/Add.5, 23 March 1992, pp. 22-23.

21. ER, *supra*, note 12, p. 103.

22. See "Confiscation and Forfeiture", Edinburgh, Scottish Law Commission Report No.147, 1994,

23. See 1999 Criminal Law Convention on Corruption, Article 19(3).

24. See 1998 Convention on the Protection of the Environment through Criminal Law, Article 7.

25. ER, *supra*, note 12, p. 205.

26. *International Legal Materials*, 1987, Washington, DC, American Society of International Law, p.1637, at p. 1690.

27. Reproduced as Appendix A to Gilmore, W, "Police Co-operation and the European Communities: Current Trends and Recent Developments", in *Action against transnational criminality: papers from the 1993 Oxford Conference on International and White Collar Crime*, London, Commonwealth Secretariat, 1994, p. 147, at pp. 154-156.

28. "Financial Action Task Force on Money Laundering: Annual Report 1995-1996", Paris, FATF, p. 8.

29. See, Recommendation 27 and the associated note.

30. Nilsson, op.cit., p. 434.

31. See, ibid., at p. 435. But see, to the same general effect, Article 12 of the 1971 UN Convention for the Suppression of Unlawful Acts against the Safety of Civil Aviation.

32. Ibid., p. 433.

33. See, for example, Article 13(4). But see, Article 18(4)(b).

34. See, ER, *supra*, note 12, at p. 198.

35. See, Article 13(1).

36. See, ER, *supra*, note 12, at pp. 217-218.

37. See, ibid., at pp. 218-219.

38. See, for example, Zander, M, *Confiscation and forfeiture law: English and American comparisons*, London, Police Foundation, 1989.

39. See generally, for example, McCutcheon, J P and Walsh, D P J (eds), *The confiscation of criminal assets: law and procedure*, Dublin, Round Hall, 1999.

40. See, Proceeds of Crime Act 2002, UK. For the policy background see generally, "Recovering the Proceeds of Crime: A Performance and Innovation Report", Cabinet Office, London, 2000.

41. ER, *supra*, note 12, p. 214.

42. "Action Plan to Combat Organised Crime", *Official Journal of the European Communities*, No. C 251/1, 15 August 1997, Part III, chapter.III, Rec. 13.

43. See, "Conclusions and Recommendations" of the Council of Europe Conference on Money Laundering in States in Transition, Strasbourg, 29 November to 1 December 1994 (typescript), at p. 2.

44. See, Council of Europe Doc. M-MINT (98) 8, 6 November 1998, at p. 2.

45. Secretariat Memorandum, "Revision of the Convention on laundering, search, seizure and confiscation of proceeds from crime", Council of Europe Doc. CDPC-BU (2002) 11, 4 November 2002, p. 1.

46. Ibid., p. 2.

47. See generally, "Draft Report on the Advisability of Drawing up an Additional Protocol to the Convention on Laundering, Search, Seizure and Confiscation of the Proceeds from Crime (ETS No.141)", Council of Europe Doc. CDPC (2002) 5, 19 April 2002.

48. See, for example, Nadelmann, E, *Cops across borders: the internationalization of US criminal law enforcement*, Pennsylvania, Pennsylvania University Press, 1993, at p. 389; and Zagaris, B and Kingma, E, "Asset Forfeiture International and Foreign Law: An Emerging Regime", *Emory International Law Review*, 1991, p. 445, at p. 467.

49. "Financial Action Task Force on Money Laundering: Annual Report 1991-1992", Paris, FATF, p. 20.

50. See, ibid.

51. "Financial Action Task Force on Money Laundering: Annual Report 1992-1993", Paris, FATF, p. 22.

52. See "Financial Action Task Force on Money Laundering: Annual Report 1993-1994", Paris, FATF, at p. 26.

53. See, for example, "Second Commission Report to the European Parliament and the Council on the implementation of the Money Laundering Directive", Commission of the European Communities, Doc. COM (1998) 401 final, Brussels, 1 July 1998, at p. 6.

54. "Select Committee of Experts on the Evaluation of Anti-Money Laundering Measures (PC-R-EV): Annual Report 1997-1998", Strasbourg, Council of Europe, 1998, p.3. With the admission of the Russian Federation to the FATF in 2003 steps were taken to permit it to retain its membership of MONEYVAL.

55. See, "Select Committee of Experts on the Evaluation of Anti-Money Laundering Measures (PC-R-EV): Annual Report 1999-2000", Strasbourg, Council of Europe, 2000, at p. 5 and p. 8. In 2004 the FATF decided to adopt a version of this system in its own work.

56. See "Select Committee of Experts on the Evaluation of Anti-Money Laundering Measures (PC-R-EV): Examiners Guide", Strasbourg, Council of Europe, 2000, at pp. 12-13. Compliance enhancing measures, at a lower level of intensity, were taken for the first time at the June 2002 plenary meeting against Albania, Georgia, Moldova and Ukraine.

57. For a most interesting analysis of the first round see, "A Review of the Anti-Money Laundering Systems in 22 Council of Europe Member States", Council of Europe Doc. PC-R-EV(01) 12 rev, 21 March 2002.

58. This will build upon a detailed analysis of the results of a self-assessment of MONEYVAL member states against the eight Special Recommendations on Terrorist Financing. This exercise, which looked at the position as of 30 September 2002, was finalised in 2003 and made public via its website; it was updated in 2004.

59. The previous version of the methodology was used on a limited basis; namely, the initial evaluation of new members of MONEYVAL. The revised version, as agreed at the 10th plenary session, will be of general application.

60. "Financial Action Task Force on Money Laundering: Annual Report 2000-2001", Paris, FATF, p. 11.

61. Dolle, S, "The Potential Impact of the European Convention on Human Rights". Paper presented to the Council of Europe Money Laundering Conference, Strasbourg, 28-30 September 1992 (typescript), p. 2.

62. Gomien, D, *Short guide to the European Convention on Human Rights*, 2nd edn, Strasbourg, Council of Europe Publishing, 1998, p. 5.

63. ER,. *supra*, note 12, p. 231.

64. Ibid., pp. 206-207.

65. Ibid., p. 222.

66. See, for example, Wilson, R, "Human Rights and Money Laundering: The Prospect of International Seizure of Defense Attorney Fees", *Criminal Law Forum*, 1991, at p. 85-103.

67. ER, *supra*, note 12, p. 208.

68. See, ibid., at p. 207.

69. See generally, Harris, D J, O'Boyle, M and Warbrick, C, *Law of the European Convention on Human Rights*, London, Butterworth, 1995.

70. Shaw, M, *International Law*, Cambridge, Cambridge University Press, 4th edn, 1997, p. 260.

71. See, for example, Finnie, W, "Rewriting the European Convention on Human Rights", *Scots Law Times*, 1994, p. 389, at p. 389.

72. Ibid., p. 390.

73. "The European Court of Human Rights: Historical Background, Organisation and Procedure". Information document issued by the Registrar of the Court and dated 4 January 1999, p. 2.

74. *Supra*, note 62, p. 140.

75. Schermers, H, "Human Rights in Europe", *Legal Studies*, 1986, p. 170, at p. 171.

76. See, ibid., at pp. 174-175. This is not to say, however, that the ECHR was regarded as entirely irrelevant in judicial proceedings. For example, a significant jurisprudence was developed in relation to the impact of the ECHR in the area of statutory interpretation. See generally, Dickson, B (ed), *Human rights and the European Convention: the effects of the Convention on the United Kingdom and Ireland*, London, Sweet and Maxwell, 1997.

77. The Scotland Act 1998 – which entered into force in July 1999 – provides another avenue for domestic consideration of ECHR issues.

78. Duffy, P, *The Police and the European Convention on Human Rights*, Directorate of Human Rights, Strasbourg, Council of Europe, 1992, p. 2.

79. See generally, Dolle, op.cit.

80. Case No. 17/1991/269/340.

81. Case No. 44/1997/828/1034, paragraph 36. See also, *Case of Edwards and Lewis v. United Kingdom* (Application Nos. 39647/98 and 40461/98), Judgment of 22 July 2003.

82. See, Decision of the Commission as to the Admissibility of Application No. 15199/89 by Nazir Chinoy against the United Kingdom.

83. See, for example, *R v. Governor of Pentonville Prison,* ex parte *Chinoy*, [1992] 1 All E.R. 317.

84. Dolle, op.cit., p. 7.

85. *Supra*, note 82, p. 9. A considerable case-law has developed on the use and admissibility of wiretap evidence in domestic criminal proceedings. See, e.g., *Case of Khan v. United Kingdom* (Application No. 35394/97), Judgment of 12 May 2000; *Case of P G and J H v. United Kingdom* (Application No. 44787/98), Judgment of 25 September 2001; and *Case of Allan v. United Kingdom* (Application No. 48539/99), Judgment of 5 November 2002. See also, "Report on Interception of Communication and Intrusive Surveillance (Best Practice Survey No. 3)", Council of Europe Doc. PC-S-CO (2000) 3.

86. See, *M v. Italy* (No. 12386/86; Decision of 15 April 1991).

87. *Case of Raimondo v. Italy* (1/1993/396/474), Judgment of 22 February 1994.

88. Dolle, op.cit., p. 8.

89. *Supra*, note 87, p. 13.

90. See, *Welch v. United Kingdom* (No. 17440/90; Decision of 15 October 1993).

91. Reproduced at 20 EHRR 247. See also, Andrew, J and Sherlock, A, "Council of Europe: European Court of Human Rights", *European Law Review*, 1996, pp. 83-86.

92. The apparent scope and severity of the limitation on state action so imposed was somewhat limited by the 10 September 1997 decision of the Commission as to the admissibility of Application No. 31209/96 by Ronald J M Taylor against the United Kingdom. See also, the decision as to admissibility of the application by Eric Fitzpatrick Danison against the United Kingdom (Application No. 45042/98).

93. Series A, No. 141, p. 16, paragraph 28.

94. Decision of the Commission as to the admissibility of Application No. 32344/96 by Bryan Leslie Elton against the United Kingdom.

95. Application No. 41087/98. See also, for example, *McIntosh v. Lord Advocate* [2003] 1 AC 1078; and, *Regina v. Benjafield* [2003] 1 AC 1099.

96. Of interest in this context is, "Reversal of the burden of proof in confiscation of the proceeds of crime: A Council of Europe Best Practice Survey", Council of Europe Doc. PC-S-CO (2000) 8 Rev.

97. Decision as to the admissibility of Application No. 52024/99.

98. Decision as to the admissibility of Application No. 41661/98.

99. Van den Wyngaert, C, "Applying the European Convention on Human Rights to Extradition: Opening Pandora's Box?", *International and Comparative Law Quarterly*, 1990, p. 757, at p. 759.

100. See also, for example, *Case of Mamatkulov and Abdurasulovic v. Turkey* (Application Nos. 46827/99 and 46951/99), Judgment of 6 February 2003. For the application of the Convention to alleged instances of state adductions from the territory of third parties see, *Case of Öcalan v. Turkey* (Application No. 46221/99), Judgment of 12 March 2003.

101. See, for example, Lush, C, "The Territorial Application of the European Convention on Human Rights: Recent Case Law", *International and Comparative Law Quarterly*, 1993, at pp. 897-906.

102. (21/1991/273/344), Judgment of 26 June 1992.

103. Ibid., p. 32.

Chapter VIII – Action within the European Union

The context

Since the 1970s the members of the European Union[1] have sought to promote closer co-operation among themselves in order to combat criminal activities with a transfrontier dimension. Prior to the entry into force of the Treaty on European Union (TEU), commonly known as the Maastricht Treaty, on 1 November 1993, discussions relating to such matters took place primarily within the framework of European political co-operation. As will be seen in greater detail below, Title VI of the Maastricht Treaty took this process further by making extensive provision for intergovernmental co-operation in the key fields of justice and home affairs.[2] Among the matters formally deemed to be of "common interest", Article K.1 mentions judicial and customs co-operation, combating fraud and drug addiction, and "police co-operation for the purposes of preventing and combating terrorism, unlawful drug trafficking and other serious forms of international crime, including if necessary certain aspects of customs cooperation, in connection with the organisation of a Union-wide system for exchanging information within a European Police Office (Europol)". Pursuant to Article K.2 such matters are to be dealt with in compliance with the European Convention on Human Rights (ECHR) and the 1951 UN Convention relating to the Status of Refugees.

However, these arrangements continue to rely primarily on the traditional intergovernmental mechanism rather than on Community initiatives and legislation to secure progress.[3] The competence of the Community in this respect remains limited. As the relevant commissioner was to note in an address to the World Ministerial Conference on Organised Transnational Crime, held in Naples in November 1994: "We do not have our own police force, nor any of the other traditional law enforcement instruments."[4]

It should be noted that a further element of complexity in this general context arises out of the Treaty of Amsterdam which was signed on 2 October 1997 and is now in force. As Walker has put it:

> ... this amendment to the constitutional architecture of the European Union responds to a general chorus of criticism to the effect that lack of involvement of Community institutions in the Third Pillar has compromised its effectiveness. It does so by announcing a new chapter on the so-called" area of freedom, security and justice". Within this chapter are to be found both a new EC Treaty Title on visas, asylum, immigration and other matters related to free movement of persons, most of which competences have been transferred from the Maastricht Third Pillar, and also a revised and truncated version of the Third Pillar restricted to police and customs cooperation and judicial cooperation in criminal matters.[5]

A further notable feature concerns the decision to incorporate the so-called "Schengen *acquis*".[6] The changes agreed to in the Treaty of Amsterdam are, in the present context, relevant primarily to the evolving mandate of Europol and will be returned to when that matter is addressed at a later stage of this chapter.

While the emphasis to date has been on securing incremental advances in the justice and home affairs sphere through intergovernmental co-operation, on occasion the constituent agreements have provided a basis on which the unification of the law of the member states through regulations, or its approximation through the use of directives, could be achieved. Such competences have provided the basis for Community action in a number of areas ranging from insider trading to the control of trade in precursor and essential chemicals to prevent diversion for the production of illicit drugs. Of more immediate relevance, they provided the necessary legal basis for the EC Directive of 10 June 1991 on Prevention of the Use of the Financial System for the Purpose of Money Laundering and the amending directive of 4 December 2001. It is to those important anti-money laundering initiatives, the texts of which are reproduced in Appendix IX and Appendix X respectively, that this study now turns.

The 1991 directive

Background and development

Although the 1991 directive was the first legislative measure to be adopted by the EC in this area it had been actively involved in earlier international initiatives. As we have seen at earlier stages of this work, the Commission participated in the negotiation of both the 1988 UN convention, which the EC has since ratified, and the Council of Europe convention of 1990. Furthermore, it is an active participant in the FATF process. For this reason the drafters of the directive were well positioned to ensure that it reinforced rather than undermined the achievements which had been recorded in those other fora.

The directive, in contrast to the 1988 and 1990 convention precedents, fully embraces the preventive approach to money laundering. As a then leading official of the Directorate of Legal Affairs of the Council of Europe was to explain to the House of Lords Select Committee on the European Communities in late 1990, the two approaches are complementary: "In principle, the directive ends where the [1990] convention begins (with the criminal investigations)."[7] Thus, while the UN and the Council of Europe initiatives were directed to articulating a repressive approach towards this issue, the directive "is primarily addressed to credit and financial institutions and imposes obligations on them which are designed to ensure that laundering is detected before the stage of criminal investigation is reached".[8]

The trigger for Community action in this area was the perceived need to ensure "the integrity and cleanliness of the financial system"[9] in the light of moves towards the creation of the Single Market. As the House of Lords committee noted, the free movement of capital and financial services "offers great scope for organised crime as well as for legitimate enterprises".[10] Similarly, it was felt that "lack of Community action against money laundering could lead member states, for the purpose of protecting their financial systems, to adopt measures which could be inconsistent with completion of the single market".[11]

Before examining the actual requirements of the 1991 directive, three points of general interest should be made. First, and as was to be expected, its content was heavily influenced by the countermeasures elaborated within a FATF context and, in particular, by the 1990 recommendations. This fact is recalled in the recitals to the directive and also finds specific mention in the domestic implementing legislation of certain member states such as the Netherlands.[12] Second, the intention was not to create a system of "complete uniformity" in relation to the treatment of this issue at the national level.[13] As Dine has remarked, "Directives are supposed to leave a measure of discretion to the member states as to the exact way to achieve the object described".[14] Indeed, Article 15 permits each country to adopt even stricter measures in this field if so wished. Finally, it was intended that the directive would have an impact beyond the internal borders of EU member countries. Of particular importance for present purposes is the fact that those European Free Trade Association (EFTA) countries which ratified the Agreement for a European Economic Area (EEA) were obliged to give effect to its terms in domestic law. Thus, Austria, Finland and Sweden were not faced with the need to address this issue anew upon entry to the EU in January 1995. Similarly, in spite of the fact that the people of Norway rejected the possibility of EU membership in a referendum in late 1994, the need for compliance with the directive remained unaffected.

The requirements of the directive and their implementation

As with the 1990 Council of Europe convention, the 1991 directive recognises the fact that:

> ... since money laundering occurs not only in relation to the proceeds of drug-related offences but also in relation to the proceeds of other criminal activities (such as organised crime and terrorism), the member states should, within the meaning of their legislation, extend the effects of the directive to include the proceeds of such activities, to the extent that they are likely to result in laundering operations justifying sanctions on that basis.

Thus, whilst the definition of laundering contained in Article 1 is derived from that used in the 1988 UN convention, it relates to "criminal activity" rather than merely serious drug trafficking offences. The term "criminal activity" is defined as "a crime specified in Article 3(1)(a) of the Vienna Convention [1988 UN convention] and any other criminal activity designated as such for the purposes of this directive by each member state".[15] Article 2 then requires all member states to ensure that laundering, as so defined, "is prohibited". As a result of differences of view as to the competence of an EC measure of this kind to require the imposition of a criminal penalty it was left to the members acting outside the Community framework to issue a statement on the same day in which they undertook: "to take all necessary steps by 31 December 1992 at the latest to enact criminal legislation enabling them to comply with their obligations ...."; a time-frame which was to experience significant slippage in practice.

In the years which followed, EU members progressively accepted the invitation to extend money laundering beyond the drug trafficking sphere. Some countries did so in relation to specified forms of serious crime while others legislated on an all-crimes basis.[16] The clear trend of moving away from a drug-specific focus in this area was well illustrated by the French law of 13 May 1996. Indeed, such was the extent of this transformation of governmental perception that in December 1998 it proved possible to reach agreement on a significant measure of harmonisation of approach. Acting within the framework of Title VI of the TEU, a Joint Action was adopted which sought to ensure that no member state makes or upholds a reservation in respect of Article 6 of the 1990 Council of Europe convention, in relation to serious offences. It provides that "[s]uch offences should in any event include offences which are punishable by deprivation of liberty or a detention order of a maximum of more than one year or, as regards those states which have a minimum threshold for offences in their legal system, offences punishable by deprivation of liberty or a detention order of a minimum of more than six months"[17] (a commitment reinforced in identical terms in the EU Council Framework Decision of 26 June 2001).[18]

Following an examination of a 1995 Commission report on the implementation of the directive, the European Parliament in 1996 called on member states to extend the scope of their money laundering legislation to embrace "all money acquired from professional and organised crime".[19] Concern was also expressed in the course of the review that the directive did not "explicitly cover the proceeds of fraud against the budget of the European Union".[20] This matter was subsequently addressed in the Second Protocol to the 1995 Convention on the Protection of the European Communities' Financial Interests. This protocol, adopted in June 1997, requires the criminalisation of laundering of the proceeds of such fraud, at least in serious cases, and of active and passive corruption.[21] Interestingly, this initiative also requires the states concerned to take measures to ensure that legal persons can be held liable when a variety of offences, including money laundering, are committed for their benefit in this context.[22]

Closely related to the question of the scope of the prohibition on money laundering is that of sanctions. In this area also there is no attempt to harmonise the penalties to be imposed for the infringement of any of the measures contained in the directive including its Article 2.[23] Consequently, individual national practices came to differ considerably.[24] Notwithstanding this fact the Commission indicated that it would monitor the practice of member countries in order to ensure that they complied with the principles of effectiveness, proportionality and dissuasion as articulated in the jurisprudence of the European Court of Justice.[25]

It is important to note that the decision was taken to seek to ensure that the 1991 directive applied to the whole financial system. This reflected the feeling that "partial coverage ... could provoke a shift in money laundering from one to another kind of financial institutions".[26] So broad were the definitions of credit and financial institutions used in Article 1 that the Commission concluded that "virtually any financial intermediary such as credit institutions, life insurance companies, credit card issuers, leasing and factoring companies, bureaux de change etc. fall under the scope of the money laundering legislation".[27] It was appreciated that in some member states not all of these institutions are subject to supervision on a prudential basis and that this poses particular problems in ensuring effective implementation. The Commission consequently followed developments in this regard with particular care.[28]

Given the understandable focus of money laundering countermeasures on banks and other credit and financial institutions, it was inevitable that launderers would increasingly seek to use non-financial businesses and professions in an effort to avoid detection. This migration of funds has, in turn, been facilitated by the emergence of professional money launderers including "solicitors, attorneys, accountants, financial advisors, notaries and other fiduciaries whose services are employed to assist in the disposal of criminal profits".[29] Mindful of this possibility, Article 12 of the directive obliged member states to extend its provisions, in whole or in part, "to include those professions and undertakings whose activities are particularly likely to be used for money laundering purposes". National implementation practices differed considerably in this regard.[30] Given the open-textured nature of this obligation the directive created, in the form of a contact committee, a mechanism through which an element of co-ordination and harmonisation of policy could be achieved in this area. Under the terms of Article 13(d) one of the functions of this body is "to examine whether a profession or category of undertaking should be included in the scope of Article 12 where it has been established that such profession or category of undertaking has been used in a Member State for money laundering". Discussions within the contact committee in this sphere were, in turn, guided by the need to "keep the balance between the burdens to be imposed and the real risk of money laundering".[31] Although it had the opportunity to formulate a common list of such professions and undertakings under consideration for some time, it proved to be difficult to fashion a consensus. Broad agreement in principle emerged on the need to extend coverage to the gaming industry (including casinos and bookmakers) and to dealers in high-value items (such as real estate agents and jewellers). However, as the Commission pointed out in 1998, "the main sticking point remains the obligations to be imposed on certain professions and in particular the legal professions".[32] Developments in other fora such as the European Parliament and the European Council were such as to compel action on this point and, as will be noted in detail below, significant coverage was included in the revised directive of December 2001.

The first specific obligations imposed upon institutions covered by the 1991 directive relate to identification of customers and record keeping. As has been pointed out elsewhere: "Keeping records of customers and their transactions is an essential part of the audit trail procedures which the authorities require to assist them in tracking down the criminals and the illicit proceeds of their money laundering activities."[33]

These measures are also designed to enable suspicious customers and transactions to be identified and reported to the appropriate national authorities for action to be taken. To these ends, Article 3 requires the identification of customers and beneficial owners when entering into business relations "particularly when opening an account or savings accounts or when offering safe custody facilities".[34]

The identification requirement also applies to those engaging in one-off transactions at or above an € 15 000 threshold "whether the transaction is carried out in a single operation or in several operations which seem to be linked".[35] The latter is specifically designed to discourage the structuring of transactions, or "smurfing" (see page 33), in an effort to evade the identification obligation. Certain derogation provisions were, however, agreed to. One such concerns the identification requirement in certain categories of insurance policy transactions.[36] As the European Commission has explained: "The exoneration from the identification requirements in small insurance operations and occupational pension schemes under certain conditions, as provided for in Article 3(3) and (4) of the directive, were introduced by the Council following an amendment proposed by the European Parliament which was aimed at facilitating insurance operations involving very low risk of money laundering".[37] While a majority of EU members have taken full advantage of these exceptions several elected not to do so and, to that extent, instituted policies stricter than those required by the directive.[38] Importantly, it is specified in Article 3(6) that: "Credit and financial institutions shall carry out such identification even where the amount of the transaction is lower than the thresholds laid down, wherever there is suspicion of money laundering."

While concrete expression is thus given by the directive to the "know your customer" principle it does not impose a standard method through which such identification requirements are to be satisfied. The decision as to the most appropriate way of making the procedure effective is left to each member country. This approach, which mirrors that taken by the FATF in its 1990 recommendations, was necessary given the diverse range of factual situations which are presented in practice. For example, identification procedures for personal customers when opening accounts may need to be varied depending on whether the individual is resident or non-resident. Different considerations apply in relation to the opening of trust accounts. An even greater range of possibilities need to be catered for in the opening of accounts for legal persons. The resulting practice has, perhaps necessarily, been far from uniform. Also of relevance in this context is the obligation, contained in Article 3(5) of the directive, to "take reasonable measures to obtain information as to the real identity of the persons on whose behalf" customers are acting when it is known or suspected that beneficial ownership rests elsewhere.

Closely allied to the requirements concerning identification is the obligation to retain certain records for specified periods of time in order to preserve the audit trail for use in any subsequent investigation. For example, pursuant to Article 4, credit and financial institutions must, in the case of transactions, keep "the supporting evidence and records, consisting of the original documents or copies admissible in court proceedings under the applicable national legislation for a period of at least five years following execution of the transactions". Though at the time a new burden for some private sector concerns it was felt that, in the wider interest, such a step was essential.

Provisions were also inserted to ensure the due diligence of credit and financial institutions. In particular, they are obliged by Article 5 to "examine with special attention any transaction which they regard as particularly likely, by its nature, to be related to money laundering". It is clear from the drafting history of this measure, and from an examination of the text as a whole, that the intention was to give effect to Recommendation 21 of the FATF programme. In doing so, it reaches two somewhat different sets of circumstances. First, it promotes a particular sensitivity to transactions involving third countries which apply no or insufficient anti-money laundering procedures. Second, it encourages the paying of special attention to unusual transactions having no apparent economic or visible lawful purpose.[39]

Articles 6, 7 and 10, considered by many to form the cornerstone of the directive, seek to ensure that the authorities responsible for combating laundering operations obtain the necessary level of co-operation in their work from both the institutions concerned and the relevant supervisory bodies.

In so far as the former is concerned, the directive embraces the view that the most effective means to accomplish this goal is through a system of mandatory reporting of suspicious transactions. To that end, Article 6 requires credit and financial institutions to inform the authorities "on their own initiative, of any fact which might be an indication of money laundering".

The directive itself does not seek either to define or to give examples of suspicious transactions and the task of making the system both operational and effective is left to member governments. In this area, practice also differs considerably from country to country. In the United Kingdom, the effort to provide substance to the concept takes place in official guidance notes rather than in the body of the primary or secondary legislation. A broadly similar approach is followed in Germany. In the Netherlands, the reporting obligation is keyed to the somewhat wider, but arguably more user-friendly, concept of unusual transactions. The question of whether or not a transaction should be regarded as unusual is assessed on the basis of established objective and subjective indicators. As has been noted elsewhere, these are "formulated and, where necessary, amended in close consultation with the relevant sectors".[40] When these reports are received by the relevant agency (the Office for the Disclosure of Unusual Transactions, MOT), they are, in conjunction with information from a variety of other sources, subject to a process of investigation and analysis. Those then deemed to be suspicious are passed on to the police and judicial authorities for further action.[41] A further significant distinction in the approach to implementation relates to the use of the criminal law in this sphere. Thus, while many member states have resorted to administrative law as the basis for giving effect to this obligation others, including the UK and Ireland, have adopted the view that failure to report should constitute a criminal offence.[42]

The directive also provides that institutions must, upon request, furnish the relevant authorities with all necessary information. The fact that such information has been transmitted must not, in order to safeguard the integrity of any subsequent investigation, be brought to the attention of the customer concerned or to that of any other third parties; an activity commonly known as "tipping off".[43] In respect of such disclosures by institutions, Article 9 provides them with an essential form of legal immunity from suit for breach of contract or other legal obligations such as customer confidentiality. The information itself may, under Article 6, "be used only in connection with the combating of money laundering. However, member states may provide that such information may also be used for other purposes".

The final element in the system of co-operation is contained in Article 7. This requires the relevant institutions to refrain from carrying out suspicious transactions until they have brought the matter to the attention of the appropriate authorities. It is up to such authorities to give instructions whether or not to execute the transaction. However, "[w]here such a transaction is suspected of giving rise to money laundering and where to refrain in such manner is impossible or is likely to frustrate efforts to pursue the beneficiaries of a suspected money-laundering operation, the institutions concerned shall apprise the authorities immediately afterwards". The flexibility of Article 7 and its sensitivity to the needs of investigators is in contrast to the original Commission proposal which would have required institutions, in all circumstances, to refrain from executing suspect transactions.

It was recognised that in reaching out to and involving the private sector to such an unprecedented extent it would be necessary to ensure that those whose participation was required would, in fact, be in a position to play their role fully and effectively. To that end the directive in Article 11(1) obliges the institutions concerned to establish adequate internal control and communications systems. It is, however, silent on such fundamental practical issues as the type of system to be introduced and the responsibilities of those within it. In addition, and of the utmost importance, credit and financial institutions must, pursuant to paragraph 2 thereof: "take appropriate measures so that their employees are aware of the provisions contained in this directive. These measures shall include participation of their relevant employees in special training programmes to help them recognise operations which may be related to money laundering as well as to instruct them as to how to proceed in such cases". The fostering of staff awareness is increasingly being facilitated in practice by the production by relevant institutions, industry associations, and others of specific training packages. The intended audiences range from senior management to bank clerks; the programmes from computer-assisted learning to videos.[44]

The 2001 directive

In the mid to late 1990s it came to be generally recognised that the directive required amendment both to cure defects, insufficiencies and ambiguities which had been revealed by practice, and to ensure consistency with evolving anti-money laundering standards. It will be recalled, in particular, that the text pre-dated the 1996 revisions to the FATF Forty Recommendations. As the Commission was to note in July 1999:

> Both the Council of Ministers and the European Parliament have called for additional measures to enhance the European Union's anti-money laundering effort. Since the Directive was adopted in 1991 both the money laundering threat and the response to that threat have evolved. It is the view of the Commission, supported by the European Parliament and the member states, that the response of the European Union must now also move forward.

While the goal was widely shared, agreement on the detailed content of the new measure proved elusive. Indeed, although the Financial Services

Commissioner announced his intention to come forward with "proposals to extend and improve the current rules" in July 1998, the second money laundering directive was to be adopted only on 4 December 2001.[46] In the course of these lengthy, and at times somewhat strained discussions,[47] involving the Council, Parliament and the Commission, two issues came to symbolise the nature and ambition of the amendment exercise. The first of these was the perceived need for the directive to contain a wider range of money laundering predicate offences. In this regard, it was widely acknowledged that the definition of criminal activity in Article 1 of the 1991 directive as drug trafficking "and any other criminal activity designated as such for the purposes of this directive by each member state" was, when viewed in the light of subsequent developments, outmoded. None the less, it was no easy matter to fashion a consensus as to the formulation which should replace it. In particular, there was a body of opinion that it was undesirable for the increasingly broad scope of the criminal offence of money laundering to be mirrored in the amended directive. Others took the view that a substantial correspondence in scope of the definition for criminal law and preventive purposes was required. In the end the latter view prevailed (Article 1(E)). However, the goal is to be achieved in two stages. Initially, the amended directive will apply to a range of serious crimes including drug trafficking, various of the activities of criminal organisations, certain categories of fraud, and corruption. However, "member states shall before 15 December 2004 amend the definition provided for in this indent in order to bring this definition into line with the definition of serious crime of Joint Action 98/699/JHA". This text, examined later in this chapter, provides a basic definition of serious offences by reference to set thresholds of punishment.

The second major area of debate was the manner in which the revised text would be extended to those professions and non-financial businesses believed to be vulnerable to abuse by money launderers. Here the concern was, in large measure, that of displacement; namely, the shift of focus by those engaged in money laundering activity from those credit and financial system actors subject to the full range of anti-money laundering measures to other sectors vulnerable to abuse which remained unregulated in this sense. As recital 13 of the 2001 text was subsequently to note: "There is evidence that the tightening of controls in the financial sector has prompted money launderers to seek alternative methods for concealing the origin of the proceeds of crime."

While the basic problem was widely recognised it proved to be extremely difficult to fashion agreement on the range of non-financial businesses and professions which should become subject to the obligations of the directive. This was a matter upon which the thinking of the Commission was heavily influenced by the content of the annual reports on money laundering typologies produced by the FATF;[48] a source of insight on such matters explicitly recorded in recital 14 of the 2001 text. The inclusion of the legal professions was particularly controversial. As Mitsilegas has noted "disagreement on this issue threatened to derail the proposal altogether, with the European Parliament advocating a broader exemption of the legal profession ... than ... could be accepted by the Council and the Commission".[49] The extension of anti-money laundering obligations to other professions and activities (auditors, external accountants and tax advisers; real estate agents; dealers in high-value goods, and, casinos) proved somewhat less problematic.

In the course of fashioning the basis for eventual agreement on coverage of the legal professions a range of both stylistic and substantive departures was made from the wording originally proposed by the Commission. It is equally the case, however, that all of the broad goals sought by the Commission were to find reflection in the text of 4 December 2001.

Central to the approach adopted is the new Article 2a by virtue of which member states are required to impose the obligations of the directive on a range of legal and natural persons "acting in the exercise of their professional activities". Among those so included are:

5. notaries and other independent legal professionals, when they participate, whether:

(a) by assisting in the planning or execution of transactions for their client concerning the

   (i) buying and selling of real property or business entities;

   (ii) managing of client money, securities or other assets;

   (iii) opening or management of bank, savings or securities accounts;

   (iv) organisation of contributions necessary for the creation, operation or management of companies;

   (v) creation, operation or management of trusts, companies or similar structures;

(b) or by acting on behalf of and for their client in any financial or real estate transaction.

It is important to stress that the intent was not to secure blanket coverage of all of the activities conducted by members of the profession. In the words of recital 16 of the text of 4 December 2001 the more limited ambition was as follows:

Notaries and independent legal professionals, as defined by the Member States, should be made subject to the provisions of the Directive when participating in financial or corporate transactions, including providing tax advice, where there is the greatest risk of the services of those legal professionals being misused for the purpose of laundering the proceeds of criminal activity.

When acting within the scope of Article 2a(5) legal professionals are subject to the key obligations of the directive including customer identification (Article 3), record keeping (Article 4) and internal control and training (Article 11). In relation to such matters they are, as a general proposition, treated in the same fashion as other obligated persons and institutions. However, it was accepted that special treatment of the legal professions would be required (notwithstanding the limited scope of Article 2a(5)) in extending to them obligations to report suspicious transactions, or other-wise to co-operate with the authorities responsible for combating money laundering. Of particular concern in this regard was the need to provide an appropriate acknowledgement of their professional duty of discretion. The two primary safeguards (both of which find some reflection in the original Commission proposal) are contained in Article 6(3) and are presented as options for individual member states. The text reads thus:

> 3. In the case of the notaries and independent legal professionals referred to in Article 2a(5), Member States may designate an appropriate self-regulatory body of the profession concerned as the authority to be informed of the facts referred to in paragraph 1(a) and in such case shall lay down the appropriate forms of cooperation between that body and the authorities responsible for combating money laundering.

> Member States shall not be obliged to apply the obligations laid down in para-graph 1 to notaries, independent legal professionals, auditors, external accoun-tants and tax advisors with regard to information they receive from or obtain on one of their clients, in the course of ascertaining the legal position for their client or performing their task of defending or representing that client in, or concern-ing judicial proceedings, including advice on instituting or avoiding proceedings, whether such information is received or obtained before, during or after such proceedings.

Several points of interest concerning this key provision should be noted. In so far as the first option is concerned, namely the ability to designate an appropriate self-regulatory body of the profession to receive the reports of suspicious transactions, individual member states are provided with the freedom to formulate the appropriate forms of co-operation between any such self-regulatory body of the profession and the relevant national anti-money laundering authorities. As recital 20 notes:

> The rules governing the treatment of such reports and their possible onward transmission to the "authorities responsible for combating money laundering" and in general the appropriate forms of cooperation between the bar associations or professional bodies and these authorities should be determined by Member States.

Given the nature of the approach adopted it is to be expected that national implementation practices in this sphere will differ significantly. The second option provided to member states relates more directly to the nature and scope of the recognition of the duty of discretion owed by the professions concerned to their clients.

Also of relevance to this part of Article 6(3) is the wording of paragraph 17 of the recital to the directive. This records the view that "legal advice remains subject to the obligation of professional secrecy unless the legal counsellor is taking part in money laundering activities, the legal advice is provided for money laundering purposes, or the lawyer knows that the client is seeking legal advice for money laundering purposes". The word "knows" in this sentence of the recital was included at the behest of the European Parliament delegation in the course of the conciliation procedure.

On the basis of the above wording it may be argued by some that the amended directive only requires lawyers within this residual area of their activities to report to the appropriate authorities in instances in which they possess actual knowledge that the client is seeking advice for the purposes of money laundering. However, such an interpretation sits uneasily with the actual wording of Article 6(1)(a). This requires that persons subject to the directive co-operate fully with the authorities "by informing those authorities, on their own initiative, of any fact which might be an indication of money laundering". There is no doubt that the wording of Article 6(1)(a) (which is, in this respect, identical to that used in the 1991 directive) includes within its scope the obligation to report suspicious transactions. The uncertainty relates to whether or not the wording "any fact which might be an indication of money laundering" as used in the directive has a scope broader than that of suspicious transactions so as to embrace, for example, instances in which suspicion is aroused prior to acceptance as a client as a consequence of which the business in question is declined.[50]

While the recitals, including recital 17, are an integral and necessary part of an EC directive, they are not part of the substantive text, and their usual legal role tends to be as an aid to interpretation.[51] In this situation, since it refers to the giving of legal advice and representation in legal proceedings, it may be suggested that, whatever the European Parliament may have intended, recital 17 amounts at most to a gloss on the special treatment of the giving of legal advice and representation in legal proceedings in Article 6(3) of the revised directive, indicating situations, in effect, of bad faith where that special treatment should not be accorded. In any event, it must be emphasised that Article 6(3) in no way requires member states to exempt the giving of legal advice and representation in legal proceedings from the obligations of Article 6(1); rather it gives them permission to grant such an exemption if they so desire, but they also remain fully at liberty not to grant such an exemption.

By way of contrast, it is of importance to note that the 2001 text provides a potentially significant form of special treatment for lawyers and other professionals of a kind not envisaged by the Commission in its 1999 proposal. Here, also, the initiative came from the European Parliament and found inclusion in the course of the conciliation process. Contained in Article 8(2) it provides member states with the option of excluding the legal professions from the scope of the obligation not to "disclose to the customer concerned nor to other third persons that information has been transmitted to the authorities ... or that a money laundering investigation is being carried out". The implications for the operation of the directive in practice for any member state availing itself of this option in relation to the legal professions are potentially significant. This is so because it would, in effect, permit lawyers to "tip off" their clients that they had informed the authorities of suspicions concerning that client, pursuant to Article 6, or were otherwise co-operating with the authorities in that context. It could readily be argued that such an action on the part of a legal professional could serve to undermine the integrity of any investigation into money laundering involving or arising out of such interactions with the competent national authorities. Indeed, in some circumstances it could serve to entirely negate the practical purpose of the reporting obligation.

From the above, it is evident that in seeking to strike the appropriate balance between the need to safeguard the traditional role of the lawyer and the desire to improve the effectiveness of efforts to combat the misuse of the services of legal and other professionals for the purpose of money laundering a series of difficult compromises was struck. This, as noted above, included making a range of optional provisions available to member states with obvious implications for harmonisation of approach in the implementation of the directive. It is therefore anticipated that the contact committee will have occasion to address this issue with some frequency and that it will be covered in the regular reports which the Commission is required to make to the European Parliament and the Council on implementation issues. The need for close monitoring of this matter is underlined by Article 2 of the 4 December 2001 text. This requires the Commission to carry out, within three years of its entry into force, a "particular examination" of aspects relating to the implementation of four issues of special interest and concern including "the specific treatment of lawyers and other independent legal professionals ... ".

The same article also extends to the identification of clients in non-face to face transactions (such as those conducted by postal, telephonic or electronic means). In this regard it will be recalled that the 1991 text contains (in Article 3(8)) only limited treatment of this difficult issue. As the Commission has recalled:

> This Article allows Member States to presume that the identification requirements regarding insurance operations have been fulfilled "when it is established that the payment for the transaction is to be debited from an account opened in the customer's name with a credit institution subject to this directive". The rationale of this provision is that insurance companies should not be obliged to follow the identification procedures when the customer has already been identified by a credit institution holding the account through which the payment must be carried out.[52]

The contact committee subsequently came to examine the adequacy of this exemption within the context of the practical issues posed in the sphere of customer identification in the case of remote financial operations more generally. The 1998 Commission report indicated that the committee had "agreed a number of principles to be applied to ensure that customers are adequately identified".[53] This matter was returned to in the course of discussion of the amending directive.[54] It was eventually decided that in addition to retaining the limited exemption from the general identification requirements from the 1991 text,[55] supplementary coverage of this issue was required. This is contained in the new Article 3(11). Pursuant to it, member states must ensure that obligated institutions and persons "take specific and adequate measures necessary to compensate for the greater risk of money laundering which arises when establishing business relations or entering into a transaction with a customer who has not been physically present for identification purposes ('non-face to face' operations)". The stipulated purpose of such measures is to "ensure that the customer's identity is established". The new directive does not, however, establish the manner in which this is to be accomplished. Rather, it provides a range of illustrations of mechanisms which might achieve the desired result. Furthermore, as Mitsilegas has noted, such measures "must be taken into account by the internal control procedures of the institutions and professions covered by the directive".[56]

The 2001 text also brought about a range of alterations of a less far reaching and mostly technical character. These include clarification that the obligations apply to the activities of investment firms, bureaux de change and money remittance offices (Article 1(B)), and special threshold requirements in respect of the identification of casino customers (Article 3(5) and (6)). Member States were to bring the amendments into force by 15 June 2003. Unsurprisingly, given the complexity and controversial character of some of the changes outlined above, there has been significant slippage on the part of several jurisdictions in satisfying this obligation. Notwithstanding this delay, discussions were underway (at the time of writing) concerning the formulation of a third money laundering directive. It will be recalled that such a process of amendment is specifically envisaged in the new Article 1(E) in the context of the scope of money laundering predicate offences. This invites the Commission to bring forward a proposal in this regard prior to 15 December 2004. All indications are, however, that the scope of this measure will not be so limited. It is likely, for example, that the opportunity will be taken to fully embrace issues concerning the financing of terrorism, to update other aspects of the directive in the light of the June 2003 revisions to the FATF Forty Recommendations, and to revisit the treatment of "tipping off" by members of the legal profession. This exercise is also expected to result in the creation of a single, consolidated, directive.

Extraterritorial issues

The directives, though elaborated within the confines of the EU, were intended to have a broader geographic impact and, for this reason, certain of their provisions contain an extraterritorial dimension. Of special importance here is the definition of money laundering contained in Article 1 of the 1991 text. This is deliberately sensitive to the increasingly international character of the problem. It provides that "[m]oney laundering shall be regarded as such even where the activities which generated the property to be laundered were perpetrated in the territory of another Member State or in that of a third country". This key provision was retained (with only minor changes of wording) in Article 1(C) of the 2001 directive.

The wider geographic relevance of the measure is also ensured by the decision, reflected in the same article of the 1991 text, to subject Community-based branch offices of non-Community financial and credit institutions to its obligations. In the course of reviewing the adequacy of the directive with a view to its amendment, it was felt that greater clarity should be brought to this issue and to the consequences which flowed from it. This was accomplished by reworking the definitions of both credit and financial institutions in Article 1. By way of illustration, the new Article 1(B) now reads, in relevant part, as follows: "This definition of financial institution includes branches located in the Community of financial institutions, whose head offices are inside or outside the Community" (see also recitals 3 and 4). Though not specifically required by the directive, some member states have subjected the branches of their financial institutions located abroad to home country rules to the extent that such rules are not inconsistent with the laws of the host state. This stance is consistent with FATF Recommendation 22 (formerly Recommendation 20 in the 1996 version).

Of greater importance is the fact that the directive applies to those European Free Trade Association (EFTA) countries which ratified the agreement for a European Economic Area (EEA). Consequently, Austria, Finland and Sweden were not faced with the need to address this issue *de novo* upon entry to the EU in January 1995. Similarly, the fact that Norway, Liechtenstein and Iceland are not EU members does not affect the need for them to comply with this measure. The eastward expansion of the influence of the directive has also been a feature of the strategy of the Commission in this sphere. This has been most obvious in the negotiation of Europe Agreements – association arrangements of the most advanced form – with various of the new democratic states of central Europe. In each of those concluded to date, the Commission has insisted upon the inclusion of specific clauses on money laundering. For example, Article 86 of the 1993 agreement with the Czech Republic reads:

1. The Parties agree on the necessity of making every effort and co-operating in order to prevent the use of their financial systems for laundering of proceeds from criminal activities in general and drug offences in particular.

2. Co-operation in this area shall include administrative and technical assistance with the purpose of establishing suitable standards against money laundering equivalent to those adopted by the Community and international fora in this field, in particular the Financial Action Task Force (FATF).

Following upon the decision in principle to broaden the membership of the EU, the directive took on an even deeper significance for applicants. As the Commission has stated: "The money laundering directive is an integral part of the *acquis communautaire* and all candidate countries will be required to implement it. Efforts to assist in this process form part of the pre-accession strategy."[57] This emphasis was strengthened and expanded by the 1998 Pre-Accession Pact on Organised Crime between the applicant countries and the member states of the EU. Principle 13 thereof expressed agreement that there should be not only full implementation of the directive but also of the FATF recommendations and the 1990 Council of Europe convention. All ten new members were formally required to be in full compliance with the obligations of both directives by the date of accession in May 2004. The states in question are: Cyprus, Czech Republic, Estonia, Hungary, Latvia, Lithuania, Malta, Poland, the Slovak Republic, and Slovenia.

While the primary focus of the European Commission is on the countries of Europe, these are not its sole concern. It is convinced that "[t]he fight against money laundering has to be seen in global terms" and that "the anti-money laundering message be delivered and be heard in every country of the world". To this end, it has been involved in the financing of anti-laundering initiatives, the provision of technical assistance, and other anti-laundering efforts on an ever-widening geographic basis. The Commission also seeks:

> ... to incorporate an anti-money laundering clause in all the agreements, of whatever type, it concludes with non-member countries. The standard clause refers to efforts and co-operation to avoid money laundering and to the establishment of suitable standards against money laundering equivalent to those adopted in the EU and in international fora such as the FATF.[58]

It should also be recalled in this context that the two directives have been listed as being among the international standards to be used in the work of the Council of Europe Select Committee of Experts on the Evaluation of Anti-Money Laundering Measures. As was seen in chapter VII, all member states of the Council of Europe (including many in eastern Europe) which are not members of the FATF are subject to periodic mutual evaluations. These evaluate the performance of such countries in complying with, among other things, the standards reflected in both directives.

Other relevant EU initiatives

As was mentioned at an earlier stage of this chapter, the member states of the EU have a longstanding tradition of co-operation in the criminal justice area.[59] Particularly in the period since the entry into force of the Maastricht Treaty, this stream of Union activity has been afforded a high priority by governments and a range of resulting initiatives, especially in the areas of police and judicial co-operation, have had both a direct and indirect influence on efforts to combat money laundering and related matters such as the confiscation of criminal proceeds.

The gradual progress which has been, and continues to be, achieved is well illustrated by the creation and evolution of a central European criminal intelligence office (Europol). Although the background to this police co-operation initiative is a complex one, it can fairly be said that it gained both momentum and political credibility as a consequence of the public support afforded to it by Germany. In May 1991 Chancellor Kohl, speaking in Edinburgh, argued strongly and publicly for a European police force "that would be able to operate without let or hindrance in all the Community countries in important matters such as the fight against drug barons or organised international crime".[60] This was followed by the discussion of a detailed German paper on the subject at the Luxembourg summit of EC heads of state and government on 28 and 29 June. Somewhat surprisingly, the underlying thrust of the German paper was favourably received by the European Council which:

> ... mandated the Trevi group of ministers to report to the European Council in Maastricht in December 1991 with their proposals on how "Europol" should be set up and what preparatory or interim steps were required. This report was adopted by the Trevi group which met at the same time as the European Council in Maastricht.[61]

Formal acceptance of the Europol concept was contained in the resulting Maastricht Treaty on European Union. It should be stressed, however, that the treaty provisions were less extensive and ambitious than those contained in the original German proposals. In particular, the treaty whilst embracing "a Union-wide system for exchanging information" made no provision for the exercise of executive policing powers on a supranational basis. This limitation, which was seen by many as necessary given the perceived absence of adequate political, legal and procedural structures needed for operational policing, was reinforced by the associated political declaration on police co-operation which indicated a willingness to adopt practical measures "in the exchange of information and experience".

Subsequent years witnessed the phased, and often halting, process of making the Europol concept a practical reality. It commenced operations in February 1994 and its restricted initial mandate was "to act as a non-operational team for the exchange and analysis of intelligence in relation to illicit drug trafficking, the criminal organisations involved and associated money-laundering activities affecting two or more member states".[62]

Following the Essen European Council in December 1994, it was decided to extend the Europol mandate to include illicit trafficking in radioactive and nuclear substances, illicit vehicle trafficking, and crimes involving clandestine immigration networks along with associated money laundering activities.[63] In 1996 its competence was extended to include trafficking in human beings.[64]

The most important objective, that of placing Europol on a firm and formal legal footing, was finally achieved with the conclusion, in July 1995, of a convention on the establishment of Europol though the associated process of bringing it into full force and effect was not completed until October 1998. While a comprehensive analysis of this lengthy and complex text, and subsequent amendments, lies beyond the scope of this work some of its more significant features should be noted.

First, the convention paved the way for a further broadening of its mandate. In this regard, it was specifically provided that within two years of entry into force of the convention Europol would start to "deal with crimes committed in the course of terrorist activities against life, limb, personal freedom or property";[65] a development which was subsequently accelerated.[66] An annex also contained an extensive list of additional forms of serious crime, ranging from fraud to environmental offences, which the member states, acting unanimously, could instruct Europol to deal with.[67] It is of particular importance to note that its competence extended from the outset to "illegal money-laundering activities in connection with these forms of crime or specific manifestations thereof".[68] Money laundering is, in turn, defined in the annex by reference to Article 6 of the 1990 Council of Europe convention. In a protocol concluded in November 2000, the Europol convention was amended so as to extend its competence to money laundering in general, regardless of the type of offence from which the proceeds originated.[69]

The objective set by the convention is for Europol to improve the effectiveness of co-operation among member states in both preventing and combating crimes falling within its mandate "where there are factual indications that an organised criminal structure is involved and two or more member states are affected by the forms of crime in question in such a way as to require a common approach by the member states owing to the scale, significance and consequences of the offences concerned".[70] To this end, it was given various tasks including facilitating the exchange of information and obtaining, collating and analysing information and intelligence.[71] In addition, as Mackarel has noted, "[a]lthough the convention primarily establishes a basis for police co-operation between member states of the EU, it also contains limited provision for co-operation with 'outside' parties".[72] On this basis, Europol has started to give effect to ambitious plans to develop an extensive network of relationships with non-member countries, Interpol and other relevant bodies: a process which was accelerated in a significant fashion following the terrorist attacks on the United States in September 2001.[73]

The policy process in relation to police co-operation is, however, a dynamic one; a fact well illustrated by the conclusion of the Amsterdam Treaty of 1997. As Walker has noted:

> For its part, Europol is allocated a range of new functions, including authority to establish joint operational teams to support national investigations, the power to ask the competent authorities of the Member States to conduct and co-ordinate investigations in specific cases, and the capacity to develop specific expertise which may be put at the disposal of Member States to assist them in investigating organised crime ....[74]

Among other matters, the effort, pursuant to the Amsterdam Treaty mandate, to develop common action in the area of police co-operation includes "the collection, storage, processing, analysis and exchange of relevant information, including information held by law enforcement services on reports on suspicious financial transactions, in particular through Europol, subject to appropriate provisions on the protection of personal data".[75]

While action under the Third Pillar has thus resulted in significant developments in the sphere of police co-operation, it has by no means been restricted to that area.[76] For example, the EU has been actively engaged in initiatives to improve various aspects of judicial co-operation and has achieved notable progress in the critical areas of extradition and mutual legal assistance. The initial phase of EU activity in the sphere of extradition was primarily evolutionary in nature and resulted in the conclusion of two relevant conventions. That of March 1995 was concerned with simplified extradition while the multilateral treaty of September 1996 was of more general application.[77] Both embodied significant modernising features.[78] However, subsequent progress towards ratification and implementation was painfully slow.

It was for that reason, among others, surprising that the Tampere European Council of October 1999 decided to include extradition within the scope of its ambitious agenda to make the principle of mutual recognition "the cornerstone of judicial cooperation in both civil and criminal matters within the Union".[79] Subsequently, a programme of measures to implement the principle of mutual recognition was formulated containing two components relevant to extradition (measures 8 and 15).[80] Interestingly, neither was afforded the highest priority. With the September 2001 attack on the Twin Towers, however, the European arrest warrant (incorporating both elements) was fast tracked. Political agreement was reached on it at the Justice and Home Affairs Council in December 2001. The Framework Decision was formally adopted in June 2002:[81] the first mutual recognition measure to be finalised in the criminal justice sphere. It entered into force on 1 January 2004.

While a comprehensive analysis of this complex and radical measure lies beyond the scope of this work,[82] it should be emphasised that through its conclusion significant strides have been taken towards the removal of some of the orthodox impediments to this form of co-operation. Indeed, it goes well beyond the benchmark set by the EU Convention on Extradition of 1996.

This is well illustrated by the stance adopted in respect to the traditional requirement of double criminality; namely, the rule which, in essence, provides that there shall be no surrender for acts which are not also categorised as criminal by the law of the state of refuge. This barrier to extradition was left largely intact by the 1996 EU Convention on Extradition (though relaxed by Article 3 for conspiracy and association to commit terrorist, organised crime and drug trafficking offences). These limited exceptions are significantly extended by Article 2(2) of the Framework Decision. As Nilsson has remarked:

> In respect of a very broad list of 32 generic types of offences, it abolished the possibility of examination of double criminality. If a foreign judge certified that he is investigating a particular offence which is punishable by imprisonment in his country of at least 3 years and if that offence is on the list of 32 offences, the judge in the executing state shall not examine the facts of the case and control double criminality.[83]

The "laundering of the proceeds of crime" is so listed; a fact of some practical significance given differing national approaches to such matters as the required mental element for the money laundering offence and the criminalisation of "own funds" or "self-laundering".

A broadly similar pattern is also evident in the sphere of EU engagement with mutual legal assistance. For example, the initial phase of EU modernisation was also of an evolutionary character placing emphasis on making judicial co-operation in criminal matters more flexible, effective and extensive. While the realisation of these goals has involved a range of initiatives, from the articulation of best practice to the creation of new institutional structures, pride of place must be afforded to the conclusion in May 2000 of the Convention on Mutual Assistance in Criminal Matters between the member states of the EU.[84] It is a text of considerable length and complexity.[85]

While in some respects it falls short of the high expectations which had been created by the influential 1997 Action Plan against Organised Crime (for example, in failing to remove double criminality as a ground for refusal of co-operation, and in not directly addressing the issue of witness protection programmes), it none the less recorded not insignificant progress. For example, in terms of expanding the range of assistance available, the 2000 EU convention on mutual assistance:

- extends assistance to cases involving corporate liability;
- provides for hearings by video-conference;
- facilitates various forms of cross-border operational policing such as covert investigations and the establishment of joint investigation teams; and
- provides the first exhaustive treatment of the complex and sensitive issue of co-operation in the interception of telecommunications.

It is of particular relevance to note that in October 2001, following a French initiative, a protocol to this convention was concluded.[86] While this includes provisions on grounds for refusal and additional requests it is Articles 1 to 4, which address the issue of assistance relating to banking information, which are of primary importance for present purposes.

Article 1 concerning requests for information on bank accounts is highly innovative. Paragraph 1 is worded thus:

> 1. Each Member State shall, under the conditions set out in this Article, take the measures necessary to determine, in answer to a request sent by another Member State, whether a natural or legal person that is the subject of a criminal investigation holds or controls one or more accounts, of whatever nature, in any bank located in its territory and, if so, provide all the details of the identified accounts.

> The information shall also, if requested and to the extent that it can be provided within a reasonable time, include accounts for which the person that is the subject of the proceedings has powers of attorney.

Subsequent paragraphs define the scope of and limits to this obligation. For example, in a departure from the norm in European mutual legal assistance, paragraph 3 indicates that the obligations under this article apply only to certain forms of offences. In the words of the official explanatory report:

> ... the offence concerned must be covered by at least one of three alternatives. The first alternative is a combination of penalty thresholds in both States – four years in the requesting Member State and two years in the requested Member State. ... The second and third alternatives are lists of crimes, namely the list of offences found in the Europol Convention ... or the offences covered by the instruments relating to the protection of the European Communities' financial interests, to the extent they are not already covered by the Europol list ... .[87]

The remaining provisions on requests for information on banking transactions (Article 2), requests for the monitoring of banking transactions (Article 3), and confidentiality (Article 4) all deal with procedures and concepts which are more firmly established in existing practice. That said, the use of the designation "confidentiality" could be misleading. Article 4, the wording of which draws heavily on that found in the money laundering directives, has as its sole focus the imposition of an obligation on banks not to "tip off" customers or third parties that information has been transmitted to the authorities or that an investigation is being carried out.

Not only are these developments important ones within an EU context they have also had, and are likely to continue to have, a broader impact on the international law and practice of mutual assistance. For instance, a new protocol has since been concluded to the 1959 Council of Europe mutual assistance convention, the content of which has been heavily influenced by the 2000 EU text.[88] Similarly, the 2003 EU-US agreement on mutual assistance includes many of the innovative features found in both the EU convention and its protocol.[89] Furthermore, it would be surprising if the new EU stance on access to bank information did not find reflection in the updated and expanded version of the 1990 Council of Europe money laundering convention the negotiations for which, as seen in the previous chapter, commenced in mid-December 2003.

It should be stressed, however, that EU innovation in this sphere is far from complete. As with extradition, mutual assistance issues form a key part of the mutual recognition agenda initiated at Tampere in October 1999. The Framework Decision on the execution of orders freezing property or evidence, finally adopted in July 2003 and due to be implemented by 2 August 2005,[90] will not be the last to intrude into this sphere of common concern. Those having a bearing on the confiscation of criminal proceeds will be of particular relevance within the present context.

Within the Third Pillar, initiatives have also been taken which are specifically focused on aspects of the anti-money laundering agenda. Of particular significance in this regard is the Joint Action of 3 December 1998 on money laundering, the identification, tracing, freezing, seizing and confiscation of instrumentalities and the proceeds from crime.[91] This seeks to build upon the participation of member countries in the 1990 Council of Europe convention. As noted earlier, it seeks to ensure that no reservations are made or upheld by its members in relation to Article 6 of the convention "in so far as serious offences are concerned". It extends the same philosophy to Article 2 on the scope of domestic confiscation legislation (though there is an exception in respect of proceeds from tax offences).[92] A number of practical steps are also to be taken to enhance the effectiveness of co-operation. These range from the preparation of user-friendly guides to national laws and practices to a requirement that the same priority be afforded to requests for assistance in this area as is given in domestic proceedings.[93]

The above measure was amended and strengthened by a European Council Framework Decision of 26 June 2001.[94] Among other things, this limits the tax-offence loophole and brings about a measure of approximation of approach to the important issue of the penalties to be applied in respect of money laundering offences.

Mention should also be made of the Council Decision of 17 October 2000 concerning arrangements for co-operation between financial intelligence units of the member states in respect of exchanging information.[95] For various reasons, which have been well summarised elsewhere,[96] neither of the directives on money laundering contains express treatment of the establishment or functioning of FIUs. In seeking to fill this gap, this Council Decision requires, among other things, that the performance of their functions "shall not be affected by their internal status, regardless of whether they are administrative, law enforcement or judicial authorities" (Article 3). Interestingly, it was specifically stated that implementation of the Decision shall be without prejudice to the member states' obligations towards Europol (Article 8).

In these and a myriad of other ways, the EU has become a significant and innovative actor in the anti-money laundering effort. As has been noted at various stages of this chapter, other relevant initiatives are in train or under active discussion. Money laundering and the targeting of the vast profits derived from criminal activity thus seem set to retain a position of prominence on the justice and home affairs agenda for some time to come.

Notes: VIII

1. As of January 2004, the fifteen members were: Austria; Belgium; Denmark; Finland; France; Germany; Greece; Ireland; Italy; Luxembourg; Netherlands; Portugal; Spain; Sweden; and the United Kingdom. In May 2004, as noted below, a further ten states were admitted.

2. For a detailed discussion see, Anderson, M et al., *Policing the European Union*, Oxford, Oxford University Press, 1995; and, Benyon, J et al., *Police co-operation in Europe: an investigation*, Leicester, University of Leicester, 1993.

3. See, for example, Dine, J, "European Community Criminal Law?", *Criminal Law Review*, 1993, at pp. 246-354. See also, Schutte, J, "The European Market of 1993: Test for a Regional Model of Supranational Criminal Justice or of Interregional Cooperation in Criminal Law", *Criminal Law Forum*, 1991, at pp. 5-83.

4. Speech of 21 November 94. Text kindly supplied by the European Commission.

5. Walker, N, "European Policing and the Politics of Regulation", in Gilmore, W and Cullen, P (eds), *Crime sans frontières: international and European legal approaches*, Edinburgh, Edinburgh University Press, 1998, p. 141, at p. 144. See also, Peers, S, *EU justice and home affairs law*, Harlow, Essex, Longman, 2000; de Zwaan, J and Vrouenraets, M, "The Future of the Third Pillar", in Heukels, T et al., *The European Union after Amsterdam*, The Hague, Kluwer, 1998, at pp. 203-214; and "Action Plan of the Council and the Commission on How Best to Implement the Provisions of the Treaty of Amsterdam on an Area of Freedom, Justice and Security", *Official Journal of the European Communities*, No. C 19/1, 23 January 1999. At the time of writing, discussions concerning the conclusion of a Treaty Establishing a Constitution for Europe were at an advanced stage. The possible impact of such a treaty on police and judicial co-operation fall outside the scope of this work.

6. See, for example, Schutte, J, "The Incorporation of the Schengen *Acquis* in the European Union"; and Genson, R, "The Schengen Agreements – Police Cooperation and Security Aspects", in Gilmore, W and Cullen, P (eds), *supra*, note 5, at p. 124 and p. 133 respectively.

7. Memorandum of H Nilsson, in House of Lords, Select Committee on the European Communities, "Money Laundering", HL Paper 6, 1990-91, Evidence, p. 35, at p. 37.

8. Cullen, P, "The European Community Directive" in MacQueen, H L (ed), *Money laundering*, Edinburgh, Edinburgh University Press, 1993, p. 34, at p. 36.

9. See, "The 1990 Commission Proposal and Explanatory Memorandum", reproduced in Gilmore, W (ed), *International efforts to combat money laundering*, Cambridge, Cambridge University Press, 1992, p. 243, at p. 244.

10. *Supra*, note 7, p. 5.

11. *Supra*, note 9, p. 251.

12. See, for example, the Netherlands Disclosure of Unusual Transactions (Financial Services) Act of 16 December 1993.

13. See, Cullen, op.cit., at p. 47.

14. Dine, op.cit., p. 247.

15. 1991 directive, Article 1.

16. Given the approach of the directive to the definition of money laundering, it is perhaps not surprising that there has not always been an exact correspondence between the scope of the criminal offence and that of the legislation formulated to implement the directive. However, as the March 1995 report from the Commission to the European Parliament and to the Council on the implementation of the directive noted, there is evidence of increasing convergence between the two thus contributing to the elimination of "any hiatus between the Member States' preventive and punitive systems as well as to facilitating interstate cooperation in this field" ("First Commission Report on the Implementation of the Money Laundering Directive (91/308/EEC) to be Submitted to the European Parliament and to the Council", COM (95) 54 final, Brussels, 03 March 1995, p. 6 (hereafter 1995 Commission report)).

17. *Official Journal of the European Communities*, No. L 333/1, 9 December 1998, Article 1(b).

18. See, *Official Journal of the European Communities*, No. L 182/1, 5 July 2001.

19. "Report on the First Commission's Report to be Submitted to the European Parliament and to the Council on the Implementation of the Directive on the Prevention of the Use of the Financial System for the Purpose of Money Laundering", European Parliament Doc. A4-0187/96 (hereafter 1996 European Parliament report), p. 5.

20. Ibid., p. 21.

21. See, *Official Journal of the European Communities*, No. C 221/11, Articles 1(e) and 2.

22. Ibid., Article 3.

23. See, 1991 directive, Article 14.

24. See, for example, Annex 7 to the 1995 Commission report, *supra*, note 16.

25. See, 1995 Commission report, *supra*, note 16, at p. 16.

26. Reproduced in Gilmore, W (ed), *supra*, note 5, p. 243, at p. 244.

27. 1995 Commission report, *supra*, note 16, pp. 6-7.

28. See, 1995 Commission report, *supra*, note 16, at p. 7; and, "Second Commission Report to the European Parliament and the Council on the Implementation of the Money Laundering Directive", COM (1998) 401 final, Brussels, 1 July 1998 (hereafter 1998 Commission report), at pp. 8-9.

29. "FATF VII Report on Money Laundering Typologies", in "Financial Action Task Force on Money Laundering: Annual Report 1995-1996", Paris, FATF, Annex 3, p. 4.

30. See, 1998 Commission report, Annex 6, *supra*, note 28, at pp. 39-40.

31. 1995 Commission report, *supra*, note 16, p. 8.

32. 1998 Commission report, *supra*, note 28, p. 10.

33. Vardon, L, "The Role of Investment Firms", in Parlour, R (ed), *Butterworths international guide to money laundering law and practice*, London, Butterworth, 1995, p.265, at p. 272.

34. 1991 directive, Article 3(1).

35. Ibid., Article 3(2).

36. See, Ibid., Article 3(3) and (4). See also, Article 3(7).

37. 1995 Commission report, *supra*, note 16, p. 10.

38. Ibid.

39. For a discussion of practice concerning implementation see, for example, 1995 Commission report, *supra*, note 16, p. 12.

40. Westerweel, J and Hillen, J, *Measures to combat money laundering in the Netherlands*, The Hague, Ministry of Finance, 1995, p. 5.

41. *The fight against money laundering*, The Hague, Ministry of Justice, Office for the Disclosure of Unusual Transactions (MOT), 1997, p. 20. See also, Schutte, J, "Police Cooperation", in Swart, B and Klip, A (eds), *International criminal law in the Netherlands*, Freiburg im Breisgau, 1997, p. 145, at pp. 161-162; and, Graff, G B and Jurgens, M, "The Netherlands", in Graham, T (ed), *Butterworths international guide to money laundering law and practice*, 2nd edn, London, Butterworth, 2003, p. 468, at pp. 480-486.

42. See, 1995 Commission report, *supra*, note 16, at p. 13.

43. 1991 directive, Article 8.

44. The 2001 directive, discussed in the following section, requires in the new Article 11(2) that members ensure that obligated institutions and persons "have access to up-to-date information on the practices of money launderers and on indications leading to the recognition of suspicious transactions".

45. "Proposal for a European Parliament and Council Directive amending Council Directive 91/308/EEC of 10 June 1991 on Prevention of the Use of the Financial System for the Purposes of Money Laundering", COM (1999) 352 final, Brussels, 14 July 1999, p. 4.

46. *Official Journal of the European Communities*, No. L 344/76, 28 December 2001.

47. See, Mitsilegas, V, *Money laundering counter-measures in the European Union, a new paradigm of security governance versus fundamental legal principles*, London, Kluwer Law International, 2003, at pp. 86-102.

48. See, 1998 Commission report, *supra*, note 28, at p.15.

49. *Supra*, note 47, p. 96.

50. The directives are regarded within the FATF as fully satisfying the requirement that members institute a mandatory suspicious transactions reporting scheme. See also, for example, the new Article 11(2) inserted by the 2001 directive.

51. See, Case 28/76 *Milac v. HZA Freiburg*, 1976 ECR 1639. I am in the debt of my colleague Professor John Usher for bringing this case to my attention and discussing related issues of European law with me.

52. 1995 Commission report, *supra*, note 16, p. 11.

53. 1998 Commission report, *supra*, note 28, p. 12.

54. See, Mitsilegas, op.cit., at pp. 92-94, and p. 100.

55. Now found in Article 3(10).

56. Mitsilegas, op.cit., p. 100.

57. 1998 Commission report, *supra*, note 28, p. 6.

58. Ibid., p. 7.

59. See generally, Anderson et al., *supra*, note 2.

60. Kohl, H, "Our Future in Europe", Edinburgh, Europa Institute, University of Edinburgh, 1991, p. 16.

61. Cullen, P, "The German Police and European Co-operation", Edinburgh, Department of Politics, University of Edinburgh, 1992, p. 79.

62. Gilmore, W, "Police Cooperation and the European Communities: Current Trends and Recent Developments", in *Action against transnational criminality: papers from the 1993 Oxford Conference on International and White Collar Crime*, London, Commonwealth Secretariat, 1994, p. 147, at p. 156.

63. See, Joint Action of 10 March 1995 concerning the Europol Drugs Unit, *Official Journal of the European Communities*, No. L 62/1, 20 March 1995.

64. See, Joint Action of 16 December 1996 extending the mandate given to the Europol Drugs Unit, *Official Journal of the European Communities*, No. L 342/4, 31 December 1996.

65. See, Convention on the Establishment of a European Police Office (Europol convention), *Official Journal of the European Communities*, No. C 316/2, 27 November 1995, Article 2(2).

66. The text of the relevant Council Decision of 3 December 1998 is reproduced at *Official Journal of the European Communities*, No. C 26/22, 30 January 1999.

67. Europol was subsequently authorised to deal with all of the annexed offences with effect from 1 January 2002. See, Council Decision of 6 December 2001, *Official Journal of the European Communities*, No. C 362/1. 18 December 2000.

68. Europol convention, Article 2(3)(1).

69. See, *Official Journal of the European Communities*, No. C 358/1, 13 December 2000.

70. Europol convention, Article 2(1).

71. See, Europol convention, Article 3.

72. Mackarel, M, "Europol", *Scottish Law and Practice Quarterly*, 1996, p. 197, at p. 203.

73. See generally, Gilmore, B, *The Twin Towers and the Third Pillar: Some Security Agenda Developments*, EUI Working Paper Law 2003/7, Florence, European University Institute, 2003.

74. Walker, op.cit., p. 145.

75. Article K.2(1)(b).

76. See, generally, for example, Barrett, G (ed), *Justice cooperation in the European Union*, Dublin, Institute of European Affairs, 1997.

77. Of these the most significant for present purposes was the latter. See, *Official Journal of the European Communities*, No. C 313/12, 23 October 1996. For the official explanatory report, see *Official Journal of the European Communities*, No. C 191/13, 23 June 1997.

78. See, for example, Vermeulen, G and Vander Beken, T, "New Conventions on Extradition in the European Union", *Dickinson Journal of International Law*, 1997, at p. 265; and, Makarel, M and Nash, S, "Extradition and the European Union", *International and Comparative Law Quarterly*, 1997, at pp. 948-957.

79. Paragraph 33 of the presidency conclusions. Reproduced in Cullen, P and Jund, S (eds), *Criminal justice co-operation in the European Union after Tampere*, Trier, Academy of European Law, 2002, p. 157, at p. 162.

80. *Official Journal of the European Communities*, No. C 12/10, 15 January 2001.

81. See, *Official Journal of the European Communities*, No. L 190/1, 18 July 2002.

82. See, Gilmore, B, "The EU Framework Decision on the European Arrest Warrant", ERA Forum, 2002, at pp. 144-147; and Plachta, M, "European Arrest Warrant: Revolution in Extradition?", *European Journal of Crime, Criminal Law and Criminal Justice*, 2003, at pp. 178-194.

83. Nilsson, H, "Mutual Recognition and Mutual Trust; new European Developments", Salerno, 2 March 2002 (typescript), pp. 4-5. Text kindly supplied by the Council.

84. See, *Official Journal of the European Communities*, No. C 197/1, 12 July 2000. For the official explanatory report see, *Official Journal of the European Communities*, No. C 379/7, 29 December 2000,

85. See generally, Denza, E, "The 2000 Convention on Mutual Assistance in Criminal Matters", *Common Market Law Review*, 2003, at pp. 1047-1074.

86. *Official Journal of the European Communities*, No. C 326/1, 21 November 2001.

87. *Official Journal of the European Communities*, No. C 257/1, 24 October 2002, p. 3.

88. Second Additional Protocol to the European Convention on Mutual Assistance in Criminal Matters, 2001.

89. See generally, House of Lords, Select Committee on the European Union, "EU-US Agreements on Extradition and Mutual Legal Assistance", HL Paper 153, 2002-03; and Mitsilegas, V, "The New EU-USA Cooperation on Extradition, Mutual Legal Assistance and the Exchange of Police Data", *European Foreign Affairs Review*, 2003, at pp. 515-536.

90. *Official Journal of the European Communities*, No. L 196/45, 2 August 2003.

91. *Supra*, note 17.

92. See, Article 1.

93. See, Articles 2 and 3.

94. *Supra*, note 18.

95. *Official Journal of the European Communities*, No. L 271/4, 24 October 2000.

96. See, *supra*, note 47, at pp. 94-95, and p. 98.

CHAPTER IX – WIDENING THE NET: AN OVERVIEW OF PROGRESS AND PROSPECTS IN OTHER REGIONS

The Caribbean basin and Latin America

Well before the demise of the cold war and the problems of transition attracted attention to central and eastern Europe, the law enforcement community and money laundering experts had identified a number of jurisdictions and regions, outside the developed financial elite represented by the members of the OECD, as sources of concern. Of these, particular attention was devoted – even before the creation of the FATF – to the countries and territories of the Caribbean basin. As the Bureau of International Narcotics Matters of the US Department of State was to remark in March 1988:

> The Caribbean Basin is the first stop for most Latin American drug dollars moving through international channels. For both the foreign suppliers and their US distributors, the Caribbean Basin has for long been a natural stop because of its proximity to the United States, high levels of corruption, and the region's many financial centers with secrecy laws and lenient taxes.[1]

This latter aspect is deserving of comment. Confronted by an inadequate natural resource base and a marked decline in the viability of the agricultural sector, a substantial number of the small island states of the Caribbean had turned to the development of offshore financial services as part of their efforts to promote rapid economic diversification. Some of these efforts met with spectacular success. By way of illustration: "In 1964 the Cayman Islands had two banks and no offshore business. By 1981 the Caymans had 360 branches of US and foreign banks, over 8,000 registered companies, and more telex machines per capita ... than any other country."[2] It is now one of the world's most significant financial centres. Other major players include Aruba, the Bahamas, the Netherlands Antilles and, in Central America, Panama.

The use of the range of facilities afforded by such emerging financial centres was of particular concern to the authorities of the United States. The absence of an established framework for co-operation and strict commercial confidentiality legislation gave rise to difficulties in efforts to secure vital evidence for use in US prosecutions. This resulted in an increasing readiness to resort to controversial unilateral measures.[3] Although such tactics not infrequently resulted in short-term success, this tended to be at the expense of creating a climate of conflict which strained international relationships.

By the mid-1980s, however, reliance on unilateral measures started to give way to an increased readiness to negotiate formal co-operative relationships on a bilateral basis. For example, in 1984 the United States and the United Kingdom entered into an agreement which established a simple and straight-forward procedure whereby the former could obtain assistance from the British dependent territory of the Cayman Islands in investigations and prosecutions involving drug trafficking. So positive was the experience of the parties with its practical operation that similar arrangements were con-cluded in respect of all of the remaining Caribbean dependencies of the UK. This experience of co-operation was to provide the foundations for efforts to deepen and widen the relationship; a process which was to lead to the conclusion of a full mutual legal assistance treaty relating to Cayman which entered into force in early 1990.[4] Somewhat similar bilateral developments were recorded in respect of other jurisdictions including the Bahamas.

It was within this context that the countries of the Caribbean and Central America met in Aruba in June 1990 in order to seek a common position on appropriate money laundering countermeasures. There, the participants took note of the fact that trafficking networks had established a drug ser-vice industry within the region, significant parts of which were believed to exist simply to facilitate the laundering of illicit proceeds. It was also acknowledged that as the United States and other highly developed indus-trialised countries moved to implement the recommendations of the FATF, the attractiveness of the region to criminal money managers was likely to increase. Consequently, they "agreed to consider the forty recommendations of the Financial Action Task Force of the G7 countries plus twenty-one additional recommendations".[5] The latter, since reduced to nineteen in number,[6] are complementary measures intended to address the problem as it has manifested itself in that area of the world.[7] Subsequently, the 11th Meeting of Heads of Government of the Caribbean Community (Caricom), held in August 1990, discussed a number of issues relating to the financial aspects of drug trafficking and took note of the active participation of many of its members at the Aruba conference.[8] The Aruba meeting also resulted in the establishment of the Caribbean Financial Action Task Force (CFATF).[9]

This major regional precedent was reinforced by an anti-laundering regional workshop which was hosted by the Government of Jamaica in May 1992.[10] This was then followed by a regional ministerial meeting held in Kingston, Jamaica, in November of the same year. At that meeting, participants "agreed that they would sign and ratify the 1988 UN Convention against Illicit Traffic in Narcotic Drugs and Psychotropic Substances and further agreed to endorse and implement both the forty FATF recommendations and the 19 Aruba recommendations".[11]

This gathering also recognised the need to create a structure to monitor and encourage progress towards implementation of the Kingston declaration. Both self-assessment and mutual evaluation processes were to be used. To further this aim and to facilitate the provision of training and technical assistance in the region, the meeting proposed the creation of a small CFATF secretariat to be based in Trinidad and Tobago.[12] With the financial support of a number of FATF "sponsoring countries" (Canada, France, Netherlands, United Kingdom, and the United States) this step was taken in early 1994.[13]

The membership of the CFATF, now standing at thirty, is drawn from the independent states of the Commonwealth Caribbean, United Kingdom dependencies (known as Overseas Territories), the Dutch associated states and Spanish-speaking states from the Caribbean, and Central America. Surinam and Venezuela are also members. After a somewhat hesitant start, this regional initiative has become firmly entrenched and has made significant progress in giving effect to an extensive programme of work. In particular, it is on course to complete its second round of mutual evaluations which commenced in July 2001. It has, in addition, undertaken several typologies exercises and developed close ties with the South American Financial Action Task Force (Gafisud). This ten-strong regional body was created in December 2000 and is serviced by a small secretariat based in Buenos Aires, Argentina.[14]

In October 1996 the CFATF, following the expression of concern by some participants over its informal nature, adopted a memorandum of understanding (MoU).[15] This codifies its objectives and formalises its structures and procedures. The MoU can be amended by the unanimous vote of a meeting of the CFATF Council. This council, which consists of one ministerial representative from each member, is the "supreme authority". It includes among its functions the adoption of mutual evaluation reports, taking decisions on policy matters (including the adoption of revised recommendations) and taking appropriate action with respect to members which fail to meet the organisation's standards.

These developments in the Caribbean and Latin America have been assisted and reinforced by initiatives taking place under the auspices of the Organization of American States (OAS), which includes among its members the independent states of the Caribbean basin as well as those located in Central and South America. The OAS, it should be stressed, has for many years identified action to counter money laundering and to confiscate proceeds as critical to the fight against drug trafficking in the Americas. Thus, the April 1986 Inter-American Program of Action of Rio de Janeiro against the Illicit Use and Production of Narcotic Drugs and Psychotropic Substances and Traffic Therein recommended the study of draft legislation designed: to strengthen the ability of the appropriate authorities to trace the origin of the funds; to criminalise drug-related laundering; and, "to forfeit assets derived from or used to facilitate drug trafficking, irrespective of where such trafficking occurred".[16] It also called for, among other measures, the creation of a regional Inter-American Drug Abuse Control Commission (Cicad).

In April 1990, a meeting of the ministers of member states responsible for the control of drug trafficking issued the Declaration and Program of Action of Ixtapa.[17] This both underlined the continuing importance attached to these law enforcement strategies and called upon Cicad to convene a group of regional experts to draft model regulations in this area which were in conformity with the 1988 UN drug trafficking convention. Out of this process there emerged the Model Regulations Concerning Laundering Offenses Connected to Illicit Drug Trafficking and Related Offenses which were approved by the OAS General Assembly in 1992.

Both influenced by and compatible with the 1988 UN convention and the FATF recommendations, the original text of the model regulations consisted of some nineteen articles which addressed all of the then key elements of a modern counterstrategy including the enhancement of the preventive role of the private sector.[18] In doing so, they reached out to cover a broad range of financial institutions and activities in addition to banks. Furthermore, the financial sector provisions, drafted with the 1990 FATF recommendations in mind, gave expression to familiar principles including those relating to customer identification, compliance with laws, co-operation with law enforcement agencies, and the introduction of internal compliance and training programmes by the institutions concerned. Finally, it should be noted that unlike the 1991 European directive and the 1990 Council of Europe money laundering convention, the 1992 model regulations were limited in their scope to drug trafficking and related offences. This was due, in the main, to the nature of the mandate given to the group of experts charged with elaborating them. However, the experts recommended that member states of the OAS consider applying them to laundering connected with other serious offences.

Subsequent years have witnessed significant developments at the policy level which have, in turn, found reflection in amendments to the model regulations. The initial developments owed much to the Declaration of Principles and Plan of Action adopted by the December 1994 Summit of the Americas. Among other matters, the action plan committed participating states to criminalise the laundering of the proceeds of all serious crimes and to work towards adopting the model regulations. In addition, they agreed to "[h]old a working-level conference, to be followed by a ministerial conference, to study and agree on a co-ordinated hemispheric response … to combat money laundering".[19]

Following working level meetings held in Washington, DC, ministers with responsibility for the money laundering issue drawn from thirty-four countries met in Buenos Aires in late 1995. They endorsed a declaration of principles and agreed to recommend a detailed and ambitious plan of action. The latter called for, among other matters, the criminalisation of the laundering of the proceeds of serious offences, the conclusion of asset-sharing agreements, the creation of national forfeiture funds to administer forfeited property, and the establishment of national FIUs. It also recorded the intention "to institute ongoing assessments of the implementation of this Plan of Action within the OAS framework".

In June of 1996, the Cicad Group of Experts to Control Money Laundering was reconvened to assist in the implementation of the December 1995 action plan. One matter to receive early attention was whether or not to amend the model regulations. Having concluded that such a modernising effort was called for, the group of experts first turned its attention to the formulation of a new provision which requires the establishment of FIUs in accordance with the Egmont Group definition. This initiative, approved in the course of 1997, was followed by further updating efforts which focused on a range of issues trailed by the ministerial meeting of December 1995. The most recent emphasis has been on extending the scope of the model regulations to include detailed treatment of the financing of terrorism.[20]

From the outset, Cicad has actively promoted the adoption of these regulations by its member countries. In this context, the key role is now played by its Anti-Money Laundering Unit (Amlu), which was established in late 1999. It affords particular priority to the provision of training and technical assistance and in so doing has formed a close and constructive relationship with, among others, the Inter-American Development Bank.

Cicad also lies at the heart of the recent emphasis within the Inter-American system on the evaluation of implementation practice. This innovation was mandated by the Second Summit of the Americas held in Santiago in April 1998. There it was agreed to move towards adopting a system of evaluation in connection with drug trafficking and other related crimes. In the words of the action plan, governments will "with the intention of strengthening mutual confidence, dialogue and hemispheric cooperation ... develop ... a singular and objective process of multilateral governmental evaluation in order to monitor the progress of their individual and collective efforts ...".

This multilateral evaluation mechanism (MEM) started functioning in 1999 and now operates on a two-year cycle. While a comprehensive review of it lies beyond the scope of this work, several points of interest are deserving of mention for present purposes. First, while it includes within its scope coverage of the issue of money laundering, its remit is much broader; namely, the nature and extent of compliance with the anti-drug strategy in the region. Second, it differs in a number of significant ways from the process of mutual evaluation used by the FATF and FATF-style regional bodies. In the Cicad system, each evaluated country provides data in response to a standard questionnaire as well as a paper on its drug problems. On this basis a governmental experts group, representing all thirty-four member countries, formulates jurisdiction-specific reports including recommendations for improvement. Importantly, this procedure is not informed by a prior on-site visit. Similarly, while the MEM includes a follow-up procedure to monitor the implementation of recommendations made, the procedure explicitly excludes recourse to sanctions of any kind. A somewhat similar procedure has now been put in place to monitor the implementation of the central obligations contained in the 1996 Inter-American Convention against Corruption.

It is of interest to note that the 1996 text specifically acknowledges the links between the profits generated by drug trafficking and the corruption problem. Article XV consequently requires the provision of "assistance in the identification, tracing, freezing, seizure and forfeiture of property or proceeds obtained, derived from or used in the commission of offences established in accordance with this convention". Similarly, significant elements of the strategy of financial devastation are incorporated in the June 2002 Inter-American Convention against Terrorism. By way of illustration, Article 4 requires the establishment of a regime to prevent, combat, and eradicate the financing of terrorism. In the implementation of this obligation, paragraph 2 requires states parties to "use as guidelines the recommendations developed by specialised international and regional entities, in particular the Financial Action Task Force and, as appropriate, the Inter-American Drug Abuse Control Commission, the Caribbean Financial Action Task Force, and the South American Financial Action Task Force".

Selected developments elsewhere

Another early priority area for the FATF's outreach programme was Asia. This regional concentration was primarily due to its pivotal role in the world trade in heroin based on the Golden Crescent and Golden Triangle production areas. It was also in the drugs sphere where initial progress was most evident. A significant cross-section of states, from Afghanistan in the west to the People's Republic of China in the east, became parties to the 1988 UN drug trafficking convention. These countries have either fully implemented their obligations to criminalise drug-related money laundering and provide for extensive international co-operation in relation to serious drug trafficking offences or claim to be in the process of doing so.

Less swiftly entrenched was the commitment towards enhancing the role of the financial sector in the effort to combat laundering or to broaden the agenda to include non-drug specific crimes. Part of the explanation lies in the vastness of the geographic area, the diversity which exists among its members in terms of socioeconomic development, and the initial absence of a regional institution to promote and facilitate progress. To this must be added the level of complexity which results from the ready availability of extensive and efficient underground and parallel banking systems (of the types discussed in chapter II), capable of acting either as a substitute for or as complement to the orthodox financial sector in international money laundering operations.

In these circumstances, the FATF concentrated its early efforts on raising the level of awareness of regional policy makers and seeking to promote a momentum towards acceptance of its package of countermeasures in a manner and form which might eventually become self-sustaining. In this it was greatly assisted by the fact that it counts Hong Kong, Japan and Singapore among its own members. Australia, and to a lesser extent New Zealand, also have special interests in securing progress in a region which is geographically proximate and of considerable economic and political importance to them.

In April 1993, the FATF combined with the Commercial Crime Unit (as it was then known) of the Commonwealth Secretariat to organise a major regional conference in Singapore. Subsequently, the decision was taken to establish a small Asia Money Laundering secretariat to support the work of the FATF in the region. Throughout this early phase of development, it was also recognised that the small island states of the Pacific faced many of the same challenges. Indeed, political leaders from those countries had collectively acknowledged the threat which they faced as a consequence of the growth of transnational criminal activity. Of particular interest in this regard was a declaration on law enforcement co-operation adopted by the South Pacific Forum in July 1992.

In this declaration they accepted that "there is a risk the South Pacific region may be targeted for such activities". Accordingly, they recommended that members consider the recommendations of the FATF and move towards the implementation of those which were deemed to be applicable to their individual circumstances. Significantly, for present purposes, the forum leaders also specifically:

> ... accepted the need to strengthen national and international legal provisions to enable the proceeds and instrumentalities of crime to be traced, frozen and seized, and acknowledged the need to regulate banking and other financial services to reduce the possible manipulation of these services to "launder" the proceeds of crime. The Forum recognised that bank secrecy laws can be used as a shield for the laundering of criminal profits and determined that it should not be permitted to obstruct the operation of mutual assistance arrangements.

Elsewhere in this document, progress was urged in the modernisation of extradition legislation and in making appropriate statutory provision for mutual assistance in criminal matters. Furthermore, members agreed to afford priority to the ratification and implementation of the 1988 UN Convention against Illicit Traffic in Narcotic Drugs and Psychotropic Substances, a step which Fiji – very much the regional leader – took in early 1993.

Eventually these two regions became fully linked for the purpose of anti-money laundering developments with the formal creation of the Asia/Pacific Group on Money Laundering (APG). It currently consists of twenty-eight members which are drawn primarily from South, Southeast and East Asia and the South Pacific. As has been pointed out elsewhere:

> In March 1998, the first annual meeting of the APG was held in Tokyo and attended by 25 jurisdictions from the region. A revised Terms of Reference was agreed, as well as an action plan for the future. The Tokyo meeting represented the full establishment of the APG as a cohesive regional group following on from the earlier awareness-raising efforts.[21]

Since that time, the APG has initiated its first round of mutual evaluations and established a positive reputation for the quality of its analysis of money laundering typologies. It has also amended its terms of reference so as to place efforts to combat terrorist financing and to implement the eight special recommendations of the FATF firmly within its mandate.

Efforts to promote greater international co-operation in the administration of justice and an acceptance of the need for comprehensive anti-money laundering measures have also been undertaken by non-regional bodies. Of particular interest in this regard is the Commonwealth – an extensive grouping of states with close ties of history, language and legal tradition. Significantly for present purposes this body includes several Task Force participants (Australia, Canada, New Zealand, Singapore, South Africa and the United Kingdom) in a membership dominated by developing countries many of which, as with the English-speaking states of Africa, are from regions where the FATF had, until recently, no representation.

The Commonwealth has for many years afforded priority to encouraging close co-operation in criminal matters and has elaborated arrangements dealing with extradition, the transfer of convicted offenders and like matters.[22] Of special relevance in this context is the 1986 Scheme Relating to Mutual Assistance in Criminal Matters (as amended).[23] Not only did this have a major impact in promoting an important mechanism of co-operation which had for long been neglected by the common law world, it also took the significant, and at the time innovative, step of making extensive provision for international action in tracing, seizing and confiscating proceeds on an all-crimes basis.[24] Another highly relevant initiative was taken by Commonwealth heads of government, meeting in Malaysia in 1989 and again in Zimbabwe in 1991, when they welcomed the conclusion of the 1988 UN convention and urged its early ratification and implementation.[25]

Such actions had a positive impact as an ever-growing number of countries took the necessary steps to modernise their legislation. This is well illustrated by the southern African Republic of Botswana which is not considered to be either a money laundering centre or to be of any special significance from a money laundering perspective.[26] It none the less acted promptly to put in place legislation which created the criminal offence of money laundering, provided for mutual assistance in the investigation and prosecution of money laundering, permitted the confiscation of the proceeds of crime, and recognised money laundering as an extraditable offence.[27] Other illustrations of such responsible international conduct can be found among Commonwealth countries in southern Africa and elsewhere.

It was, however, also recognised that some of its developing country members – and in particular the small island states of the Caribbean and the Pacific – faced particular difficulties in elaborating policy and modernising legislation in such a complex area. Accordingly, the Legal and Constitutional Affairs Division of the Commonwealth Secretariat has prepared model legislation for the prohibition of money laundering on which such countries can draw. Following the terrorist attacks against the United States of September 2001, it acted swiftly to provide its membership with model legislative provisions on measures to combat terrorism;[28] an initiative which has had a positive impact throughout the common law world. It also provides a range of other forms of technical assistance to these and other members. All Commonwealth countries also benefit from the provision of constantly updated information on legislative, case-law and other relevant developments.[29]

The issue of money laundering has also been considered with some frequency at the highest level. For instance, in October 1993 Commonwealth heads of government, at their meeting in Cyprus, "commended" the Forty FATF Recommendations, "urged steps for their early implementation" and mandated law and finance ministers to examine the matter further.[30] The first opportunity to do so was provided by the Meeting of Commonwealth Law Ministers, which took place in Mauritius in November 1993. In the final communiqué, ministers:

> ...expressed their desire that this issue be addressed as a matter of urgency and their resolve, individually and collectively, to put in place comprehensive provisions criminalising money laundering in respect of the proceeds of all serious crimes, facilitating the disclosure by financial institutions of information giving rise to suspicion of money laundering activities, enabling confiscation of the proceeds of crime, making money laundering extraditable, and promoting international co-operation in the investigation and prosecution of money laundering and in confiscation proceedings.[31]

In June of 1998 a joint meeting of Commonwealth law and finance officials was convened in London to ensure that a co-ordinated approach to the money laundering issue was followed and to consider further measures which could be taken by members. Among the major issues discussed in the latter context was the strengthening of regional initiatives; a matter of particular significance given the FATF decision, announced later the same month, to emphasise this as a central feature of its mandate. Importantly, as early as October 1996, the Commonwealth Secretariat had joined with the FATF to sponsor the first Southern and Eastern African Money Laundering Conference. Convened in Cape Town and attended by thirteen African states, representatives agreed in principle to move towards the formation of a sub-regional task force. The Commonwealth thereafter played a central role in the realisation of this goal. The Eastern and Southern African Anti-Money Laundering Group (ESAAMLG) was launched in August 1999. Consisting of fourteen members (including the two Indian Ocean island states of Mauritius and the Seychelles), it has now become operational and embarked on its first round of evaluations.[32] By way of contrast the efforts to create similar regional bodies in western and central Africa are at a far less advanced stage of development.[33]

Conclusions

The primary focus for action beyond the confines of the restricted membership of the FATF was initially on the laundering of the proceeds of drug trafficking as represented by the ever-increasing spread of participation in the 1988 UN convention regime and the resulting implementation of its criminal justice obligations. However, more recently there has been a growing awareness that a broader multifaceted approach is required. As this selective overview has demonstrated, while this more comprehensive agenda has been widely embraced at the political and policy levels there are significant differences both between and within the regions of the developing world concerning the pace of practical implementation.

Notes: IX

1. "International Narcotics Control Strategy Report", Washington, DC, Bureau of International Narcotics Matters, US Department of State, 1988, p. 45.

2. Nadelmann, E, "Negotiations in Criminal Law Assistance Treaties", *American Journal of Comparative Law*, 1985, p.467, at p. 499.

3. See, for example, Gilmore, W, "International Action against Drug Trafficking: Trends in United Kingdom Law and Practice", *International Lawyer*, 1990, p. 365, at pp. 380-381.

4. See, ibid., at pp. 381-388.

5. Zagaris, B, "Caribbean Financial Action Task Force Aruba Meeting Presages Cooperation by Caribbean Jurisdictions", *International Enforcement Law Reporter*, 1990, pp. 217-218.

6. Recommendations 11 and 17 have been deleted.

7. Reproduced in Gilmore, W (ed), *International efforts to combat money laundering*, Cambridge, Cambridge University Press, 1992, pp. 25-30.

8. See, Zagaris, B and Kingma, E, "Asset Forfeiture International and Foreign Law: An Emerging Regime", *Emory International Law Review*, 1991, p. 445, at p. 477.

9. See, Smellie, A, "The Work of the Caribbean Regional Division of the Financial Action Task Force", in *Action against transnational criminality: papers from the 1993 Oxford Conference on International and White Collar Crime*, London, Commonwealth Secretariat, 1994, at pp. 17-38.

10. See, Gilmore, W, "Money Laundering: The International Aspect", in MacQueen, H L (ed), *Money laundering*, Edinburgh, Edinburgh University Press, 1993, p. 1, at p. 10.

11. The Kingston declaration is reproduced in full by Smellie, op. cit., pp. 34-37. Subsequently the CFATF has used both the 1996 version of the FATF recommendations and the NCCT criteria in its work.

12. See, "Financial Action Task Force on Money Laundering: Annual Report 1992-1993", Paris, FATF, at p.21. Since that time, Spain and Mexico have also become co-operating and supporting nations (Cosuns).

13. See, "Caribbean Financial Action Task Force: Annual Report 1994-1995", Trinidad and Tobago, CFATF, at p. 5.

14. See, "Financial Action Task Force on Money Laundering: Annual Report 2002-2003", Paris, FATF, at p. 21.

15. See, "Caribbean Financial Action Task Force: Annual Report 1995-1996", Trinidad and Tobago, CFATF, at p. 4.

16. Gilmore, W (ed), op.cit., p. 271.

17. Reproduced in relevant part in ibid., pp. 290-295.

18. See, e.g., Jiminez, H, "Inter-American Measures to Combat Money Laundering", *International Enforcement Law Reporter*, 1992, at pp.165-169; and, Solomon, P, "Are Money Launderers All Washed Up in the Western Hemisphere? The OAS Model Regulations", *Hastings International and Comparative Law Review*, 1994, pp.433-455.

19. See, *International Legal Materials*, Vol. 34 1995, Washington, DC, American Society of International Law, p.808, at p.820.

20. See the text as amended in Montreal in November 2003.

21. "Financial Action Task Force on Money Laundering: Annual Report 1997-1998", Paris, FATF, p. 31.

22. See, for example, Gilmore, W, "International Cooperation in the Administration of Justice: Developments and Prospects", in *Action against transnational criminality: Papers from the 1992 Oxford Conference on International and White Collar Crime*, London, Commonwealth Secretariat, 1993, at pp. 147-154.

23. See, McClean, J D, *International cooperation in civil and criminal matters*, Oxford, Oxford University Press, 2002, at pp. 196-211.

24. See, ibid., at p. 319.

25. See, for example, Brown, A, "Money Laundering: International Law and the Commonwealth", *Commonwealth Judicial Journal*, 1994, p. 23, at p. 23.

26. See, for example, "International Narcotics Control Strategy Report", Washington, DC, Bureau of International Narcotics Matters, US Department of State, 1998.

27. See, Segopolo, S M, "Mutual Assistance in Criminal Matters – Developing Country Perspectives", in Gilmore, *supra*, note 22, at pp. 135-140.

28. See, *Model legislative provisions on measures to combat terrorism*, London, Commonwealth Secretariat, 2002. In a closely related initiative, it has produced implementation kits for all of the international counter-terrorism conventions to assist with their legislative implementation.

29. See generally, Stafford, D, "Combating Transnational Crime: The Role of the Commonwealth", in Cullen, P and Gilmore, W (eds), *Crimes sans frontières: international and European legal approaches*, Edinburgh, Edinburgh University Press, 1998, at pp. 44-49.

30. Reproduced in *Commonwealth Law Bulletin*, 1993, p. 2003, at p. 2004. See also, p. 2006.

31. Ibid., p. 2009.

32. See, *supra*, note 14, at pp. 20-21.

33. See, ibid., p. 21.

Chapter X – Conclusions

In the course of the last fifteen years there has been unprecedented action by the world community to combat what is perceived to be a significant and increasing threat from drug trafficking and other forms of serious crime. Those activities which generate significant profits and possess transnational features have been singled out for especially aggressive treatment. Furthermore, a broad consensus has emerged that both domestic and international strategies should be directed towards undermining the economic power of the criminals and organised crime groups involved.

In order to achieve this goal, three closely interconnected ingredients have been identified as essential. The first, and most orthodox, is based on enhancing domestic criminal justice systems in order to increase the "law enforcement risk". In addition to the traditional threat posed by prosecution and conviction for the underlying profit-generating offence, this element of the strategy has come to emphasise the need to criminalise money laundering and to provide for the tracing, freezing and confiscation of the profits accumulated through involvement in illicit activities. These criminal justice measures are essentially offensive in nature and intent. Thanks to the innovative work of the Basel committee, the Council of Europe, and the FATF, among others, they have come to be supplemented and complemented by a series of defensive or preventive measures which reach out to involve private sector actors to an extent never before attempted. Here, as we have seen, the policy seeks "to reduce the opportunities for accumulating profits through illicit activities, and to reduce the vulnerability of societies and governments to infiltration by organised crime".[1]

The final element of the strategy stems from the recognition that such is the ingenuity, sophistication and flexibility of modern money launderers, and of the organised crime groups whose needs they service, that domestic initiatives are, in and of themselves, necessary but insufficient preconditions for effective action. Greatly enhanced levels of international co-operation are essential if the "seizure risk" is not be rendered illusory when launderers make use, as they frequently do in practice, of the facilities of the global financial system in their efforts to disguise and break the money trail.

Progress towards the formulation and implementation of this multifaceted strategy has been greatly assisted by the importance which has been afforded to the issues of laundering and the confiscation of criminal proceeds at the highest political levels. They are matters which, far from remaining in the secretive confines of law enforcement discussions, now arise with considerable frequency at the meetings of heads of state or government and those of their ministerial colleagues. Such political support has produced the environment and created the momentum out of which concrete achievements have been recorded.

Progress at the global level was, in the initial phase, driven by concern over international drug trafficking. Here the 1988 UN convention deserves pride of place. Its requirement that drug-related money laundering be criminalised, its approach to the problem of bank secrecy, and the range of the obligations imposed in relation to the provision of international assistance laid the foundations on which subsequent initiatives have been built. The centrality of this UN precedent was recognised, both explicitly and implicitly, by the highly influential package of countermeasures elaborated by the FATF.

The 1990 report of that specialised group was, of course, much more ambitious than the 1988 UN convention in its scope. Drawing upon earlier work undertaken by the Council of Europe and the Basel committee, it contributed decisively to the broad acceptance which the preventive aspects of the strategy now enjoy. In this regard the relevant FATF recommendations exercised a considerable influence on supportive actions undertaken by the EU, the OAS, the CFATF and others. Furthermore, the FATF has, in spite of its limited and (preponderantly) advanced financial centre jurisdiction membership, played a highly significant role in the continuing process of policy formulation, best illustrated by the 1996 and 2003 revisions to its package of countermeasures, and in the equally important task of generating a much greater awareness of the complex issues involved.

With the advent of the second round of the mutual evaluation process, the Task Force entered into a phase in which the major concern was with the effectiveness of the strategies put in place by its members rather than, as had previously been the case, with formal legislative, administrative and regulatory compliance therewith. Both formal compliance and effective implementation concerns are to be brought to bear in the third round of the evaluation process which is expected to commence prior to the end of 2004. Based on a common methodology elaborated in conjunction with the IMF, the World Bank and others, this procedure will assess progress against both the revised recommendations of June 2003 and, significantly, the eight Special Recommendations on the Financing of Terrorism which were adopted in the aftermath of the September 2001 attacks against the United States. As was noted at an earlier stage of this work, together these are intended to "create a comprehensive, consistent and substantially strengthened international framework for combating money laundering and terrorist financing".[2]

It is to be hoped that in this and other contexts the Task Force does not lose sight of one of the most significant lessons learned from its activities throughout the 1990s; namely, the need to focus on how best to improve the somewhat disappointing results achieved thus far. As has been noted on various occasions, when viewed in terms of activity measures or "outcome indicators", such as the number of (professional) money launderers convicted or of proceeds confiscated, it is clear that performance to date has been, at best, mixed.[3] Importantly, much the same picture emerges from the work of FATF-style regional bodies such as MONEYVAL.[4]

A compelling argument can be made that the time has now come to consider a deliberate rebalancing of priorities with the intention of affording greater emphasis to the tracing, freezing and confiscation of criminal profits. This (and not money laundering) was, of course, the original point of criminal justice emphasis in both the 1988 UN convention and the 1990 Council of Europe convention. Notwithstanding this fact, no complete examination of national confiscation laws has been undertaken in either of the evaluation rounds concluded by the FATF to date. What the process did reveal was a high level of formal compliance with what was then Recommendation 7 (now Recommendation 3). However, as a subsequent Task Force review was to remark: "What is more problematic is whether the confiscation legislation and administrative structures are effective in depriving criminals of their illegal proceeds."[5] Again the MONEYVAL experience has been similar. A review of its first round of evaluations found that "operationally, confiscation systems were, to varying degrees, under-used and experience in them was only beginning to develop".[6] Worryingly, "experience with provisional measures was mixed" and there were many jurisdictions in which "there was a high risk of assets being dissipated before any confiscation order could be made".[7]

Some states have acknowledged these difficulties and have sought to address them. One such is the United Kingdom. As a Cabinet Office report noted in June 2000: "What little data exists shows that, despite legislation that provides for confiscation upon conviction for all crimes, the UK's confiscation track record is poor. Very little is ordered to be confiscated, even less is collected."[8] It was accordingly decided to launch a comprehensive package of reforms designed to maximise the efficiency of the pursuit of criminal proceeds. While most attention has been paid to the consequential introduction, under the Proceeds of Crime Act 2002, of a system of civil asset recovery the changes went much further. They included, among others, such practical measures as better trained and supported law enforcement officers and a more robust use of existing tax investigation powers.

While the stance taken by the UK in this regard is not unique, the impression remains that many FATF members continue to focus on a much narrower, money laundering-specific, set of priorities. Further efforts to assist them to reconceptualise the nature of the challenge they face would be welcome.

It would also be timely given the priority which has been afforded by the international community in the period since the attack on the Twin Towers to the seizure of terrorist funds.

This and other issues of effectiveness cannot, however, be addressed solely within the confines of the world's leading financial centre jurisdictions. As the *Economist* noted in a leading article in July 1997: "Fighting money laundering is rather like tackling global warming: unless everybody joins in, there is little hope of curbing the problem."[9] To its credit the FATF has, from the outset, fully recognised this fact. Working in conjunction with other leading organisations and bodies with a mandate in the area of money laundering, it has actively promoted the greatest possible geographic spread of the anti-money laundering message. Largely as a consequence of these efforts there are clear indications of an ever-growing acceptance of the contention that "[e]very corner of the globe is affected by money laundering ...".[10] Although at its most advanced state in North America and Europe, substantial progress has also been achieved in the Caribbean, Asia, the Pacific, and elsewhere. However, much remains to be done if the remaining gaps in the anti-money laundering net are to be closed. The highly ambitious regional strategy announced by the FATF in June 1998 has been the major element of its plan to address this critical issue. As was seen in chapter IX, this has resulted in the creation of several new, regional anti-money laundering bodies and yet others are in prospect.

This strategy of spreading the anti-money laundering message to all continents and regions is not without its difficulties. For example, even when the political will to take action is present many nations face very real problems and constraints in enacting the complex domestic legislation and adapting administrative and regulatory systems in order to reflect best international practice. Making such a structure effective in operational terms is even more demanding. Some appreciation of the nature and extent of the challenge faced by the states of central and eastern Europe throughout the 1990s will have been gleaned from this study. Great as those problems were (and in some cases still are) they are of a different and lesser order of magnitude than those which confront many of the world's least developed countries for which the complexity and sophistication of the countermeasures which have been elaborated sometimes seem to sit uneasily with domestic realities. Some of these difficulties can be tackled on the basis of a substantial programme of technical assistance and support. Others are essentially issues of social and economic development and can be addressed properly only in the longer term and in that wider context. It is essential that the OECD and financial centre jurisdictions, individually and collectively, remain fully sensitive to such issues as they press for progress. A renewed willingness to admit that, in spite of their best efforts, many of the major money laundering centres continue to be located in FATF jurisdictions would assist in the formulation of a balanced attitude.

These leading nations must also be prepared to adopt a flexible and constructive stance when presented with initiatives from developing countries and states in transition which are intended to increase the relevance or improve the functioning of the strategy in the light of particular local or regional circumstances. Here the track record is not particularly encouraging. One example is provided by the debate within the UN on proposals to create an international criminal court. Although the idea that the international community should establish a judicial body to exercise criminal jurisdiction over individuals, as opposed to states, has a lengthy history it was not until it was revived by the Prime Minister of Trinidad and Tobago in the late 1980s that it came to gather substantial political momentum.[11] In taking this step, the Trinidadian leader was responding to the magnitude of the problem posed by the international drugs trade for countries such as his own. As the Commonwealth Secretary General subsequently remarked, "small countries cannot often handle the complex, expensive and sometimes dangerous consequences of a major trial involving international criminals".[12]

In spite of the considerable technical problems which arise as a consequence of moving beyond crimes under general international law,[13] the International Law Commission, to which the issue was remitted for expert study, suggested that the proposed international criminal court be given jurisdiction, under certain circumstances, over serious drug trafficking offences, including money laundering, which possess an international dimension. However, leading industrialised nations, including the United States and the United Kingdom, resisted this concession with the result that the Statute of the International Criminal Court, as approved in Rome in mid-1998, excludes such matters from its subject-matter jurisdiction. The issue will, however, arise for reconsideration in a few years time.

While the great majority of countries indicated a willingness to adopt a positive approach to the notion of participation in the global fight against money laundering a small minority stood aside, at least in some measure, because of a desire to attract criminal money. Many would agree with Savona and De Feo that this group of countries was "inviting sanctions from the responsible elements of the world financial and law enforcement community, and deserve them".[14]

The question of sanctions and inducements has been discussed on occasion within the FATF. This was the case, for instance, during the 1990-91 round of meetings. Among the options discussed at that time were the production of a blacklist of non-co-operative jurisdictions and, alternatively, the production of a whitelist of countries which had satisfactorily implemented its Forty Recommendations.[15] It was felt at that time that it was too early in the process to arrive at common and definitive assessments. Consequently, in its report of May 1991 it was decided to continue to rely on peer and public pressure to achieve the desired results. It was agreed, however, that should this approach not bear fruit "additional measures might be envisaged in the future".[16]

Throughout much of the 1990s the emphasis remained on providing help, assistance and encouragement. However, as the decade drew to a close there emerged growing sympathy for the view that the time had come to reconsider this position; to examine, with much increased seriousness, the benefits to be derived from the imposition of practical and progressive financial or political sanctions to reinforce efforts to effectively combat this form of serious transnational criminality.[17] As was seen in chapter VI, it was within this context that the Task Force launched its NCCT process; a name, shame and punish strategy. There can be no doubt that it had the effect of triggering significant improvements in the blacklisted jurisdictions.[18] Nor, given its exclusive focus in practice on non-FATF members, is it surprising that it proved to be highly controversial within the wider international community. For instance, the oft-repeated claim by the Task Force as to the "openness, fairness and objectivity" of the process[19] has been received with bemusement by some outside the confines of its membership. While we appear to have now moved, due in large measure to the influence of the IMF and the World Bank, into a less confrontational period it is not beyond the realms of possibility that the position will be reached in the future where recourse to such a strategy (for example, in the sphere of terrorist financing) again comes to command attention. For that reason both the positive and negative lessons of the NCCT exercise must be subject to analysis. In the latter context, it is of particular importance that the FATF countries never again lay themselves open to the suggestion that they are collectively holding non-members to a higher standard of conduct than they have set for, or been prepared to enforce against, themselves.

It is to be hoped, of course, that coercive action of this kind will not have to be resorted to again and that the widespread and increasing commitment of governments to participate as fully and effectively as possible in the fight against money laundering and related forms of serious criminality will eventually become, to all intents and purposes, universal. Even now the international community is in a position to take co-ordinated action against the financial power of drug trafficking networks and other criminal organisations of a kind and to an extent which seemed hardly possible a decade ago. It should not be thought, however, that action against money laundering and the confis- cation of proceeds constitutes, even potentially, some form of panacea of crime control. The strategy will not eradicate international drug trafficking or transnational organised crime let alone terrorism. It will, however, create an increasingly hostile and inhospitable environment for the terrorist financier, the money launderer and others involved in highly lucrative forms of criminal behaviour and afford new elements of protection to economic and political systems. To achieve this is to achieve something of real and lasting value.

Notes: X

1. "National Legislation and its Adequacy to Deal with the Various Forms of Organised Transnational Crime: Appropriate Guidelines for Legislative and Other Measures to be Taken at the National Level", UN Doc. E/CONF.88/3, 25 August 1994, p. 2.

2. Introduction to the FATF Forty Recommendations of June 2003.

3. See, for example, "Review of FATF Anti-Money Laundering Systems and Mutual Evaluation Procedures 1992-1999", Paris, FATF 2001, at pp. 7-14.

4. See, e.g., "A Review of the Anti-Money Laundering Systems in 22 Council of Europe member states, 1998-2001", Council of Europe Doc. PC-R-EV (01) 12 rev.

5. *Supra*, note 3, p. 11.

6. *Supra*, note 4, p. 16.

7. Ibid., p. 17.

8. "Recovering the Proceeds of Crime", London, Cabinet Office, 2000, p. 29.

9. "Cleaning up Dirty Money", *Economist*, London, 26 July 1997.

10. Sherman, T, "International Efforts to Combat Money Laundering: The Role of the Financial Action Task Force", in MacQueen, H L (ed), *Money laundering*, Edinburgh, Edinburgh University Press, 1993, p. 12, at p. 13.

11. See, for example, Patel, F, "Crime Without Frontiers: A Proposal For an International Narcotics Court", *New York University Journal of International Law and Politics*, 1990, at pp. 709-747.

12. Speech of the Commonwealth Secretary General to the September 1993 Oxford Conference on International and White Collar Crime (typescript), p. 8.

13. See, for example, Crawford, J, "The ILC's Draft Statute for an International Criminal Tribunal", *American Journal of International Law*, 1994, p.140, at pp. 145-146; and, Gilmore, W, "The Proposed International Criminal Court: Recent Developments", *Transnational Law and Contemporary Problems*, 1995, at p. 264.

14. Savona, E and De Feo, M, "Money Trails: International Money Laundering Trends and Prevention/Control Policies". Paper presented to the International Conference on Preventing and Controlling Money Laundering and the Use of the Proceeds of Crime, Courmayeur Mont Blanc, Italy, 18-20 June 1994 (typescript), p. 101.

15. See, "Proposals for the Future of the Financial Action Task Force: Report to the FATF from Working Group 3", in "Financial Action Task Force on Money Laundering: Annexes to the Report 1990-1991", Paris, FATF, at p. 6.

16. Reproduced in Gilmore, W (ed) *International efforts to combat money laundering*, Cambridge, Cambridge University Press, 1992, p. 31, at p. 49.

17. See, for example, Kerry, J, *The new war: the web of crime that threatens America's security*, New York, Simon & Schuster, 1997. See also, Tanzi, V, "Money Laundering and the International Financial System", IMF Working Paper, WP/96/55, May 1996, at p. 12.

18. See, for example, "Financial Action Task Force on Money Laundering: Annual Report 2002-2003", Paris, FATF, at p. 26.

19. Ibid., p. 25.

APPENDICES

Appendix I – The 1990 recommendations of the FATF on money laundering[1]

A. General framework of the recommendations

1. Each country should, without further delay, take steps to fully implement the Vienna Convention, and proceed to ratify it.

2. Financial institution secrecy laws should be conceived so as not to inhibit implementation of the recommendations of this group.

3. An effective money laundering enforcement program should include increased multilateral cooperation and mutual legal assistance in money laundering investigations and prosecutions and extradition in money laundering cases, where possible.

B. Improvement of national legal systems to combat money laundering

Definition of the criminal offense of money laundering

4. Each country should take such measures as may be necessary, including legislative ones, to enable it to criminalize drug money laundering as set forth in the Vienna Convention.

5. Each country should consider extending the offense of drug money laundering to any other crimes for which there is a link to narcotics; an alternative approach is to criminalize money laundering based on all serious offenses, and/or on all offenses that generate a significant amount of proceeds, or on certain serious offenses.

6. As provided in the Vienna Convention, the offense of money laundering should apply at least to knowing money laundering activity, including the concept that knowledge may be inferred from objective factual circumstances.

7. Where possible, corporations themselves – not only their employees – should be subject to criminal liability.

---

1. These are referred to as the forty guidelines.

Provisional Measures and Confiscation

8. Countries should adopt measures similar to those set forth in the Vienna Convention, as may be necessary, including legislative ones, to enable their competent authorities to confiscate property laundered, proceeds from, instrumentalities used in or intended for use in the commission of any money laundering offense, or property of corresponding value. Such measures should include the authority to: 1) identify, trace and evaluate property which is subject to confiscation; 2) carry out provisional measures, such as freezing and seizing, to prevent any dealing, transfer or disposal of such property; and 3) take any appropriate investigative measures.

    In addition to confiscation and criminal sanctions, countries also should consider monetary and civil penalties, and/or proceedings including civil proceedings, to void contracts entered by parties, where parties knew or should have known that as a result of the contract, the State would be prejudiced in its ability to recover financial claims, e.g. through confiscation or collection of fines and penalties.

C. Enhancement of the role of the financial system

Scope of the following Recommendations

9. Recommendations 12 to 29 of this paper should apply not only to banks, but also to non-bank financial institutions.

10. The appropriate national authorities should take steps to ensure that these Recommendations are implemented on as broad a front as is practically possible.

11. A working group should further examine the possibility of establishing a common minimal list of non-bank financial institutions and other professions dealing with cash subject to these Recommendations.

Customer identification and record-keeping rules

12. Financial institutions should not keep anonymous accounts or accounts in obviously fictitious names: they should be required (by law, by regulations, by agreements between supervisory authorities and financial institutions or by self-regulatory agreements among financial institutions) to identify, on the basis of an official or other reliable identifying document, and record the identity of their clients, either occasional or usual, when establishing business relations or conducting transactions (in particular opening of accounts or passbooks, entering into fiduciary transactions, renting of safe deposit boxes, performing large cash transactions).

13. Financial institutions should take reasonable measures to obtain information about the true identity of the persons on whose behalf an account is opened or a transaction conducted if there are any doubts as to whether these clients or customers are not acting on their own behalf, in particular, in the case of domiciliary companies (i.e. institutions, corporations, foundations, trusts, etc. that do not conduct any commercial or manufacturing business or any other form of commercial operation in the country where their registered office is located).

14. Financial institutions should maintain, for at least five years, all necessary records on transactions, both domestic or international, to enable them to comply swiftly with information requests from the competent authorities. Such records must be sufficient to permit reconstruction of individual transactions (including the amounts and types of currency involved if any) so as to provide, if necessary, evidence for prosecution of criminal behaviour. Financial institutions should keep records on customer identification (e.g. copies or records of official identification documents like passports, identity cards, driving licenses or similar documents), account files and business correspondence for at least five years after the account is closed.

    These documents should be available to domestic competent authorities in the context of relevant criminal prosecutions and investigations.

Increased diligence of financial institutions

15. Financial institutions should pay special attention to all complex, unusual large transactions, and all unusual patterns of transactions, which have no apparent economic or visible lawful purpose. The background and purpose of such transactions should, as far as possible, be examined, the findings established in writing, and be available to help supervisors, auditors and law enforcement agencies.

16. If financial institutions suspect that funds stem from a criminal activity, they should be permitted or required to report promptly their suspicions to the competent authorities. Accordingly, there should be legal provisions to protect financial institutions and their employees from criminal or civil liability for breach of any restriction on disclosure of information imposed by contract or by any legislative, regulatory or administrative provision, if they report in good faith, in disclosing suspected criminal activity to the competent authorities, even if they did not know precisely what the underlying criminal activity was, and regardless of whether illegal activity actually occurred.

17. Financial institutions, their directors and employees, should not, or, where appropriate, should not be allowed to, warn their customers when information relating to them is being reported to the competent authorities.

18. In the case of a mandatory reporting system, or in the case of a voluntary reporting system where appropriate, financial institutions reporting their suspicions should comply with instructions from the competent authorities.

19. When a financial institution develops suspicions about the operations of a customer, and when no obligation of reporting these suspicious exists, makes no report to the competent authorities, it should deny assistance to this customer, sever relations with him and close his accounts.

20. Financial institutions should develop programs against money laundering. These programs should include, as a minimum:
    (a) the development of internal policies, procedures and controls, including the designation of compliance officers at management level, and adequate screening procedures to ensure high standards when hiring employees;
    (b) an ongoing employee training programme;
    (c) an audit function to test the system.

Measures to cope with the problem of countries with no or insufficient anti-money laundering measures

21. Financial institutions should give special attention to business relations and transactions with persons, including companies and financial institutions, from countries which do not or insufficiently apply these Recommendations. Whenever these transactions have no apparent economic or visible lawful purpose, their background and purpose should, as far as possible, be examined, the findings established in writing, and be available to help supervisors, auditors and law enforcement agencies.

22. Financial institutions should ensure that the principles mentioned above are also applied to branches and majority owned subsidiaries located abroad, especially in countries which do not or insufficiently apply these Recommendations, to the extent that local applicable laws and regulations permit. When local applicable laws and regulations prohibit this implementation, competent authorities in the country of the mother institution should be informed by the financial institutions that they cannot apply these Recommendations.

Other measures to avoid currency laundering

23. The feasibility of measures to detect or monitor cash at the border should be studied, subject to strict safeguards to ensure proper use of information and without impeding in any way the freedom of capital movements.

24. Countries should consider the feasibility and utility of a system where banks and other financial institutions and intermediaries would report all domestic and international currency transactions above a fixed amount, to a national central agency with a computerised data base, available to competent authorities for use in money laundering cases, subject to strict safeguards to ensure proper use of the information.

25. Countries should further encourage in general the development of modern and secure techniques of money management, including increased use of checks, payment cards, direct deposit of salary checks, and book entry recording of securities, as a means to encourage the replacement of cash transfers.

Implementation, and role of regulatory and other administrative authorities

26. The competent authorities supervising banks or other financial institutions or intermediaries, or other competent authorities, should ensure that the supervised institutions have adequate programs to guard against money laundering. These authorities should cooperate and lend expertise spontaneously or on request with other domestic judicial or law enforcement authorities in money laundering investigations and prosecutions.

27. Competent authorities should be designated to ensure an effective implementation of all these Recommendations, through administrative supervision and regulation, in other professions dealing with cash as defined by each country.

28. The competent authorities should establish guidelines which will assist financial institutions in detecting suspicious patterns of behaviour by their customers. It is understood that such guidelines must develop over time, and will never be exhaustive. It is further understood that such guidelines will primarily serve as an educational tool for financial institutions' personnel.

29. The competent authorities regulating or supervising financial institutions should take the necessary legal or regulatory measures to guard against control or acquisition of a significant participation in financial institutions by criminals or their confederates.

D. Strengthening of international co-operation

Administrative co-operation

   (a) Exchange of general information

30. National administrations should consider recording, at least in the aggregate, international flows of cash in whatever currency, so that estimates can be made of cash flows and reflows from various sources abroad, when this is combined with central bank information. Such information should be made available to the IMF and BIS to facilitate international studies.

31. International competent authorities, perhaps Interpol and the Customs Cooperation Council, should be given responsibility for gathering and disseminating information to competent authorities about the latest developments in money laundering and money laundering techniques.

   Central banks and bank regulators could do the same on their network. National authorities in various spheres, in consultation with trade associations, could then disseminate this to financial institutions in individual countries.

   (b) Exchange of information relating to suspicious transactions

32. Each country should make efforts to improve a spontaneous or "upon request" international information exchange relating to suspicious transactions, persons and corporations involved in those transactions between competent authorities. Strict safeguards should be established to ensure that this exchange of information is consistent with national and international provisions on privacy and data protection.

Co-operation between legal authorities

   (a) Basis and means for co-operation in confiscation, mutual assistance and extradition

33. Countries should try to ensure, on a bilateral or multilateral basis, that different knowledge standards in national definitions – i.e. different standards concerning the intentional element of the infraction – do not affect the ability or willingness of countries to provide each other with mutual legal assistance.

34. International cooperation should be supported by a network of bilateral and multilateral agreements and arrangements based on generally shared legal concepts with the aim of providing practical measures to affect the widest possible range of mutual assistance.

35. Countries should encourage international conventions such as the draft Convention of the Council of Europe on Confiscation of the Proceeds from Offenses.

   (b) Focus of improved mutual assistance on money laundering issues

36. Co-operative investigations among appropriate competent authorities of countries should be encouraged.

37. There should be procedures for mutual assistance in criminal matters regarding the use of compulsory measures including the production of records by financial institutions and other persons, the search of persons and premises, seizure and obtaining of evidence for use in money laundering investigations and prosecutions and in related actions in foreign jurisdictions.

38. There should be authority to take expeditious action in response to requests by foreign countries to identify, freeze, seize and confiscate proceeds or other property of corresponding value to such proceeds, based on money laundering or the crimes underlying the laundering activity. There should also be arrangements for coordinating seizure and confiscation proceedings which may include the sharing of confiscated assets.

39. To avoid conflicts of jurisdiction, consideration should be given to devising and applying mechanisms for determining the best venue for prosecution of defendants in the interests of justice in cases that are subject to prosecution in more than one country. Similarly, there should be arrangements for coordinating seizure and confiscation proceedings which may include the sharing of confiscated assets.

40. Countries should have procedures in place to extradite, where possible, individuals charged with a money laundering offense or related offenses. With respect to its national legal system, each country should recognise money laundering as an extraditable offense. Subject to their legal frameworks, countries may consider simplifying extradition by allowing direct transmission of extradition requests between appropriate ministries, extraditing persons based only on warrants of arrests or judgments, extraditing their nationals, and/or introducing a simplified extradition of consenting persons who waive formal extradition proceedings.

Appendix II – The 1996 Revised FATF Recommendations

A. General framework of the recommendations

1. Each country should take immediate steps to ratify and to implement fully, the 1988 United Nations Convention against Illicit Traffic in Narcotic Drugs and Psychotropic Substances (the Vienna Convention).

2. Financial institution secrecy laws should be conceived so as not to inhibit implementation of these recommendations.

3. An effective money laundering enforcement program should include increased multilateral cooperation and mutual legal assistance in money laundering investigations and prosecutions and extradition in money laundering cases, where possible.

B. Role of national legal systems in combating money laundering

Scope of the criminal offence of money laundering

4. Each country should take such measures as may be necessary, including legislative ones, to enable it to criminalise money laundering as set forth in the Vienna Convention. Each country should extend the offence of drug money laundering to one based on serious offences. Each country would determine which serious crimes would be designated as money laundering predicate offences.

5. As provided in the Vienna Convention, the offence of money laundering should apply at least to knowing money laundering activity, including the concept that knowledge may be inferred from objective factual circumstances.

6. Where possible, corporations themselves – not only their employees – should be subject to criminal liability.

Provisional measures and confiscation

7. Countries should adopt measures similar to those set forth in the Vienna Convention, as may be necessary, including legislative ones, to enable their competent authorities to confiscate property laundered, proceeds from, instrumentalities used in or intended for use in the commission of any money laundering offence, or property of corresponding value, without prejudicing the rights of bona fide third parties.

Such measures should include the authority to: (1) identify, trace and evaluate property which is subject to confiscation; (2) carry out provisional measures, such as freezing and seizing, to prevent any dealing, transfer or disposal of such property; and (3) take any appropriate investigative measures.

In addition to confiscation and criminal sanctions, countries also should consider monetary and civil penalties, and/or proceedings including civil proceedings, to void contracts entered into by parties, where parties knew or should have known that as a result of the contract, the State would be prejudiced in its ability to recover financial claims, e.g. through confiscation or collection of fines and penalties.

C. Role of the financial system in combating money laundering

8. Recommendations 10 to 29 should apply not only to banks, but also to non-bank financial institutions. Even for those non-bank financial institutions which are not subject to a formal prudential supervisory regime in all countries, for example bureaux de change, governments should ensure that these institutions are subject to the same anti-money laundering laws or regulations as all other financial institutions and that these laws or regulations are implemented effectively.

9. The appropriate national authorities should consider applying Recommendations 10 to 21 and 23 to the conduct of financial activities as a commercial undertaking by businesses or professions which are not financial institutions, where such conduct is allowed or not prohibited. Financial activities include, but are not limited to, those listed in the attached annex. It is left to each country to decide whether special situations should be defined where the application of anti-money laundering measures is not necessary, for example, when a financial activity is carried out on an occasional or limited basis.

Customer identification and record-keeping rules

10. Financial institutions should not keep anonymous accounts or accounts in obviously fictitious names: they should be required (by law, by regulations, by agreements between supervisory authorities and financial institutions or by self-regulatory agreements among financial institutions) to identify, on the basis of an official or other reliable identifying document, and record the identity of their clients, either occasional or usual, when establishing business relations or conducting transactions (in particular opening of accounts or passbooks, entering into fiduciary transactions, renting of safe deposit boxes, performing large cash transactions).

In order to fulfil identification requirements concerning legal entities, financial institutions should, when necessary, take measures:

(i) to verify the legal existence and structure of the customer by obtaining either from a public register or from the customer or both, proof of incorporation, including information concerning the customer's name, legal form, address, directors and provisions regulating the power to bind the entity.

(ii) to verify that any person purporting to act on behalf of the customer is so authorised and identify that person.

11. Financial institutions should take reasonable measures about the true identity of the persons on whose behalf an account is opened or a transaction conducted if there are any doubts as to whether these clients or customers are acting on their own behalf, for example, in the case of domiciliary companies (i.e. institutions, corporations, foundations, trusts, etc. that do not conduct any commercial or manufacturing business or any other form of commercial operation in the country where their registered office is located).

12. Financial institutions should maintain, for at least five years, all necessary records on transactions, both domestic or international, to enable them to comply swiftly with information requests from the competent authorities. Such records must be sufficient to permit reconstruction of individual transactions (including the amounts and types of currency involved if any) so as to provide, if necessary, evidence for prosecution of criminal behaviour.

Financial institutions should keep records on customer identification (e.g. copies or records of official identification documents like passports, identity cards, driving licenses or similar documents), account files and business correspondence for at least five years after the account is closed.

These documents should be available to domestic competent authorities in the context of relevant criminal prosecutions and investigations.

13. Countries should pay special attention to money laundering threats inherent in new or developing technologies that might favour anonymity, and take measures, if needed, to prevent their use in money laundering schemes.

Increased diligence of finanacial institutions

14. Financial institutions should pay special attention to all complex, unusual large transactions, and all unusual patterns of transactions, which have no apparent economic or visible lawful purpose. The background and purpose of such transactions should, as far as possible, be examined, the findings established in writing, and be available to help supervisors, auditors and law enforcement agencies.

15. If financial institutions suspect that funds stem from a criminal activity, they should be required to report promptly their suspicions to the competent authorities.

16. Financial institutions, their directors, officers and employees should be protected by legal provisions from criminal or civil liability for breach of any restriction on disclosure of information imposed by contract or by any legislative, regulatory or administrative provision, if they report their suspicions in good faith to the competent authorities, even if they did not know precisely what the underlying criminal activity was, and regardless of whether illegal activity actually occurred.

17. Financial institutions, their directors, officers and employees, should not, or, where appropriate, should not be allowed to, warn their customers when information relating to them is being reported to the competent authorities.

18. Financial institutions reporting their suspicions should comply with instructions from the competent authorities.

19. Financial institutions should develop programs against money laundering. These programs should include, as a minimum:

    (i) the development of internal policies, procedures and controls, including the designation of compliance officers at management level, and adequate screening procedures to ensure high standards when hiring employees;

    (ii) an ongoing employee training programme;

    (iii) an audit function to test the system.

Measures to cope with the problems of countries with no or insufficient anti-money laundering measures

20. Financial institutions should ensure that the principles mentioned above are also applied to branches and majority owned subsidiaries located abroad, especially in countries which do not or insufficiently apply these Recommendations, to the extent that local applicable laws and regulations permit. When local applicable laws and regulations prohibit this implementation, competent authorities in the country of the mother institution should be informed by the financial institutions that they cannot apply these Recommendations.

21. Financial institutions should give special attention to business relations and transactions with persons, including companies and financial institutions, from countries which do not or insufficiently apply these Recommendations. Whenever these transactions have no apparent economic or visible lawful purpose, their background and purpose should, as far as possible, be examined, the findings established in writing, and be available to help supervisors, auditors and law enforcement agencies.

Other measures to avoid money laundering

22. Countries should consider implementing feasible measures to detect or monitor the physical crossborder transportation of cash and bearer negotiable instruments, subject to strict safeguards to ensure proper use of information and without impeding in any way the freedom of capital movements.

23. Countries should consider the feasibility and utility of a system where banks and other financial institutions and intermediaries would report all domestic and international currency transactions above a fixed amount, to a national central agency with a computerised data base, available to competent authorities for use in money laundering cases, subject to strict safeguards to ensure proper use of the information.

24. Countries should further encourage in general the development of modern and secure techniques of money management, including increased use of checks, payment cards, direct deposit of salary checks, and book entry recording of securities, as a means to encourage the replacement of cash transfers.

25. Countries should take notice of the potential for abuse of shell corporations by money launderers and should consider whether additional measures are required to prevent unlawful use of such entities.

Implementation and role of regulatory and other administrative authorities

26. The competent authorities supervising banks or other financial institutions or intermediaries, or other competent authorities, should ensure that the supervised institutions have adequate programs to guard against money laundering. These authorities should co-operate and lend expertise spontaneously or on request with other domestic judicial or law enforcement authorities in money laundering investigations and prosecutions.

27. Competent authorities should be designated to ensure an effective implementation of all these Recommendations, through administrative supervision and regulation, in other professions dealing with cash as defined by each country.

28. The competent authorities should establish guidelines which will assist financial institutions in detecting suspicious patterns of behaviour by their customers. It is understood that such guidelines must develop over time, and will never be exhaustive. It is further understood that such guidelines will primarily serve as an educational tool for financial institutions' personnel.

29. The competent authorities regulating or supervising financial institutions should take the necessary legal or regulatory measures to guard against control or acquisition of a significant participation in financial institutions by criminals or their confederates.

D. Strengthening of international co-operation

Administative co-operation

Exchange of general information

30. National administrations should consider recording, at least in the aggregate, international flows of cash in whatever currency, so that estimates can be made of cash flows and reflows from various sources abroad, when this is combined with central bank information. Such information should be made available to the International Monetary Fund and the Bank for International Settlements to facilitate international studies.

31. International competent authorities, perhaps Interpol and the World Customs Organisation, should be given responsibility for gathering and disseminating information to competent authorities about the latest developments in money laundering and money laundering techniques. Central banks and bank regulators could do the same on their network. National authorities in various spheres, in consultation with trade associations, could then disseminate this to financial institutions in individual countries.

Exchange of information relating to suspicious transfers

32. Each country should make efforts to improve a spontaneous or "upon request" international information exchange relating to suspicious transactions, persons and corporations involved in those transactions between competent authorities. Strict safeguards should be established to ensure that this exchange of information is consistent with national and international provisions on privacy and data protection.

Other forms of co-operation

Basic and means for co-operation in confiscation, mutual assistance and extradition

33. Countries should try to ensure, on a bilateral or multilateral basis, that different knowledge standards in national definitions – i.e. different standards concerning the intentional element of the infraction – do not affect the ability or willingness of countries to provide each other with mutual legal assistance.

34. International co-operation should be supported by a network of bilateral and multilateral agreements and arrangements based on generally shared legal concepts with the aim of providing practical measures to affect the widest possible range of mutual assistance.

35. Countries should be encouraged to ratify and implement relevant international conventions on money laundering such as the 1990 Council of Europe Convention on Laundering, Search, Seizure and Confiscation of the Proceeds from Crime.

Focus on improved mutual assistance on money laundering issues

36. Co-operative investigations among countries' appropriate competent authorities should be encouraged. One valid and effective investigative technique in this respect is controlled delivery related to assets known or suspected to be the proceeds of crime. Countries are encouraged to support this technique, where possible.

37. There should be procedures for mutual assistance in criminal matters regarding the use of compulsory measures including the production of records by financial institutions and other persons, the search of persons and premises, seizure and obtaining of evidence for use in money laundering investigations and prosecutions and in related actions in foreign jurisdictions.

38. There should be authority to take expeditious action in response to requests by foreign countries to identify, freeze, seize and confiscate proceeds or other property of corresponding value to such proceeds, based on money laundering or the crimes underlying the laundering activity. There should also be arrangements for co-ordinating seizure and confiscation proceedings which may include the sharing of confiscated assets.

39. To avoid conflicts of jurisdiction, consideration should be given to devising and applying mechanisms for determining the best venue for prosecution of defendants in the interests of justice in cases that are subject to prosecution in more than one country. Similarly, there should be arrangements for coordinating seizure and confiscation proceedings which may include the sharing of confiscated assets.

40. Countries should have procedures in place to extradite, where possible, individuals charged with a money laundering offence or related offences. With respect to its national legal system, each country should recognise money laundering as an extraditable offence. Subject to their legal frameworks, countries may consider simplifying extradition by allowing direct transmission of extradition requests between appropriate ministries, extraditing persons based only on warrants of arrests or judgments, extraditing their nationals, and/or introducing a simplified extradition of consenting persons who waive formal extradition proceedings.

Appendix III – The 2003 revised FATF recommendations and interpretative notes

A. Legal systems

Scope of the criminal offence of money laundering

1. Countries should criminalise money laundering on the basis of the United Nations Convention against Illicit Traffic in Narcotic Drugs and Psychotropic Substances, 1988 (the Vienna Convention) and the United Nations Convention against Transnational Organized Crime, 2000 (the Palermo Convention).

    Countries should apply the crime of money laundering to all serious offences, with a view to including the widest range of predicate offences. Predicate offences may be described by reference to all offences, or to a threshold linked either to a category of serious offences or to the penalty of imprisonment applicable to the predicate offence (threshold approach), or to a list of predicate offences, or a combination of these approaches.

    Where countries apply a threshold approach, predicate offences should at a minimum comprise all offences that fall within the category of serious offences under their national law or should include offences which are punishable by a maximum penalty of more than one year's imprisonment or for those countries that have a minimum threshold for offences in their legal system, predicate offences should comprise all offences, which are punished by a minimum penalty of more than six months imprisonment.

    Whichever approach is adopted, each country should at a minimum include a range of offences within each of the designated categories of offences.[1]

    Predicate offences for money laundering should extend to conduct that occurred in another country, which constitutes an offence in that country, and which would have constituted a predicate offence had it occurred domestically. Countries may provide that the only prerequisite is that the conduct would have constituted a predicate offence had it occurred domestically.

    Countries may provide that the offence of money laundering does not apply to persons who committed the predicate offence, where this is required by fundamental principles of their domestic law.

---

1. See the definition of "designated categories of offences" in the glossary.

2. Countries should ensure that:

   a) The intent and knowledge required to prove the offence of money laundering is consistent with the standards set forth in the Vienna and Palermo Conventions, including the concept that such mental state may be inferred from objective factual circumstances.

   b) Criminal liability, and, where that is not possible, civil or administrative liability, should apply to legal persons. This should not preclude parallel criminal, civil or administrative proceedings with respect to legal persons in countries in which such forms of liability are available. Legal persons should be subject to effective, proportionate and dissuasive sanctions. Such measures should be without prejudice to the criminal liability of individuals.

Provisonal measures and confiscation

3. Countries should adopt measures similar to those set forth in the Vienna and Palermo Conventions, including legislative measures, to enable their competent authorities to confiscate property laundered, proceeds from money laundering or predicate offences, instrumentalities used in or intended for use in the commission of these offences, or property of corresponding value, without prejudicing the rights of bona fide third parties.

   Such measures should include the authority to: (a) identify, trace and evaluate property which is subject to confiscation; (b) carry out provisional measures, such as freezing and seizing, to prevent any dealing, transfer or disposal of such property; (c) take steps that will prevent or void actions that prejudice the State's ability to recover property that is subject to confiscation; and (d) take any appropriate investigative measures.

   Countries may consider adopting measures that allow such proceeds or instrumentalities to be confiscated without requiring a criminal conviction, or which require an offender to demonstrate the lawful origin of the property alleged to be liable to confiscation, to the extent that such a requirement is consistent with the principles of their domestic law.

B. Measures to be taken by financial institutions and non-financial businesses and professions to prevent money laundering and terrorist financing

4. Countries should ensure that financial institution secrecy laws do not inhibit implementation of the FATF Recommendations.

Customer due diligence and record-keeping

5.* Financial institutions should not keep anonymous accounts or accounts in obviously fictitious names.

---

* Recommendations marked with an asterisk should be read in conjunction with their interpretative note.

Financial institutions should undertake customer due diligence measures, including identifying and verifying the identity of their customers, when:

- establishing business relations;
- carrying out occasional transactions: (i) above the applicable designated threshold; or (ii) that are wire transfers in the circumstances covered by the Interpretative Note to Special Recommendation VII;
- there is a suspicion of money laundering or terrorist financing; or
- the financial institution has doubts about the veracity or adequacy of previously obtained customer identification data.

The customer due diligence (CDD) measures to be taken are as follows:

a) Identifying the customer and verifying that customer's identity using reliable, independent source documents, data or information.[2]

b) Identifying the beneficial owner, and taking reasonable measures to verify the identity of the beneficial owner such that the financial institution is satisfied that it knows who the beneficial owner is. For legal persons and arrangements this should include financial institutions taking reasonable measures to understand the ownership and control structure of the customer.

c) Obtaining information on the purpose and intended nature of the business relationship.

d) Conducting ongoing due diligence on the business relationship and scrutiny of transactions undertaken throughout the course of that relationship to ensure that the transactions being conducted are consistent with the institution's knowledge of the customer, their business and risk profile, including, where necessary, the source of funds.

Financial institutions should apply each of the CDD measures under (a) to (d) above, but may determine the extent of such measures on a risk sensitive basis depending on the type of customer, business relationship or transaction. The measures that are taken should be consistent with any guidelines issued by competent authorities. For higher risk categories, financial institutions should perform enhanced due diligence. In certain circumstances, where there are low risks, countries may decide that financial institutions can apply reduced or simplified measures.

Financial institutions should verify the identity of the customer and beneficial owner before or during the course of establishing a business relationship or conducting transactions for occasional customers. Countries may permit financial institutions to complete the verification as soon as

---

2. Reliable, independent source documents, data or information will hereafter be referred to as "identification data".

reasonably practicable following the establishment of the relationship, where the money laundering risks are effectively managed and where this is essential not to interrupt the normal conduct of business.

Where the financial institution is unable to comply with paragraphs (a) to (c) above, it should not open the account, commence business relations or perform the transaction; or should terminate the business relationship; and should consider making a suspicious transactions report in relation to the customer.

These requirements should apply to all new customers, though financial institutions should also apply this Recommendation to existing customers on the basis of materiality and risk, and should conduct due diligence on such existing relationships at appropriate times.

6.* Financial institutions should, in relation to politically exposed persons, in addition to performing normal due diligence measures:

    a) Have appropriate risk management systems to determine whether the customer is a politically exposed person.

    b) Obtain senior management approval for establishing business relationships with such customers.

    c) Take reasonable measures to establish the source of wealth and source of funds.

    d) Conduct enhanced ongoing monitoring of the business relationship.

7. Financial institutions should, in relation to cross-border correspondent banking and other similar relationships, in addition to performing normal due diligence measures:

    a) Gather sufficient information about a respondent institution to understand fully the nature of the respondent's business and to determine from publicly available information the reputation of the institution and the quality of supervision, including whether it has been subject to a money laundering or terrorist financing investigation or regulatory action.

    b) Assess the respondent institution's anti-money laundering and terrorist financing controls.

    c) Obtain approval from senior management before establishing new correspondent relationships.

    d) Document the respective responsibilities of each institution.

e) With respect to "payable-through accounts", be satisfied that the respondent bank has verified the identity of and performed on-going due diligence on the customers having direct access to accounts of the correspondent and that it is able to provide relevant customer identification data upon request to the correspondent bank.

8. Financial institutions should pay special attention to any money launder-ing threats that may arise from new or developing technologies that might favour anonymity, and take measures, if needed, to prevent their use in money laundering schemes. In particular, financial institutions should have policies and procedures in place to address any specific risks associated with non-face to face business relationships or transactions.

9.* Countries may permit financial institutions to rely on intermediaries or other third parties to perform elements (a) – (c) of the CDD process or to introduce business, provided that the criteria set out below are met. Where such reliance is permitted, the ultimate responsibility for customer identification and verification remains with the financial institution rely-ing on the third party.

The criteria that should be met are as follows:

a) A financial institution relying upon a third party should immediate-ly obtain the necessary information concerning elements (a) – (c) of the CDD process. Financial institutions should take adequate steps to satisfy themselves that copies of identification data and other relevant documentation relating to the CDD requirements will be made available from the third party upon request without delay.

b) The financial institution should satisfy itself that the third party is regulated and supervised for, and has measures in place to comply with CDD requirements in line with Recommendations 5 and 10.

It is left to each country to determine in which countries the third party that meets the conditions can be based, having regard to information available on countries that do not or do not adequately apply the FATF Recommendations.

10.* Financial institutions should maintain, for at least five years, all necessary records on transactions, both domestic or international, to enable them to comply swiftly with information requests from the competent authorities. Such records must be sufficient to permit reconstruction of individual trans-actions (including the amounts and types of currency involved if any) so as to provide, if necessary, evidence for prosecution of criminal activity.

Financial institutions should keep records on the identification data obtained through the customer due diligence process (e.g. copies or records of official identification documents like passports, identity cards, driving licenses or similar documents), account files and business cor-respondence for at least five years after the business relationship is ended.

The identification data and transaction records should be available to domestic competent authorities upon appropriate authority.

11.* Financial institutions should pay special attention to all complex, unusual large transactions, and all unusual patterns of transactions, which have no apparent economic or visible lawful purpose. The background and purpose of such transactions should, as far as possible, be examined, the findings established in writing, and be available to help competent authorities and auditors.

12.* The customer due diligence and record-keeping requirements set out in Recommendations 5, 6, and 8 to 11 apply to designated non-financial businesses and professions in the following situations:

a) Casinos – when customers engage in financial transactions equal to or above the applicable designated threshold.

b) Real estate agents – when they are involved in transactions for their client concerning the buying and selling of real estate.

c) Dealers in precious metals and dealers in precious stones – when they engage in any cash transaction with a customer equal to or above the applicable designated threshold.

d) Lawyers, notaries, other independent legal professionals and accountants when they prepare for or carry out transactions for their client concerning the following activities:

- buying and selling of real estate;
- managing of client money, securities or other assets;
- management of bank, savings or securities accounts;
- organisation of contributions for the creation, operation or management of companies;
- creation, operation or management of legal persons or arrangements, and buying and selling of business entities.

e) Trust and company service providers when they prepare for or carry out transactions for a client concerning the activities listed in the definition in the Glossary.

Reporting of suspicious transactions and compliance

13.* If a financial institution suspects or has reasonable grounds to suspect that funds are the proceeds of a criminal activity, or are related to terrorist financing, it should be required, directly by law or regulation, to report promptly its suspicions to the financial intelligence unit (FIU).

14.* Financial institutions, their directors, officers and employees should be:

a) Protected by legal provisions from criminal and civil liability for breach of any restriction on disclosure of information imposed by contract or by any legislative, regulatory or administrative provision, if they report their suspicions in good faith to the FIU, even if they did not know precisely what the underlying criminal activity was, and regardless of whether illegal activity actually occurred.

b) Prohibited by law from disclosing the fact that a suspicious transaction report (STR) or related information is being reported to the FIU.

15.* Financial institutions should develop programmes against money laundering and terrorist financing. These programmes should include:

a) The development of internal policies, procedures and controls, including appropriate compliance management arrangements, and adequate screening procedures to ensure high standards when hiring employees.

b) An ongoing employee training programme.

c) An audit function to test the system.

16.* The requirements set out in Recommendations 13 to 15, and 21 apply to all designated non-financial businesses and professions, subject to the following qualifications:

a) Lawyers, notaries, other independent legal professionals and accountants should be required to report suspicious transactions when, on behalf of or for a client, they engage in a financial transaction in relation to the activities described in Recommendation 12(d). Countries are strongly encouraged to extend the reporting requirement to the rest of the professional activities of accountants, including auditing.

b) Dealers in precious metals and dealers in precious stones should be required to report suspicious transactions when they engage in any cash transaction with a customer equal to or above the applicable designated threshold.

c) Trust and company service providers should be required to report suspicious transactions for a client when, on behalf of or for a client, they engage in a transaction in relation to the activities referred to Recommendation 12(e).

Lawyers, notaries, other independent legal professionals, and accountants acting as independent legal professionals, are not required to report their suspicions if the relevant information was obtained in circumstances where they are subject to professional secrecy or legal professional privilege.

Other measures to deter money laundering and terrorist financing

17. Countries should ensure that effective, proportionate and dissuasive sanctions, whether criminal, civil or administrative, are available to deal with natural or legal persons covered by these Recommendations that fail to comply with anti-money laundering or terrorist financing requirements.

18. Countries should not approve the establishment or accept the continued operation of shell banks. Financial institutions should refuse to enter into, or continue, a correspondent banking relationship with shell banks. Financial institutions should also guard against establishing relations with respondent foreign financial institutions that permit their accounts to be used by shell banks.

19.˙ Countries should consider:

   a) Implementing feasible measures to detect or monitor the physical cross-border transportation of currency and bearer negotiable instruments, subject to strict safeguards to ensure proper use of information and without impeding in any way the freedom of capital movements.

   b) The feasibility and utility of a system where banks and other financial institutions and intermediaries would report all domestic and international currency transactions above a fixed amount, to a national central agency with a computerised data base, available to competent authorities for use in money laundering or terrorist financing cases, subject to strict safeguards to ensure proper use of the information.

20. Countries should consider applying the FATF Recommendations to businesses and professions, other than designated non-financial businesses and professions, that pose a money laundering or terrorist financing risk.

   Countries should further encourage the development of modern and secure techniques of money management that are less vulnerable to money laundering.

Measures to be taken with respect to countries that do not or insufficiently comply with the FATF Recommendations

21. Financial institutions should give special attention to business relationships and transactions with persons, including companies and financial institutions, from countries which do not or insufficiently apply the FATF Recommendations. Whenever these transactions have no apparent economic or visible lawful purpose, their background and purpose should, as far as possible, be examined, the findings established in writing, and be available to help competent authorities. Where such a country continues not to apply or insufficiently applies the FATF Recommendations, countries should be able to apply appropriate countermeasures.

22. Financial institutions should ensure that the principles applicable to financial institutions, which are mentioned above are also applied to branches and majority owned subsidiaries located abroad, especially in countries which do not or insufficiently apply the FATF Recommendations, to the extent that local applicable laws and regulations permit. When local applicable laws and regulations prohibit this implementation, competent authorities in the country of the parent institution should be informed by the financial institutions that they cannot apply the FATF Recommendations.

Regulation and supervision

23.* Countries should ensure that financial institutions are subject to adequate regulation and supervision and are effectively implementing the FATF Recommendations. Competent authorities should take the necessary legal or regulatory measures to prevent criminals or their associates from holding or being the beneficial owner of a significant or controlling interest or holding a management function in a financial institution.

For financial institutions subject to the Core Principles, the regulatory and supervisory measures that apply for prudential purposes and which are also relevant to money laundering, should apply in a similar manner for anti-money laundering and terrorist financing purposes.

Other financial institutions should be licensed or registered and appropriately regulated, and subject to supervision or oversight for anti-money laundering purposes, having regard to the risk of money laundering or terrorist financing in that sector. At a minimum, businesses providing a service of money or value transfer, or of money or currency changing should be licensed or registered, and subject to effective systems for monitoring and ensuring compliance with national requirements to combat money laundering and terrorist financing.

24. Designated non-financial businesses and professions should be subject to regulatory and supervisory measures as set out below.

   a) Casinos should be subject to a comprehensive regulatory and supervisory regime that ensures that they have effectively implemented the necessary anti-money laundering and terrorist-financing measures. At a minimum:

   - casinos should be licensed;
   - competent authorities should take the necessary legal or regulatory measures to prevent criminals or their associates from holding or being the beneficial owner of a significant or controlling interest, holding a management function in, or being an operator of a casino;
   - competent authorities should ensure that casinos are effectively supervised for compliance with requirements to combat money laundering and terrorist financing.

b) Countries should ensure that the other categories of designated non-financial businesses and professions are subject to effective systems for monitoring and ensuring their compliance with requirements to combat money laundering and terrorist financing. This should be performed on a risk-sensitive basis. This may be performed by a government authority or by an appropriate self-regulatory organisation, provided that such an organisation can ensure that its members comply with their obligations to combat money laundering and terrorist financing.

25.* The competent authorities should establish guidelines, and provide feedback which will assist financial institutions and designated non-financial businesses and professions in applying national measures to combat money laundering and terrorist financing, and in particular, in detecting and reporting suspicious transactions.

C. Institutional and other measures necessary in systems for combating money laundering and terrorist financing

Competent authorities, their powers and resources

26.* Countries should establish a FIU that serves as a national centre for the receiving (and, as permitted, requesting), analysis and dissemination of STR and other information regarding potential money laundering or terrorist financing. The FIU should have access, directly or indirectly, on a timely basis to the financial, administrative and law enforcement information that it requires to properly undertake its functions, including the analysis of STR.

27.* Countries should ensure that designated law enforcement authorities have responsibility for money laundering and terrorist financing investigations. Countries are encouraged to support and develop, as far as possible, special investigative techniques suitable for the investigation of money laundering, such as controlled delivery, undercover operations and other relevant techniques. Countries are also encouraged to use other effective mechanisms such as the use of permanent or temporary groups specialised in asset investigation, and co-operative investigations with appropriate competent authorities in other countries.

28. When conducting investigations of money laundering and underlying predicate offences, competent authorities should be able to obtain documents and information for use in those investigations, and in prosecutions and related actions. This should include powers to use compulsory measures for the production of records held by financial institutions and other persons, for the search of persons and premises, and for the seizure and obtaining of evidence.

29. Supervisors should have adequate powers to monitor and ensure compliance by financial institutions with requirements to combat money laundering and terrorist financing, including the authority to conduct inspections. They should be authorised to compel production of any information from financial institutions that is relevant to monitoring such compliance, and to impose adequate administrative sanctions for failure to comply with such requirements.

30. Countries should provide their competent authorities involved in combating money laundering and terrorist financing with adequate financial, human and technical resources. Countries should have in place processes to ensure that the staff of those authorities are of high integrity.

31. Countries should ensure that policy makers, the FIU, law enforcement and supervisors have effective mechanisms in place which enable them to co-operate, and where appropriate co-ordinate domestically with each other concerning the development and implementation of policies and activities to combat money laundering and terrorist financing.

32. Countries should ensure that their competent authorities can review the effectiveness of their systems to combat money laundering and terrorist financing systems by maintaining comprehensive statistics on matters relevant to the effectiveness and efficiency of such systems. This should include statistics on the STR received and disseminated; on money laundering and terrorist financing investigations, prosecutions and convictions; on property frozen, seized and confiscated; and on mutual legal assistance or other international requests for co-operation.

Transparency of legal persons and arrangements

33. Countries should take measures to prevent the unlawful use of legal persons by money launderers. Countries should ensure that there is adequate, accurate and timely information on the beneficial ownership and control of legal persons that can be obtained or accessed in a timely fashion by competent authorities. In particular, countries that have legal persons that are able to issue bearer shares should take appropriate measures to ensure that they are not misused for money laundering and be able to demonstrate the adequacy of those measures.

    Countries could consider measures to facilitate access to beneficial ownership and control information to financial institutions undertaking the requirements set out in Recommendation 5.

34. Countries should take measures to prevent the unlawful use of legal arrangements by money launderers. In particular, countries should ensure that there is adequate, accurate and timely information on express trusts,

271

including information on the settlor, trustee and beneficiaries, that can be obtained or accessed in a timely fashion by competent authorities. Countries could consider measures to facilitate access to beneficial ownership and control information to financial institutions undertaking the requirements set out in Recommendation 5.

D. International co-operation

35. Countries should take immediate steps to become party to and implement fully the Vienna Convention, the Palermo Convention, and the 1999 United Nations International Convention for the Suppression of the Financing of Terrorism. Countries are also encouraged to ratify and implement other relevant international conventions, such as the 1990 Council of Europe Convention on Laundering, Search, Seizure and Confiscation of the Proceeds from Crime and the 2002 Inter-American Convention against Terrorism.

Mutual legal assistance and extradition

36. Countries should rapidly, constructively and effectively provide the widest possible range of mutual legal assistance in relation to money laundering and terrorist financing investigations, prosecutions, and related proceedings. In particular, countries should:

    a) Not prohibit or place unreasonable or unduly restrictive conditions on the provision of mutual legal assistance.

    b) Ensure that they have clear and efficient processes for the execution of mutual legal assistance requests.

    c) Not refuse to execute a request for mutual legal assistance on the sole ground that the offence is also considered to involve fiscal matters.

    d) Not refuse to execute a request for mutual legal assistance on the grounds that laws require financial institutions to maintain secrecy or confidentiality.

    Countries should ensure that the powers of their competent authorities required under Recommendation 28 are also available for use in response to requests for mutual legal assistance, and if consistent with their domestic framework, in response to direct requests from foreign judicial or law enforcement authorities to domestic counterparts.

    To avoid conflicts of jurisdiction, consideration should be given to devising and applying mechanisms for determining the best venue for prosecution of defendants in the interests of justice in cases that are subject to prosecution in more than one country.

37. Countries should, to the greatest extent possible, render mutual legal assistance notwithstanding the absence of dual criminality.

Where dual criminality is required for mutual legal assistance or extradition, that requirement should be deemed to be satisfied regardless of whether both countries place the offence within the same category of offence or denominate the offence by the same terminology, provided that both countries criminalise the conduct underlying the offence.

38.* There should be authority to take expeditious action in response to requests by foreign countries to identify, freeze, seize and confiscate property laundered, proceeds from money laundering or predicate offences, instrumentalities used in or intended for use in the commission of these offences, or property of corresponding value. There should also be arrangements for co-ordinating seizure and confiscation proceedings, which may include the sharing of confiscated assets.

39. Countries should recognise money laundering as an extraditable offence. Each country should either extradite its own nationals, or where a country does not do so solely on the grounds of nationality, that country should, at the request of the country seeking extradition, submit the case without undue delay to its competent authorities for the purpose of prosecution of the offences set forth in the request. Those authorities should take their decision and conduct their proceedings in the same manner as in the case of any other offence of a serious nature under the domestic law of that country. The countries concerned should cooperate with each other, in particular on procedural and evidentiary aspects, to ensure the efficiency of such prosecutions.

Subject to their legal frameworks, countries may consider simplifying extradition by allowing direct transmission of extradition requests between appropriate ministries, extraditing persons based only on warrants of arrests or judgments, and/or introducing a simplified extradition of consenting persons who waive formal extradition proceedings.

Other forms of co-operation

40.* Countries should ensure that their competent authorities provide the widest possible range of international co-operation to their foreign counterparts. There should be clear and effective gateways to facilitate the prompt and constructive exchange directly between counterparts, either spontaneously or upon request, of information relating to both money laundering and the underlying predicate offences. Exchanges should be permitted without unduly restrictive conditions. In particular:

a) Competent authorities should not refuse a request for assistance on the sole ground that the request is also considered to involve fiscal matters.

b) Countries should not invoke laws that require financial institutions to maintain secrecy or confidentiality as a ground for refusing to provide co-operation.

c) Competent authorities should be able to conduct inquiries; and where possible, investigations; on behalf of foreign counterparts.

Where the ability to obtain information sought by a foreign competent authority is not within the mandate of its counterpart, countries are also encouraged to permit a prompt and constructive exchange of information with non-counterparts. Co-operation with foreign authorities other than counterparts could occur directly or indirectly. When uncertain about the appropriate avenue to follow, competent authorities should first contact their foreign counterparts for assistance.

Countries should establish controls and safeguards to ensure that information exchanged by competent authorities is used only in an authorised manner, consistent with their obligations concerning privacy and data protection.

Glossary

In these Recommendations the following abbreviations and references are used:

"Beneficial owner" refers to the natural person(s) who ultimately owns or controls a customer and/or the person on whose behalf a transaction is being conducted. It also incorporates those persons who exercise ultimate effective control over a legal person or arrangement.

"Core Principles" refers to the Core Principles for Effective Banking Supervision issued by the Basel Committee on Banking Supervision, the Objectives and Principles for Securities Regulation issued by the International Organization of Securities Commissions, and the Insurance Supervisory Principles issued by the International Association of Insurance Supervisors.

"Designated categories of offences" means:
- participation in an organised criminal group and racketeering;
- terrorism, including terrorist financing;
- trafficking in human beings and migrant smuggling;
- sexual exploitation, including sexual exploitation of children;
- illicit trafficking in narcotic drugs and psychotropic substances;
- illicit arms trafficking;
- illicit trafficking in stolen and other goods;
- corruption and bribery;
- fraud;
- counterfeiting currency;
- counterfeiting and piracy of products;

- environmental crime;
- murder, grievous bodily injury;
- kidnapping, illegal restraint and hostage-taking;
- robbery or theft;
- smuggling;
- extortion;
- forgery;
- piracy; and
- insider trading and market manipulation.

When deciding on the range of offences to be covered as predicate offences under each of the categories listed above, each country may decide, in accordance with its domestic law, how it will define those offences and the nature of any particular elements of those offences that make them serious offences.

"Designated non-financial businesses and professions" means:

a) Casinos (which also includes internet casinos).
b) Real estate agents.
c) Dealers in precious metals.
d) Dealers in precious stones.
e) Lawyers, notaries, other independent legal professionals and accountants – this refers to sole practitioners, partners or employed professionals within professional firms. It is not meant to refer to 'internal' professionals that are employees of other types of businesses, nor to professionals working for government agencies, who may already be subject to measures that would combat money laundering.
f) Trust and Company Service Providers refers to all persons or businesses that are not covered elsewhere under these Recommendations, and which as a business, provide any of the following services to third parties:
  - acting as a formation agent of legal persons;
  - acting as (or arranging for another person to act as) a director or secretary of a company, a partner of a partnership, or a similar position in relation to other legal persons;
  - providing a registered office; business address or accommodation, correspondence or administrative address for a company, a partnership or any other legal person or arrangement;
  - acting as (or arranging for another person to act as) a trustee of an express trust;
  - acting as (or arranging for another person to act as) a nominee shareholder for another person.

"Designated threshold" refers to the amount set out in the Interpretative Notes.

"Financial institutions" means any person or entity who conducts as a business one or more of the following activities or operations for or on behalf of a customer:

1.   Acceptance of deposits and other repayable funds from the public.[3]

2.   Lending.[4]

3.   Financial leasing.[5]

4.   The transfer of money or value.[6]

5.   Issuing and managing means of payment (e.g. credit and debit cards, cheques, traveller's cheques, money orders and bankers' drafts, electronic money).

6.   Financial guarantees and commitments.

7.   Trading in:

   (a) money market instruments (cheques, bills, CDs, derivatives etc.);

   (b) foreign exchange;

   (c) exchange, interest rate and index instruments;

   (d) transferable securities;

   (e) commodity futures trading.

8.   Participation in securities issues and the provision of financial services related to such issues.

9.   Individual and collective portfolio management.

10. Safekeeping and administration of cash or liquid securities on behalf of other persons.

11. Otherwise investing, administering or managing funds or money on behalf of other persons.

12. Underwriting and placement of life insurance and other invest-ment related insurance.[7]

---

3. This also captures private banking.

4. This includes: consumer credit; mortgage credit; factoring, with or without recourse; and finance of commercial transactions (including forfeiting).

5. This does not extend to financial leasing arrangements in relation to consumer products.

6. This applies to financial activity in both the formal or informal sector e.g. alternative remit-tance activity. See the Interpretative Note to Special Recommendation VI. It does not apply to any natural or legal person that provides financial institutions solely with message or other support systems for transmitting funds. See the Interpretative Note to Special Recommendation VII.

7. This applies both to insurance undertakings and to insurance intermediaries (agents and brokers).

13. Money and currency changing.

14. When a financial activity is carried out by a person or entity on an occasional or very limited basis (having regard to quantitative and absolute criteria) such that there is little risk of money laundering activity occurring, a country may decide that the application of anti-money laundering measures is not necessary, either fully or partially.

    In strictly limited and justified circumstances, and based on a proven low risk of money laundering, a country may decide not to apply some or all of the Forty Recommendations to some of the financial activities stated above.

    "FIU" means financial intelligence unit.

    "Legal arrangements" refers to express trusts or other similar legal arrangements.

    "Legal persons" refers to bodies corporate, foundations, anstalt, partnerships, or associations, or any similar bodies that can establish a permanent customer relationship with a financial institution or otherwise own property.

    "Payable-through accounts" refers to correspondent accounts that are used directly by third parties to transact business on their own behalf.

    "Politically Exposed Persons" (PEPs) are individuals who are or have been entrusted with prominent public functions in a foreign country, for example Heads of State or of government, senior politicians, senior government, judicial or military officials, senior executives of state owned corporations, important political party officials. Business relationships with family members or close associates of PEPs involve reputational risks similar to those with PEPs themselves. The definition is not intended to cover middle ranking or more junior individuals in the foregoing categories.

    "Shell bank" means a bank incorporated in a jurisdiction in which it has no physical presence and which is unaffiliated with a regulated financial group.

    "STR" refers to suspicious transaction reports.

    "Supervisors" refers to the designated competent authorities responsible for ensuring compliance by financial institutions with requirements to combat money laundering and terrorist financing.

    "the FATF Recommendations" refers to these Recommendations and to the FATF Special Recommendations on Terrorist Financing.

Annex

Interpretative Notes to the Forty Recommendations

General

1. Reference in this document to "countries" should be taken to apply equally to "territories" or "jurisdictions".

2. Recommendations 5-16 and 21-22 state that financial institutions or designated non-financial businesses and professions should take certain actions. These references require countries to take measures that will oblige financial institutions or designated non-financial businesses and professions to comply with each Recommendation. The basic obligations under Recommendations 5, 10 and 13 should be set out in law or regulation, while more detailed elements in those Recommendations, as well as obligations under other Recommendations, could be required either by law or regulation or by other enforceable means issued by a competent authority.

3. Where reference is made to a financial institution being satisfied as to a matter, that institution must be able to justify its assessment to competent authorities.

4. To comply with Recommendations 12 and 16, countries do not need to issue laws or regulations that relate exclusively to lawyers, notaries, accountants and the other designated non-financial businesses and professions so long as these businesses or professions are included in laws or regulations covering the underlying activities.

5. The Interpretative Notes that apply to financial institutions are also relevant to designated non-financial businesses and professions, where applicable.

Recommendations 5, 12 and 16

The designated thresholds for transactions (under Recommendations 5 and 12) are as follows:

- Financial institutions (for occasional customers under Recommendation 5) – USD/EUR 15,000.
- Casinos, including internet casinos (under Recommendation 12) – USD/EUR 3000
- For dealers in precious metals and dealers in precious stones when engaged in any cash transaction (under Recommendations 12 and 16) – USD/EUR 15,000.

Financial transactions above a designated threshold include situations where the transaction is carried out in a single operation or in several operations that appear to be linked.

Recommendation 5

Customer due diligence and tipping off

1. If, during the establishment or course of the customer relationship, or when conducting occasional transactions, a financial institution suspects that transactions relate to money laundering or terrorist financing, then the institution should:

    a) Normally seek to identify and verify the identity of the customer and the beneficial owner, whether permanent or occasional, and irrespective of any exemption or any designated threshold that might otherwise apply.

    b) Make a STR to the FIU in accordance with Recommendation 13.

2. Recommendation 14 prohibits financial institutions, their directors, officers and employees from disclosing the fact that an STR or related information is being reported to the FIU. A risk exists that customers could be unintentionally tipped off when the financial institution is seeking to perform its customer due diligence (CDD) obligations in these circumstances. The customer's awareness of a possible STR or investigation could compromise future efforts to investigate the suspected money laundering or terrorist financing operation.

3. Therefore, if financial institutions form a suspicion that transactions relate to money laundering or terrorist financing, they should take into account the risk of tipping off when performing the customer due diligence process. If the institution reasonably believes that performing the CDD process will tip-off the customer or potential customer, it may choose not to pursue that process, and should file an STR. Institutions should ensure that their employees are aware of and sensitive to these issues when conducting CDD.

CDD for legal persons and arrangements

4. When performing elements (a) and (b) of the CDD process in relation to legal persons or arrangements, financial institutions should:

    a) Verify that any person purporting to act on behalf of the customer is so authorised, and identify that person.

    b) Identify the customer and verify its identity – the types of measures that would be normally needed to satisfactorily perform this function would require obtaining proof of incorporation or similar evidence of the legal status of the legal person or arrangement, as well as information concerning the customer's name, the names of trustees, legal form, address, directors, and provisions regulating the power to bind the legal person or arrangement.

c) Identify the beneficial owners, including forming an understanding of the ownership and control structure, and take reasonable measures to verify the identity of such persons. The types of measures that would be normally needed to satisfactorily perform this function would require identifying the natural persons with a controlling interest and identifying the natural persons who comprise the mind and management of the legal person or arrangement. Where the customer or the owner of the controlling interest is a public company that is subject to regulatory disclosure requirements, it is not necessary to seek to identify and verify the identity of any shareholder of that company.

The relevant information or data may be obtained from a public register, from the customer or from other reliable sources.

Reliance on identification and verification already performed

5. The CDD measures set out in Recommendation 5 do not imply that financial institutions have to repeatedly identify and verify the identity of each customer every time that a customer conducts a transaction. An institution is entitled to rely on the identification and verification steps that it has already undertaken unless it has doubts about the veracity of that information.

Examples of situations that might lead an institution to have such doubts could be where there is a suspicion of money laundering in relation to that customer, or where there is a material change in the way that the customer's account is operated which is not consistent with the customer's business profile.

Timing of verification

6. Examples of the types of circumstances where it would be permissible for verification to be completed after the establishment of the business relationship, because it would be essential not to interrupt the normal conduct of business include:

- Non face-to-face business.

- Securities transactions. In the securities industry, companies and intermediaries may be required to perform transactions very rapidly, according to the market conditions at the time the customer is contacting them, and the performance of the transaction may be required before verification of identity is completed.

- Life insurance business. In relation to life insurance business, countries may permit the identification and verification of the beneficiary under the policy to take place after having established the business relationship with the policyholder. However, in all such cases, identification and verification should occur at or before the time of payout or the time where the beneficiary intends to exercise vested rights under the policy.

7. Financial institutions will also need to adopt risk management procedures with respect to the conditions under which a customer may use the business relationship prior to verification.

These procedures should include a set of measures such as a limitation of the number, types and/or amount of transactions that can be performed and the monitoring of large or complex transactions being carried out outside of expected norms for that type of relationship.

Financial institutions should refer to the Basel CDD paper[8] (section 2.2.6.) for specific guidance on examples of risk management measures for non-face to face business.

Requirement to identify existing customers

8. The principles set out in the Basel CDD paper concerning the identification of existing customers should serve as guidance when applying customer due diligence processes to institutions engaged in banking activity, and could apply to other financial institutions where relevant.

Simplified or reduced CDD measures

9. The general rule is that customers must be subject to the full range of CDD measures, including the requirement to identify the beneficial owner. Nevertheless there are circumstances where the risk of money laundering or terrorist financing is lower, where information on the identity of the customer and the beneficial owner of a customer is publicly available, or where adequate checks and controls exist elsewhere in national systems. In such circumstances it could be reasonable for a country to allow its financial institutions to apply simplified or reduced CDD measures when identifying and verifying the identity of the customer and the beneficial owner.

10. Examples of customers where simplified or reduced CDD measures could apply are:

- Financial institutions – where they are subject to requirements to combat money laundering and terrorist financing consistent with the FATF Recommendations and are supervised for compliance with those controls.

- Public companies that are subject to regulatory disclosure requirements.

- Government administrations or enterprises.

---

8. "Basel CDD paper" refers to the guidance paper on customer due diligence for banks issued by the Basel Committee on Banking Supervision in October 2001.

11. Simplified or reduced CDD measures could also apply to the beneficial owners of pooled accounts held by designated non financial businesses or professions provided that those businesses or professions are subject to requirements to combat money laundering and terrorist financing consistent with the FATF Recommendations and are subject to effective systems for monitoring and ensuring their compliance with those requirements. Banks should also refer to the Basel CDD paper (section 2.2.4.), which provides specific guidance concerning situations where an account holding institution may rely on a customer that is a professional financial intermediary to perform the customer due diligence on his or its own customers (i.e. the beneficial owners of the bank account). Where relevant, the CDD Paper could also provide guidance in relation to similar accounts held by other types of financial institutions.

12. Simplified CDD or reduced measures could also be acceptable for various types of products or transactions such as (examples only):

   • Life insurance policies where the annual premium is no more than USD/EUR 1000 or a single premium of no more than USD/EUR 2500.

   • Insurance policies for pension schemes if there is no surrender clause and the policy cannot be used as collateral.

   • A pension, superannuation or similar scheme that provides retirement benefits to employees, where contributions are made by way of deduction from wages and the scheme rules do not permit the assignment of a member's interest under the scheme.

13. Countries could also decide whether financial institutions could apply these simplified measures only to customers in its own jurisdiction or allow them to do for customers from any other jurisdiction that the original country is satisfied is in compliance with and has effectively implemented the FATF Recommendations.

   Simplified CDD measures are not acceptable whenever there is suspicion of money laundering or terrorist financing or specific higher risk scenarios apply.

Recommendation 6

Countries are encouraged to extend the requirements of Recommendation 6 to individuals who hold prominent public functions in their own country.

Recommendation 9

This Recommendation does not apply to outsourcing or agency relationships.

This Recommendation also does not apply to relationships, accounts or transactions between financial institutions for their clients. Those relationships are addressed by Recommendations 5 and 7.

Recommendations 10 and 11

In relation to insurance business, the word "transactions" should be understood to refer to the insurance product itself, the premium payment and the benefits.

Recommendation 13

1. The reference to criminal activity in Recommendation 13 refers to:

    a) all criminal acts that would constitute a predicate offence for money laundering in the jurisdiction; or

    b) at a minimum to those offences that would constitute a predicate offence as required by Recommendation 1.

    Countries are strongly encouraged to adopt alternative (a). All suspicious transactions, including attempted transactions, should be reported regardless of the amount of the transaction.

2. In implementing Recommendation 13, suspicious transactions should be reported by financial institutions regardless of whether they are also thought to involve tax matters. Countries should take into account that, in order to deter financial institutions from reporting a suspicious transaction, money launderers may seek to state *inter alia* that their transactions relate to tax matters.

Recommendation 14 (tipping off)

Where lawyers, notaries, other independent legal professionals and accountants acting as independent legal professionals seek to dissuade a client from engaging in illegal activity, this does not amount to tipping off.

Recommendation 15

The type and extent of measures to be taken for each of the requirements set out in the Recommendation should be appropriate having regard to the risk of money laundering and terrorist financing and the size of the business. For financial institutions, compliance management arrangements should include the appointment of a compliance officer at the management level.

Recommendation 16

1. It is for each jurisdiction to determine the matters that would fall under legal professional privilege or professional secrecy. This would normally cover information lawyers, notaries or other independent legal professionals receive from or obtain through one of their clients: (a) in the

course of ascertaining the legal position of their client, or (b) in performing their task of defending or representing that client in, or concerning judicial, administrative, arbitration or mediation proceedings. Where accountants are subject to the same obligations of secrecy or privilege, then they are also not required to report suspicious transactions.

2. Countries may allow lawyers, notaries, other independent legal professionals and accountants to send their STR to their appropriate self-regulatory organisations, provided that there are appropriate forms of co-operation between these organisations and the FIU.

Recommendation 19

1. To facilitate detection and monitoring of cash transactions, without impeding in any way the freedom of capital movements, countries could consider the feasibility of subjecting all cross-border transfers, above a given threshold, to verification, administrative monitoring, declaration or record keeping requirements.

2. If a country discovers an unusual international shipment of currency, monetary instruments, precious metals, or gems, etc., it should consider notifying, as appropriate, the Customs Service or other competent authorities of the countries from which the shipment originated and/or to which it is destined, and should co-operate with a view toward establishing the source, destination, and purpose of such shipment and toward the taking of appropriate action.

Recommendation 23

Recommendation 23 should not be read as to require the introduction of a system of regular review of licensing of controlling interests in financial institutions merely for anti-money laundering purposes, but as to stress the desirability of suitability review for controlling shareholders in financial institutions (banks and non-banks in particular) from a FATF point of view. Hence, where shareholder suitability (or "fit and proper") tests exist, the attention of supervisors should be drawn to their relevance for anti-money laundering purposes.

Recommendation 25

When considering the feedback that should be provided, countries should have regard to the FATF Best Practice Guidelines on Providing Feedback to Reporting Financial Institutions and Other Persons.

Recommendation 26

Where a country has created an FIU, it should consider applying for membership in the Egmont Group. Countries should have regard to the Egmont Group Statement of Purpose, and its Principles for Information Exchange Between Financial Intelligence Units for Money Laundering Cases. These documents set out important guidance concerning the role and functions of FIUs, and the mechanisms for exchanging information between FIU.

Recommendation 27

Countries should consider taking measures, including legislative ones, at the national level, to allow their competent authorities investigating money laundering cases to postpone or waive the arrest of suspected persons and/or the seizure of the money for the purpose of identifying persons involved in such activities or for evidence gathering. Without such measures the use of procedures such as controlled deliveries and undercover operations are precluded.

Recommendation 38

Countries should consider:

a) Establishing an asset forfeiture fund in its respective country into which all or a portion of confiscated property will be deposited for law enforcement, health, education, or other appropriate purposes.

b) Taking such measures as may be necessary to enable it to share among or between other countries confiscated property, in particular, when confiscation is directly or indirectly a result of co-ordinated law enforcement actions.

Recommendation 40

1. For the purposes of this Recommendation:

   • "Counterparts" refers to authorities that exercise similar responsibilities and functions.

   • "Competent authority" refers to all administrative and law enforcement authorities concerned with combating money laundering and terrorist financing, including the FIU and supervisors.

2. Depending on the type of competent authority involved and the nature and purpose of the co-operation, different channels can be appropriate for the exchange of information. Examples of mechanisms or channels that are used to exchange information include: bilateral or multilateral agreements or arrangements, memoranda of understanding, exchanges on the basis of reciprocity, or through appropriate international or regional organisations. However, this Recommendation is not intended to cover co-operation in relation to mutual legal assistance or extradition.

3. The reference to indirect exchange of information with foreign authorities other than counterparts covers the situation where the requested

information passes from the foreign authority through one or more domestic or foreign authorities before being received by the requesting authority. The competent authority that requests the information should always make it clear for what purpose and on whose behalf the request is made.

4. FIUs should be able to make inquiries on behalf of foreign counterparts where this could be relevant to an analysis of financial transactions. At a minimum, inquiries should include:

- Searching its own databases, which would include information related to suspicious transaction reports.

- Searching other databases to which it may have direct or indirect access, including law enforcement databases, public databases, administrative databases and commercially available databases.

Where permitted to do so, FIUs should also contact other competent authorities and financial institutions in order to obtain relevant information.

Appendix IV – The 2001 FATF Special Recommendations on Terrorist Financing

Recognising the vital importance of taking action to combat the financing of terrorism, the FATF has agreed these Recommendations, which, when combined with the FATF Forty Recommendations on money laundering, set out the basic framework to detect, prevent and suppress the financing of terrorism and terrorist acts.

I. Ratification and implementation of UN instruments

Each country should take immediate steps to ratify and to implement fully the 1999 United Nations International Convention for the Suppression of the Financing of Terrorism.

Countries should also immediately implement the United Nations resolutions relating to the prevention and suppression of the financing of terrorist acts, particularly United Nations Security Council Resolution 1373.

II. Criminalising the financing of terrorism and associated money laundering

Each country should criminalise the financing of terrorism, terrorist acts and terrorist organisations. Countries should ensure that such offences are designated as money laundering predicate offences.

III. Freezing and confiscating terrorist assets

Each country should implement measures to freeze without delay funds or other assets of terrorists, those who finance terrorism and terrorist organisations in accordance with the United Nations resolutions relating to the prevention and suppression of the financing of terrorist acts.

Each country should also adopt and implement measures, including legislative ones, which would enable the competent authorities to seize and confiscate property that is the proceeds of, or used in, or intended or allocated for use in, the financing of terrorism, terrorist acts or terrorist organisations.

IV. Reporting suspicious transactions related to terrorism

If financial institutions, or other businesses or entities subject to anti-money laundering obligations, suspect or have reasonable grounds to suspect that funds are linked or related to, or are to be used for terrorism, terrorist acts or by terrorist organisations, they should be required to report promptly their suspicions to the competent authorities.

V. International co-operation

Each country should afford another country, on the basis of a treaty, arrangement or other mechanism for mutual legal assistance or information exchange, the greatest possible measure of assistance in connection with criminal, civil enforcement, and administrative investigations, inquiries and proceedings relating to the financing of terrorism, terrorist acts and terrorist organisations.

Countries should also take all possible measures to ensure that they do not provide safe havens for individuals charged with the financing of terrorism, terrorist acts or terrorist organisations, and should have procedures in place to extradite, where possible, such individuals.

VI. Alternative remittance

Each country should take measures to ensure that persons or legal entities, including agents, that provide a service for the transmission of money or value, including transmission through an informal money or value transfer system or network, should be licensed or registered and subject to all the FATF Recommendations that apply to banks and non-bank financial institutions. Each country should ensure that persons or legal entities that carry out this service illegally are subject to administrative, civil or criminal sanctions.

VII. Wire transfers

Countries should take measures to require financial institutions, including money remitters, to include accurate and meaningful originator information (name, address and account number) on funds transfers and related messages that are sent, and the information should remain with the transfer or related message through the payment chain.

Countries should take measures to ensure that financial institutions, including money remitters, conduct enhanced scrutiny of and monitor for suspicious activity funds transfers which do not contain complete originator information (name, address and account number).

VIII. Non-profit organsations

Countries should review the adequacy of laws and regulations that relate to entities that can be abused for the financing of terrorism. Non-profit organisations are particularly vulnerable, and countries should ensure that they cannot be misused:

(i) by terrorist organisations posing as legitimate entities;

(ii) to exploit legitimate entities as conduits for terrorist financing, including for the purpose of escaping asset freezing measures; and

(iii) to conceal or obscure the clandestine diversion of funds intended for legitimate purposes to terrorist organisations.

Appendix V – Interpretative note to Special Recommendation VII: wire transfers[1]

Objective

1. Special Recommendation VII (SR VII) was developed with the objective of preventing terrorists and other criminals from having unfettered access to wire transfers for moving their funds and for detecting such misuse when it occurs. Specifically, it aims to ensure that basic information on the originator of wire transfers is immediately available (1) to appropriate law enforcement and/or prosecutorial authorities to assist them in detecting, investigating, prosecuting terrorists or other criminals and tracing the assets of terrorists or other criminals, (2) to financial intelligence units for analysing suspicious or unusual activity and disseminating it as necessary, and (3) to beneficiary financial institutions to facilitate the identification and reporting of suspicious transactions. It is not the intention of the FATF to impose rigid standards or to mandate a single operating process that would negatively affect the payment system.

Definitions

2. For the purposes of this interpretative note, the following definitions apply.

    a. The terms *wire transfer* and *funds transfer* refer to any transaction carried out on behalf of an originator person (both natural and legal) through a financial institution by electronic means with a view to making an amount of money available to a beneficiary person at another financial institution. The originator and the beneficiary may be the same person.

    b. *Cross-border transfer* means any wire transfer where the originator and beneficiary institutions are located in different jurisdictions. This term also refers to any chain of wire transfers that has at least one cross-border element.

    c. *Domestic transfer* means any wire transfer where the originator and beneficiary institutions are located in the same jurisdiction. This term therefore refers to any chain of wire transfers that takes place entirely within the borders of a single jurisdiction, even though the system used to effect the wire transfer may be located in another jurisdiction.

---

1. It is recognised that jurisdictions will need time to make relevant legislative or regulatory changes and to allow financial institutions to make necessary adaptations to their systems and procedures. This period should not be longer than two years after the adoption of this Interpretative Note.

d. The term *financial institution* is as defined by the FATF Forty Recommendations (2003).[2] The term does not apply to any persons or entities that provide financial institutions solely with message or other support systems for transmitting funds.[3]

e. The *originator* is the account holder, or where there is no account, the person (natural or legal) that places the order with the financial institution to perform the wire transfer.

Scope

3. SR VII applies, under the conditions set out below, to cross-border and domestic transfers between financial institutions.

Cross-border wire transfers

4. Cross-border wire transfers should be accompanied by accurate and meaningful originator information.[4]

5. Information accompanying cross-border wire transfers must always contain the name of the originator and where an account exists, the number of that account. In the absence of an account, a unique reference number must be included.

6. Information accompanying the wire transfer should also contain the address of the originator. However, jurisdictions may permit financial institutions to substitute the address with a national identity number, customer identification number, or date and place of birth.

7. Cross-border wire transfers that are contained within batch transfers, except for those sent by money remitters, will be treated as domestic wire transfers. In such cases, the ordering institutions must retain the information necessary to identify all originators and make it available on

---

2. When this Interpretative Note was originally issued, these references were to the 1996 FATF Forty Recommendations. Subsequent to the publication of the revised FATF Forty Recommendations in June 2003, this text was updated accordingly. All references are now to the 2003 FATF Forty Recommendations.

3. However, these systems do have a role in providing the necessary means for the financial institutions to fulfil their obligations under Special Recommendation VII and, in particular, in preserving the integrity of the information transmitted with a wire transfer.

4. Jurisdictions may have a *de minimis* threshold (no higher than US$3 000) for a one-year period from publication of this Interpretative Note. At the end of this period, the FATF will undertake a review of this issue to determine whether the use of a *de minimis* threshold is acceptable. Notwithstanding any thresholds, accurate and meaningful originator information must be retained and made available by the ordering financing institution as set forth in paragraph 9.

request to the authorities and to the beneficiary financial institution. Financial institutions should ensure that non-routine transactions are not batched where this would increase the risk of money laundering or terrorist financing.

Domestic wire transfers

8. Information accompanying domestic wire transfers must also include originator information as indicated for cross-border wire transfers, unless full originator information can be made available to the beneficiary financial institution and appropriate authorities by other means.

    In this latter case, financial institutions need only include the account number or a unique identifier provided that this number or identifier will permit the transaction to be traced back to the originator.

9. The information must be made available by the ordering financial institution within three business days of receiving the request either from the beneficiary financial institution or from appropriate authorities. Law enforcement authorities should be able to compel immediate production of such information.

Exemptions from SR VII

10. SR VII is not intended to cover the following types of payments:

    a. Any transfer that flows from a transaction carried out using a credit or debit card so long as the credit or debit card number accompanies all transfers flowing from the transaction. However, when credit or debit cards are used as a payment system to effect a money transfer, they are covered by SR VII, and the necessary information should be included in the message.

    b. Financial institution-to-financial institution transfers and settlements where both the originator person and the beneficiary person are financial institutions acting on their own behalf.

Role of ordering, intermediary and beneficiary financial institutions

Ordering financial institution

11. The ordering financial institution must ensure that qualifying wire transfers contain complete originator information. The ordering financial institution must also verify this information for accuracy and maintain this information in accordance with the standards set out in the FATF Forty Recommendations (2003).[5]

---

5. See footnote [2, page 290.]

Intermediary financial institution

12. For both cross-border and domestic wire transfers, financial institutions processing an intermediary element of such chains of wire transfers must ensure that all originator information that accompanies a wire transfer is retained with the transfer.

13. Where technical limitations prevent the full originator information accompanying a cross-border wire transfer from remaining with a related domestic wire transfer (during the necessary time to adapt payment systems), a record must be kept for five years by the receiving intermediary financial institution of all the information received from the ordering financial institution.

Beneficiary financial institution

14. Beneficiary financial institutions should have effective risk-based procedures in place to identify wire transfers lacking complete originator information. The lack of complete originator information may be considered as a factor in assessing whether a wire transfer or related transactions are suspicious and, as appropriate, whether they are thus required to be reported to the financial intelligence unit or other competent authorities. In some cases, the beneficiary financial institution should consider restricting or even terminating its business relationship with financial institutions that fail to meet SRVII standards.

Enforcement mechanisms for financial institutions that do not comply with wire transfer rules and regulations

15. Jurisdictions should adopt appropriate measures to monitor effectively the compliance of financial institutions with rules and regulations governing wire transfers. Financial institutions that fail to comply with such rules and regulations should be subject to civil, administrative or criminal sanctions.

Appendix VI – Interpretative note to Special Recommendation VI: alternative remittance

General

1. Money or value transfer systems have shown themselves vulnerable to misuse for money laundering and terrorist financing purposes. The objective of Special Recommendation VI is to increase the transparency of payment flows by ensuring that jurisdictions impose consistent anti-money laundering and counter-terrorist financing measures on all forms of money/value transfer systems, particularly those traditionally operating outside the conventional financial sector and not currently subject to the FATF Recommendations. This Recommendation and Interpretative Note underscore the need to bring all money or value transfer services, whether formal or informal, within the ambit of certain minimum legal and regulatory requirements in accordance with the relevant FATF Recommendations.

2. Special Recommendation VI consists of three core elements:

   a. Jurisdictions should require licensing or registration of persons (natural or legal) that provide money/value transfer services, including through informal systems;

   b. Jurisdictions should ensure that money/value transmission services, including informal systems (as described in paragraph 5 below), are subject to applicable FATF Forty Recommendations (2003) (in particular, Recommendations 4-16 and 21-25)[1] and the Eight Special Recommendations (in particular SR VII); and

   c. Jurisdictions should be able to impose sanctions on money/value transfer services, including informal systems, that operate without a license or registration and that fail to comply with relevant FATF Recommendations.

Scope and application

3. For the purposes of this Recommendation, the following definitions are used.

---

1. When this Interpretative Note was originally issued, these references were to the 1996 FATF Forty Recommendations. Subsequent to the publication of the revised FATF Forty Recommendations in June 2003, this text was updated accordingly. All references are now to the 2003 FATF Forty Recommendations.

4. *Money or value transfer service* refers to a financial service that accepts cash, cheques, other monetary instruments or other stores of value in one location and pays a corresponding sum in cash or other form to a beneficiary in another location by means of a communication, message, transfer or through a clearing network to which the money/value transfer service belongs. Transactions performed by such services can involve one or more intermediaries and a third party final payment.

5. A money or value transfer service may be provided by persons (natural or legal) formally through the regulated financial system or informally through non-bank financial institutions or other business entities or any other mechanism either through the regulated financial system (for example, use of bank accounts) or through a network or mechanism that operates outside the regulated system.

    In some jurisdictions, informal systems are frequently referred to as *alternative remittance services* or *underground* (or *parallel*) *banking systems*. Often these systems have ties to particular geographic regions and are therefore described using a variety of specific terms. Some examples of these terms include *hawala, hundi, fei-chien*, and the *black market peso exchange*.[2]

6. Licensing means a requirement to obtain permission from a designated competent authority in order to operate a money/value transfer service legally.

7. *Registration* in this Recommendation means a requirement to register with or declare to a designated competent authority the existence of a money/value transfer service in order for the business to operate legally.

8. The obligation of licensing or registration applies to agents. At a minimum, the principal business must maintain a current list of agents which must be made available to the designated competent authority. An agent is any person who provides money or value transfer service under the direction of or by contract with a legally registered or licensed remitter (for example, licensees, franchisees, concessionaires).

Applicability of Special Recommendation VI

9. Special Recommendation VI should apply to all persons (natural or legal), which conduct for or on behalf of another person (natural or legal) the types of activity described in paragraphs 4 and 5 above as a primary or substantial part of their business or when such activity is undertaken on a regular or recurring basis, including as an ancillary part of a separate business enterprise.

---

2. The inclusion of these examples does not suggest that such systems are legal in any particular jurisdiction.

10. Jurisdictions need not impose a separate licensing/registration system or designate another competent authority in respect to persons (natural or legal) already licensed or registered as financial institutions (as defined by the FATF Forty Recommendations (2003)) within a particular jurisdiction, which under such license or registration are permitted to perform activities indicated in paragraphs 4 and 5 above and which are already subject to the full range of applicable obligations under the FATF Forty Recommendations (2003) (in particular, Recommendations 4-16 and 21-25) and the Eight Special Recommendations (in particular SR VII).

Licensing or Registration and Compliance

11. Jurisdictions should designate an authority to grant licences and/or carry out registration and ensure that the requirement is observed. There should be an authority responsible for ensuring compliance by money/value transfer services with the FATF Recommendations (including the Eight Special Recommendations). There should also be effective systems in place for monitoring and ensuring such compliance. This interpretation of Special Recommendation VI (i.e., the need for designation of competent authorities) is consistent with FATF Recommendation 23.

Sanctions

12. Persons providing money/value transfer services without a license or registration should be subject to appropriate administrative, civil or criminal sanctions.[3] Licensed or registered money/value transfer services which fail to comply fully with the relevant measures called for in the FATF Forty Recommendations (2003) or the Eight Special Recommendations should also be subject to appropriate sanctions.

---

3. Jurisdictions may authorise temporary or provisional operation of money/value transfer services that are already in existence at the time of implementing this Special Recommendation to permit such services to obtain a license or to register.

Appendix VII – Interpretative Note to Special Recommendation III:
FREEZING AND CONFISCATING TERRORIST ASSETS

Objectives

1. FATF Special Recommendation III consists of two obligations. The first requires jurisdictions to implement measures that will freeze or, if appropriate, seize terrorist-related funds or other assets without delay in accordance with relevant United Nations resolutions. The second obligation of Special Recommendation III is to have measures in place that permit a jurisdiction to seize or confiscate terrorist funds or other assets on the basis of an order or mechanism issued by a competent authority or a court.

2. The objective of the first requirement is to freeze terrorist-related funds or other assets based on reasonable grounds, or a reasonable basis, to suspect or believe that such funds or other assets could be used to finance terrorist activity. The objective of the second requirement is to deprive terrorists of these funds or other assets if and when links have been adequately established between the funds or other assets and terrorists or terrorist activity. The intent of the first objective is preventative, while the intent of the second objective is mainly preventative and punitive. Both requirements are necessary to deprive terrorists and terrorist networks of the means to conduct future terrorist activity and maintain their infrastructure and operations.

Scope

3. Special Recommendation III is intended, with regard to its first requirement, to complement the obligations in the context of the United Nations Security Council (UNSC) resolutions relating to the prevention and suppression of the financing of terrorist acts – S/RES/1267(1999) and its successor resolutions,[1] S/RES/1373(2001) and any prospective resolutions related to the freezing, or if appropriate seizure, of terrorist assets. It should be stressed that none of the obligations in Special Recommendation III is intended to replace other measures or obligations that may already be in place for dealing with funds or other assets

---

1. When issued, S/RES/1267(1999) had a time limit of one year. A series of resolutions have been issued by the United Nations Security Council (UNSC) to extend and further refine provisions of S/RES/1267(1999). By "successor resolutions" are meant those resolutions that extend and are directly related to the original resolution S/RES/1267(1999). At the time of issue of this Interpretative Note, these resolutions included S/RES/1333(2000), S/RES/1363(2001), S/RES/1390(2002) and S/RES/1455(2003). In this Interpretative Note, the term *S/RES/1267(1999)* refers to S/RES/1267(1999) and its successor resolutions.

in the context of a criminal, civil or administrative investigation or proceeding.[2] The focus of Special Recommendation III instead is on the preventative measures that are necessary and unique in the context of stopping the flow or use of funds or other assets to terrorist groups.

4. S/RES/1267(1999) and S/RES/1373(2001) differ in the persons and entities whose funds or other assets are to be frozen, the authorities responsible for making these designations, and the effect of these designations.

5. S/RES/1267(1999) and its successor resolutions obligate jurisdictions to freeze without delay the funds or other assets owned or controlled by Al-Qaida, the Taliban, Usama bin Laden, or persons and entities associated with them as designated by the United Nations Al-Qaida and Taliban Sanctions Committee established pursuant to United Nations Security Council Resolution 1267 (the Al-Qaida and Taliban Sanctions Committee), including funds derived from funds or other assets owned or controlled, directly or indirectly, by them or by persons acting on their behalf or at their direction, and ensure that neither these nor any other funds or other assets are made available, directly or indirectly, for such persons' benefit, by their nationals or by any person within their territory. The Al-Qaida and Taliban Sanctions Committee is the authority responsible for designating the persons and entities that should have their funds or other assets frozen under S/RES/1267(1999). All jurisdictions that are members of the United Nations are obligated by S/RES/1267(1999) to freeze the assets of persons and entities so designated by the Al-Qaida and Taliban Sanctions Committee.[3]

6. S/RES/1373(2001) obligates jurisdictions[4] to freeze without delay the funds or other assets of persons who commit, or attempt to commit, terrorist acts or participate in or facilitate the commission of terrorist acts; of entities owned or controlled directly or indirectly by such persons; and of persons and entities acting on behalf of, or at the direction of such persons and entities, including funds or other assets derived or generated from property owned or controlled, directly or indirectly, by such persons and associated persons and entities. Each

---

2. For instance, both the *UN Convention against Illicit Traffic in Narcotic Drugs and Psychotropic Substances (1988)* and *UN Convention against Transnational Organised Crime (2000)* contain obligations regarding freezing, seizure and confiscation in the context of combating transnational crime. Those obligations exist separately and apart from obligations that are set forth in S/RES/1267(1999), S/RES/1373(2001) and Special Recommendation III.

3. When the UNSC acts under Chapter VII of the UN Charter, the resolutions it issues are mandatory for all UN members.

4. The UNSC was acting under Chapter VII of the UN Charter in issuing S/RES/1373(2001) (see previous footnote).

individual jurisdiction has the authority to designate the persons and entities that should have their funds or other assets frozen. Additionally, to ensure that effective co-operation is developed among jurisdictions, jurisdictions should examine and give effect to, if appropriate, the actions initiated under the freezing mechanisms of other jurisdictions. When (i) a specific notification or communication is sent and (ii) the jurisdiction receiving the request is satisfied, according to applicable legal principles, that a requested designation is supported by reasonable grounds, or a reasonable basis, to suspect or believe that the proposed designee is a terrorist, one who finances terrorism or a terrorist organisation, the jurisdiction receiving the request must ensure that the funds or other assets of the designated person are frozen without delay.

Definitions

7. For the purposes of Special Recommendation III and this Interpretive Note, the following definitions apply:

    a) The term *freeze* means to prohibit the transfer, conversion, disposition or movement of funds or other assets on the basis of, and for the duration of the validity of, an action initiated by a competent authority or a court under a freezing mechanism. The frozen funds or other assets remain the property of the person(s) or entity(ies) that held an interest in the specified funds or other assets at the time of the freezing and may continue to be administered by the financial institution or other arrangements designated by such person(s) or entity(ies) prior to the initiation of an action under a freezing mechanism.

    b) The term *seize* means to prohibit the transfer, conversion, disposition or movement of funds or other assets on the basis of an action initiated by a competent authority or a court under a freezing mechanism. However, unlike a freezing action, a seizure is effected by a mechanism that allows the competent authority or court to take control of specified funds or other assets. The seized funds or other assets remain the property of the person(s) or entity(ies) that held an interest in the specified funds or other assets at the time of the seizure, although the competent authority or court will often take over possession, administration or management of the seized funds or other assets.

    c) The term *confiscate*, which includes forfeiture where applicable, means the permanent deprivation of funds or other assets by order of a competent authority or a court. Confiscation or forfeiture takes place through a judicial or administrative procedure that transfers the ownership of specified funds or other assets to be transferred to the State. In this case, the person(s) or entity(ies) that held an interest in the specified funds or other assets at the time of the confiscation or forfeiture loses all rights, in principle, to the confiscated or forfeited funds or other assets.[5]

d) The term *funds or other assets* means financial assets, property of every kind, whether tangible or intangible, movable or immovable, however acquired, and legal documents or instruments in any form, including electronic or digital, evidencing title to, or interest in, such funds or other assets, including, but not limited to, bank credits, travellers cheques, bank cheques, money orders, shares, securities, bonds, drafts, or letters of credit, and any interest, dividends or other income on or value accruing from or generated by such funds or other assets.

e) The term *terrorist* refers to any natural person who: (i) commits, or attempts to commit, terrorist acts[6] by any means, directly or indirectly, unlawfully and wilfully; (ii) participates as an accomplice in terrorist acts or terrorist financing; (iii) organises or directs others to commit terrorist acts or terrorist financing; or (iv) contributes to the commission of terrorist acts or terrorist financing by a group of persons acting with a common purpose where the contribution is made intentionally and with the aim of furthering the terrorist act or terrorist financing or with the knowledge of the intention of the group to commit a terrorist act or terrorist financing.

f) The phrase *those who finance terrorism* refers to any person, group, undertaking or other entity that provides or collects, by any means, directly or indirectly, funds or other assets that may be used, in full or in part, to facilitate the commission of terrorist acts, or to any persons or entities acting on behalf of, or at the direction of such persons, groups, undertakings or other entities. This includes those who provide or collect funds or other assets with the intention that they should be used or in the knowledge that they are to be used, in full or in part, in order to carry out terrorist acts.

---

5. Confiscation or forfeiture orders are usually linked to a criminal conviction or a court decision whereby the confiscated or forfeited property is determined to have been derived from or intended for use in a violation of the law.

6. A *terrorist* act includes an act which constitutes an offence within the scope of, and as defined in one of the following treaties: Convention for the Suppression of Unlawful Seizure of Aircraft, Convention for the Suppression of Unlawful Acts against the Safety of Civil Aviation, Convention on the Prevention and Punishment of Crimes against Internationally Protected Persons, including Diplomatic Agents, International Convention against the Taking of Hostages, Convention on the Physical Protection of Nuclear Material, Protocol for the Suppression of Unlawful Acts of Violence at Airports Serving International Civil Aviation, supplementary to the Convention for the Suppression of Unlawful Acts against the Safety of Civil Aviation, Convention for the Suppression of Unlawful Acts against the Safety of Maritime Navigation, Protocol for the Suppression of Unlawful Acts against the Safety of Fixed Platforms located on the Continental Shelf, International Convention for the Suppression of Terrorist Bombings, and the International Convention for the Suppression of the Financing of Terrorism (1999).

g) The term *terrorist organisation* refers to any legal person, group, undertaking or other entity owned or controlled directly or indirectly by a terrorist(s).

h) The term *designated* persons refers to those persons or entities designated by the Al-Qaida and Taliban Sanctions Committee pursuant to S/RES/1267(1999) or those persons or entities designated and accepted, as appropriate, by jurisdictions pursuant to S/RES/1373(2001).

i) The phrase *without delay*, for the purposes of S/RES/1267(1999), means, ideally, within a matter of hours of a designation by the Al-Qaida and Taliban Sanctions Committee. For the purposes of S/RES/1373(2001), the phrase *without delay* means upon having reasonable grounds, or a reasonable basis, to suspect or believe that a person or entity is a terrorist, one who finances terrorism or a terrorist organisation. The phrase *without delay* should be interpreted in the context of the need to prevent the flight or dissipation of terrorist-linked funds or other assets, and the need for global, concerted action to interdict and disrupt their flow swiftly.

Freezing without delay terrorist-related funds or other assets

8. In order to fulfil the preventive intent of Special Recommendation III, jurisdictions should establish the necessary authority and adopt the following standards and procedures to freeze the funds or other assets of terrorists, those who finance terrorism and terrorist organisations in accordance with both S/RES/1267(1999) and S/RES/1373(2001):

a) *Authority to freeze, unfreeze and prohibit dealing in funds or other assets of designated persons.* Jurisdictions should prohibit by enforceable means the transfer, conversion, disposition or movement of funds or other assets. Options for providing the authority to freeze and unfreeze terrorist funds or other assets include:

(i) empowering or designating a competent authority or a court to issue, administer and enforce freezing and unfreezing actions under relevant mechanisms, or

(ii) enacting legislation that places responsibility for freezing the funds or other assets of designated persons publicly identified by a competent authority or a court on the person or entity holding the funds or other assets and subjecting them to sanctions for non-compliance.

The authority to freeze and unfreeze funds or other assets should also extend to funds or other assets derived or generated from funds or other assets owned or controlled directly or indirectly by such terrorists, those who finance terrorism, or terrorist organisations.

Whatever option is chosen there should be clearly identifiable competent authorities responsible for enforcing the measures.

The competent authorities shall ensure that their nationals or any persons and entities within their territories are prohibited from making any funds or other assets, economic resources or financial or other related services available, directly or indirectly, wholly or jointly, for the benefit of: designated persons, terrorists; those who finance terrorism; terrorist organisations; entities owned or controlled, directly or indirectly, by such persons or entities; and persons and entities acting on behalf of or at the direction of such persons or entities.

b) *Freezing procedures.* Jurisdictions should develop and implement procedures to freeze the funds or other assets specified in paragraph (c) below without delay and without giving prior notice to the persons or entities concerned. Persons or entities holding such funds or other assets should be required by law to freeze them and should furthermore be subject to sanctions for non-compliance with this requirement. Any delay between the official receipt of information provided in support of a designation and the actual freezing of the funds or other assets of designated persons undermines the effectiveness of designation by affording designated persons time to remove funds or other assets from identifiable accounts and places. Consequently, these procedures must ensure (i) the prompt determination whether reasonable grounds or a reasonable basis exists to initiate an action under a freezing mechanism and (ii) the subsequent freezing of funds or other assets without delay upon determination that such grounds or basis for freezing exist. Jurisdictions should develop efficient and effective systems for communicating actions taken under their freezing mechanisms to the financial sector immediately upon taking such action. As well, they should provide clear guidance, particularly financial institutions and other persons or entities that may be holding targeted funds or other assets on obligations in taking action under freezing mechanisms.

c) *Funds or other assets to be frozen or, if appropriate, seized.* Under Special Recommendation III, funds or other assets to be frozen include those subject to freezing under S/RES/1267(1999) and S/RES/1373(2001). Such funds or other assets would also include those wholly or jointly owned or controlled, directly or indirectly, by designated persons. In accordance with their obligations under the United Nations International Convention for the Suppression of the Financing of Terrorism (1999) (the Terrorist Financing Convention (1999)), jurisdictions should be able to freeze or, if appropriate, seize any funds or other assets that they identify, detect, and verify, in accordance with applicable legal principles, as being used by, allocated for, or being made available to terrorists, those who finance terrorists or terrorist organisations. Freezing or seizing under the Terrorist Financing Convention (1999) may be conducted by freezing or seizing in the context of a criminal investigation or proceeding. Freezing action taken under Special Recommendation III shall be without prejudice to the rights of third parties acting in good faith.

d) *De-listing and unfreezing procedures.* Jurisdictions should develop and implement publicly known procedures to consider de-listing requests upon satisfaction of certain criteria consistent with international obligations and applicable legal principles, and to unfreeze the funds or other assets of de-listed persons or entities in a timely manner. For persons and entities designated under S/RES/1267(1999), such procedures and criteria should be in accordance with procedures adopted by the Al-Qaida and Taliban Sanctions Committee under S/RES/1267(1999).

e) *Unfreezing upon verification of identity.* For persons or entities with the same or similar name as designated persons, who are inadvertently affected by a freezing mechanism, jurisdictions should develop and implement publicly known procedures to unfreeze the funds or other assets of such persons or entities in a timely manner upon verification that the person or entity involved is not a designated person.

f) *Providing access to frozen funds or other assets in certain circumstances.* Where jurisdictions have determined that funds or other assets, which are otherwise subject to freezing pursuant to the obligations under S/RES/1267(1999), are necessary for basic expenses; for the payment of certain types of fees, expenses and service charges, or for extraordinary expenses,[7] jurisdictions should authorise access to such funds or other assets in accordance with the procedures set out in S/RES/1452(2002) and subject to approval of the Al-Qaida and Taliban Sanctions Committee. On the same grounds, jurisdictions may authorise access to funds or other assets, if freezing measures are applied pursuant to S/RES/1373(2001).

g) *Remedies.* Jurisdictions should provide for a mechanism through which a person or an entity that is the target of a freezing mechanism in the context of terrorist financing can challenge that measure with a view to having it reviewed by a competent authority or a court.

h) *Sanctions.* Jurisdictions should adopt appropriate measures to monitor effectively the compliance with relevant legislation, rules or regulations governing freezing mechanisms by financial institutions

---

7. See Article 1, S/RES/1452(2002) for the specific types of expenses that are covered.

and other persons or entities that may be holding funds or other assets as indicated in paragraph 8(c) above. Failure to comply with such legislation, rules or regulations should be subject to civil, administrative or criminal sanctions.

Seizure and confiscation

9. Consistent with FATF Recommendation 3, jurisdictions should adopt measures similar to those set forth in Article V of the United Nations Convention against Illicit Traffic in Narcotic Drugs and Psychotropic Substances (1988), Articles 12 to 14 of the United Nations Convention on Transnational Organised Crime (2000), and Article 8 of the Terrorist Financing Convention (1999), including legislative measures, to enable their courts or competent authorities to seize and confiscate terrorist funds or other assets.

Appendix VIII – The 1990 Council of Europe Convention on Laundering, Search, Seizure and Confiscation of the Proceeds from Crime

Preamble

The member States of the Council of Europe and the other States signatory hereto,

Considering that the aim of the Council of Europe is to achieve a greater unity between its members;

Convinced of the need to pursue a common criminal policy aimed at the protection of society;

Considering that the fight against serious crime, which has become an increasingly international problem, calls for the use of modern and effective methods on an international scale;

Believing that one of these methods consists in depriving criminals of the proceeds from crime;

Considering that for the attainment of this aim a well-functioning system of international co-operation also must be established,

Have agreed as follows:

Chapter I – Use of terms

Article I – Use of terms

For the purposes of this Convention:

    a. "proceeds" means any economic advantage from criminal offences. It may consist of any property as defined in sub-paragraph b of this article;

    b. "property" includes property of any description, whether corporeal or incorporeal, movable or immovable, and legal documents or instruments evidencing title to, or interest in such property;

    c. "instrumentalities" means any property used or intended to be used, in any manner, wholly or in part, to commit a criminal offence or criminal offences;

    d. "confiscation" means a penalty or a measure, ordered by a court following proceedings in relation to a criminal offence or criminal offences resulting in the final deprivation of property;

e. "predicate offence" means any criminal offence as a result of which proceeds were generated that may become the subject of an offence as defined in Article 6 of this Convention.

Chapter II – Measures to be taken at national level

Article 2 – Confiscation measures

1. Each Party shall adopt such legislative and other measures as may be necessary to enable it to confiscate instrumentalities and proceeds or property the value of which corresponds to such proceeds.

2. Each Party may, at the time of signature or when depositing its instrument of ratification, acceptance, approval or accession, by a declaration addressed to the Secretary General of the Council of Europe, declare that paragraph 1 of this article applies only to offences or categories of offences specified in such declaration.

Article 3 – Investigative and provisional measures

Each Party shall adopt such legislative and other measures as may be necessary to enable it to identify and trace property which is liable to confiscation pursuant to Article 2, paragraph 1, and to prevent any dealing in, transfer or disposal of such property.

Article 4 – Special investigative powers and techniques

1. Each Party shall adopt such legislative and other measures as may be necessary to empower its courts or other competent authorities to order that bank, financial or commercial records be made available or be seized in order to carry out the actions referred to in Articles 2 and 3. A Party shall not decline to act under the provisions of this article on grounds of bank secrecy.

2. Each Party shall consider adopting such legislative and other measures as may be necessary to enable it to use special investigative techniques facilitating the identification and tracing of proceeds and the gathering of evidence related thereto. Such techniques may include monitoring orders, observation, interception of telecommunications, access to computer systems and orders to produce specific documents.

Article 5 – Legal remedies

Each Party shall adopt such legislative and other measures as may be necessary to ensure that interested parties affected by measures under Articles 2 and 3 shall have effective legal remedies in order to preserve their rights.

Article 6 – Laundering offences

1. Each Party shall adopt such legislative and other measures as may be necessary to establish as offences under its domestic law, when committed intentionally:

   a. the conversion or transfer of property, knowing that such property is proceeds, for the purpose of concealing or disguising the illicit origin of the property or of assisting any person who is involved in the commission of the predicate offence to evade the legal consequences of his actions;

   b. the concealment or disguise of the true nature, source, location, disposition, movement, rights with respect to, or ownership of, property, knowing that such property is proceeds; and, subject to its constitutional principles and the basic concepts of its legal system;

   c. the acquisition, possession or use of property, knowing, at the time of receipt, that such property was proceeds;

   d. participation in, association or conspiracy to commit, attempts to commit and aiding, abetting, facilitating and counselling the commission of any of the offences established in accordance with this article.

2. For the purposes of implementing or applying paragraph 1 of this article:

   a. it shall not matter whether the predicate offence was subject to the criminal jurisdiction of the Party;

   b. it may be provided that the offences set forth in that paragraph do not apply to the persons who committed the predicate offence;

   c. knowledge, intent or purpose required as an element of an offence set forth in that paragraph may be inferred from objective, factual circumstances.

3. Each Party may adopt such measures as it considers necessary to establish also as offences under its domestic law all or some of the acts referred to in paragraph 1 of this article, in any or all of the following cases where the offender:

   a. ought to have assumed that the property was proceeds;

   b. acted for the purpose of making profit;

   c. acted for the purpose of promoting the carrying on of further criminal activity.

4. Each Party may, at the time of signature or when depositing its instrument of ratification, acceptance, approval or accession, by declaration addressed to the Secretary General of the Council of Europe declare that paragraph 1 of this article applies only to predicate offences or categories of such offences specified in such declaration.

Chapter III – International co-operation

Section 1 – Principles of international co-operation

Article 7 – General principles and measures for international co-operation

1. The Parties shall co-operate with each other to the widest extent possible for the purposes of investigations and proceedings aiming at the confiscation of instrumentalities and proceeds.

2. Each Party shall adopt such legislative or other measures as may be necessary to enable it to comply, under the conditions provided for in this chapter, with requests:

   a. for confiscation of specific items of property representing proceeds or instrumentalities, as well as for confiscation of proceeds consisting in a requirement to pay a sum of money corresponding to the value of proceeds;

   b. for investigative assistance and provisional measures with a view to either form of confiscation referred to under a above.

Section 2 – Investigative assistance

Article 8 – Obligation to assist

The Parties shall afford each other, upon request, the widest possible measure of assistance in the identification and tracing of instrumentalities, proceeds and other property liable to confiscation. Such assistance shall include any measure providing and securing evidence as to the existence, location or movement, nature, legal status or value of the aforementioned property.

Article 9 – Execution of assistance

The assistance pursuant to Article 8 shall be carried out as permitted by and in accordance with the domestic law of the requested Party and, to the extent not incompatible with such law, in accordance with the procedures specified in the request.

Article 10 – Spontaneous information

Without prejudice to its own investigations or proceedings, a Party may without prior request forward to another Party information on instrumentalities and proceeds, when it considers that the disclosure of such information might assist the receiving Party in initiating or carrying out investigations or proceedings or might lead to a request by that Party under this chapter.

Section 3 – Provisional measures

Article 11 – Obligation to take provisional measures

1. At the request of another Party which has instituted criminal proceedings or proceedings for the purpose of confiscation, a Party shall take the necessary provisional measures, such as freezing or seizing, to prevent any dealing in, transfer or disposal of property which, at a later stage, may be the subject of a request for confiscation or which might be such as to satisfy the request.

2. A Party which has received a request for confiscation pursuant to Article 13 shall, if so requested, take the measures mentioned in paragraph 1 of this article in respect of any property which is the subject of the request or which might be such as to satisfy the request.

Article 12 – Execution of provisional measures

1. The provisional measures mentioned in Article 11 shall be carried out as permitted by and in accordance with the domestic law of the requested Party and, to the extent not incompatible with such law, in accordance with the procedures specified in the request.

2. Before lifting any provisional measure taken pursuant to this article, the requested Party shall, wherever possible, give the requesting Party an opportunity to present its reasons in favour of continuing the measure.

Section 4 – Confiscation

Article 13 – Obligation to confiscate

1. A Party, which has received a request made by another Party for confiscation concerning instrumentalities or proceeds, situated in its territory, shall:

    a. enforce a confiscation order made by a court of a requesting Party in relation to such instrumentalities or proceeds; or

    b. submit the request to its competent authorities for the purpose of obtaining an order of confiscation and, if such order is granted, enforce it.

2. For the purposes of applying paragraph 1.b of this article, any Party shall whenever necessary have competence to institute confiscation proceedings under its own law.

3. The provisions of paragraph 1 of this article shall also apply to confiscation consisting in a requirement to pay a sum of money corresponding to the value of proceeds, if property on which the confiscation can be enforced is located in the requested Party. In such cases, when enforcing confiscation pursuant to paragraph 1, the requested Party shall, if payment is not obtained, realise the claim on any property available for that purpose.

4. If a request for confiscation concerns a specific item of property, the Parties may agree that the requested Party may enforce the confiscation in the form of a requirement to pay a sum of money corresponding to the value of the property.

Article 14 – Execution of confiscation

1. The procedures for obtaining and enforcing the confiscation under Article 13 shall be governed by the law of the requested Party.

2. The requested Party shall be bound by the findings as to the facts in so far as they are stated in a conviction or judicial decision of the requesting Party or in so far as such conviction or judicial decision is implicitly based on them.

3. Each Party may, at the time of signature or when depositing its instrument of ratification, acceptance, approval or accession, by a declaration addressed to the Secretary General of the Council of Europe, declare that paragraph 2 of this article applies only subject to its constitutional principles and the basic concepts of its legal system.

4. If the confiscation consists in the requirement to pay a sum of money, the competent authority of the requested Party shall convert the amount thereof into the currency of that Party at the rate of exchange ruling at the time when the decision to enforce the confiscation is taken.

5. In the case of Article 13, paragraph 1.a, the requesting Party alone shall have the right to decide on any application for review of the confiscation order.

Article 15 – Confiscated property

Any property confiscated by the requested Party shall be disposed of by that Party in accordance with its domestic law, unless otherwise agreed by the Parties concerned.

Article 16 – Right of enforcement and maximum amount of confiscation

1. A request for confiscation made under Article 13 does not affect the right of the requesting Party to enforce itself the confiscation order.

2. Nothing in this Convention shall be so interpreted as to permit the total value of the confiscation to exceed the amount of the sum of money specified in the confiscation order. If a Party finds that this might occur, the Parties concerned shall enter into consultations to avoid such an effect.

Article 17 – Imprisonment in default

The requested Party shall not impose imprisonment in default or any other measure restricting the liberty of a person as a result of a request under Article 13, if the requesting Party has so specified in the request.

Section 5 – Refusal and postponement of co-operation

Article 18 – Grounds for refusal

1. Co-operation under this chapter may be refused if:

    a. the action sought would be contrary to the fundamental principles of the legal system of the requested Party; or

    b. the execution of the request is likely to prejudice the sovereignty, security, *ordre public* or other essential interests of the requested Party; or

    c. in the opinion of the requested Party, the importance of the case to which the request relates does not justify the taking of the action sought; or

    d. the offence to which the request relates is a political or fiscal offence; or

    e. the requested Party considers that compliance with the action sought would be contrary to the principle of *ne bis in idem*; or

    f. the offence to which the request relates would not be an offence under the law of the requested Party if committed within its jurisdiction. However, this ground for refusal applies to co-operation under Section 2 only in so far as the assistance sought involves coercive action.

2. Co-operation under Section 2, in so far as the assistance sought involves coercive action, and under Section 3 of this chapter, may also be refused if the measures sought could not be taken under the domestic law of the requested Party for the purposes of investigations or proceedings, had it been a similar domestic case.

3. Where the law of the requested Party so requires, co-operation under Section 2, in so far as the assistance sought involves coercive action, and under Section 3 of this chapter may also be refused if the measures sought or any other measures having similar effects would not be permitted under the law of the requesting Party, or, as regards the competent authorities of the requesting Party, if the request is not authorised by either a judge or another judicial authority, including public prosecutors, any of these authorities acting in relation to criminal offences.

4. Co-operation under Section 4 of this chapter may also be refused if:

   a. under the law of the requested Party confiscation is not provided for in respect of the type of offence to which the request relates; or

   b. without prejudice to the obligation pursuant to Article 13, paragraph 3, it would be contrary to the principles of the domestic laws of the requested Party concerning the limits of confiscation in respect of the relationship between an offence and:

      i. an economic advantage that might be qualified as its proceeds; or

      ii. property that might be qualified as its instrumentalities; or

   c. under the law of the requested Party confiscation may no longer be imposed or enforced because of the lapse of time; or

   d. the request does not relate to a previous conviction, or a decision of a judicial nature or a statement in such a decision that an offence or several offences have been committed, on the basis of which the confiscation has been ordered or is sought; or

   e. confiscation is either not enforceable in the requesting Party, or it is still subject to ordinary means of appeal; or

   f. the request relates to a confiscation order resulting from a decision rendered *in absentia* of the person against whom the order was issued and, in the opinion of the requested Party, the proceedings conducted by the requesting Party leading to such decision did not satisfy the minimum rights of defence recognised as due to everyone against whom a criminal charge is made.

5. For the purpose of paragraph 4.f of this article a decision is not considered to have been rendered *in absentia* if:

   a. it has been confirmed or pronounced after opposition by the person concerned; or

   b. it has been rendered on appeal, provided that the appeal was lodged by the person concerned.

6. When considering, for the purposes of paragraph 4.f of this article if the minimum rights of defence have been satisfied, the requested Party shall take into account the fact that the person concerned has deliberately sought to evade justice or the fact that that person, having had the possibility of lodging a legal remedy against the decision made *in absentia*, elected not to do so. The same will apply when the person concerned, having been duly served with the summons to appear, elected not to do so nor to ask for adjournment.

7. A Party shall not invoke bank secrecy as a ground to refuse any co-operation under this chapter. Where its domestic law so requires, a Party may require that a request for co-operation which would involve the lifting of bank secrecy be authorised by either a judge or another judicial authority, including public prosecutors, any of these authorities acting in relation to criminal offences.

8. Without prejudice to the ground for refusal provided for in paragraph 1.a of this article:

    a. the fact that the person under investigation or subjected to a confiscation order by the authorities of the requesting Party is a legal person shall not be invoked by the requested Party as an obstacle to affording any co-operation under this chapter;

    b. the fact that the natural person against whom an order of confiscation of proceeds has been issued has subsequently died or the fact that a legal person against whom an order of confiscation of proceeds has been issued has subsequently been dissolved shall not be invoked as an obstacle to render assistance in accordance with Article 13, paragraph 1.a.

Article 19 – Postponement

The requested Party may postpone action on a request if such action would prejudice investigations or proceedings by its authorities.

Article 20 – Partial or conditional granting of a request

Before refusing or postponing co-operation under this chapter, the requested Party shall, where appropriate after having consulted the requesting Party, consider whether the request may be granted partially or subject to such conditions as it deems necessary.

Section 6 – Notification and protection of third parties' rights

Article 21 – Notification of documents

1. The Parties shall afford each other the widest measure of mutual assistance in the serving of judicial documents to persons affected by provisional measures and confiscation.

2. Nothing in this article is intended to interfere with:

   a. the possibility of sending judicial documents, by postal channels, directly to persons abroad;

   b. the possibility for judicial officers, officials or other competent authorities of the Party of origin to effect service of judicial documents directly through the consular authorities of that Party or through judicial officers, officials or other competent authorities of the Party of destination,

   unless the Party of destination makes a declaration to the contrary to the Secretary General of the Council of Europe at the time of signature or when depositing its instrument of ratification, acceptance, approval or accession.

3. When serving judicial documents to persons abroad affected by provisional measures or confiscation orders issued in the sending Party, this Party shall indicate what legal remedies are available under its law to such persons.

Article 22 – Recognition of foreign decisions

1. When dealing with a request for co-operation under Sections 3 and 4, the requested Party shall recognise any judicial decision taken in the requesting Party regarding rights claimed by third parties.

2. Recognition may be refused if:

   a. third parties did not have adequate opportunity to assert their rights; or

   b. the decision is incompatible with a decision already taken in the requested Party on the same matter; or

   c. it is incompatible with the *ordre public* of the requested Party; or

   d. the decision was taken contrary to provisions on exclusive jurisdiction provided for by the law of the requested Party.

Section 7 – Procedural and other general rules

Article 23 – Central authority

1. The Parties shall designate a central authority or, if necessary, authorities, which shall be responsible for sending and answering requests made under this chapter, the execution of such requests or the transmission of them to the authorities competent for their execution.

2. Each Party shall, at the time of signature or when depositing its instrument of ratification, acceptance, approval or accession, communicate to the Secretary General of the Council of Europe the names and addresses of the authorities designated in pursuance of paragraph 1 of this article.

Article 24 – Direct communication

1. The central authorities shall communicate directly with one another.

2. In the event of urgency, requests or communications under this chapter may be sent directly by the judicial authorities, including public prosecutors, of the requesting Party to such authorities of the requested Party. In such cases a copy shall be sent at the same time to the central authority of the requested Party through the central authority of the requesting Party.

3. Any request or communication under paragraphs 1 and 2 of this article may be made through the International Criminal Police Organisation (Interpol).

4. Where a request is made pursuant to paragraph 2 of this article and the authority is not competent to deal with the request, it shall refer the request to the competent national authority and inform directly the requesting Party that it has done so.

5. Requests or communications under Section 2 of this chapter, which do not involve coercive action, may be directly transmitted by the competent authorities of the requesting Party to the competent authorities of the requested Party.

Article 25 – Form of request and languages

1. All requests under this chapter shall be made in writing. Modern means of telecommunications, such as telefax, may be used.

2. Subject to the provisions of paragraph 3 of this article, translations of the requests or supporting documents shall not be required.

3. At the time of signature or when depositing its instrument of ratification, acceptance, approval or accession, any Party may communicate to the Secretary General of the Council of Europe a declaration that it reserves the right to require that requests made to it and documents supporting such requests be accompanied by a translation into its own language or into one of the official languages of the Council of Europe or into such one of these languages as it shall indicate. It may on that occasion declare its readiness to accept translations in any other language as it may specify. The other Parties may apply the reciprocity rule.

Article 26 – Legalisation

Documents transmitted in application of this chapter shall be exempt from all legalisation formalities.

Article 27 – Content of request

1. Any request for co-operation under this chapter shall specify:

    a. the authority making the request and the authority carrying out the investigations or proceedings;

b. the object of and the reason for the request;

c. the matters, including the relevant facts (such as date, place and circumstances of the offence) to which the investigations or proceedings relate, except in the case of a request for notification;

d. in so far as the co-operation involves coercive action:

  i. the text of the statutory provisions or, where this is not possible, a statement of the relevant law applicable; and

  ii. an indication that the measure sought or any other measures having similar effects could be taken in the territory of the requesting Party under its own law;

e. where necessary and in so far as possible:

  i. details of the person or persons concerned, including name, date and place of birth, nationality and location, and, in the case of a legal person, its seat; and

  ii. the property in relation to which co-operation is sought, its location, its connection with the person or persons concerned, any connection with the offence, as well as any available information about other persons, interests in the property; and

f. any particular procedure the requesting Party wishes to be followed.

2. A request for provisional measures under Section 3 in relation to seizure of property on which a confiscation order consisting in the requirement to pay a sum of money may be realised shall also indicate a maximum amount for which recovery is sought in that property.

3. In addition to the indications mentioned in paragraph 1, any request under Section 4 shall contain:

a. in the case of Article 13, paragraph 1.a:

  i. a certified true copy of the confiscation order made by the court in the requesting Party and a statement of the grounds on the basis of which the order was made, if they are not indicated in the order itself;

  ii. an attestation by the competent authority of the requesting Party that the confiscation order is enforceable and not subject to ordinary means of appeal;

  iii. information as to the extent to which the enforcement of the order is requested; and

  iv. information as to the necessity of taking any provisional measures;

b. in the case of Article 13, paragraph 1.b, a statement of the facts relied upon by the requesting Party sufficient to enable the requested Party to seek the order under its domestic law;

c. when third parties have had the opportunity to claim rights, documents demonstrating that this has been the case.

Article 28 – Defective requests

1. If a request does not comply with the provisions of this chapter or the information supplied is not sufficient to enable the requested Party to deal with the request, that Party may ask the requesting Party to amend the request or to complete it with additional information.

2. The requested Party may set a time-limit for the receipt of such amendments or information.

3. Pending receipt of the requested amendments or information in relation to a request under Section 4 of this chapter, the requested Party may take any of the measures referred to in Sections 2 or 3 of this chapter.

Article 29 – Plurality of requests

1. Where the requested Party receives more than one request under Sections 3 or 4 of this chapter in respect of the same person or property, the plurality of requests shall not prevent that Party from dealing with the requests involving the taking of provisional measures.

2. In the case of plurality of requests under Section 4 of this chapter, the requested Party shall consider consulting the requesting Parties.

Article 30 – Obligation to give reasons

The requested Party shall give reasons for any decision to refuse, postpone or make conditional any co-operation under this chapter.

Article 31 – Information

1. The requested Party shall promptly inform the requesting Party of:

a. the action initiated on a request under this chapter;

b. the final result of the action carried out on the basis of the request;

c. a decision to refuse, postpone or make conditional, in whole or in part, any co-operation under this chapter;

d. any circumstances which render impossible the carrying out of the action sought or are likely to delay it significantly; and

e. in the event of provisional measures taken pursuant to a request under Sections 2 or 3 of this chapter, such provisions of its domestic law as would automatically lead to the lifting of the provisional measure.

2. The requesting Party shall promptly inform the requested Party of:

a. any review, decision or any other fact by reason of which the confiscation order ceases to be wholly or partially enforceable; and

b. any development, factual or legal, by reason of which any action under this chapter is no longer justified.

3. Where a Party, on the basis of the same confiscation order, requests confiscation in more than one Party, it shall inform all Parties which are affected by an enforcement of the order about the request.

Article 32 – Restriction of use

1. The requested Party may make the execution of a request dependent on the condition that the information or evidence obtained will not, without its prior consent, be used or transmitted by the authorities of the requesting Party for investigations or proceedings other than those specified in the request.

2. Each Party may, at the time of signature or when depositing its instrument of ratification, acceptance, approval or accession, by declaration addressed to the Secretary General of the Council of Europe, declare that, without its prior consent, information or evidence provided by it under this chapter may not be used or transmitted by the authorities of the requesting Party in investigations or proceedings other than those specified in the request.

Article 33 – Confidentiality

1. The requesting Party may require that the requested Party keep confidential the facts and substance of the request, except to the extent necessary to execute the request. If the requested Party cannot comply with the requirement of confidentiality, it shall promptly inform the requesting Party.

2. The requesting Party shall, if not contrary to basic principles of its national law and if so requested, keep confidential any evidence and information provided by the requested Party, except to the extent that its disclosure is necessary for the investigations or proceedings described in the request.

3. Subject to the provisions of its domestic law, a Party which has received spontaneous information under Article 10 shall comply with any requirement of confidentiality as required by the Party which supplies the information. If the other Party cannot comply with such requirement, it shall promptly inform the transmitting Party.

Article 34 – Costs

The ordinary costs of complying with a request shall be borne by the requested Party. Where costs of a substantial or extraordinary nature are necessary to comply with a request, the Parties shall consult in order to agree the conditions on which the request is to be executed and how the costs shall be borne.

Article 35 – Damages

1. When legal action on liability for damages resulting from an act or omission in relation to co-operation under this chapter has been initiated by a person, the Parties concerned shall consider consulting each other, where appropriate, to determine how to apportion any sum of damages due.

2. A Party which has become subject of a litigation for damages shall endeavour to inform the other Party of such litigation if that Party might have an interest in the case.

Chapter IV – Final provisions

Article 36 – Signature and entry into force

1. This Convention shall be open for signature by the member States of the Council of Europe and non-member States which have participated in its elaboration. Such States may express their consent to be bound by:

   a. signature without reservation as to ratification, acceptance or approval; or

   b. signature subject to ratification, acceptance or approval, followed by ratification, acceptance or approval.

2. Instruments of ratification, acceptance or approval shall be deposited with the Secretary General of the Council of Europe.

3. This Convention shall enter into force on the first day of the month following the expiration of a period of three months after the date on which three States, of which at least two are member States of the Council of Europe, have expressed their consent to be bound by the Convention in accordance with the provisions of paragraph 1.

4.   In respect of any signatory State which subsequently expresses its consent to be bound by it, the Convention shall enter into force on the first day of the month following the expiration of a period of three months after the date of the expression of its consent to be bound by the Convention in accordance with the provisions of paragraph 1.

Article 37 – Accession to the Convention

1.   After the entry into force of this Convention, the Committee of Ministers of the Council of Europe, after consulting the Contracting States to the Convention, may invite any State not a member of the Council and not having participated in its elaboration to accede to this Convention, by a decision taken by the majority provided for in Article 20.d. of the Statute of the Council of Europe and by the unanimous vote of the representatives of the Contracting States entitled to sit on the Committee.

2.   In respect of any acceding State the Convention shall enter into force on the first day of the month following the expiration of a period of three months after the date of deposit of the instrument of accession with the Secretary General of the Council of Europe.

Article 38 – Territorial application

1.   Any State may, at the time of signature or when depositing its instrument of ratification, acceptance, approval or accession, specify the territory or territories to which this Convention shall apply.

2.   Any State may, at any later date, by a declaration addressed to the Secretary General of the Council of Europe, extend the application of this Convention to any other territory specified in the declaration. In respect of such territory the Convention shall enter into force on the first day of the month following the expiration of a period of three months after the date of receipt of such declaration by the Secretary General.

3.   Any declaration made under the two preceding paragraphs may, in respect of any territory specified in such declaration, be withdrawn by a notification addressed to the Secretary General. The withdrawal shall become effective on the first day of the month following the expiration of a period of three months after the date of receipt of such notification by the Secretary General.

Article 39 – Relationship to other conventions and agreements

1.   This Convention does not affect the rights and undertakings derived from international multilateral conventions concerning special matters.

2. The Parties to the Convention may conclude bilateral or multilateral agreements with one another on the matters dealt with in this Convention, for purposes of supplementing or strengthening its provisions or facilitating the application of the principles embodied in it.

3. If two or more Parties have already concluded an agreement or treaty in respect of a subject which is dealt with in this Convention or otherwise have established their relations in respect of that subject, they shall be entitled to apply that agreement or treaty or to regulate those relations accordingly, in lieu of the present Convention, if it facilitates international co-operation.

Article 40 – Reservations

1. Any State may, at the time of signature or when depositing its instrument of ratification, acceptance, approval or accession, declare that it avails itself of one or more of the reservations provided for in Article 2, paragraph 2, Article 6, paragraph 4, Article 14, paragraph 3, Article 21, paragraph 2, Article 25, paragraph 3 and Article 32, paragraph 2. No other reservation may be made.

2. Any State which has made a reservation under the preceding paragraph may wholly or partly withdraw it by means of a notification addressed to the Secretary General of the Council of Europe. The withdrawal shall take effect on the date of receipt of such notification by the Secretary General.

3. A Party which has made a reservation in respect of a provision of this Convention may not claim the application of that provision by any other Party; it may, however, if its reservation is partial or conditional, claim the application of that provision in so far as it has itself accepted it.

Article 41 – Amendments

1. Amendments to this Convention may be proposed by any Party, and shall be communicated by the Secretary General of the Council of Europe to the member States of the Council of Europe and to every non-member State which has acceded to or has been invited to accede to this Convention in accordance with the provisions of Article 37.

2. Any amendment proposed by a Party shall be communicated to the European Committee on Crime Problems which shall submit to the Committee of Ministers its opinion on that proposed amendment.

3. The Committee of Ministers shall consider the proposed amendment and the opinion submitted by the European Committee on Crime Problems and may adopt the amendment.

4. The text of any amendment adopted by the Committee of Ministers in accordance with paragraph 3 of this article shall be forwarded to the Parties for acceptance.

5. Any amendment adopted in accordance with paragraph 3 of this article shall come into force on the thirtieth day after all Parties have informed the Secretary General of their acceptance thereof.

Article 42 – Settlement of disputes

1. The European Committee on Crime Problems of the Council of Europe shall be kept informed regarding the interpretation and application of this Convention.

2. In case of a dispute between Parties as to the interpretation or application of this Convention, they shall seek a settlement of the dispute through negotiation or any other peaceful means of their choice, including submission of the dispute to the European Committee on Crime Problems, to an arbitral tribunal whose decisions shall be binding upon the Parties, or to the International Court of Justice, as agreed upon by the Parties concerned.

Article 43 – Denunciation

1. Any Party may, at any time, denounce this Convention by means of a notification addressed to the Secretary General of the Council of Europe.

2. Such denunciation shall become effective on the first day of the month following the expiration of a period of three months after the date of receipt of the notification by the Secretary General.

3. The present Convention shall, however, continue to apply to the enforcement under Article 14 of confiscation for which a request has been made in conformity with the provisions of this Convention before the date on which such a denunciation takes effect.

Article 44 – Notifications

The Secretary General of the Council of Europe shall notify the member States of the Council and any State which has acceded to this Convention of:

a. any signature;

b. the deposit of any instrument of ratification, acceptance, approval or accession;

c. any date of entry into force of this Convention in accordance with Articles 36 and 37;

d. any reservation made under Article 40, paragraph 1;

e. any other act, notification or communication relating to this Convention.

In witness whereof the undersigned, being duly authorised thereto, have signed this Convention.

Done at Strasbourg, the 8th day of November 1990, in English and in French, both texts being equally authentic, in a single copy which shall be deposited in the archives of the Council of Europe. The Secretary General of the Council of Europe shall transmit certified copies to each member State of the Council of Europe, to the non-member States which have participated in the elaboration of this Convention, and to any State invited to accede to it.

Appendix IX – The 1991 European Communities Directive on Prevention of the Use of the Financial System for the Purpose of Money Laundering (91/308/EEC)

COUNCIL DIRECTIVE of 10 June 1991 on prevention of the use of the financial system for the purpose of money laundering (91/308/EEC)

THE COUNCIL OF THE EUROPEAN COMMUNITIES,

Having regard to the Treaty establishing the European Economic Community, and in particular Article 57 (2), first and third sentences, and Article 100a thereof,

Having regard to the proposal from the Commission[1],

In cooperation with the European Parliament [2],

Having regard to the opinion of the Economic and Social Committee[3],

Whereas when credit and financial institutions are used to launder proceeds from criminal activities (hereinafter referred to as "money laundering"), the soundness and stability of the institution concerned and confidence in the financial system as a whole could be seriously jeopardized, thereby losing the trust of the public;

Whereas lack of Community action against money laundering could lead Member States, for the purpose of protecting their financial systems, to adopt measures which could be inconsistent with completion of the single market; whereas, in order to facilitate their criminal activities, launderers could try to take advantage of the freedom of capital movement and freedom to supply financial services which the integrated financial area involves, if certain coordinating measures are not adopted at Community level;

Whereas money laundering has an evident influence on the rise of organized crime in general and drug trafficking in particular; whereas there is more and more awareness that combating money laundering is one of the most effective means of opposing this form of criminal activity, which constitutes a particular threat to Member States' societies;

Whereas money laundering must be combated mainly by penal means and within the framework of international cooperation among judicial and law

---

1. OJ No. C 106, 28.4.1990, p. 6; and C 319, 19.12.1990, p. 9.

2. OJ No. C 324, 24.12.1990, p. 264; and C 129, 20.5.1991.

3. OJ No. C 332, 31.12.1990, p. 86.

enforcement authorities, as has been undertaken, in the field of drugs, by the United Nations Convention Against Illicit Traffic in Narcotic Drugs and Psychotropic Substances, adopted on 19 December 1988 in Vienna (hereinafter referred to as the "Vienna Convention") and more generally in relation to all criminal activities, by the Council of Europe Convention on laundering, tracing, seizure and confiscation of proceeds of crime, opened for signature on 8 November 1990 in Strasbourg;

Whereas a penal approach should, however, not be the only way to combat money laundering, since the financial system can play a highly effective role; whereas reference must be made in this context to the recommendation of the Council of Europe of 27 June 1980 and to the declaration of principles adopted in December 1988 in Basle by the banking supervisory authorities of the Group of Ten, both of which constitute major steps towards preventing the use of the financial system for money laundering;

Whereas money laundering is usually carried out in an international context so that the criminal origin of the funds can be better disguised; whereas measures exclusively adopted at a national level, without taking account of international coordination and cooperation, would have very limited effects;

Whereas any measures adopted by the Community in this field should be consistent with other action undertaken in other international fora; whereas in this respect any Community action should take particular account of the recommendations adopted by the financial action task force on money laundering, set up in July 1989 by the Paris summit of the seven most developed countries;

Whereas the European Parliament has requested, in several resolutions, the establishment of a global Community programme to combat drug trafficking, including provisions on prevention of money laundering;

Whereas for the purposes of this Directive the definition of money laundering is taken from that adopted in the Vienna Convention; whereas, however, since money laundering occurs not only in relation to the proceeds of drug-related offences but also in relation to the proceeds of other criminal activities (such as organized crime and terrorism), the Member States should, within the meaning of their legislation, extend the effects of the Directive to include the proceeds of such activities, to the extent that they are likely to result in laundering operations justifying sanctions on that basis;

Whereas prohibition of money laundering in Member States' legislation backed by appropriate measures and penalties is a necessary condition for combating this phenomenon;

Whereas ensuring that credit and financial institutions require identification of their customers when entering into business relations or conducting transactions, exceeding certain thresholds, are necessary to avoid launderers' taking advantage of anonymity to carry out their criminal activities; whereas such provisions must also be extended, as far as possible, to any beneficial owners;

Whereas credit and financial institutions must keep for at least five years copies or references of the identification documents required as well as supporting evidence and records consisting of documents relating to transactions or copies thereof similarly admissible in court proceedings under the applicable national legislation for use as evidence in any investigation into money laundering;

Whereas ensuring that credit and financial institutions examine with special attention any transaction which they regard as particularly likely, by its nature, to be related to money laundering is necessary in order to preserve the soundness and integrity of the financial system as well as to contribute to combating this phenomenon; whereas to this end they should pay special attention to transactions with third countries which do not apply comparable standards against money laundering to those established by the Community or to other equivalent standards set out by international fora and endorsed by the Community;

Whereas, for those purposes, Member States may ask credit and financial institutions to record in writing the results of the examination they are required to carry out and to ensure that those results are available to the authorities responsible for efforts to eliminate money laundering;

Whereas preventing the financial system from being used for money laundering is a task which cannot be carried out by the authorities responsible for combating this phenomenon without the cooperation of credit and financial institutions and their supervisory authorities; whereas banking secrecy must be lifted in such cases; whereas a mandatory system of reporting suspicious transactions which ensures that information is transmitted to the abovementioned authorities without alerting the customers concerned, is the most effective way to accomplish such cooperation; whereas a special protection clause is necessary to exempt credit and financial institutions, their employees and their directors from responsibility for breaching restrictions on disclosure of information;

Whereas the information received by the authorities pursuant to this Directive may be used only in connection with combating money laundering; whereas Member States may nevertheless provide that this information may be used for other purposes;

Whereas establishment by credit and financial institutions of procedures of internal control and training programmes in this field are complementary provisions without which the other measures contained in this Directive could become ineffective;

Whereas, since money laundering can be carried out not only through credit and financial institutions but also through other types of professions and categories of undertakings, Member States must extend the provisions of this Directive in whole or in part, to include those professions and undertakings whose activities are particularly likely to be used for money laundering purposes;

Whereas it is important that the Member States should take particular care to ensure that coordinated action is taken in the Community where there are strong grounds for believing that professions or activities the conditions governing the pursuit of which have been harmonized at Community level are being used for laundering money;

Whereas the effectiveness of efforts to eliminate money laundering is particularly dependent on the close coordination and harmonization of national implementing measures; whereas such coordination and harmonization which is being carried out in various international bodies requires, in the Community context, cooperation between Member States and the Commission in the framework of a contact committee;

Whereas it is for each Member State to adopt appropriate measures and to penalize infringement of such measures in an appropriate manner to ensure full application of this Directive,

HAS ADOPTED THIS DIRECTIVE:

Article 1 For the purpose of this Directive:

- "credit institution" means a credit institution, as defined as in the first indent of Article 1 of Directive 77/780/EEC[4], as last amended by Directive 89/646/EEC[5], and includes branches within the meaning of the third indent of that Article and located in the Community, of credit institutions having their head offices outside the Community,

- "financial institution" means an undertaking other than a credit institution whose principal activity is to carry out one or more of the operations included in numbers 2 to 12 and number 14 of the list annexed to Directive 89/646/EEC, or an insurance company duly authorized in accordance with Directive 79/267/EEC[6], as last amended by Directive 90/619/EEC[7], in so far as it carries out activities covered by that Directive; this definition includes branches located in the Community of financial institutions whose head offices are outside the Community,

---

4. OJ No. L 322, 17.12.1977, p. 30.
5. OJ No. L 386, 30.12.1989, p. 1.
6. OJ No. L 63, 13.3.1979, p. 1.
7. OJ No. L 330, 29.11.1990, p. 50.

- "money laundering" means the following conduct when committed intentionally:
  - the conversion or transfer of property, knowing that such property is derived from criminal activity or from an act of participation in such activity, for the purpose of concealing or disguising the illicit origin of the property or of assisting any person who is involved in the commission of such activity to evade the legal consequences of his action,
  - the concealment or disguise of the true nature, source, location, disposition, movement, rights with respect to, or ownership of property, knowing that such property is derived from criminal activity or from an act of participation in such activity,
  - the acquisition, possession or use of property, knowing, at the time of receipt, that such property was derived from criminal activity or from an act of participation in such activity,
  - participation in, association to commit, attempts to commit and aiding, abetting, facilitating and counselling the commission of any of the actions mentioned in the foregoing paragraphs.

Knowledge, intent or purpose required as an element of the above-mentioned activities may be inferred from objective factual circumstances.

Money laundering shall be regarded as such even where the activities which generated the property to be laundered were perpetrated in the territory of another Member State or in that of a third country.

- "Property" means assets of every kind, whether corporeal or incorporeal, movable or immovable, tangible or intangible, and legal documents or instruments evidencing title to or interests in such assets.
- "Criminal activity" means a crime specified in Article 3 (1) (a) of the Vienna Convention and any other criminal activity designated as such for the purposes of this Directive by each Member State.
- "Competent authorities" means the national authorities empowered by law or regulation to supervise credit or financial institutions.

Article 2

Member States shall ensure that money laundering as defined in this Directive is prohibited.

Article 3

1.   Member States shall ensure that credit and financial institutions require identification of their customers by means of supporting evidence when entering into business relations, particularly when opening an account or savings accounts, or when offering safe custody facilities.

2.   The identification requirement shall also apply for any transaction with customers other than those referred to in paragraph 1, involving a sum

amounting to ECU 15 000 or more, whether the transaction is carried out in a single operation or in several operations which seem to be linked. Where the sum is not known at the time when the transaction is undertaken, the institution concerned shall proceed with identification as soon as it is apprised of the sum and establishes that the threshold has been reached.

3.   By way of derogation from paragraphs 1 and 2, the identification requirements with regard to insurance policies written by insurance undertakings within the meaning of Directive 79/267/EEC, where they perform activities which fall within the scope of that Directive shall not be required where the periodic premium amount or amounts to be paid in any given year does or do not exceed ECU 1 000 or where a single premium is paid amounting to ECU 2 500 or less. If the periodic premium amount or amounts to be paid in any given year is or are increased so as to exceed the ECU 1 000 threshold, identification shall be required.

4.   Member States may provide that the identification requirement is not compulsory for insurance policies in respect of pension schemes taken out by virtue of a contract of employment or the insured's occupation, provided that such policies contain no surrender clause and may not be used as collateral for a loan.

5.   In the event of doubt as to whether the customers referred to in the above paragraphs are acting on their own behalf, or where it is certain that they are not acting on their own behalf, the credit and financial institutions shall take reasonable measures to obtain information as to the real identity of the persons on whose behalf those customers are acting.

6.   Credit and financial institutions shall carry out such identification, even where the amount of the transaction is lower than the threshold laid down, wherever there is suspicion of money laundering.

7.   Credit and financial institutions shall not be subject to the identification requirements provided for in this Article where the customer is also a credit or financial institution covered by this Directive.

8.   Member States may provide that the identification requirements regarding transactions referred to in paragraphs 3 and 4 are fulfilled when it is established that the payment for the transaction is to be debited from an account opened in the customer's name with a credit institution subject to this Directive according to the requirements of paragraph 1.

Article 4

Member States shall ensure that credit and financial institutions keep the following for use as evidence in any investigation into money laundering:

-    in the case of identification, a copy or the references of the evidence required, for a period of at least five years after the relationship with their customer has ended,

- in the case of transactions, the supporting evidence and records, consisting of the original documents or copies admissible in court proceedings under the applicable national legislation for a period of at least five years following execution of the transactions.

Article 5

Member States shall ensure that credit and financial institutions examine with special attention any transaction which they regard as particularly likely, by its nature, to be related to money laundering.

Article 6

Member States shall ensure that credit and financial institutions and their directors and employees cooperate fully with the authorities responsible for combating money laundering:

- by informing those authorities, on their own initiative, of any fact which might be an indication of money laundering,
- by furnishing those authorities, at their request, with all necessary information, in accordance with the procedures established by the applicable legislation.

The information referred to in the first paragraph shall be forwarded to the authorities responsible for combating money laundering of the Member State in whose territory the institution forwarding the information is situated. The person or persons designated by the credit and financial institutions in accordance with the procedures provided for in Article 11 (1) shall normally forward the information.

Information supplied to the authorities in accordance with the first paragraph may be used only in connection with the combating of money laundering. However, Member States may provide that such information may also be used for other purposes.

Article 7

Member States shall ensure that credit and financial institutions refrain from carrying out transactions which they know or suspect to be related to money laundering until they have apprised the authorities referred to in Article 6. Those authorities may, under conditions determined by their national legislation, give instructions not to execute the operation. Where such a transaction is suspected of giving rise to money laundering and where to refrain in such manner is impossible or is likely to frustrate efforts to pursue the beneficiaries of a suspected money-laundering operation, the institutions concerned shall apprise the authorities immediately afterwards.

Article 8

Credit and financial institutions and their directors and employees shall not disclose to the customer concerned nor to other third persons that information has been transmitted to the authorities in accordance with Articles 6 and 7 or that a money laundering investigation is being carried out.

Article 9

The disclosure in good faith to the authorities responsible for combating money laundering by an employee or director of a credit or financial institution of the information referred to in Articles 6 and 7 shall not constitute a breach of any restriction on disclosure of information imposed by contract or by any legislative, regulatory or administrative provision, and shall not involve the credit or financial institution, its directors or employees in liability of any kind.

Article 10

Member States shall ensure that if, in the course of inspections carried out in credit or financial institutions by the competent authorities, or in any other way, those authorities discover facts that could constitute evidence of money laundering, they inform the authorities responsible for combating money laundering.

Article 11

Member States shall ensure that credit and financial institutions:

1.   establish adequate procedures of internal control and communication in order to forestall and prevent operations related to money laundering,

2.   take appropriate measures so that their employees are aware of the provisions contained in this Directive. These measures shall include participation of their relevant employees in special training programmes to help them recognize operations which may be related to money laundering as well as to instruct them as to how to proceed in such cases.

Article 12

Member States shall ensure that the provisions of this Directive are extended in whole or in part to professions and to categories of undertakings, other than the credit and financial institutions referred to in Article 1, which engage in activities which are particularly likely to be used for money-laundering purposes.

Article 13

1.   A contact committee (hereinafter referred to as "the Committee") shall be set up under the aegis of the Commission. Its function shall be:

    (a) without prejudice to Articles 169 and 170 of the Treaty, to facilitate harmonized implementation of this Directive through regular consultation on any practical problems arising from its application and on which exchanges of view are deemed useful;

(b) to facilitate consultation between the Member States on the more stringent or additional conditions and obligations which they may lay down at national level;

(c) to advise the Commission, if necessary, on any supplements or amendments to be made to this Directive or on any adjustments deemed necessary, in particular to harmonize the effects of Article 12;

(d) to examine whether a profession or a category of undertaking should be included in the scope of Article 12 where it has been established that such profession or category of undertaking has been used in a Member State for money laundering.

2.   It shall not be the function of the Committee to appraise the merits of decisions taken by the competent authorities in individual cases.

3.   The Committee shall be composed of persons appointed by the Member States and of representatives of the Commission. The secretariat shall be provided by the Commission. The chairman shall be a representative of the Commission. It shall be convened by its chairman, either on his own initiative or at the request of the delegation of a Member State.

Article 14

Each Member State shall take appropriate measures to ensure full application of all the provisions of this Directive and shall in particular determine the penalties to be applied for infringement of the measures adopted pursuant to this Directive.

Article 15

The Member States may adopt or retain in force stricter provisions in the field covered by this Directive to prevent money laundering.

Article 16

1.   Member States shall bring into force the laws, regulations and administrative decisions necessary to comply with this Directive before 1 January 1993 at the latest.

2.   Where Member States adopt these measures, they shall contain a reference to this Directive or shall be accompanied by such reference on the occasion of their official publication. The methods of making such a reference shall be laid down by the Member States.

3.   Member States shall communicate to the Commission the text of the main provisions of national law which they adopt in the field governed by this Directive..

Article 17

One year after 1 January 1993, whenever necessary and at least at three yearly intervals thereafter, the Commission shall draw up a report on the implementation of this Directive and submit it to the European Parliament and the Council.

Article 18

This Directive is addressed to the Member States.

Done at Luxembourg, 10 June 1991.

For the Council
The President
J.-C. JUNCKER

Statement by the representatives of the Governments of the Member States meeting within the Council

The representatives of the Governments of the Member States, meeting within the Council,

Recalling that the Member States signed the United Nations Convention against illicit traffic in narcotic drugs and psychotropic substances, adopted on 19 December 1988 in Vienna;

Recalling also that most Member States have already signed the Council of Europe Convention on laundering, tracing, seizure and confiscation of proceeds of crime on 8 November 1990 in Strasbourg;

Conscious of the fact that the description of money laundering contained in Article 1 of Council Directive 91/308/EEC[8] derives its wording from the relevant provisions of the aforementioned Conventions;

Hereby undertake to take all necessary steps by 31 December 1992 at the latest to enact criminal legislation enabling them to comply with their obligations under the aforementioned instruments.

---

8. See page 77 of this Official Journal.

APPENDIX X – THE 2001 DIRECTIVE AMENDING COUNCIL DIRECTIVE 91/308/EEC ON PREVENTION OF THE USE OF THE FINANCIAL SYSTEM FOR THE PURPOSE OF MONEY LAUNDERING

Directive 2001/97/EC of the European Parliament and of the Council of 4 December 2001

amending Council Directive 91/308/EEC on prevention of the use of the financial system for the purpose of money laundering

THE EUROPEAN PARLIAMENT AND THE COUNCIL OF THE EUROPEAN UNION,

Having regard to the Treaty establishing the European Community, and in particular Article 47(2), first and third sentences, and Article 95 thereof,

Having regard to the proposal from the Commission[1],

Having regard to the opinion of the Economic and Social Committee[2],

Acting in accordance with the procedure laid down in Article 251 of the Treaty[3], in the light of the joint text approved by the Conciliation Committee on 18 September 2001,

Whereas:

(1)   It is appropriate that Directive 91/308/EEC[4], hereinafter referred to as "the Directive", as one of the main international instruments in the fight against money laundering, should be updated in line with the conclusions of the Commission and the wishes expressed by the European Parliament and the Member States. In this way the Directive should not only reflect best international practice in this area but should also continue to set a high standard in protecting the financial sector and other vulnerable activities from the harmful effects of the proceeds of crime.

(2)   The General Agreement on Trade in Services (GATS) allows Members to adopt measures necessary to protect public morals and to adopt measures for prudential reasons, including for ensuring the stability and integrity of the financial system. Such measures should not impose restrictions that go beyond what is necessary to achieve those objectives.

---

1. OJ C 177 E, 27.6.2000, p. 14.

2. OJ C 75, 15.3.2000, p. 22.

3. Opinion of the European Parliament of 5 July 2000 (OJ C 121, 24.4.2001, p. 133), Council Common Position of 30 November 2000 (OJ C 36, 2.2.2001, p. 24) and Decision of the European Parliament of 5 April 2001 (not yet published in the Official Journal). Decision of the European Parliament of 13 November 2001 and Decision of the Council of 19 November 2001.

4. OJ L 166, 28.6.1991, p. 77.

(3)   The Directive does not establish clearly which Member State's authorities should receive suspicious transaction reports from branches of credit and financial institutions having their head office in another Member State nor which Member State's authorities are responsible for ensuring that such branches comply with the Directive. The authorities of the Member States in which the branch is located should receive such reports and exercise the above responsibilities.

(4)   This allocation of responsibilities should be set out clearly in the Directive by means of an amendment to the definition of "credit institution" and "financial institution".

(5)   The European Parliament has expressed concerns that the activities of currency exchange offices ("bureaux de change") and money transmitters (money remittance offices) are vulnerable to money laundering. These activities should already fall within the scope of the Directive. In order to dispel any doubt in this matter the Directive should clearly confirm that these activities are covered.

(6)   To ensure the fullest possible coverage of the financial sector it should also be made clear that the Directive applies to the activities of investment firms as defined in Council Directive 93/22/EEC of 10 May 1993 on investment services in the securities field[5].

(7)   The Directive obliges Member States only to combat the laundering of the proceeds of drugs offences. There has been a trend in recent years towards a much wider definition of money laundering based on a broader range of predicate or underlying offences, as reflected for example in the 1996 revision of the Forty Recommendations of the Financial Action Task Force (FATF), the leading international body devoted to the fight against money laundering.

(8)   A wider range of predicate offences facilitates suspicious transaction reporting and international cooperation in this area. Therefore, the Directive should be brought up to date in this respect.

(9)   In Joint Action 98/699/JHA of 3 December 1998 adopted by the Council on money laundering, the identification, tracing, freezing, seizing and confiscation of instrumentalities and the proceeds from crime[6], the Member States agreed to make all serious offences, as defined in the Joint Action, predicate offences for the purpose of the criminalisation of money laundering.

(10) The suppression of organised crime in particular is closely linked to measures to combat money laundering. The list of predicate offences should therefore be adapted accordingly.

---

5. OJ L 141, 11.6.1993, p. 27. Directive as last amended by Directive 97/9/EC of the European Parliament and of the Council (OJ L 84, 26.3.1997, p. 22).
6. OJ L 333, 9.12.1998, p. 1.

(11) The Directive imposes obligations regarding in particular the reporting of suspicious transactions. It would be more appropriate and in line with the philosophy of the Action Plan to Combat Organised Crime[7] for the prohibition of money laundering under the Directive to be extended.

(12) On 21 December 1998 the Council adopted Joint Action 98/733/JHA on making it a criminal offence to participate in a criminal organisation in the Member States of the European Union[8]. This Joint Action reflects the Member States' agreement on the need for a common approach in this area.

(13) As required by the Directive, suspicious transaction reports are being made by the financial sector, and particularly by the credit institutions, in every Member State. There is evidence that the tightening of controls in the financial sector has prompted money launderers to seek alternative methods for concealing the origin of the proceeds of crime.

(14) There is a trend towards the increased use by money launderers of non-financial businesses. This is confirmed by the work of the FATF on money laundering techniques and typologies.

(15) The obligations of the Directive concerning customer identification, record keeping and the reporting of suspicious transactions should be extended to a limited number of activities and professions which have been shown to be vulnerable to money laundering.

(16) Notaries and independent legal professionals, as defined by the Member States, should be made subject to the provisions of the Directive when participating in financial or corporate transactions, including providing tax advice, where there is the greatest risk of the services of those legal professionals being misused for the purpose of laundering the proceeds of criminal activity.

(17) However, where independent members of professions providing legal advice which are legally recognised and controlled, such as lawyers, are ascertaining the legal position of a client or representing a client in legal proceedings, it would not be appropriate under the Directive to put these legal professionals in respect of these activities under an obligation to report suspicions of money laundering. There must be exemptions from any obligation to report information obtained either before, during or after judicial proceedings, or in the course of ascertaining the legal position for a client. Thus, legal advice remains subject to the obligation of professional secrecy unless the legal counsellor is taking part in money laundering activities, the legal advice is provided for money laundering purposes, or the lawyer knows that the client is seeking legal advice for money laundering purposes.

---

7. OJ C 251, 15.8.1997, p. 1.
8. OJ L 351, 29.12.1998, p. 1.

(18) Directly comparable services need to be treated in the same manner when practised by any of the professionals covered by the Directive. In order to preserve the rights laid down in the European Convention for the Protection of Human Rights and Fundamental Freedoms (ECHR) and the Treaty of the European Union, in the case of auditors, external accountants and tax advisors who, in some Member States, may defend or represent a client in the context of judicial proceedings or ascertain a client's legal position, the information they obtain in the performance of these tasks should not be subject to the reporting obligations in accordance with the Directive.

(19) The Directive makes reference to "the authorities responsible for combating money laundering" to which reports of suspicious operations must be made on the one hand, and to authorities empowered by law or regulation to supervise the activity of any of the institutions or persons subject to this Directive ("competent authorities") on the other hand. It is understood that the Directive does not oblige Member States to create such "competent authorities" where they do not exist, and that bar associations and other self-regulatory bodies for independent professionals do not fall under the term "competent authorities".

(20) In the case of notaries and independent legal professionals, Member States should be allowed, in order to take proper account of these professionals' duty of discretion owed to their clients, to nominate the bar association or other self-regulatory bodies for independent professionals as the body to which reports on possible money laundering cases may be addressed by these professionals. The rules governing the treatment of such reports and their possible onward transmission to the "authorities responsible for combating money laundering" and in general the appropriate forms of cooperation between the bar associations or professional bodies and these authorities should be determined by the Member States,

HAVE ADOPTED THIS DIRECTIVE:

Article 1

Directive 91/308/EEC is hereby amended as follows:

1.   Article 1 shall be replaced by the following:

"Article 1

For the purpose of this Directive:

(A) Credit institution means a credit institution, as defined in Article 1(1) first subparagraph of Directive 2000/12/EC[9] and includes branches

---

9. OJ L 126, 26.5.2000, p. 1. Directive as amended by Directive 2000/28/EC (OJ L 275, 27.10.2000, p. 37).

within the meaning of Article 1(3) of that Directive and located in the Community, of credit institutions having their head offices inside or outside the Community;

(B) 'Financial institution' means:

1. an undertaking other than a credit institution whose principal activity is to carry out one or more of the operations included in numbers 2 to 12 and number 14 of the list set out in Annex I to Directive 2000/12/EC; these include the activities of currency exchange offices (bureaux de change) and of money transmission/remittance offices;

2. an insurance company duly authorised in accordance with Directive 79/267/EEC[10], insofar as it carries out activities covered by that Directive;

3. an investment firm as defined in Article 1(2) of Directive 93/22/EEC3[11];

4. a collective investment undertaking marketing its units or shares.

This definition of financial institution includes branches located in the Community of financial institutions, whose head offices are inside or outside the Community,

(C) 'Money laundering' means the following conduct when committed intentionally:

– the conversion or transfer of property, knowing that such property is derived from criminal activity or from an act of participation in such activity, for the purpose of concealing or disguising the illicit origin of the property or of assisting any person who is involved in the commission of such activity to evade the legal consequences of his action;

– the concealment or disguise of the true nature, source, location, disposition, movement, rights with respect to, or ownership of property, knowing that such property is derived from criminal activity or from an act of participation in such activity;

– the acquisition, possession or use of property, knowing, at the time of receipt, that such property was derived from criminal activity or from an act of participation in such activity;

10. OJ L 63, 13.3.1979, p. 1. Directive as last amended by Directive 95/26/EC of the European Parliament and of the Council (OJ L 168, 18.7.1995, p. 7).
11. OJ L 141, 11.6.1993, p. 27. Directive as last amended by Directive 97/9/EC of the European Parliament and of the Council (OJ L 84, 26.3.1997, p. 22).

– participation in, association to commit, attempts to commit and aiding, abetting, facilitating and counselling the commission of any of the actions mentioned in the foregoing indents.

Knowledge, intent or purpose required as an element of the abovementioned activities may be inferred from objective factual circumstances.

Money laundering shall be regarded as such even where the activities which generated the property to be laundered were carried out in the territory of another Member State or in that of a third country.

(D) 'Property' means assets of every kind, whether corporeal or incorporeal, movable or immovable, tangible or intangible, and legal documents or instruments evidencing title to or interests in such assets.

(E) 'Criminal activity' means any kind of criminal involvement in the commission of a serious crime.

Serious crimes are, at least:

– any of the offences defined in Article 3(1)(a) of the Vienna Convention;

– the activities of criminal organisations as defined in Article 1 of Joint Action 98/733/JHA[12];

– fraud, at least serious, as defined in Article 1(1) and Article 2 of the Convention on the protection of the European Communities' financial interests[13];

– corruption;

– an offence which may generate substantial proceeds and which is punishable by a severe sentence of imprisonment in accordance with the penal law of the Member State.

Member States shall before 15 December 2004 amend the definition provided for in this indent in order to bring this definition into line with the definition of serious crime of Joint Action 98/699/JHA. The Council invites the Commission to present before 15 December 2004 a proposal for a Directive amending in that respect this Directive.

---

12. OJ L 351, 29.12.1998, p. 1.
13. OJ C 316, 27.11.1995, p. 48.

Member States may designate any other offence as a criminal activity for the purposes of this Directive.

(F) 'Competent authorities' means the national authorities empowered by law or regulation to supervise the activity of any of the institutions or persons subject to this Directive."

2. The following Article shall be inserted:

"Article 2a

Member States shall ensure that the obligations laid down in this Directive are imposed on the following institutions:

1. credit institutions as defined in point A of Article 1;

2. financial institutions as defined in point B of Article 1;

and on the following legal or natural persons acting in the exercise of their professional activities:

3. auditors, external accountants and tax advisors;

4. real estate agents;

5. notaries and other independent legal professionals, when they participate, whether:

  (a) by assisting in the planning or execution of transactions for their client concerning the

    (i) buying and selling of real property or business entities;

    (ii) managing of client money, securities or other assets;

    (iii) opening or management of bank, savings or securities accounts;

    (iv) organisation of contributions necessary for the creation, operation or management of companies;

    (v) creation, operation or management of trusts, companies or similar structures;

  (b) or by acting on behalf of and for their client in any financial or real estate transaction;

6. dealers in high-value goods, such as precious stones or metals, or works of art, auctioneers, whenever payment is made in cash, and in an amount of EUR 15 000 or more;

7. casinos."

3. Article 3 shall be replaced by the following:

"Article 3

1. Member States shall ensure that the institutions and persons subject to this Directive require identification of their customers by means of supporting evidence when entering into business relations, particularly, in the case of the institutions, when opening an account or savings accounts, or when offering safe custody facilities.

2. The identification requirement shall also apply for any transaction with customers other than those referred to in paragraph 1, involving a sum amounting to EUR 15000 or more, whether the transaction is carried out in a single operation or in several operations which seem to be linked. Where the sum is not known at the time when the transaction is undertaken, the institution or person concerned shall proceed with identification as soon as it or he is apprised of the sum and establishes that the threshold has been reached.

3. By way of derogation from the preceding paragraphs, the identification requirements with regard to insurance policies written by insurance undertakings within the meaning of Council Directive 92/96/EEC of 10 November 1992 on the coordination of laws, regulations and administrative provisions relating to direct life assurance (third life assurance Directive)[14], where they perform activities which fall within the scope of that Directive shall not be required where the periodic premium amount or amounts to be paid in any given year does or do not exceed EUR 1000 or where a single premium is paid amounting to EUR 2500 or less. If the periodic premium amount or amounts to be paid in any given year is or are increased so as to exceed the EUR 1000 threshold, identification shall be required.

4. Member States may provide that the identification requirement is not compulsory for insurance policies in respect of pension schemes taken out by virtue of a contract of employment or the insured's occupation, provided that such policies contain no surrender clause and may not be used as collateral for a loan.

5. By way of derogation from the preceding paragraphs, all casino customers shall be identified if they purchase or sell gambling chips with a value of EUR 1000 or more.

6. Casinos subject to State supervision shall be deemed in any event to have complied with the identification requirement laid down in this Directive if they register and identify their customers immediately on entry, regardless of the number of gambling chips purchased.

---

14. OJ L 360, 9.12.1992, p. 1. Directive as last amended by Directive 2000/64/EC of the European Parliament and of the Council (OJ L 290, 17.11.2000, p. 27).

7. In the event of doubt as to whether the customers referred to in the above paragraphs are acting on their own behalf, or where it is certain that they are not acting on their own behalf, the institutions and persons subject to this Directive shall take reasonable measures to obtain information as to the real identity of the persons on whose behalf those customers are acting.

8. The institutions and persons subject to this Directive shall carry out such identification, even where the amount of the transaction is lower than the threshold laid down, wherever there is suspicion of money laundering.

9. The institutions and persons subject to this Directive shall not be subject to the identification requirements provided for in this Article where the customer is a credit or financial institution covered by this Directive or a credit or financial institution situated in a third country which imposes, in the opinion of the relevant Member States, equivalent requirements to those laid down by this Directive.

10. Member States may provide that the identification requirements regarding transactions referred to in paragraphs 3 and 4 are fulfilled when it is established that the payment for the transaction is to be debited from an account opened in the customer's name with a credit institution subject to this Directive according to the requirements of paragraph 1.

11. Member States shall, in any case, ensure that the institutions and persons subject to this Directive take specific and adequate measures necessary to compensate for the greater risk of money laundering which arises when establishing business relations or entering into a transaction with a customer who has not been physically present for identification purposes ('non-face to face' operations). Such measures shall ensure that the customer's identity is established, for example, by requiring additional documentary evidence, or supplementary measures to verify or certify the documents supplied, or confirmatory certification by an institution subject to this Directive, or by requiring that the first payment of the operations is carried out through an account opened in the customer's name with a credit institution subject to this Directive. The internal control procedures laid down in Article 11(1) shall take specific account of these measures."

4. In Articles 4, 5, 8 and 10 the terms "credit and financial institutions" shall be replaced by "the institutions and persons subject to this Directive".

5. Article 6 shall be replaced by the following:

"Article 6

1. Member States shall ensure that the institutions and persons subject to this Directive and their directors and employees cooperate fully with the authorities responsible for combating money laundering:

(a) by informing those authorities, on their own initiative, of any fact which might be an indication of money laundering;

(b) by furnishing those authorities, at their request, with all necessary information, in accordance with the procedures established by the applicable legislation.

2. The information referred to in paragraph 1 shall be forwarded to the authorities responsible for combating money laundering of the Member State in whose territory the institution or person forwarding the information is situated. The person or persons designated by the institutions and persons in accordance with the procedures provided for in Article 11(1)(a) shall normally forward the information.

3. In the case of the notaries and independent legal professionals referred to in Article 2a(5), Member States may designate an appropriate self-regulatory body of the profession concerned as the authority to be informed of the facts referred to in paragraph 1(a) and in such case shall lay down the appropriate forms of cooperation between that body and the authorities responsible for combating money laundering.

Member States shall not be obliged to apply the obligations laid down in paragraph 1 to notaries, independent legal professionals, auditors, external accountants and tax advisors with regard to information they receive from or obtain on one of their clients, in the course of ascertaining the legal position for their client or performing their task of defending or representing that client in, or concerning judicial proceedings, including advice on instituting or avoiding proceedings, whether such information is received or obtained before, during or after such proceedings."

6. Article 7 shall be replaced by the following:

"Article 7

Member States shall ensure that the institutions and persons subject to this Directive refrain from carrying out transactions which they know or suspect to be related to money laundering until they have apprised the authorities referred to in Article 6. Those authorities may, under conditions determined by their national legislation, give instructions not to execute the operation. Where such a transaction is suspected of giving rise to money laundering and where to refrain in such manner is impossible or is likely to frustrate efforts to pursue the beneficiaries of a suspected money-laundering operation, the institutions and persons concerned shall apprise the authorities immediately afterwards."

7. The current text becomes paragraph 1 and the following shall be added to Article 8:

"2. Member States shall not be obliged under this Directive to apply the obligation laid down in paragraph 1 to the professions mentioned in the second paragraph of Article 6(3)."

8.   Article 9 shall be replaced by the following:

"Article 9

The disclosure in good faith to the authorities responsible for combating money laundering by an institution or person subject to this Directive or by an employee or director of such an institution or person of the information referred to in Articles 6 and 7 shall not constitute a breach of any restriction on disclosure of information imposed by contract or by any legislative, regulatory or administrative provision, and shall not involve the institution or person or its directors or employees in liability of any kind."

9.   The following paragraph shall be added to Article 10

"Member States shall ensure that supervisory bodies empowered by law or regulation to oversee the stock, foreign exchange and financial derivatives markets inform the authorities responsible for combating money laundering if they discover facts that could constitute evidence of money laundering."

10. Article 11 shall be replaced by the following:

"Article 11

1.   Member States shall ensure that the institutions and persons subject to this Directive:

(a)   establish adequate procedures of internal control and communication in order to forestall and prevent operations related to money laundering;

(b)   take appropriate measures so that their employees are aware of the provisions contained in this Directive. These measures shall include participation of their relevant employees in special training programmes to help them recognise operations which may be related to money laundering as well as to instruct them as to how to proceed in such cases.

Where a natural person falling within any of Article 2a(3) to (7) undertakes his professional activities as an employee of a legal person, the obligations in this Article shall apply to that legal person rather than to the natural person.

2.   Member States shall ensure that the institutions and persons subject to this Directive have access to up-to-date information on the practices of money launderers and on indications leading to the recognition of suspicious transactions."

11. In Article 12 the words "credit or financial institutions referred to in Article 1" shall be replaced by "institutions and persons referred to in Article 2a." .

Article 2

Within three years of the entry into force of this Directive, the Commission shall carry out a particular examination, in the context of the report provided for in Article 17 of Directive 91/308/EEC, of aspects relating to the implementation of the fifth indent of Article 1(E), the specific treatment of lawyers and other independent legal professionals, the identification of clients in non-face to face transactions and possible implications for electronic commerce.

Article 3

1.   Member States shall bring into force the laws, regulations and administrative provisions necessary to comply with this Directive by 15 June 2003 at the latest. They shall forthwith inform the Commission thereof.

Where Member States adopt these measures, they shall contain a reference to this Directive or shall be accompanied by such reference on the occasion of their official publication. The methods of making such a reference shall be laid down by the Member States.

2.   Member States shall communicate to the Commission the text of the main provisions of domestic law which they adopt in the field governed by this Directive.

Article 4

This Directive shall enter into force on the day of its publication in the Official Journal of the European Communities.

Article 5

This Directive is addressed to the Member States.

Done at Brussels, 4 December 2001.

For the European Parliament	For the Council
The President	The President
N. Fontaine	D. Reynders

Commission Declaration

The Commission reiterates the commitment made in its work programme 2001 to launch a proposal before the end of this year for a Regulation of the European Parliament and of the Council establishing a cooperation mechanism between the competent national authorities of the Member States and the Commission in order to ensure the protection of the Communities' financial interests against illegal activities, including Value Added Tax (VAT) fraud and money laundering. This commitment has been confirmed in the Communication from the Commission concerning the Action Plan for 2001-2003 on protecting the Communities' financial interests – Fight against fraud – of 15 May 2001[15].

---

15.   COM (2001) 254 final: see paragraph 2.2.1.

Selected Websites[1]

Asia/Pacific Group on Money Laundering	www.apgml.org
Caribbean Financial Action Task Force	www.cfatf.org
Commonwealth Secretariat	www.thecommonwealth.org
Council of Europe	www.coe.int
Egmont Group	www.egmontgroup.org
European Commission: Justice and Home Affairs	europa.eu.int/comm/ justice_home/index_en.htm
Europol	www.europol.eu.int
Financial Action Task Force	www.fatf-gafi.org
G8	www.g8.utoronto.ca
International Monetary Fund	www.imf.org
International Organisation of Securities Commissions	www.iosco.org
Interpol	www.interpol.int
Organisation for Economic Co-operation and Development	www.oecd.org
Organisation of American States	www.oea.org
United Nations	www.un.org
World Bank	www.worldbank.org

---

1. As of January 2004.

Sales agents for publications of the Council of Europe
Agents de vente des publications du Conseil de l'Europe

AUSTRALIA/AUSTRALIE
Hunter Publications, 58A, Gipps Street
AUS-3066 COLLINGWOOD, Victoria
Tel.: (61) 3 9417 5361
Fax: (61) 3 9419 7154
E-mail: Sales@hunter-pubs.com.au
http://www.hunter-pubs.com.au

BELGIUM/BELGIQUE
La Librairie européenne SA
50, avenue A. Jonnart
B-1200 BRUXELLES 20
Tel.: (32) 2 734 0281
Fax: (32) 2 735 0860
E-mail: info@libeurop.be
http://www.libeurop.be

Jean de Lannoy
202, avenue du Roi
B-1190 BRUXELLES
Tel.: (32) 2 538 4308
Fax: (32) 2 538 0841
E-mail: jean.de.lannoy@euronet.be
http://www.jean-de-lannoy.be

CANADA
Renouf Publishing Company Limited
5369 Chemin Canotek Road
CDN-OTTAWA, Ontario, K1J 9J3
Tel.: (1) 613 745 2665
Fax: (1) 613 745 7660
E-mail: order.dept@renoufbooks.com
http://www.renoufbooks.com

CZECH REPUBLIC/
RÉPUBLIQUE TCHÈQUE
Suweco Cz Dovoz Tisku Praha
Ceskomoravska 21
CZ-18021 PRAHA 9
Tel.: (420) 2 660 35 364
Fax: (420) 2 683 30 42
E-mail: import@suweco.cz

DENMARK/DANEMARK
GAD Direct
Fiolstaede 31-33
DK-1171 COPENHAGEN K
Tel.: (45) 33 13 72 33
Fax: (45) 33 12 54 94
E-mail: info@gaddirect.dk

FINLAND/FINLANDE
Akateeminen Kirjakauppa
Keskuskatu 1, PO Box 218
FIN-00381 HELSINKI
Tel.: (358) 9 121 41
Fax: (358) 9 121 4450
E-mail: akatilaus@stockmann.fi
http://www.akatilaus.akateeminen.com

FRANCE
La Documentation française
(Diffusion/Vente France entière)
124, rue H. Barbusse
F-93308 AUBERVILLIERS Cedex
Tel.: (33) 01 40 15 70 00
Fax: (33) 01 40 15 68 00
E-mail: commandes.vel@ladocfrancaise.gouv.fr
http://www.ladocfrancaise.gouv.fr

Librairie Kléber (Vente Strasbourg)
Palais de l'Europe
F-67075 STRASBOURG Cedex
Fax: (33) 03 88 52 91 21
E-mail: librairie.kleber@coe.int

GERMANY/ALLEMAGNE
AUSTRIA/AUTRICHE
UNO Verlag
Am Hofgarten 10
D-53113 BONN
Tel.: (49) 2 28 94 90 20
Fax: (49) 2 28 94 90 222
E-mail: bestellung@uno-verlag.de
http://www.uno-verlag.de

GREECE/GRÈCE
Librairie Kauffmann
28, rue Stadiou
GR-ATHINAI 10564
Tel.: (30) 1 32 22 160
Fax: (30) 1 32 30 320
E-mail: ord@otenet.gr

HUNGARY/HONGRIE
Euro Info Service
Hungexpo Europa Kozpont ter 1
H-1101 BUDAPEST
Tel.: (361) 264 8270
Fax: (361) 264 8271
E-mail: euroinfo@euroinfo.hu
http://www.euroinfo.hu

ITALY/ITALIE
Libreria Commissionaria Sansoni
Via Duca di Calabria 1/1, CP 552
I-50125 FIRENZE
Tel.: (39) 556 4831
Fax: (39) 556 41257
E-mail: licosa@licosa.com
http://www.licosa.com

NETHERLANDS/PAYS-BAS
De Lindeboom Internationale Publikaties
PO Box 202, MA de Ruyterstraat 20 A
NL-7480 AE HAAKSBERGEN
Tel.: (31) 53 574 0004
Fax: (31) 53 572 9296
E-mail: books@delindeboom.com
http://home-1-worldonline.nl/~lindeboo/

NORWAY/NORVÈGE
Akademika, A/S Universitetsbokhan
PO Box 84, Blindern
N-0314 OSLO
Tel.: (47) 22 85 30 30
Fax: (47) 23 12 24 20

POLAND/POLOGNE
Głowna Księgarnia Naukowa
im. B. Prusa
Krakowskie Przedmiescie 7
PL-00-068 WARSZAWA
Tel.: (48) 29 22 66
Fax: (48) 22 26 64 49
E-mail: inter@internews.com.pl
http://www.internews.com.pl

PORTUGAL
Livraria Portugal
Rua do Carmo, 70
P-1200 LISBOA
Tel.: (351) 13 47 49 82
Fax: (351) 13 47 02 64
E-mail: liv.portugal@mail.telepac.pt

SPAIN/ESPAGNE
Mundi-Prensa Libros SA
Castelló 37
E-28001 MADRID
Tel.: (34) 914 36 37 00
Fax: (34) 915 75 39 98
E-mail: libreria@mundiprensa.es
http://www.mundiprensa.com

SWITZERLAND/SUISSE
Adeco – Van Diermen
Chemin du Lacuez 41
CH-1807 BLONAY
Tel.: (41) 21 943 26 73
Fax: (41) 21 943 36 05
E-mail: info@adeco.org

UNITED KINGDOM/ROYAUME-U
TSO (formerly HMSO)
51 Nine Elms Lane
GB-LONDON SW8 5DR
Tel.: (44) 207 873 8372
Fax: (44) 207 873 8200
E-mail: customer.services@theso.cc
http://www.the-stationery-office.c
http://www.itsofficial.net

UNITED STATES and CANADA/
ÉTATS-UNIS et CANADA
Manhattan Publishing Company
2036 Albany Post Road
CROTON-ON-HUDSON,
NY 10520, USA
Tel.: (1) 914 271 5194
Fax: (1) 914 271 5856
E-mail: Info@manhattanpublishing
http://www.manhattanpublishing

Council of Europe Publishing/Editions du Conseil de l'Europe
F-67075 Strasbourg Cedex
Tel.: (33) 03 88 41 25 81 – Fax: (33) 03 88 41 39 10 – E-mail: publishing@coe.int – Website: http://book.coe.int